WOMEN IN THE NEW ASIA

WOMEN
IN THE
NEW ASIA

*The changing social roles of men
and women in South and South-East Asia*

Edited by
BARBARA E. WARD

UNESCO

*Published in 1963 by the United Nations
Educational, Scientific and Cultural Organization,
Place de Fontenoy, Paris-7e
Printed by Arbeiderspers, Amsterdam*

In January 1958, Unesco convened at Calcutta a meeting of social scientists to discuss the contribution which the social sciences could make towards furthering the objectives of Unesco's Major Project on the Mutual Appreciation of Eastern and Western Cultural Values. In general terms, this contribution was already seen as the task of placing cultural values in their socio-economic context, of acquainting the general public with the contemporary evolution of these values and of clarifying the new conditions of relations among peoples. The conference was concerned with the particular areas of study which could most usefully be selected for special emphasis in the fulfilment of this threefold task.

About one such area there was little dispute. It is an undeniable fact that almost the whole world has seen revolutionary changes in the status of women—politically, legally, economically, educationally. In country after country during the last fifty years women have gained the right to vote, to enter all forms of paid employment and to seek educational qualifications on equal terms with men. What do these revolutionary changes amount to in practice?

This collection of studies tries to answer the question by describing the impact of the new public status of women upon the private, domestic lives of both sexes in the various countries of South and South-East Asia. Part I contains contributions by social scientists and personal autobiographical chapters concerning the following countries: Burma, Ceylon, India, Indonesia, Laos, Malaya, Pakistan, Philippines, Singapore, Thailand and Viet-Nam. Part II contains a study of women's emancipation movements in South Asia and a demographic survey, with appendixes, on the existing state of women's rights in the countries concerned and the measures for family planning being taken in these countries.

The facts stated in this volume, or the opinions expressed with regard to these facts, are the sole responsibility of the authors and are not necessarily an expression of the views of the Organization.

Contents

PART III

by Her Excellency
MRS. VIJAYA LAKSHMI PANDIT

Ideas about woman's place in a man's world are constantly changing. It would be incorrect to assume that the position of woman in ancient societies was one of thraldom, and that all changes since have been for the better. Nor can it be denied that definite progress has been made in recent years towards equality between men and women in the eyes of the law in some countries. But we are only too familiar with situations where the spirit of the law can be frustrated by the social prejudice and mental reservations of large sections of the community.

Time was when a woman espousing the cause of equality between the sexes was considered aggressive and essentially unfeminine. In the past fifty-odd years, universal education in some parts of the world has thrown up many distinguished and talented women in almost all fields of human endeavour, and has rendered such concepts obsolete. Men have, in varying degrees, come to accept the equal partnership of women without thinking any the less of them as women.

In this context a study of the relationship between men and women in South and South-East Asia should prove interesting and valuable. Current notions about the status and personality of the Asian woman are often based on oversimplified generalizations. In the East, for instance, there is a time-honoured concept of her as a symbol of purity, faithfulness and 'queen of the home'. In some Western countries the Indian woman is considered backward, oppressed and no more than a chattel of man. I would, therefore, welcome this symposium in the hope that it will enable a more realistic appraisal of the past, present and future of millions of women in Asia.

London, August 1961

Acknowledgements

No editor can ever have been more in debt for kindness, hospitality, ideas, suggestions and criticism, practical help of every kind. I can only trust that the many to whom I owe lasting gratitude will accept this public expression of my thanks, and will, if ever the occasion arises, give me a chance to do as I was done by. What merits this book has are altogether theirs; for its shortcomings—for which I trust they will forgive me—I alone am responsible.

My first thanks must be paid to those whose contributions form the body of the book. Their names and brief notes about each of them appear elsewhere; their articles speak for themselves.

An equal debt of gratitude is due to the late Dr. Alfred Métraux, of the Department of Social Sciences of Unesco, for his constant encouragement, ever ready help and apparently unwearying patience, and to Dr. Eric de Dampièrre who took over his unenviable task. I must also express my thanks to the members of the Steering Committee appointed under Unesco's auspices by the International Association: Professor Isaac Schapera, Dr. Maurice Freedman, Mrs. Jean Floud and Mr. Thomas Bottomore, and to Birkbeck College, University of London, for granting me leave of absence.

Before leaving for Asia I was fortunate enough to receive most valuable advice and help from many people, including in particular: Miss I. Bunberry, Mr. A. Christie, Professor Lionel Elvin, Professor C. von Führer-Haimendorf, Miss Valerie Hinge, Khin Myint Myint, Dr. L. P. Mair, Miss Sally Martin, Professor Margaret Mead, Her Excellency Mrs. A. Myrdal, Miss C. Rustom, Dr. Marian Smith, Mr. T. E. Smith and the Secretary to the International Federation of University Women. In addition, I visited the Embassies of Burma,

Indonesia, Nepal and Viet-Nam and the High Commissions of Ceylon, India, Malaya and Pakistan, from all of which I received kind assistance.

To people in Asia my debts of gratitude are literally innumerable, for they extend to many casually met acquaintances in conversations on board ships—and aeroplanes—street and shop encounters, and so on, whose names I never knew. In addition, of course, there are the many whose help was personal and direct, who gave hospitality, practical assistance, good advice, wise opinion and, above all, that most precious commodity, time—and gave them so generously that I was never allowed to feel my importunity a nuisance.

Especially I must mention: Mr. John Blofeld, Mr. and Mrs. W. Carson, Dr. Irene Cheng, Mrs. Ezlynn Deraniyagala, Mrs. Sylvia Fernando, Dr. Garina, Mr. and Mrs. G. T. Gooding, Professor T. L. Green, Miss Daphne Ho, Mrs. R. Prawer Jhabvala, Daw Khin Khin U, Miss Mary Khin Thet, Mr. Lawrence, Miss Dorothy Lee, Dr. and Mrs. G. E. D. Lewis, Dr. D. Lim, Mr. Ma Meng, Mrs. Yay Marking, Mrs. F. B. de Mel, Mrs. P. P. Naidu, Mr. Conrad Opper, Mrs. G. Pecson, Khun Pinthorn, Dr. Philps, Professor E. Shils, Professor N. Srinivas, Mr. and Mrs. Lawrence Wilson, Mr. Douglas Williams, Mr. and Mrs. H. Y. H. Wong.

For their skill in typing and additional editing I would like to thank Mrs. M. Alfandary, Mrs. Li Mei-Li and Miss A. Bibby; for the maps, Mr. Alan Dyson and Mr. Arthur Enright; and for English translation, Mrs. B. Hooke.

Finally, the most generous creditors of all: George, John and Beryl, who came with me, my sister Janet Ward and Ah Ho, who cheerfully accepted us into their household for many months, and my husband who stayed behind in London; without their true friendship nothing could have been accomplished.

BARBARA E. WARD
London, 1961

12

Preface

In this book Unesco is daring to ask for trouble—for to study the relations between the roles of two sexes is to do just that. Probably no other topic excites more argument and less agreement, and probably on no other topic is the argument more heated and the disagreement more profound. Nevertheless, we have endeavoured to set out facts and suggest conclusions for the common reader in the West, and also—we hope—in the East, to ponder upon. We hope our endeavour will provoke new argument—perhaps less heated and more enlightened; we even dare to hope that it may produce some measure of agreement here and there.

Our object is quite simple. It is to put before the ordinary reader in the West the fruits of a two years' gathering of material made under the auspices of the Unesco Major Project on Mutual Appreciation of Eastern and Western Cultural Values. We are not writing for academics or officials; we are simply hoping to interest ordinary people, men and women in the West, in the experiences and problems of their fellows in the East. (If Easterners also find the book interesting—written as it is mostly by other Easterners—so much the better.)

But we would like to think that we could do a little more. After all, a mere dilettante interest is somewhat unrewarding. And the topics we have written about are far from that. As any newspaper editor knows, one has only to start a correspondence on the position of women—at home or at work, cooking or typing, superior or inferior, angels or devils—to make sure of having a supply of material for the next six months. At the present moment of history all Western countries are undergoing social changes as profound in their own ways as those occurring in Africa or Asia. Foremost among them are the

13

changes in the position of women. We do not hope only to interest our readers, but also to suggest lines of thinking that may be of assistance to them—men and women, both—in facing and dealing with their own personal problems.

For the 'woman question', as it was once called in England, is also the 'man question'. One cannot meaningfully discuss the status and role of women without discussing also—if only by implication—the status and role of the other half of the human race. The title of this book is misleading if it is read without its supplementary sub-title: the changing social roles of men and women in South and South-East Asia. What concerns us primarily is not simply the change in the political and legal status of women, or even their advance in economic and educational opportunity as such, but the bearing of all these things, and other concomitant changes too, upon everyday living. And this must include both sexes.

Most of us spend by far the larger part of everyday living in families, a fact which necessarily involves us closely with one another, and forces us to consider the reciprocal social roles of males and females. The kinds of family we live in are very various, the relationships that exist between male and female members, both in personal terms and as regards the division of labour, are also various. But all this variety represents merely different methods of dealing with similar problems: problems of child-rearing, of domestic happiness, of social security. In a time of rapid change, such as the one we all live in now, when our own views upon how best to meet these perennial and ubiquitous problems are in a state of flux, we may be helped at least towards clarity of thinking by considering some of the ways in which other peoples have been tackling them.

The book had its origin in Calcutta, to which central point of South Asia a distinguished gathering of social scientists was convened by the Department of Social Sciences of Unesco in January 1958. Their discussions centred upon the contribution which the social sciences could make towards furthering the objectives of the Unesco Major Project on the Mutual Appreciation of Eastern and Western Cultural Values. In general terms this contribution was already clearly seen as the 'task of placing cultural values in their socio-economic context, of acquainting the general public with the contemporary evolution of these values, and of clarifying the new conditions of relations among peoples'. The conference was concerned with the particular areas of

14

study which could most usefully be selected for special emphasis in the fulfilment of this threefold task.

About one such area there was little dispute. It is an undeniable fact of recent history that almost the whole world has seen revolutionary changes in the status of women—politically, legally, economically, educationally. The formal changes are not hard to discover. In country after country during the last fifty years, women have gained the right to vote, to stand for election, to hold property in their own right, to plead their own cases at law, to enter all forms of paid employment and to seek educational qualifications on equal terms with men. That there still remain certain anomalies and inequalities which are the special concern of the United Nations Commission on the Status of Women, does not alter the general picture. It is one of revolutionary change—*de jure*. What is harder to evaluate is the meaning of the change *de facto*. What, so far, do these revolutionary formal changes amount to in practice?

There is more than one way of tackling this question. First (perhaps most obvious) is what might be called the feminist approach. For this one would study the formal situation, as laid down in the statute books, country by country, comparing it at every step with the practical results so far observable. Looked at in terms of numbers these are sometimes said to be uninspiring results, but this is a view which is both too simple and too short-sighted. Too simple partly because sociological explanation requires far more than a merely numerical analysis, and partly because contributions in the areas of life to which the figures refer cannot be measured in terms of numbers alone; too short-sighted because, measured against the extremely brief period of time for which they have been eligible for high position, it is nothing less than astonishing that so many women should have attained eminence. To take the sphere of international diplomacy alone, who could have imagined fifty years ago the achievement of Mrs. Pandit, Mrs. Meir or Mrs. Alva Myrdal?

Studies in this vein are valuable in precisely the same way as studies of slavery, or the remaining examples of colonial, racial, religious or ideological discrimination are valuable. By drawing attention to injustice and to gaps between theory and practice they can act as a spur to further endeavour and a needle in the side of prejudice. As far as special discrimination against women is concerned, the continued existence in the United Nations of a Special Commission for

15

the Status of Women indicates how necessary this feminist argument still is.

And it has not been neglected.

It was, indeed, partly because of the prior existence of numerous distinguished works of this nature that the Calcutta conference decided there was no need for yet another. Unesco's concern was rather different. Political and legal rights, economic and educational opportunities—all these things which might be summed up as the public status of women could be taken as given. What was wanted now was information about the effect of this newly granted public status upon the minutiae of day-to-day domestic living. There, in the homes of the people, lies the place where men and women most constantly and characteristically interact, where the sexual division of labour is most obvious and most telling, where techniques are most conservative and attitudes least easily changed. Or so one might expect. What was the effect there of the newly achieved political status of women? Of legal changes? Of economic opportunity and educational advance? This was what Unesco was interested in now.

And so this book was born. It is not a feminist treatise, though feminist arguments appear in it and are implicit throughout; it is not concerned primarily with the public life of women at all, though many of its contributors are themselves women distinguished in public life and the public role of women is crucial to the general subject matter; it is simply a study, or rather a collection of studies, of the impact of the new public status of women upon the private, domestic lives of both sexes—of families, in fact—in the various countries of South and South-East Asia.

The book's form is quite straightforward. Neither time nor funds made it possible for us to launch out on new research. It was therefore necessary to rely on existing material and experience. This we have done in two ways: first, by calling for contributions written by social scientists who have already been working on these or allied topics in South and South-East Asia; second, by inviting personal autobiographical accounts from nationals of the countries concerned.

It happens that some of the social scientists are also nationals of the countries they describe, others are not. The criteria for selection here did not include nationality but only first-hand field experience, sociological ability and willingness to contribute. The criteria for selecting the writers of autobiographical memoirs were—apart, of course, from willingness—quite different: nationality, sex, education all came in, the selection falling invariably upon a national, a woman, and one able to write in either French or English. Not everyone who was approached was free or willing to contribute, not quite everyone who promised to do so did in fact send in his manuscript in time for publication (though perhaps it should go on record that it was never the autobiographical amateurs but only the sociological professionals—and very few of them—who fell down in this way!). But that the general response was enthusiastic, lively and interesting our readers can see for themselves.

The book is divided into three parts, the first being an introductory essay written by the editor.

Part II contains the real meat. Each of eleven countries from Southern Asia is there listed in alphabetical order: Burma, Ceylon, India, Indonesia, Laos, Malaya, Pakistan, the Philippines, Singapore, Thailand and Viet-Nam. A small map and a few words pointing out the salient geographical features and adding some historical reminders introduce each country, which is then made the subject of one or two (in the case of India, three) chapters of description and analysis. Burma, Malaya, the Philippines, Singapore, Thailand, have two chapters each: one a sociological study, the other a personal narrative; India, because of her immense size and variety, has two personal chapters alongside her one sociological study; Pakistan's two chapters are both written in a personal, autobiographical style, but the first (by Professor A. K. Nazmul Karim) is the work of a social scientist using his own family as a framework for his analysis; Ceylon has a single chapter written by an educationist giving in one article both a sociological and a personal account; the writer of Indonesia's autobiographical study, besides her many other qualifications, is also a trained social anthropologist; Laos and Viet-Nam are represented by personal memoirs alone.

A word should perhaps be said about the form of the two kinds of chapter in Part II: sociological and autobiographical. A considerable effort was made to obtain true comparability, but without much success. Originally it had been hoped that a general meeting of at least the social scientists could be arranged so that a common approach could be thrashed out in face-to-face discussion. Unfortunately, this proved impossible. Unfortunately, too, the present state of the social sciences makes true comparability of presentation without continued face-to-face discussion almost impossible. Differences in training and

17

outlook, as well as in orientation of interest, are too profound. The circulation of identical instructions to each contributor, including a projected outline and notes on the use of terminology, did go some way towards providing a common approach, but contributors had necessarily to be allowed to present the material they had, and that, and the kind of analysis they made, inevitably depended upon their own particular interests. Only when sociological investigation in Asia is much more developed than at present will it be possible to produce truly comparable studies from different regions. We are only too well aware that we have not succeeded in this.

The writers of the autobiographical memoirs were also given instructions, or rather suggestions, about the outline they might like to follow and the topics they might like to include. Their instructions were far more flexible than those given to the social scientists, and they were urged over and over again to feel completely free to express their own experiences in their own way. All that was definitely required of them was a general account of the changes that have occurred in their own families from the days of their grandmothers up to now. Our readers can judge for themselves how far the experiences of women in different parts of Asia in the last three generations have been really comparable. Certainly they have been intensely interesting.

Part III contains two chapters of essential background information: the first, by Dr. Romila Tharpar, a study of the women's emancipation movements in Southern Asia, the second a demographic survey by Mr. T. E. Smith in which the prospects of an explosively expanding population are discussed. An appendix to Dr. Tharpar's chapter sets out the formally existing state of women's rights in the countries we have discussed earlier in the book; an appendix to Mr. Smith's chapter describes the measures for family planning which are being developed in these countries.

Mrs. ANGELINA ARCEO-ORTEGA, A.B. Descended from Spanish-speaking ancestors, educated in Manila and the United States, deeply attached to her rural background, Angelina (Eileen) Arceo-Ortega is in many ways typical of the energetic and go-ahead yet intensely home-loving professional women of the modern Philippines.

Mrs. BARBARA CADBURY. Proud of being the daughter of a mother who went to prison for the right of women to vote, Barbara Cadbury has herself played an active part in local government in England, was the first woman to be elected to the board of management of the largest consumers' co-operative in Canada, and was at one time a member of the Jamaica Social Welfare Commission. Though both born and educated in England, Mr. and Mrs. Cadbury now live in Toronto (Canada). He is an economist, employed for ten years by the Technical Assistance Administration of the United Nations.

Mrs. PRAMUAN DICKINSON, B.A. The young Thai wife of a Canadian, Pramuan Dickinson lives in Bangkok where she holds a research post in the Unesco Institute for the Study of Child Development.

Professor S. C. DUBE, Ph.D. Professor Dube's contributions to Indian sociology are well known, and he has held several important academic and advisory posts. He has travelled widely in Europe and the United States as well as in India. His publications include *Indian Village* (1955) and *India's Changing Villages* (1959). At present Director of Research at the Central Institute of Study and Research in Community Development, Mussoorie.

ROBERT E. FOX, Ph.D. Bob Fox has lived in the Philippines for many years with his Filipina wife and their son. As head of the anthropology section of the National Museum in Manila, he is constantly travelling throughout the country in order to add to the rich collections already there.

Begum AMNA GANI, B.A. Begum Amna Gani came to Pakistan from Bombay in 1947. She is a trained social worker and is at present engaged in pioneering

19

social work in some of the poorest districts of Karachi, for which she has emerged from some eight years in *purdah*.

DAW NI NI GYI, B.A. Wife of U Hla Myunt, one of Burma's foremost scientists, Daw Ni Ni is at present living with him in Vienna. Educated in Rangoon and the United States, she is a leading figure in Rangoon social life and has held several interesting literary posts.

LUCIEN M. HANKS JR., Ph.D. and JANE R. HANKS, Ph.D. A husband-and-wife team who have together made field expeditions in Thailand, taking their three sons with them. Mr. and Mrs. Hanks have published several articles in anthropological and sociological journals. Dr. Lucien Hanks holds a post at Bennington College, Vermont (U.S.A.).

Professor A. K. NAZMUL KARIM, M.A. Head of the Department of Sociology, Dacca University, Professor Karim comes from a family with a long tradition of devotion to the cause of education. He has studied in the United States and in England, and published several articles and a book, *Changing Society in India and Pakistan* (1956). His wife is also an educationist.

DAW MI MI KHAING, M.A. Daw Mi Mi Khaing, author of the well-known book, *The Burmese Family*, and several other publications, is at present Principal of Kanbawsa College, a co-educational boarding school at Taung-gyi in the Southern Shan States.

MRS. LE KWANG KIM. A leading personality in Viet-Namese social life and in the women's movement in Asia, Mrs. Kim was trained as a pharmacist in France some time after the second world war. She is a widow, with one son, who succeeds in combining her professional career with both her family duties and her outstanding contributions to national and international women's organizations and civic and social welfare projects. She has travelled very widely since the war, and now lives in Cholon (Saigon).

MRS. BANYEN PHIMMASONE LÉVY. The first Loatian girl ever to attain the *baccalauréat*, Mrs. Paul Lévy is now the wife of one of the foremost Western scholars in the field of Oriental studies.

SUSHILLA NAYER, M.B.B.S., M.D., Dr.P.H., M.P. (Lok Sabha). At one time personal physician to Mahatma Gandhi, Dr. Nayer has played a leading part in Indian political life. At present she is Minister of Health in Mr. Nehru's Government. Her main interests are health, education, social welfare and external affairs, and she has published several papers on these and other topics in addition to being a most active member of various advisory bodies. She has travelled extensively in Europe and the United States as well as in Asia and throughout India.

CHE HASHIMAH ROOSE, B.A. The eldest daughter of the Head of the Malayan

Civil Service, Mrs. Roose teaches at one of Malaya's largest and most famous secondary schools, the Federation of the Victoria Institution.

JYOTIRMOYEE SARMA, Ph.D. Jyoti Sarma lectures in sociology at Cuttack University in Orissa, and has written several articles on Indian sociology.

Mrs. B. S. SIRIWARDENA, M.A. An enthusiastic educationist, Subadra Siri-wardena is working for a Ph.D. degree in education and hopes to publish a work on 'Growing Up in a Ceylon Village' in the near future.

T. E. SMITH, O.B.E., M.A. Now working in the Institute of Commonwealth Studies, University of London, Ted Smith earlier served in the Malayan Civil Service for seventeen years. He has published two books, *Population Growth in Malaya* (1952) and *Elections in Developing Countries* (1960), and several articles on demographic matters.

HURUSTIATI SUBANDRIO, M.D. A.P.D.A. The wife of Indonesia's Minister for Foreign Affairs, Dr. Subandrio is also an outstanding public figure in her own right. She has played a leading part in the women's movement in Indonesia, in connexion with which, and her medical and anthropological interests, she has published several articles in both Indonesian and English. She has also written two books, one a biography of the Indonesian woman pioneer Kartini and the other a book for expectant mothers, in Indonesia. She is at present a Senior Officer in the Ministry of Health, Republic of Indonesia, a Member of the National Planning Council and a Member of the People's Consultative Assembly.

MICHAEL SWIFT, Ph.D. Now a lecturer at the University of Sydney (Australia), Michael Swift lived for several years in the Federation of Malaya, where he was a lecturer in the Department of Malay Studies, University of Malaya, and has published several articles on Malayan sociology.

ROMILA THARPAR, Ph.D. Romila Tharpar, who has travelled very widely in connexion with her interests in history and archaeology, is an accomplished broadcaster and writer in addition to being an experienced university lecturer, in which capacity she has held posts in both India and England.

Mrs. ANN WEE, M.A. The English wife of a Chinese lawyer in Singapore, Ann Wee is a tutor in the Social Science Department of the University of Malaya. She has written several articles on the sociology of Singapore.

FOONG WONG's vivid autobiography speaks for itself. She is a qualified social worker at present combining, like so many of our contributors, the double roles of housewife-mother and career-woman, in Singapore.

PART I

Men, women and change: an essay in understanding social roles in South and South-East Asia

by BARBARA E. WARD

INTRODUCTION: WORDS AND CONCEPTS

It is important to explain at the outset what this book does not do. We have already insisted that it is not a study of the emancipation of women in the feminist sense and that it is not intended to be an academic treatise but a book for the general reader. Though it is certainly not our intention to discourage professional social scientists from reading it, we have not written particularly for them. Yet this is a sociological work. Aimed at a wider public than usual, it is nonetheless concerned with matters of sociological interest, treated in a sociological framework.

The general reader should therefore beware. This is not a psychological study, nor is it concerned with sexual relations in the narrow sense. No doubt a complete analysis of the changing roles of the two sexes should cover a study of the ways of making love and of mutual psychological adaptations. This book does not include these things. It takes its stand upon social facts and discusses only sociological differences between the sexes—in other words: the division of labour, of interest and of status.

What exactly we mean by these terms will appear in due course, for the final *caveat* we wish to enter concerns our use of words. Though intended for the common reader, the language of this book does not, is not meant to, conform entirely to common usage. This requires some explanation.

It is one of the difficulties of the social sciences that they have not, in general, produced a special technical language. Unlike, say, botanists or physicists, who use terms peculiar to their own subject matter

25

and therefore relatively easily definable, social scientists rely in the main upon the use of words already current in ordinary speech. Hence arise many misunderstandings—and much of the layman's mistrust. For the sake of accuracy it is, of course, essential for social scientists to try to pin-point their usages, to narrow them down so that the referrents are as nearly as possible clear and unambiguous. But common speech is nearer poetry than science, its tendency usually towards wider connotations and evocative rather than indicative meaning. Thus many of the words social scientists use—'family', for instance, or 'social class' (to take but two examples)—have extremely wide, if not positively vague, connotations in everyday speech. As a result, a layman's reading of a professional sociologist's article on, say, the family in the class system of Western Germany, may be sadly distorted if, with the ordinary poetic overtones of everyday speech in mind, he fails to grasp the essential limitations of scientific terminology. Faced with an article on plant genetics he may also encounter difficulties, but they will not be those of over-familiarity with the terms used. Though to non-specialists the proliferation of 'jargon' at times appears excessive, there is a sense in which social scientists may envy the natural scientists' technical vocabulary.

For our present purposes, however, it is enough to let the reader be warned. Technical usages are explained in the text, and their limiting nature should not be forgotten.

The concept of 'social role'

There is, however, one particular terminological warning that must be made here. In this book the term 'social role' appears in the sub-title and, frequently, elsewhere. This is a quite specific technical term referring to the expected kinds of social behaviour associated with a particular social position. Thus the position 'teacher' is associated with a role which includes all the activities of teaching and also a number of other associated items of expected social behaviour—usually a middle-class standard of living, often a certain demeanour, and so on. Similarly the position 'unmarried adult daughter' in English society today is associated with a certain expected role which includes willingness to live within reach of her elderly parents, or with them if they are old and incapacitated, and to take over their full care and a large measure of their financial support if necessary.

These two simple examples should make it clear that the sociological concept to which the term 'social role' refers is an artificial construct. We are not talking of the social behaviour of any individual 'teacher' or 'unmarried adult daughter' (or 'businessman', 'father', 'clergyman', 'civil servant', 'teenager' or what you will). Instead, we are constructing types, and labelling them with the kinds of behaviour considered appropriate to each one. Considered appropriate, that is, by local and contemporary pleople. 'In Russia today the role of doctor of medicine is thus and thus'; 'In India the role of village welfare worker is to do this and this'; 'Among the Malays the role of father includes that and that'—and so on.

A number of sociological writers use the term 'social status' as a correlative to 'social role'. 'Status' in this phrase refers not primarily to a placing in a graded order of power or rank or esteem, but to 'position' in the sense in which that word has been used in the preceding paragraph. Thus one can talk of the 'status' of teacher, of adult unmarried daughter, businessman, father, and the rest. Because of the almost inescapable suggestion of grading which is attached to the word 'status' in everyday speech (which most sociologists also have in mind in using the word in other contexts) this is a difficult usage to maintain. We do not, therefore, use 'status' in this way (if a word other than 'position' in this general, non-grading sense is required, the Latin *locus* might be more appropriate). When, earlier, we referred to differences in the status of men and women, we used the word in its more common sense. Status in this chapter thus refers simply to placement in a graded order of access to power and legal and economic independence. This is the usage which appears, for example, in the title of the United Nations' Commission on the Status of Women. (In talking of placement in a graded order of esteem, as distinct from—though, of course, often correlated with—power, we use the term 'prestige'.)

Readers who wish to follow up the concept of social role in more detail may be referred to the short bibliography at the end of this volume. For the present only three further points need to be made. First, it is clearly possible for one individual to take several roles. The derivation from dramatic usage is obvious, and each man not only in his life, but even in each day, plays many parts. 'Father', 'farmer', 'churchman', and so on; these are not mutually exclusive roles. It is not difficult to list the various different roles in which any given individual—oneself included—appears from time to time. Nor is it difficult

27

to see that whereas some roles are, like those just mentioned, merely mutually compatible, other roles are actually inclusive of others—whether necessarily or by custom. Think, for example, of the number of roles comprised under the label 'mother'. This is a point to which we return later on.

But if some roles are compatible and others inclusive, still others are obviously incompatible or even mutually exclusive. One cannot, for instance, act as teacher and as pupil at the same time. This would be a sheer contradiction. On the other hand, nothing in either physical necessity or social custom prevents one from switching fairly easily from one of these roles to the other. It is otherwise with, to take extreme examples, either a Roman Catholic priest or a Hinayana Buddhist monk who breaks his vows of chastity. There is no physical bar to his being both priest (or monk) and parent; but the religious bar is absolute. Thus social sanctions can, and indeed often do, make incompatible what physical possibility has not divided. This question of the compatibility of social roles is crucial to our argument below.

The second point we wish to stress is closely connected with the foregoing, and equally obvious. We express it here as a generalization: the more complex the society, the greater the number of social roles that exist, and, in general (though this requires qualification, as we shall see) the greater the number of social roles available to each individual. In a very small-scale, simple band of primitive hunters and gatherers all men must be hunters and gatherers; for, with the exception of those of kinship and of rather rudimentary leadership, there are no other roles available. This, again, is an extreme example, but it illustrates another point to which we shall have to return below. For the new nations of the Orient are those whose social structures, for centuries already highly complex, are daily growing more and more so, through industrialization and its concomitants, and therefore those in which new social roles are daily emerging for both men and women.

Social role and social change

This, indeed, is one of the most striking features of current social change: the proliferation of possible roles. New kinds of paid employment, new types of leadership, new opportunities for the development of new skills of all kinds—these are some of the concomitants of industrialization and urbanization, political independence and development, and technological and educational advance. For the individuals who inhabit the new nations of the world, this is one of the most significant and often exciting factors of their lives: social roles which did not exist before are now becoming available.

At the same time old roles are changing. All the chapters in Part II of this book, particularly the autobiographical chapters, draw attention to the many patterns of behaviour accepted as proper and normal in the past which have drastically altered or which are in process of being recast.

Here, too, the concept of social role can aid our understanding. We have stated that in talking of roles social scientists are talking of types, not individuals. It is more accurate to say that we are talking of norms, that is matters which the consensus of reasonable opinion in any particular social group considers correct or appropriate. It is important to note that social roles are abstracted not from actual behaviour but from opinion about what behaviour ought to be. In other words, in this instance the social scientist does not watch what one hundred teachers do and construct the social role of teacher from that, but discusses with both teachers themselves and others what teachers ought to do, watches the reactions, verbal and other, to what teachers in fact do (and say), and constructs the role from the outcome of these discussions and observations. (It would be inaccurate but not altogether misleading to say that any particular social role is compounded from all the current prejudices about the particular social position to which it is attached.)

But—and here is the nub of the third point to which we wish to draw attention—prejudices are not immutable. If the actual behaviour of most teachers (to continue with our same example) begins to deviate from the hitherto accepted norm, it is likely that in time the norm too will change; similarly in certain circumstances changes in norms may lead to changes in behaviour. Thus—as in the drama—there is room for individual interpretation of roles, and a successful new interpretation of an old role may well be the starting-point of one kind of social change. Where such new interpretations are the result of conscious planning (whether based on general principles for social betterment or personal self-interest, or a mixture of the two) they may be copied by other people or not, according to circumstances and the innovator's powers of leadership. But probably, more often than not, a new interpretation of an old role is simply the accidental outcome of *ad hoc*

29

adaptations to changed circumstances. If such changes affect many people similarly and more or less simultaneously, a kind of consensus of individual adaptations is likely to emerge, and remain more or less fixed as the new norm for the time being. So-called 'static' societies are those in which the role patterns have remained relatively stable for a considerable period of time; in developing societies roles are constantly being added to and reinterpreted.

It must not be thought that we wish to contend that the phenomena of social change can be explained entirely in terms of a theory of social roles. This is very far indeed from being our standpoint. But we do wish to suggest that the concept of social role can be useful in the kind of enterprise which we are engaged in here. By making it possible to distinguish between an individual and the roles he plays it allows us to escape from the difficulties inherent in popular psychological types of explanation, and thus makes genuinely sociological comparison between personal relationships in different societies possible.

In our own everyday social life we constantly find ourselves erecting stereotypes of the kinds of behaviour we consider appropriate (or 'proper') to certain kinds of persons. Indeed, as we have seen, it is largely from the consensus of such stereotypes that a social scientist constructs the social roles we have been discussing. But there are two essential differences between the social scientists' 'roles' and our own 'stereotypes'. The scientist abstracts his roles objectively by recording the norms held by the people of the society he is studying, and having abstracted them he regards them simply as patterns, models of behaviour which individuals occupying certain social positions are expected to follow while acting in these positions. For him as sociologist they are merely roles, not moral imperatives. For ourselves, the contemporary people under observation, it is different. Our stereotypes come from the teaching and learning which have been our constant experiences since birth in our own particular social environments. They are largely subjective: the believed-in justifications of our own attitudes. They are not merely roles, distinguishable from the individuals who play them, and valid only for particular positions in social life; instead many of them are highly charged with moral value and attached firmly in our minds to the personalities of individuals. Thus where the social scientists speaking as such might say: 'In this society the teachers' role is thus and thus . . .', we, speaking as ordinary contemporary members of that same society, would say: 'Teachers are—and ought to be—thus and thus . . .'. In other words, we are usually prejudiced; the concept of social roles can help us not to be so.

It is probably the main justification of a symposium of this kind that it may help us to emerge a little from the cocoon of our preconceptions, including our own culturally derived stereotypes about what are truly 'masculine' and what 'feminine' social roles—and also about what are really 'Eastern' and what 'Western' patterns of living.

CLEARING THE GROUND: THE DANGER OF OVERSIMPLIFICATION

To make any sort of sense of the welter of information and opinion that can be collected on such a challenging topic as ours it is essential to attempt to sort out the various factors at work and analyse their differing, though interdependent, significance. As far as the sociological understanding of personal relationships is concerned we believe that analysis in terms of new and changing social roles is one of the keys. But we are still left with the questions: Whence the new roles? Why the changes?

It is always easy to talk in a general way about the causes of this, that or the other example of social change. According to prevailing fashion, one can blame something called 'Westernization', or something else called 'urbanization', or 'the breakdown of religion', or 'the collapse of the traditional family system' and so on. But all these are no more than question-begging phrases. Simply calling the processes of change and their results 'Westernization' (for example) does next to nothing towards helping us understand them.

Indeed, it may be positively misleading. Historically it is, of course, a fact that recent and contemporary changes in Oriental societies have been connected with the period of Occidental economic and political dominance. But except in some strictly economic and political spheres, and where Western educational institutions have been unusually influential, it is probably true to say that comparatively little is directly and simply ascribable to Western influence or Western example. The relationship is more complicated than that. Thus to use the term 'Westernization' as an explanation is to introduce a false simplification. Orientals, if they do not resent it, may shrug their shoulders; but Occidentals, vaguely flattered, are often lulled by it into an unrealistic dream of elder-sisterly understanding—for we think we know what

31

Western patterns are, and therefore we tend to look upon ourselves as the fore-ordained guides and patrons for 'Westernizing' Orientals. But patronage is always morally dangerous—especially for the patrons—and doubly so when based upon false premises. It is not only that the peoples of the East may not want to follow Western patterns (and, as our contributors show us, they often do not), it is not only even that they are increasingly (and rightly) rejecting our self-assumed leadership: it is also that many of the changes that are taking place have very little to do with 'Westernization' in any direct sense at all.

Similarly with 'urbanization': undoubtedly the rapid development of huge modern commercial and industrial towns all over the Orient has had and is having profound effects upon almost every aspect of economic and social relationships, including political and legal relationships, family grouping and the upbringing of children; but present-day changes are various, their starting-points different, and their explanation by no means solely to be sought in the modern surge of population towards the towns. Analysis must be more subtle than this.

Again, 'religion', 'the traditional family system'—these too are blanket terms. Religious beliefs and rituals and the effectiveness and range of application of religious sanctions are by no means uniform even within the borders of a single nation in which a single faith is officially proposed. Between different nations the differences may be manifold and profound. Christianity in Italy is not the same thing as Christianity in Sweden, nor is the Buddhism of Ceylon to be equated with the Buddhism of the Overseas Chinese; and it should go without saying that Moslems, Hindus, Buddhists and Roman Catholics—all of whom are to be found predominating in different Asian States—have very different approaches to such matters as family structure and the status of women.

As for 'the traditional family'—more nonsense is talked about this, both in the East and the West, than about almost any other subject. What was it? Who lived in it? Was it everywhere the same? How did it relate to the laws and customs governing property, marriage, the wider kinship system, politics and the economic division of labour? These and similar questions have to be answered before one can make valid pronouncements about the effect (or even the fact) of its decline. But how often are they even asked?

One of our troubles is that, Easterners and Westerners alike, we are too quick to put up straw figures, stereotypes of social patterns and cultural forms (as well as social roles) which we label 'Eastern' and 'Western' respectively. We forget the enormous variety within the West, let alone the even greater variety within the much larger East. We forget, too, that most Europeans—and similarly most Asians—are ignorant of their neighbours' customs and traditions. We generalize from our own experience of the one or two places we know something about to the very many places of which we have no experience and know nothing at all. And we all forget that social patterns and cultural forms are never simple and never develop along single-line tracks, but are always complex and always mutually interdependent in a multiplicity of different ways.

The chapters in the main body of this book (Part II below) demonstrate both the complexities of change and the variety which exists in the countries of South and South-East Asia. (And almost incidentally, among other things they make it quite clear that the cherished Western notion of typical Oriental womanhood is an illusion.)

Nevertheless, when all that can be said about variety and the falsity of blanket explanations has been said, it remains true that the chapters in Part II of this book do also show remarkable similarities: the same themes do recur. Similar technical, economic and political changes and above all similar educational advances appear in nearly all of them. And the effects of these things do seem to tend in the same direction, towards similar patterns of urban in place of rural living, wage- and salary-earning in place of self-subsistence, buying and selling of factory-made goods in place of home handicraft production, universal suffrage and a national bureaucracy in place of colonial administration or absolute monarchy, modern schools and universities in place of traditional religious and home education, and so on and so forth. Not that all these tendencies are everywhere apparent at the same rate, nor that none of them has anywhere appeared before—towns are far older in Asia than in Europe, and a system of advanced competitive examination for entry into the national bureaucracy had already existed for a thousand years in China before it was taken as a model for Great Britain in the nineteenth century—but their scale, their widespread nature and the particular type of technological and economic system which underlies their present-day manifestations are new. The novelty is not least in the universality of the changes and their world-wide interconnectedness. What in the past were largely separate civilizations, though never completely isolated nor without influence upon each other, are becoming in the twentieth century ever more closely connected by the single network of economic and political relations which now enmeshes the whole world. At the same time their own economic and governmental systems are all being remade after a limited number of Western-type models.

Were we then wrong to denounce explanation in terms of Westernization? In so far as the large-scale economic and governmental institutions of the present day—together with the technological features which enable them to work—are European in origin and form, the whole world may be said to have become Westernized. But it is still true to say that the effects of the working of these large-scale Western-type economic and governmental institutions (and their world-wide interconnexions) upon the everyday lives of ordinary people and the personal relations of men and women can only be ascribed indirectly to Western influence. Moreover, because of such things as original difference in culture and social structure and variations in the speed and intensity of economic and political change, they are not felt everywhere in the same way. At this level, to speak of the whole world becoming Westernized is to beg all the questions this book is designed to investigate.

Moreover, the West, too, is changing. 'Westernization' no longer has meaning as an explanation for a general process in which the West itself is also caught up, by reason of the interconnectedness of world events which, paradoxically enough, is greater now than in the colonial era, and because Western institutions themselves are altering. We are all in this together. Is it this, perhaps, which gives us today an opportunity for mutual understanding that has never really existed before?

Be that as it may, the ground has now been cleared for the next steps in our argument. These are as follows: first, an examination of some of the ways in which the rather similar new institutional developments in South and South-East Asia are opening new roles and new opportunities, especially for women; second, an examination of some of the ways in which these new features are affecting older institutions and bringing about changes in traditional roles—particularly the family roles of women; and finally a discussion of what may be the factors which make changes in the relative role patterns of the two sexes easy or difficult, acceptable or otherwise. The argument refers in particular to South and South-East Asia, but its general applicability is much wider, and we do not hesitate to point the comparisons.

Social change is no respecter of persons. Hardly any of the profound changes which have been occurring in South and South-East Asia have in themselves discriminated between the sexes. The trend towards urban living, for example, although it usually draws in men first, nevertheless also affects women (and children) whether they follow in their turn to the towns or stay behind in the villages. Improved health services, DDT spraying, inoculation and so on are not available for one sex only, nor are lowered death rates with their results in population pressure sexually selective. Most political, economic and religious changes are similarly impartial. Only a few special measures—women's suffrage, girls' education, the provision of maternity services, for example—have been deliberately devised for a single sex, and all these, together with recent legal alterations in such matters as marriage and inheritance, inevitably have repercussions upon men as well.

Nevertheless, existing differences in roles have necessarily meant that changes affecting all equally have not affected all similarly. The rich respond differently from the poor, town dwellers differently from country people, women differently from men. Our brief is to direct attention primarily to the women's response, and in this section we concentrate upon the ways in which these general changes are opening up new roles, or the potentiality of them, for women.

Obviously we cannot cover the whole canvas, but we shall select from the general changes certain aspects which appear particularly significant: modern medical measures, improved communications, increasing urbanization, new openings for paid employment, education, political emancipation and legal change. Our illustrations will be drawn primarily, though not exclusively, from the evidence provided in the articles which follow.

Modern medical measures

We have pointed out that the changes brought about in human social life by the application of modern medical measures are not limited to women's affairs only; nor, of course, are they unique to Asia. Many of the effects of postponing the age of death which are now beginning to appear in the East were first consciously experienced in Europe and the United States about a hundred to a hundred and fifty years ago.

35

My husband's great-grandfather died in 1870. He left among his effects a small locket in which was framed the picture of a weeping willow tree embroidered entirely in seven different shades of fine golden hair, from the heads of the seven of his brothers and sisters who had died before reaching the age of ten years; several of the remaining thirteen died in adolescence. He himself successfully raised six children, one of whom was my husband's maternal grandfather who lost only one of his five, and that in battle. The daughter who was my mother-in-law bore one child only; we in our turn have two.

The same story appears over and over again in the history of middle-class Westerners in the last hundred years. Their families in the later nineteenth century were unusual not in the numbers who were born but in the numbers who survived. After about two generations of this, parents no longer in constant dread of bereavement started to control the number of births.

So far, as Ted Smith's article points out, only Japan in the whole of Asia shows a similar trend towards slowing the rate of population growth. Whether or not other Asian nations will follow suit is a matter of open debate; certainly, as Barbara Cadbury explains, much is being done to encourage them to do so.

At the level of national (and international) policy making, control of population growth is largely a matter of economic or military calculation. For individuals, too, economic thinking is often paramount though in a different way. Small-holding farmers who depend upon their children for increasing production naturally want large families, especially if they live under a family system which keeps adult children at home, or still more, one which maintains property (especially land) undivided for as long as possible. Wage-earners, particularly white-collared salary-earners who see a need for educating their children, do not want too many dependents. The validity of this argument is commonly borne out in the experience of family planning clinics whose *clientèle* is predominantly from the white-collar classes and above (though standards of education, availability of clinics and degree of acceptance of Western-type medicine also play a part in determining who shall attend and where). The evidence of the articles in the body of this book points to a future development of contraception on much the same lines as that which has taken place in the West, though some of the populations concerned are larger, and the time lag may be considerable.

36

This is a new thing in the world. Its full effects on the role of women are not yet clear even in those countries of the West where it has been longer apparent. But undoubtedly it is one of the crucial factors. For the first time in human history there is a promise of potential freedom from the physiological and social effects of the more or less continuous period of pregnancy, parturition and lactation which, with numerous miscarriages, has been the lot of the majority of women between the ages of about 15 and about 50 in all societies.

And the babies they do have need not die.

This, too, is crucial. A modern Westerner reads the pathetic inscriptions on the tiny graves which are scattered throughout the old burial grounds of Europe with pity; most modern Easterners would read them with a sympathy born of experience. One of the most striking differences between conversations with women in most parts of the West and most parts of the East today is that in the West one says: 'And how many children have you got?', in the East: 'How many have you reared?' Increasingly, as the former question becomes safer to ask in Asia as well—and this is happening—the roles of mother and wife will be affected by a new freedom from fear.

Moreover, this has been fear not of personal bereavement only, but of failure in marriage in the present and lack of support in the future. Foong Wong's article gives a telling account of a situation which is common in most extended family systems, such as exist in India and Pakistan and among the Chinese, for example: a wife must bear children (in patrilineal systems, such as these, especially sons) in order to justify her position in her husband's home. Children who die are almost as little use in this respect as children unborn, and certainly a widow without children to support her may be in a desperate plight. In countries like Burma, Thailand, the Philippines, where the true extended family does not obtain (except among some minority peoples) there is still a need for children to justify a woman's position in marriage (marriages in which there are no children are far more likely to end in divorce) and to support her in her old age. Modern medicine saves very many of the babies who formerly would have died and family-planning clinics can help restore fertility to couples who previously would have remained barren.

These are matters of peculiarly personal concern to women. Together with men they share also, of course, in the other benefits of modern preventive and curative medicine. And here the countries of

37

South and South-East Asia are probably more greatly affected than the West, for 'the West' is on the whole a temperate zone, whereas the regions described in this volume all fall largely within the Tropics where diseases have been more lowering and more difficult to eradicate. Freedom from malaria, for instance, is one of the greatest boons that the twentieth century has brought. Cholera still strikes, but it can be controlled; leprosy can be cured; the typhoids become less and less common as sanitation improves; yaws can be easily eliminated. The list could be much longer. Dr. Smith's article describes how death-rates have already been falling—often dramatically.

But Dr. Smith's article also tells us something else about current death-rates in our region, namely that they are somewhat higher for women than for men. Here is a measurable contrast with the West. In most economically developed countries the number of adult women exceeds the number of adult men, and it is well known that the actuarial figures for a woman's expectation of life are higher than those for a man's. However, it does not follow that this difference between East and West is evidence of a low valuation of females in the East. Despite some popular beliefs, there is no demographic evidence that female infanticide anywhere in the region makes a noticeable difference to the sex ratio of infants and small children. Indeed, infant mortality in India, for example, is believed to be higher for male than for female babies. It is possible that among people whose family system shows a strong patrilineal bias girl children may not be given quite the same care as their brothers, but any such discrimination, in so far as it still exists, is likely to be of diminishing importance. It is much more likely that slowness in adopting modern methods of midwifery is to blame, whether because of their inadequate supply or from prejudice—and this is an area in which prejudice dies hard, as Begum Amna Gani points out. Compared with economically developed countries, relatively large numbers of women do still die in child-birth. But this is likely to be a temporary state of affairs.

What new social roles have all these developments brought? (Their effect upon old roles, particularly those of wife and mother, is discussed later on.) In the first place there are new opportunities for employment. Doctors, nurses, midwives, medical assistants of all kinds, social workers in the fields of health and nutrition, pharmacists and so on are required in increasing numbers together with the host of other technologists and administrators and the developed system of

38

communications without which a modern medical service cannot operate. In most of these occupations women (including at least five of our own contributors) are to be found as well as men, though, except in nursing, in lesser numbers. (It is interesting to notice a recent regulation restricting the numbers of women medical students in Bangkok because they were fast outnumbering the men to the detriment, so it was thought, of the future of the Thai health services.)

The role of 'healer' is, of course, not a new one; traditionally in different countries it was performed in varying ways, often closely connected with magical and religious rituals, sometimes by men and sometimes by women. Madame Lévy and Dr. Nayer both describe the high esteem in which their fathers' and grandfathers' healing powers were held. Nevertheless the full apparatus of modern medicine is a break with tradition, and the modern occupations of doctor, nurse and so on are the framework of what are essentially new roles for educated men and women in South and South-East Asia.

But those who become nurses or doctors are few. For most people the effects of modern medical measures upon their social roles are indirect. Freedom from ill-health (including the burden of continuous pregnancy and the bearing of too many children) and from fear of early death can lead to the reinterpretation of old roles in the family and the opportunity to develop other new roles outside it. Already in the West women are beginning to think in terms of a 'third period' of life in which, the tasks of motherhood completed, they still have time to re-enter the world of employment. The current campaign to draw married women in the United Kingdom back into the teaching profession is only one example. But we return to this and other aspects of what has been called 'the dual role' of women later on.

Communications

Pramuan Dickinson describes graphically how a journey which took her grandfather two months by elephant and her father a fortnight by train and on foot can now be accomplished in a few hours by fast motor-car. Romila Tharpar draws the moral that modern means of travel have been one of the most liberating influences upon women whose mothers were in full *purdah*. Eileen Arceo-Ortega and Subadra Siriwardena explain how driving their own automobiles makes it possible for each of them to combine successfully the roles of housewife, mother and professional educationist. Very many of our contributors have travelled the world around in search of higher education, on professional business, or for pleasure. Like modern medicine, modern transport is a kind of enabling measure making new roles possible and forcing the reinterpretation of old ones through the freedom which it confers.

This kind of freedom—to go about easily, speedily, over long distances, and if necessary by oneself—is a new thing in the world's history; not unique to Asia. It has been well said that even Napoleon's armies could travel no faster than Julius Caesar's—or, for that matter, Akbar's or Ghengis Khan's. The writer's own grandfather was born in the first heyday of railway building in England (the first, that is, in the world); her father watched the early motor-cars proceeding, as by law they were bound to do, behind a man walking with a red flag, and later saw Blériot fly the English Channel; her mother made social history in the West of England by being one of the first women to ride a motor-bicycle—in 1922. (Her son cheered Major Gagarin when he visited London in 1961.) Thus the development of modern transport is almost as recent in the West as in the East. The difference is one of degree only—and anyone who has been caught in the rush hour traffic jams of Bangkok or Manila or Calcutta might be forgiven if he doubted even that!

In some of the countries of our region (notably, from the evidence of our contributors, Burma and Thailand) women have apparently always had relative freedom to travel on their own affairs; in others (notably India and Pakistan) it has not been so. It is particularly in these latter countries that Dr. Tharpar's point that modern methods of transport have been indirectly one of the most influential factors in the practical emancipation of women is well taken. Traditional customs are not always easy to maintain on modern vehicles, distance from the familiar social environment may make them seem unnecessary, even ridiculous. Dr. Sushilla Nayer describes how her mother used to keep full *purdah* while travelling by train; a complicated business, requiring among other things a large staff of servants. There is a station on the line from Bombay to Delhi through which large numbers of the Indians resident in East Africa pass on their way to and from that continent. The women know it as 'Anand-raise-the-veil' or 'Anand-lower-the-veil' according to whether they are journeying towards their ancestral villages in India or their newer homes across the sea.

It is not necessary to labour the obvious points about travel broadening the mind, helping to break down ethnocentricity, leading to new personal contacts, economic and educational opportunities, even inter-marriage. Our contributors make them very clear.

But travel is only one part of the modern system of communications. Not only people, but goods and ideas too are being distributed more and more widely. Clothes which once had to be hand-made (even to the spinning of the threads, as Madame Le Kwang Kim explains) can now be bought ready-made; pots and pans can be of plastic and aluminium; soap, cosmetics, medicaments, surgical plaster, even comfortable and hygienic sanitary towels, are easily available almost every-where; food-stuffs, once laboriously planted, weeded, harvested and processed by family hand labour, can be bought ready wrapped in the stores. There is electricity and piped water. These things are by no means true for all the people of our area, not yet; but they are for many. And their effects upon the lives and roles of men and women and the way they spend their time are profound. (Moreover, they are among the several modern developments which are making the lives of Easterners and Westerners more alike—and, therefore, presumably mutually more comprehensible.)

As for ideas—the spread of books and newspapers, and the tele-phone, radio, cinema, and television (already in 1961 popular tele-vision is a regular feature of life in Hong Kong, Manila, Bangkok, Singapore) marks a whole series of social revolutions. In education, the arts and entertainment their influence is obvious, producing new knowledge, new concepts, new and modified social attitudes, new ways of passing time, and new openings for employment. The husband who refused to countenance the education of women 'because my wife might learn to write and read love letters from other men' saw only a very small part of the complications that improved communications would bring. Perhaps the most striking tales of family change among those which follow in Part II of this book are those written by women university graduates whose own grandmothers, even mothers, were illiterate.

The surge to the towns

In 1953 something quite new happened in the Chinese fishing village of Kau Sai, which lies on one of the many islands in the territory of

Hong Kong: several fishermen sent their daughters to school. Previously this had been the privilege of sons only. But in the early 1950s Kau Sai was becoming prosperous. Some of the fishing junks were fitted with diesel engines; catches were larger and more regular, incomes higher. With higher incomes, wives and daughters, as well as sons and grandsons, wanted to buy things. The city had plenty of things to sell, but to find the shops you needed to be able to read—read the shop signs, the street names, the figures on the buses and their destinations. Modern communications were all laid on, travel and goods were at the women's disposal—but first they had to be able to read.

In the village literacy was not necessary; town living, even town visiting, was difficult without it. The schoolgirls of Kau Sai illustrate very neatly the interdependence of the many different factors in contemporary social change.

More than that, they illustrate also the surge towards the towns. Between 1951 and 1959 four young fisher boys left the village—prosperous though their families undoubtedly were—for work in the city, and one girl was lucky enough to marry a townsman. This, which made her the envy of every other woman and the ideal of every schoolgirl in the village, meant that she went to live in a windowless cubicle about 9 feet long and 5 feet broad, whose hardboard walls reached a height of about 7 feet and which was flanked by six or seven similar cubicles with whose occupants (together with those who slept in the passageway) she now shares a common kitchen-cum-lavatory about 10 feet square. The fourth floor of the tenement which contains this cubicle is reached by a steep, straight stairway, a yard wide, down which all refuse—including night-soil—has to be carried, and which, being no tenant's property, is no tenant's business to keep clean. The tenement is, of course, only one in a street of such buildings, and in scores of such streets. There is a standpipe for water about a hundred yards away. The good fortune of this girl, who now has two children both under 3 years old, is still the talk of her old friends in the village. She has achieved their highest ambition: she lives in town.

What has she gained? In the eyes of her friends and herself two precious things: freedom from the ceaselessness of toil in the village, and access to glamour and excitement. Both the 'push' from the country and the 'pull' to the towns are here reflected. There is no doubt that in most countries peasant rural life is an endless round of physically demanding work. Chinese fishing families are perhaps an extreme example, since they live always (men, women and children) on their boats and many of them work far into the night; moreover they are driven all the time by the constant desire to make good in the material sense. By no means all the other nationalities in South and South-East Asia share this motivation, and, without it, most of them, living in a climate and environment which do not force absolutely continuous effort, do in fact lead a less strenuous life. Nevertheless, even for them, the work is usually demanding and unending; often especially so for the women who, in addition to the inescapable daily chores of child care, cooking, cleaning, collecting water and firewood, laundering, and other domestic duties, usually have the more continuous, if less arduous, tasks of agriculture laid upon them—planting out, for instance, and weeding.

In the towns those tasks disappear; water comes from a tap (what is a hundred yards or so down the street compared with a quarter of a mile or more on rough village path?); food can quite often be bought ready cooked; charcoal and firewood are in the market; there is electricity. All this and glamour too: things to see, shops to look at, the cinema, a fire engine, buses, crowded pavements, curious foreigners, rich people, perhaps processions for funerals and weddings. The fascination of town life for the imaginations of peasant women is not hard to understand.

The question how far their expectations are fulfilled can hardly be answered. For the fisherman's daughter from Kau Sai they undoubtedly were. Though to midde-class Western eyes she may appear to have exchanged a healthy open-air life in some of the most beautiful scenery in the world for an overcrowded slum, she is a truly happy woman. She told me so; and I could see that it was true. But for the pavement sleepers of other parts of Hong Kong (or Calcutta, or Bombay, or elsewhere) I cannot say. Overcrowding, unemployment, slum housing—these are common in all large Asian cities and there are probably many who wish they had never left the land. But we do not always see the alternatives. We need more information, more factual studies of the relative advantages of poor town and poor country living and the actual reasons behind the decisions to migrate.

Moreover it is as misleading to think solely in terms of poverty and overcrowding as it is to ignore them. Asian towns have their well-to-do inhabitants too. Furthermore, in Asia as elsewhere it is town life that gives the greatest opportunities for recreation, cultural activities of all

43

kinds, education, diversified employment—after all, as the derivation of the word shows, towns are the seats of civilization. And, as Professor Karim points out, as often as not they are also the places in which it is easiest for traditionally secluded women to emerge from *purdah*. None of our Asian women contributors can be described as a mere countrywoman.

In this they are atypical. Dr. Smith tells us that, apart from city-states like Singapore, the proportion of the total population living in towns containing a population of 20,000 or more nowhere in our region exceeds 22 per cent, and the average is not much above 10 per cent. In North America it is (1950) 42 per cent, in Europe (excluding Russia) 35 per cent, in the U.S.S.R. 31 per cent. One of the difficulties in the way of mutual understanding between East and West is that the overwhelming majority of Asians are villagers—or small-town dwellers—still.

Nevertheless it is certain that there is a surge towards the towns in Asia, and that it is increasing. The figures in Table 1 were among those presented to a joint United Nations/Unesco seminar in August 1956 on urbanization in Asia and the Far East.

TABLE 1. Trends in percentage of the total population in towns of 20,000 inhabitants or more, 1910-51

Year	India	Federation of Malaya
1910	5.1	8.3
1920	5.4	10.1
1930	6.3	12.2
1940	8.2	—
1947	—	17.0
1951	12.0	—

Source: Proceedings of the Joint United Nations/Unesco Seminar on Urbanization in the ECAFE Region, Bangkok, 8-18 August 1956, edited by Philip M. Hauser, Calcutta, 1957, p. 103.

It is equally certain that the change from rural to urban living is accompanied by profound changes in social roles. What this may mean for traditional family roles we discuss below; the development of new types of role in towns is one of the topics we consider under our next heading.

New employment

When economists discuss increasing urbanization in terms of a 'pull' to the towns or a 'push' from the country they are referring to opportunities for making a living. Most of the new (that is, non-traditional) concerns are in the towns, and despite much serious urban unemployment and poverty the continuing processes of economic specialization and industrialization do mean that the towns offer a multitude of new jobs. For most men, whether 'pushed out' or 'pulled in'—or, more commonly, a bit of both—going to town and looking for work are more or less synonymous.

This is not necessarily true of women. Indeed, it seems likely that most of the migrant women who seek employment in the towns of Asia do so rather as a response to the economic necessity they find pressing upon them after they have arrived than as their intended goal on arriving. We must beware of equating the numbers of women living in towns with the numbers in employment: on the one hand, many women (and, of course, many men too) are employed in the country and, on the other hand, in both town and country many are not employed at all.

The recorded numbers of gainfully employed women are in fact always less than the total female population in any given place. This is not only because, as with men, a fairly large proportion consists of people who are either too young or too old to be included, but also because the tasks which engage most of the time and energy of most women everywhere are not included in the statistics of economic activity. Housework in one's own home is a job which has no money value put upon it; it is therefore excluded from the statistics and classed as 'uneconomic'. This fact, which complicates every discussion of the division of labour between the sexes, tends also to depreciate the social contribution of women—difficulties which could be avoided if it were possible (as surely it should be?) to set a money value upon housework at home (and, also, one might add, upon the strictly productive work of bearing and rearing children, which is likewise regarded as an uneconomic activity).

Be that as it may (and proverbial comment notwithstanding), the fact remains that most women do not 'work', including usually a large proportion of those who are of working age. In the United Kingdom, about half of the women between 15 and 59 are thus economically inactive. In India, of women aged 15 to 56, 58 per cent are inactive; in the Philippines, of women over 10, 60 per cent are inactive. Comparable information does not exist for the other countries of South and South-East Asia, which is especially unfortunate since (as will become clearer later on) the common Western assumption that women in all Oriental countries have a similar position is far indeed from the facts.

In any case, we are not so much concerned here with the extent of women's employment in general as with their employment in such ways as may be expected to bring about role changes. For some assistance with this topic we can turn to such statistics as do exist on the distribution of women workers between the three sectors of the economy: agriculture, industry, services, and on their distribution by status as employers and workers on their own account, unpaid family workers, and employees.[1]

TABLE 2. Percentage of female labour force in each economic sector

Country	Agriculture	Industry	Services
India	82	7	11
Federation of Malaya	79	8	13
Pakistan	82	9	9
Philippines	44	23	33
Thailand	90	2	8

Two points stand out: first, the high proportion of women employed in agriculture; second, the predominance of service over industrial employment. The first point reflects the preponderance of agriculture over industry in all contemporary South and South-East Asian economies. It also suggests that a large proportion of the employed women of this region have not left the countryside. The second is a feature of

1. For Tables 2 and 3 and much of their interpretation, we are indebted to a paper presented by Sir Alexander Carr Saunders to the thirty-first meeting of the International Institute of Differing Civilizations (INCIDI) held in Brussels on 17, 18, 19 and 20 September 1958, and published in the report entitled *Women's Role in the Development of Tropical and Subtropical Countries*, Brussels, 1959, p. 500-516. The figures are taken from an article, 'Women in the Labour Force', *International Labour Review*, Vol. LXXVII, No. 3, March 1958.

the industrialized West as well, but the kinds of services performed and the conditions under which they are carried out are usually different. It is perhaps worth recalling that 'services' include commerce and transport as well as domestic service.

Further light is thrown on these points by the figures in Table 3.

TABLE 3. Distribution of the female labour force by status (percentage of total)

Country	Employers and workers on own account	Unpaid family workers	Employees
India	26	60	14
Federation of Malaya	29	23	48
Pakistan	83	2	15
Philippines	11	60	29

In fully industrialized countries the proportion of women classed as employers and workers on their own account never reaches 20 per cent; in the United States, Canada and the United Kingdom, it is around 5 per cent. In other words, in those countries where industrialization has gone furthest, relatively few women are employers or workers on their own account, more than 90 per cent of the female labour force being engaged as employees. This is partly because of the greater number of women workers engaged in manufacturing, but also partly because the services in such countries tend to be organized on a larger scale. In less industrialized countries quite a large proportion of the women working in traditional ways in agriculture are employers or working on their own account, as would be expected; it is less often remembered that relatively many of the women engaged in trade or business are of this status too. This is especially so in Thailand (and also Burma, the Philippines and Indonesia which are not on this list). But these are traditional, not new, roles in these countries. When to those facts is added the probability that a large proportion of the women who are listed as employees are in fact domestic servants (another traditional occupation, and one which has dramatically decreased in importance in the West), it will be seen that probably the great majority of the gainfully employed women in South and South-East Asia today have not entered new kinds of employment at all.

47

But some undoubtedly have, and not only in towns. Agriculture has its own non-traditional side, particularly in plantation work which employs very large numbers of women especially in Ceylon, Federation of Malaya, Indonesia and parts of India. This accounts for the big discrepancy between the proportion of women workers in agriculture (79 per cent) and the proportion engaged as unpaid family workers (23 per cent) in Malaya, for example.

Plantation employment is rather a special case. Although certainly not part of the indigenous traditional economies, it has in most places now been going on for a fairly long time, and in any case being mainly rural and often engaging whole families at a time, it might be expected to bring about less fundamental change in the lives of the women engaged in it, and their families, than occupations which require a move to the towns. On the other hand, many plantation workers are immigrants, or the descendants of immigrants, from overseas (like the workers of South Indian origin in Ceylon's tea and Malaya's rubber plantations). And however true it may be that rural women of the poorer classes have almost everywhere and almost always taken part in their families' agricultural work, there are important differences between being a wage-earner working for someone else, and being a co-worker in your own family enterprise.

Nevertheless, it is when the wage-earning takes place in a completely non-traditional occupation in town that there are likely to be the greatest number of other differences too. And though the proportion of Asian women so affected is small, the number is not—and it is rapidly increasing. We should be exceedingly unwise to underestimate its extent, or play down its significance.

A great deal has been written about the effect of the change from subsistence agriculture in a stable village setting to wage-earning in the slum conditions of many modern towns. We have been told how the family ceases to be a unit of production, and how the bread-winner becomes for the first time a hired hand paid as an individual; how the dependants, who have hitherto been co-workers in a joint enterprise, find themselves in a new and lower status and how they may even be left behind in the villages; how when women, too, become wage-earners the disruption is even greater, children are not properly cared for, sexual morality is weakened, and the traditional family system undermined if not destroyed. This is hardly an exaggeration of a familiar line of argument.

There is some truth in it. Subsistence agriculture, which is the traditional occupation for the large majority of people in our region, is often bound up with the existence of closely integrated groups of kinsmen. It would not be surprising if, when individual wage-earning took the place of shared productive labour, some of the cement holding such groups together were removed. In the next section of this chapter (on changing family roles) we examine the relative viability of different kinds of family and kinship structure in this respect. But it does not need an excursion into kinship theory to demonstrate that by no means all the traditional Asian family systems are in fact so fragile as some writers believe. We have already noted the traditional role of women as traders in Burma, Thailand, Indonesia and the Philippines. These women have long enjoyed an independently earned income. And it should go without saying that all the countries of our region have had traditionally differentiated economies, such that money rewards for work have a long history for large numbers of men everywhere. Yet it is not suggested that these things have undermined the traditional family systems. (There is, however, ample evidence that the traditional family systems in the countries where women have freely engaged in trade are very different from those, of, say, India, or Pakistan; but that is just the point at issue.)

Reading some of the literature on urbanization and industrialization in Asia, one cannot help feeling that it has been written by Westerners suffering from a deep-seated, possibly unconscious, romantic yearning for a rural Golden Age in which the climate is always balmy, the season always just after harvest—and electricity and running water are not far away. It is true that the social cost of urbanization and industrialization has usually been extremely high. It is true that housing in rapidly expanding towns is often poor, insanitary and overcrowded. But we have already suggested that agricultural poverty and overcrowding may be at least as hard to bear. Experience shows that given industrialization (and only then) the extreme conditions of both rural and urban wretchedness can be mitigated. And may it not be these, rather than wage-earning, which are the significant factors in family break-up where it occurs?

Where women are concerned it is probably not wage-earning as such but the necessity of working to fixed hours which is more important in bringing about changes in interpretation of roles and patterns of family living. Hours of work on family agricultural plots, in traditional small-scale trading and cottage-industry, even, to some extent, in plantation work, are flexibly adaptable to the worker. A modern factory, big store, transport business, office, or school has a fixed time-table and pay is usually according to hours worked. People who have prior obligations to housework, catering, cooking, and, above all, children, find this extremely difficult, and very tiring. Only those who for economic reasons must, or for domestic reasons can, are likely to seek out employment of this kind. If this is so, then it helps to explain why it is that in several countries of our region, it appears to be commoner to find gainfully employed women among the poor and the fairly well-to-do, uncommon to find them from the middle ranges, or, of course, the very rich. Where the women of the poorest classes work from necessity, those of the next higher income groups tend to stay at home, partly because domestic work demands their presence, partly because social prestige for their families may depend upon their being different in this respect from the poor. The upper strata who can afford to give their girls both education and freedom from domestic tasks can also afford to ignore this particular badge of social prestige. (Indeed, for them prestige often comes more from having highly educated daughters or wives engaged in professional work and imbued with ideas of service to the community.) In some of the more highly industrialized countries of the West there is now a much wider scatter throughout the socio-economic scale.

But this difference in social class distribution goes with another difference; in the West a very large proportion of working women are unmarried; in the East nearly all are married. And this applies not only to traditional occupations and plantation work where the flexibility of time-table might be expected to facilitate the employment of married women, but throughout. (Widows, and women deserted by their husbands, who have children to support are an important minority, of course, everywhere.) This is not altogether surprising, for in some countries—notably, but not exclusively, India and Pakistan—girls marry young, and almost everywhere arranged marriages (usually implying the careful chaperonage of young women) are still the normal practice and spinsters hardly exist. Only among the later generations of town-dwellers in the East is there a tendency for girls to marry later and, with a higher standard of education, to seek a job as soon as they are old enough to work.

We may surmise from this that more differences between Western and Eastern patterns are likely to disappear in time. For if Eastern girls are beginning to marry later and go to work earlier, Western girls are beginning to marry earlier and stay at work later, and fewer and fewer are remaining unmarried. It is now not marriage which forces a girl's retirement from paid employment in the West, but the arrival of babies. The significance of child care in this respect is further demonstrated by the recent tendency noted widely in the West for married women to return to work after their children have grown up. We have already linked this with the increased expectancy of life and the decreased expectancy of pregnancy. We could also link it with the mobility of population which often denies a mother the support and help of nearby relatives, and with the decline in the number of domestic servants. All these are developments which are very likely to follow in Eastern countries later on. Will it also follow that there, too, the majority of the female labour force will be either pre- or post-child bearing? Or will other methods of organizing domestic work and child care—together, perhaps, with more flexible working hours, or less restricting housing programmes—be developed on a large scale? And will recognition be paid to the economic contribution of the child-bearing years?

These are crucial issues in any discussion of the division of labour between the sexes and the changing roles of women.

They are crucial also in any consideration of the status of women in employment. Table 4 shows how small is the number of women in higher grade posts in our region.

This is a many-sided subject, to which we return in the later sections of this essay. Here we simply draw attention to one practical obstacle to successful participation in the professions and to promotion which affects men and women unequally: the years during which a person of talent and ambition consolidates his knowledge and skill, builds up his reputation and makes his important contacts are just the years in which a woman with children is most fully occupied at home. It is not an accident that so many Western women in high positions and in the professions have been spinsters. Up to now few Asian women have had seriously to face the choice between marriage and a career. Both are possible as long as domestic servants are easily available, or relatives are at hand, though even with good domestic help a professional woman with young children still has the problem of reconciling two responsibilities.

TABLE 4. The proportion of women gainfully employed expressed as a percentage[1] of the total number employed; selected countries and selected occupations[2]

	Philippines (1960)	Thailand (1960)	Burma (1953)	Federation of Malaya (1957)[3]	Ceylon (1953)	Singapore (1957)	India (1951)	Pakistan (1951)
Total employed population	35	40	27	23	24	18	16	6
Agricultural and related occupations	25	52	22	27	27	27	18	6
Non-agricultural occupations	50	29	28	16	20	17	14	5
Professional, technical and related occupations	39	52	23	22	28	34	4(?)	4
Managerial, administrative and clerical occupations	5	17	9	0.09	8	9	4(?)	0.5
Sales and related occupations	57	44	48	27	11	10	10	3
Manufacturing occupations	61	28	31	12	25	16	14	6
Service occupations	61	51	15	10	24	37	19	8

1. These percentages were calculated to the nearest whole number from round thousands. They are only approximate.
2. Original figures were obtained from the most recent (as dates) census reports for each country, except the Philippines for which the data were taken from the *ILO Yearbook of Labour Statistics, 1960*.
3. Malays only.

Note: Comparisons must be treated with caution because the criteria for allocation to occupational divisions, and for the category 'gainfully employed', are not always identical in different censuses. The figures for India, Burma and Thailand require special mention: the Indian census of 1951 employed a new method of classifying occupations from which the above figures were compiled with as near accuracy as possible; the Burmese figures refer to a sample census of 252 Burmese towns only; the Thai figures were calculated from data from two administrative divisions (*changwad*) only, one urban and one rural.

Nearly all our women contributors refer to these matters. Many are beginning to wonder what their daughters and grand-daughters will decide to do, for they are well aware that given small families of father, mother and unmarried children, isolated from close relatives, unable to engage domestic servants, and with a tradition that each family lives, eats, and brings up its young children separately, there is a genuine incompatibility between the role of mother and the role of professional worker or higher grade executive.

But this cannot be the sole obstacle to women's participation in the professions and promotion or our table would not show such marked contrasts between different countries. It is clear that proportionately it is much more than ten times easier for a women to enter these occupations in the Philippines than in Pakistan. Thailand, Singapore, India, Ceylon and Federation of Malaya—more or less in that order—lie between these two extremes. Our readers are invited to read the articles in the body of this book (especially those written by professional women) with the object of finding out why this should be so. We ourselves offer certain hypotheses in the remaining sections of this essay.

Note on equal pay

In 1960 the United Nations published a special pamphlet (E/CN/6/341/Rev. 1) on equal pay for the two sexes. In an appendix to this appear summaries of the measures taken in seventy different countries to give effect to the International Labour Office Equal Remuneration Convention and Recommendation of 1951. In almost all of them (the notable exceptions are South Africa, Australia and the Sudan) governmental and/or trade union policies endorse the principle of equal pay and seek to extend its application. Up to 15 October 1960, thirty-four governments had ratified this ILO convention, among them India, Indonesia and the Philippines. No other South Asian countries appear on the list of ratifications, but neither do over a dozen Western countries, including the United Kingdom and the United States.

It is, however, only fair to point out that ratification implies accepting the principle of equal pay, application of the principle does not automatically follow; moreover, failure to ratify does not imply rejection of either the principle or its application. The practice of paying equal reward for equal work regardless of sex is, in fact, more common in some of the non-ratifying than in some of the ratifying countries.

From our present point of view, however, the significant facts are that all South and South-East Asian governments endorse the principle of equal pay, and nearly all of them apply it in the public administrative and other services while at the same time endeavouring to promote its application in the private sectors of employment.

Two further points should be noted: first that sex-linked pay differences are common for unskilled and semi-skilled work in all countries where they exist at all; and second, that a relatively larger majority of women than of men workers are in unskilled and semi-skilled occupations. This also is true everywhere.

Modern education

If there is any single point on which our contributors are all agreed, it is the immense significance of education. This is not surprising. Although our region has been the seat and cultural domain of all the classical civilizations of India, and the sphere also of Chinese and Arabian influences (both long ante-dating the contacts with Europe, which themselves began as many as 400 years ago), most of the ordinary people have remained illiterate. Education in the formal sense was the privilege of a limited proportion of the population, to which, though with quite numerous and often notable exceptions, women did not usually belong.

There was, of course, nothing peculiarly Oriental about this. Universal education was nowhere even envisaged much before the twentieth century. Only advancing industrialism, ready to take virtually whole populations into its employ and depending for its further development upon vast numbers of relatively educated consumers, has begun to make general literacy (and numeracy) an economic necessity. This has been a recent occurrence even in the West, which was the cradle of industrialism. And even there the education of women has everywhere lagged behind.

There are certain rather obvious difficulties in the way of estimating a country's degree of literacy, but even if we allow for these we still have to admit that there are large variations not only between the industrialized and the non-industrialized nations of the world but also within each of these two categories. The report published in 1959 by the International Institute of Differing Civilizations, which we have already quoted, gives the following proportions of non-literate women in the total female population: Ceylon 46 per cent, Thailand 64, Federation of Malaya 84, India 92. In Viet-Nam, we are told, 30 per cent of those who have received at least primary education are female; in the Philippines, more than 40 per cent. The statistics for Indonesia are less definite, but it is reported that no more than 35 per cent of the total population were illiterate in 1958. From evidence that girls are less freely given access to education in Indonesia than boys, we have to assume that the ratio of females in this 35 per cent is high. The figures for Pakistan appear in a different form; in 1956 enrolments in all Pakistani places of education taken together were: males, 4,893,265; females, 566,834 (rather less than 11 per cent).

Although Pakistan's is the extreme case, it is clear that women are everywhere at an educational disadvantage. The Philippines goes nearest to affording equality in this, as in most other, respects. Our other countries lie at successive points along a continuum of which these two represent the respective poles.

One attempt at working out some of the possible social correlates of this variety appears in the political section of this essay. It omits, however, several important features which are particularly relevant to education: for example, governmental policy (and in the case of colonial governments the influence of contemporary metropolitan views on the education of girls) and the demands made by the economy for large numbers of literate female workers and consumers. Broadly speaking, the economic demand for female education is only now beginning to become apparent in South and South-East Asia. Furthermore, it is not to be expected that industrial development will occur evenly, or that existing differences will be quickly eliminated. In the Philippines women already and traditionally do most of the shopping; in traditional Pakistan they do virtually none. It is noteworthy, too, that India, which is without doubt industrially the most advanced of our countries, still has one of the highest rates of female illiteracy.

What have already told about the fisher-girls and boys of Hong Kong shows well enough the desire for literacy. Some of its potential effects upon traditional roles are also discussed elsewhere. The demand for it creates the new roles of primary school teachers, mass education workers and so on, and beyond these it acts as a kind of lubricant for almost all the other changes we discuss. It is probably fair to describe it as the enabling measure *par excellence*.

But industrialized countries have already found that literacy is not enough. The achievement of universal primary schooling (which we are, for brevity's sake, equating with the achievement of general literacy) has been followed by the development of universal secondary education. Here, too, the Orient is beginning to follow suit, but as yet there is everywhere a much smaller proportion of pupils in secondary than in primary schools and a still smaller proportion of these are girls. Once again there are national differences, the Philippines, where 44 per cent of the secondary school pupils are females, being well ahead of the rest (Ceylon 30 per cent, Thailand 28, Viet-Nam 25, Cambodia 16, India 13).

In so far as we are considering the approach towards universal education—whether primary or secondary—we are considering something which is in a substantial sense much less of a novelty for boys in the East than in the West. In Ceylon, Burma, Thailand, Cambodia, Laos and indeed anywhere where Theravāda (Hinayana) Buddhism is practised, all boys traditionally enter the monasteries for a shorter or longer period before attaining manhood. This novitiate includes training in the scriptures, with the result that in these countries all boys have long had the opportunity of becoming literate. Girls, however, had to depend upon such teaching as their brothers, fathers, husbands or other male relatives were willing to give, for no monk is permitted any personal relationship with a female. In Moslem areas (and in addition to the predominantly Moslem populations in Pakistan, the Federation of Malaya and Indonesia there are quite large Moslem minorities in every country of our region) a somewhat similar custom obtains for scriptural training in the Holy Koran, which is often given to girls as well as boys. It would therefore be quite untrue to say that universal education is in every sense a new thing in the East.

Nevertheless, in content and aims and in its ideal extension to both sexes equally modern education is certainly very different. Literacy is no longer sought mainly for the sake of reading holy texts; and going to school nowadays is an important step towards personal advantage in this world as well as the next. Even if widespread formal education is not the new idea to South and South-East Asia that it is to the West, its modern manifestations are quite unlike the traditional ones.

Much the same can be said about higher education. In so far as this is thought of as the training of *élites* rather than an extension of general education it—or something like it—has long been familiar in our region. What is peculiar to the modern situation is not that such a training exists but that its content is vastly changed and its scope vastly extended, both as regards more and new subjects of study and as regards a greatly enlarged student body. And for the first time this now includes women—again only a little later in the East than in the West. This is something really new.

Here, indeed, is one of the crucial points for studying the emergence of new roles for women. To what extent are they now being trained intellectually to enter the *élite*? It is common knowledge that there is no country anywhere in which the number of women receiving post-secondary education is as great as the number of men. It is worth pointing out, too, that the highest proportions of women students are not always found in the West, for Burma, the Philippines and Thailand, in each of which women make up about 36 per cent of the total number of post-secondary students, are among the most progressive in this respect in the world.

Table 5 shows the increases which occurred in four countries of our region in the ten years following the second world war compared with

TABLE 5. Changes in number and proportion of women students enrolled in institutes of post-secondary education[1] for the academic years beginning in 1945, 1950 and 1954, in selected countries

Country	1945			1950			1955		
	A	B	C	A	B	C	A	B	C
Ceylon	133	8.1	—	387	14.7	5.1	664[2]	16.0	7.9
India	20844	9.8	6.2	43185	11.2	12.1	83751	12.4	26.4
Philippines (public institutions only)	965	42.9	5.3	2749	42.6	12.5	—	—	—
Thailand	2908[3]	15.5	17.0	2522	8.4	13.9	9554	36.5	47.1
Netherlands	3245	14.9	35.0	4346	15.4	43.0	5152	17.4	47.9
United Kingdom	17907	33.4	36.4	19904	22.7	39.5	20420	24.6	40.3
Sweden	3048	21.7	45.9	3942	23.3	56.2	6387	28.5	87.9
France	40211	32.6	102.8	47260	33.9	113.2	58534	33.8	135.3
U.S.S.R.	—	—	—	—	—	—	967600	51.8	483.0
United States	585431	41.7	418.4	724609[4]	29.4	485.7	791234	34.4	487.2

1. A=Number of women students enrolled; B=Percentage of total enrolment; C=Number per 100,000 of total population.
2. 1954.
3. 1946.
4. 1949.

57

figures from six selected Western countries (including the four major colonial powers of our region) for the same dates.[1]

It is clear that the expansion in numbers of post-secondary students is fairly general, and that this has included in many countries an expansion not only of numbers but actually of proportions of women students. (It is noteworthy that this has not always been true in the West.) Nevertheless women are still in a minority, usually very much so. Most of the several reasons for this are discussed elsewhere. The strictly educational factors include the late entry of women into the field of formal education of any kind, the still very much smaller number of girls than boys in primary and secondary schools, and the various special curricula for girls which are often directed mainly towards preparing them for their traditional roles in the home at the expense of their intellectual advancement. This is not the place to pursue these and the other educational arguments further. They are well known. It may, however, be worth suggesting the probable value of a con-

TABLE 6. Degrees and diplomas awarded to women students in the years 1950 and 1954, in selected countries

Country	1950		1954	
	Number awarded to women	Percentage of total awarded	Number awarded to women	Percentage of total awarded
Burma	74	27.0	189	30.2
Ceylon	—	—	90	20.6
India	7329	12.4	10483	13.1
Thailand	140	56.0	179	46.7
Viet-Nam	10	14.7	35	11.4
Netherlands	352	12.4	395[1]	12.1
Sweden	657	20.9	2297	31.7
France	5465	33.8	1051	37.8
United States	123861	27.9	122954	34.9

1. 1953

1. The figures for this and the following two tables have been taken from lists supplied by the Statistical Department of Unesco to the International Federation of University Women. All references to countries of our region have been included.

trolled inquiry into the question of whether the segregation of the sexes in education is compatible with equality.

Table 6 refers not to the numbers of students but their successes. In the countries of our region the proportion of women receiving degrees is higher than the contemporary proportion of women to men students. The answer to our former question is, then, that women are now being given *élite* training, but almost everywhere in small numbers. If education alone was the criterion for entry, we should expect to find many fewer women than men in the professions, and in executive and managerial positions in general.

But we should not expect the discrepancy to be as great as it is. Even in the Philippines where girls have very nearly equal educational advantages and there are, as we have seen, remarkably large numbers of women in the professions, administration, and relatively high posts in commerce and industry, the really leading positions are almost all held by men. A comparison between Table 7 and the two preceding tables shows what differences exist between the proportions of women who appear as students and the proportions who appear as teachers in post-secondary institutions.

TABLE 7. Numbers and proportions of women teaching in institutions of higher education, 1950 and 1954, in selected countries

Country	1950		1954	
	Number	Percentage of total	Number	Percentage of total
Burma	51	20.9	181	37.8
Ceylon	13	5.8	12	4.9
India	2053	8.7	2976	9.9
Singapore	5	5.5	...	...
Thailand	108	18.7	179	24.6
Philippines	...	...	—	39.3
Japan	3097	6.5	4358	7.2
Sweden	45	3.0	44	2.6
United States	44492[1]	23.4	...	...

1. 1949, including administrative staff.

Note: The figures for Japanese, Swedish and United States institutes of higher education are included for comparison. The relatively lower proportion of women employed in these than in some of the institutes of our region will not pass unnoticed.

... Data not available.

The discrepancies between these figures and those in Tables 5 and 6 make obvious what we expect already: that selective processes additional to those of educational attainment are at work. The fact that the differences between the countries of our region on this list follow much the same kind of graduation as we found in the preceding section of this essay—with the Philippines, Burma and Thailand standing at the opposite pole to India and Ceylon—makes it seem likely that these other processes are fairly constant. We discuss this further below.

Political emancipation

It is often forgotten how recent is the achievement of political equality between the sexes. Fifty years ago only one country in Europe (Finland) had granted women the vote, and certainly no Western woman could hold political office except for those very few who in certain exceptional circumstances happened to inherit royal positions. Today no country in South or South-East Asia discriminates between the sexes in this respect. Where the right to vote exists at all (and that is almost everywhere) it is held equally by women and by men, and in almost every State all political offices are similarly open to both sexes. Whereas in European Portugal and Switzerland women are still in 1961 denied the right to vote in national elections, Ceylon in 1960 elected the world's first woman Prime Minister.

This is a revolution indeed. There are many questions one could ask about it. For our present purposes we will confine ourselves to two: How has it come about? What does it mean in practice?

For the first question, the most striking thing for a Western observer is the relative ease of the revolution. Not for the East, it seems, the rigours of a militant campaign, but simply a quiet and quick advance. Indeed, one can often hear ladies in South Asia decrying what they regard as the hysterical excesses of the Western (particularly the British) feminist movements, whose small and short-lived (but spectacular and long-remembered) militant branches are so often wrongly assumed to have been representative of the whole, and whose historical and sociological backgrounds were very different from their own; whose success, moreover, undoubtedly influenced theirs. Despite quite considerable national variations in background, and in the speed and effectiveness of advance, it seems likely that the relative smoothness and rapidity of the political emancipation of women in Asia may be largely ascribed to the immediately prior (in some cases contemporary) success of the feminist movements in the West. The table showing the chronological order in which voting rights were granted in different countries (appended to Dr. Romila Tharpar's article) should be studied in this connexion.

But it is not necessary for us to dwell on chronology; Romila Tharpar deals with it brilliantly. What we are concerned with here is sociological analysis. So, of course, to a considerable extent is she. She mentions the relevance of types of family structure and religion, both of which we examine again here, and points to the connexions between the movements for women's education and women's emancipation both in the West and the East which we have also mentioned. She shows, too, how to some extent Western experience was paralleled in the East, for much as the two world wars in Europe, so the anti-colonial struggles in southern Asia provided opportunities for women to play roles which had not been open to them before, and thus to demonstrate their capabilities and prove themselves actively welcome as fellow fighters with men. It is not surprising that in such circumstances national emancipation and female emancipation went hand in hand, or that in those places where political rights had already been given to women by the colonial powers they should not be rescinded but rather enlarged.

It would not be surprising, either, if once national independence had been gained there should have appeared some reaction against the new political status of women, at least in countries where their previous subordination had been most marked. Dr. Vreede de Stuers (quoted by Dr. Tharpar below) has drawn attention to just such a reaction in Indonesia. But time has been too short to tell whether it will have much success there, or whether something similar may appear elsewhere too.

On the whole, it would seem rather unlikely. Though women may well have to overcome great difficulties in winning office or promotion, perhaps more so in some countries than in others, the general trends of world opinion—and, much more important than that, of world economic development which more and more requires the contribution of women both as workers and as consumers—makes it unlikely that there will be a general return to second-class citizenship for women as a category.

This opinion of ours implies an important distinction between actually holding political office, on the one hand, and simply exercising the full rights of ordinary citizenship, on the other. It is obvious that for the majority of both men and women office is in any case unattainable, but as long as the number of girls at school remains markedly less than the number of boys, as long as they continue to leave school earlier, attend less regularly, or receive a different quality of education, so long will there be proportionately fewer women likely to enter office than men. The exercise of the franchise is quite another matter. Nowhere in our region are educational qualifications required for this, and, in any case, 'wisdom' in voting cannot be measured except by untestable opinion. The only valid measurement is the number of people taking the trouble to cast their votes, and such figures as exist for the countries in our region so far show a marked consistency between men and women in this respect.

There are other differences. Whereas voting is an individual's personal concern, holding political office is a matter of exercising power over others, and the necessary qualifications for that cannot be inculcated in schools alone. People who are expected from earliest youth to submit to the demands of others and not to assert domination, given few or no opportunities to build up personal followings or practise the exercise of authority, may be expected to find it difficult to develop the traits required for active political life—the more so if they have to compete in a world populated mainly by those to whom they have been taught to defer and who, at the same time, expect their deference and have not suffered the same disabilities. This, which is the common situation of any politically subordinate people, is aggravated if the individuals concerned live largely separated from one another in such a way that they meet too seldom to make their common organization possible, or if the roles they play are so limited that they get little practice in wielding power even amongst themselves. All these disadvantages—and others which we will leave aside for the present—apply in a greater or lesser degree to women in different countries; but the franchise having been granted they are relevant much more to the holding of office than the casting of votes.

We shall return to this distinction, and mention others, a little later.

Now, in some parts of our region the roles traditionally open to a woman were very few in number, and almost all incompatible with the assertion of power. As 'daughter', 'daughter-in-law', 'wife', even 'mother', a girl living in a patrilocal extended family household, with few or no property rights of her own, has virtually no power. Such

62

would have been the situation in the traditional three-generation family households of Hindu India, Moslem Pakistan and Confucian China. And for a respectable girl there were no other roles available. The limitations implicit in this situation were narrowed still further by the conventions which insisted—still insist, in many cases—upon *purdah*, backed by religious sanctions, as in Pakistan and parts of India, or at least upon careful seclusion backed by the full force of moral disapproval (not to mention foot binding) as in the gentry families of pre-1911 China. Granted seniority, sons, long life and a strong personality, a woman might expect to reach a position of authority in her husband's household later on. She might even come to exercise almost complete control—within the home. Outside it her traditional power was always officially nil, though indirectly by working upon the men who came under her domination at home (or, if she was not of the respectable class, elsewhere) she could possibly exercise considerable influence. Only in the most exceptional circumstances, however, could exceptional characters have any decisive effect upon political life. Information, contacts, experience, all were lacking; neither training nor opportunity was present.

Today opportunity (in the shape of formally granted rights) is open, but where schooling is still inadequate and the traditional attitudes pertaining to the type of family we have just described are changing only slowly, training often lags behind. It is probably not an accident that out of all the South and South-East Asian peoples for whom the patrilocal extended family was traditional the women who have so far shown themselves most politically advanced come from the upper-middle and middle classes of India, and, in rather lesser numbers, Pakistan. These are the classes in which modern education has made most headway, and where family structure has been much modified, as we shall see; they are also those where women took an active, often leading, part in the struggles for national independence. Dr. Nayer and Dr. Dube both underline the significance of this practical training.

By contrast, political consciousness is apparently less highly developed among Overseas Chinese women. Both Ann Wee and Foong Wong mention the modifications of traditional Chinese family structure brought about in Singapore by the effects of migration, urbanization and the influence of British colonial law, and it is well known that schooling there is widespread, even for girls; but these things alone have clearly not been enough, or Ann Wee could not have described

63

Chinese women in Singapore as being uninterested in politics as she did in an article published in 1954 in the book, *The Status of Women in South-East Asia,* edited by Dr. A. Appadorai. At least until more recently than that they have had little practice in active political campaigning.

Where the traditional kinship structure did not produce patrilocal extended family households, where there is no tradition of *purdah* or close seclusion, or where recent political history has followed different lines, the situation is different. In Burma or Thailand, for example, women have long held property in their own right, and often managed it, and have been accustomed to handling business of many kinds on their own behalf outside the family circle. Our figures of women retail traders in these two countries make this quite clear. Members of small, simple (or 'nuclear') two-generation family households usually with near relatives living close at hand, these Asian women have been subjected neither to the overriding rule of mother-in-law as in India or China, nor to the overriding demands of domesticity, as in the West. The number of roles open to them having long been relatively large, 'the vote' is not regarded as the necessary precondition and guarantee of other kinds of freedom, which it undoubtedly was (and probably still is) in most countries of the West. Moreover Burma's attainment of national independence was not preceded by a long country-wide campaign of anti-colonial resistance in which women could learn the practices of political activity, and Thailand is the one country of our whole region which never came under colonial rule at all. In each of these countries, too, the franchise was granted fairly freely (and early). Considerations such as these probably go far towards explaining the relative 'apathy' towards political affairs which our contributors report. If our diagnosis so far has been correct, we are now in a position to suggest a number of hypotheses to explain how it came about that out of the very various conditions prevailing in the different countries of our region have issued apparently very similar, smooth and rapid revolutions in the political status of women. However, before doing so we must clarify our use of terms a little further.

We earlier drew a distinction between holding the franchise and holding political office, both of which are comprised in the idea of emancipation. We now draw attention to two further usages: the first refers to a general level of freedom to engage in social and economic as well as political activity without restriction or supervision; this is the most generalized usage. The second refers to a degree of active political awareness, such as would be implied if one heard it said: 'Of course, only the women who have actually joined in [such and such political organization or activity] can be said to be truly emancipated.'

There are thus at least four quite separate notions included under the one label 'emancipation of women'; it is not useful to confuse them. In the following analysis, which has relevance for all four, they are distinguished as: the holding of the franchise, the holding of office, ability to engage in activities outside the home, and level of political awareness, respectively. With the exception of the last, all are easily measurable in terms of the numbers of women taking part. The level of political awareness can only be gauged by opinion, though the extent of women's membership in organized political associations could perhaps be used as a more objective measure were full data on the subject available.

Let us now consider the countries we have already discussed briefly. If we set aside the common modern factors (such as Western-type education) which differ mainly only in degree throughout, we can isolate three other main sets of conditions which appear to have relevance for all four kinds of emancipation.

First, there are sociological conditions: in Burma and Thailand the social structure of family households, their location and the division of labour between the sexes have traditionally tolerated the relative mobility of women and their engaging in occupations outside the home. In these countries we found a minimum of opposition to their being granted the franchise at the same time as men, but very few women are in political office and there is a generally rather low degree of political awareness. On the other hand, the present-day level of ability to engage in activities outside the home is still high—as witness the figures we have already quoted. In India, Pakistan and the homeland of the Overseas Chinese, by contrast, family structure and the traditional division of labour and responsibility between the sexes largely immobilized women except in the lower economic ranges. Equal franchise was not granted early in these societies, nor is the general freedom to engage in occupations outside the home even yet very marked. Among the Overseas Chinese the political apathy we might expect from such conditions does appear, but in India and Pakistan this is not so. There, albeit overwhelmingly among the upper-middle and middle classes in the towns, there is a relatively high level of political awareness and India at least can even show a relatively large number of women holding political office.

To explain this apparent contradiction we must turn to our second set of conditions: namely, historical. The active part that Indian and Pakistani women, especially—but not exclusively—of these social classes, took in anti-colonial struggles is sufficient to account for their political awareness. It is also probably the explanation for the relatively high number of women in office in India, and the ease with which the franchise was granted after Independence in both countries. A cynic might suggest that it was a series of lucky chances which brought the hardships and opportunities of anti-colonial struggle to just those countries whose women most needed them.

He would have to add, however, that they appear to have been less successful agents of change in Pakistan than in India. To explain this difference we refer to a third set of factors: religion.

We do not follow the lead of most previous writers on the position of women in the Orient who have, almost without exception, emphasized the paramount significance of religion. We find this unsatisfactory partly because the differences in this respect between the major religions of the region are often not clearly explained, and partly because it tends to mask other factors which we consider sociologically more significant. It is always sociologically unsound to argue as if social facts were derived from religious beliefs and rituals and did not exist in their own right. There is enough evidence from other parts of the world to show that the two basically different types of traditional family structure we have just mentioned as pertaining respectively to India, Pakistan and China, on the one hand, and Burma and Thailand, on the other, would have had their own characteristic effects upon the status of women in these countries quite irrespective of the prevailing religious systems. The various divisions of Hinduism and Islam and the mixture of Confucianism, Taoism and Buddhism, which was the religious background of traditional China, deeply influenced the social systems in which they have flourished, but they did not produce them. Perhaps we should add that we do not argue the other way (namely, that religious beliefs and rituals are simply a product of social structure) either. The relationship is one of subtle mutual influence, differing with different religious and social systems, and at different historical periods.

66

These differences are important. Although it is always to be expected that traditional religious attitudes will reflect and support traditional social practices and will probably be rather slow to change, the degree and effectiveness of their conservative influence differ considerably with differences in dogma and ecclesiastical organization. This is not the place, nor have we the space, to develop this argument fully, but very briefly stated it is that of the four major religions found in South and South-East Asia, only one, Islam, is inevitably resistant to change in general, and change in the position of women in particular.

Hinduism, despite its close hold over family and marriage, its special ideals of womanhood, its theories of caste and pollution, comprises an essentially flexible system of dogma, inclusive rather than exclusive, in which there is room for a huge variety of interpretations and many sects. Its long perspective, with its cyclical view of history as an endless rhythm of good and evil and its doctrine of reincarnation, teaches a sovereign non-attachment which is ultimately incompatible with too close a concern with the details of secular life. Moreover, its organization is far indeed from the monolithic, theocratic ideal which is Islam's, and gives no scope for enforcing an over-all supervision of secular matters. India today is a secular State. Very similar remarks can be made about the Buddhism of Burma, Cambodia, Ceylon, Laos and Thailand. Philosophically and doctrinally it shares the ideal of non-attachment to the things of this world which an unendingly long view of history and a firm belief in reincarnation render essentially illusory. For Hinayana Buddhists the true religious life is lived apart from the world, in the monasteries; the details of secular social organization are therefore of secondary importance, and change in them is not necessarily intolerable. Daw Mi Mi Khaing's article below adds practical evidence of this state of affairs.

For Christianity and Islam the situation is otherwise. Both monotheisms, both based upon revealed scriptures, they are both also exclusive religions with histories of the persecution and fighting of heretics and unbelievers. Unlike Hindus and Buddhists, neither Christians nor Moslems regard the experience of earthly life as an illusion, both (in most of their forms) maintaining that a truly religious life can be lived in the world. For each this necessarily argues a very close concern indeed with even the smallest details of everyday secular life. But Christianity is both more flexible in its interpretation of scripture

67

(many forms of Christianity allowing also for new revelation through the Church) and less all-embracing in its organization than Islam. Christian doctrine, even at the height of the temporal power of the Church, has always looked upon the State as a separate entity, a necessary concession to human sinfulness, not as a means to attain the other-worldly purposes of life which are the business of the Church. Thus change is allowed for, and a separation between secular and sacred maintained. But this is not so in Islam. There, in theory at least, there can be no distinction between sacred and secular, with the result that not only the life of the individual but the whole of society, the State, the army, all things are subject to specific prescriptions issued by the Lord, and issued once for all, through His Prophet.[1] In such a system any social change is necessarily difficult to accommodate. And the roles and statuses of women, being laid down in the Holy Koran, are at least as immutable as anything else. We have no need to feel surprised at the greater conservatism of Pakistan.

Our hypothesis is, then, that the general freedom of women to engage in activities outside their homes, their holding the franchise, their holding public office, and their political consciousness are connected with (among other things) one or more of the following sets of factors: first, a non-restricting traditional family structure and division of labour (what we mean by this will be made more clear in the fourth section of this essay); second, a history of prolonged anti-colonial (or possibly other) political struggle in which women played a full part; third, a religious system which can accommodate at least a fair degree of social change.

Tables 8A and 8B are set out for comparison. They demonstrate (8A) the different incidence of these three factors in the five countries we have discussed so far, and (8B) the relative distribution of the four aspects of women's emancipation which we have distinguished.

Some of the variations are fairly clearly concomitant. Experience of political struggle and degree of political awareness appear to vary together; so, too, it seems do family structure and the relative ability of women to engage in activities outside their homes; Pakistan differs from all the rest in type of religion, and from those with similar kinds of family structure in the relative slowness of her women to enter

---

1. This exposition follows that of Grunebaun, in *Islam, Essays in the Nature and Growth of a Cultural Tradition,* 1955.

68

TABLE 8A. Women's emancipation in Burma, India, Pakistan, Singapore, Thailand

	Burma	India	Pakistan	Singapore	Thailand
Traditional family and division of labour non-restricting	+	—	—	—	+
Women's participation in prolonged anti-colonial or other political struggle	—	+	+	—	—
Dominant religion relatively tolerant of change[1]	+	+	—	+	+
TABLE 8B					
(a) Early franchise	+				+
(b) Franchise with independence		+	+	+	
Relatively many women in political office	—	+	—	—	—
Relative freedom to engage in activities outside the home (present day)[2]	+	Increasing	Increasing only slowly	Increasing	+
Relative political awareness of women[3]	—	+	?	—	—

+ = presence of trait.   — = absence of trait.   ? = data not adequate.
1. The table distinguishes between Islam on the one hand, and Hinduism, Buddhism, etc., on the other. This is obviously an oversimplification.
2. Educational standards of women, and degree of economic development are assumed to be constant. This is obviously not true to the facts (see below).
3. 'Relative political awareness' is a subjective estimate based mainly on the estimates made in the articles which follow, and first-hand experience of the Chinese groups.

employment. None of these correlations occasions any surprise, but setting them out side by side does help to make them clearer.

Let us now tabulate what we know of the other countries of our region in a similar way (see Tables 9A and 9B). Our readers can then, if they wish, further test our whole analysis against their readings in Part II of this book.

We confine our detailed discussion of these tables to the data from Ceylon, Indonesia (Java), and the Philippines.

It might have been expected that the women of Ceylon would have been granted the vote only after the attainment of national independence, but in fact it came in 1931—the first in Asia. Just under thirty years later Ceylon produced the world's first woman Prime Minister. Neither of these two 'firsts' could have been predicted from the facts

TABLE 9A. Women's emancipation in Cambodia, Ceylon, Indonesia (Java), Laos, Federation of Malaya, Philippines, Viet-Nam

	Cambodia	Ceylon	Indonesia (Java)	Laos	Federation of Malaya	Philippines	Viet-Nam
Traditional family and division of labour non-restricting	+	—	+	+	+	+	—
Women's participation in prolonged anti-colonial or other political struggle	Post-1945	—	+	Post-1945	—	+	Post-1945
Dominant religion relatively tolerant of social change	+	+	—	+	—	+	+

TABLE 9B

	Cambodia	Ceylon	Indonesia (Java)	Laos	Federation of Malaya	Philippines	Viet-Nam
(a) Early franchise		+				+	
(b) Franchise granted with independence	+		+	+	+		+
Relatively many women in political office	—	—	—	—	—	—	—
Relative freedom to engage in activities outside the home	+	—	+	+	—	+	+?
Relative political awareness of women	—?	—	+	—?	—	+	+?

+ = presence of trait.   — = absence of trait.   ? = data not adequate.

70

recorded in Table 9A, nor, indeed, from Mrs. Siriwardena's picture of the life of Ceylon women. But they are somewhat misleading. Great though Mrs. Bandaranaike's achievement is, her position is partly a legacy from her deceased husband; and the early granting of the franchise was due to the then British Colonial Government's decision to take advantage of the 1931 revision of the constitution in an attempt to draw in women's personal interest in such matters as the incidence of maternal mortality, at that time very high. The fact remains that there is a very big disparity between the very few who have achieved highest position or do show political awareness and the general many in Ceylon.

It should go without saying that this kind of disparity exists everywhere, and by no means only in the East (or only among women). Our discussion of India and Pakistan, for example, has been seriously lopsided because we have concentrated upon the upper and middle classes. It remains our general impression, however, that even comparing similar social classes, Ceylon's politically advanced women are proportionately fewer than India's. We connect this with the fact that they have not had to struggle either for national independence or the franchise.

What of Indonesia? For the sake of simplicity (and for no other reason) we have confined our tabulation to those parts of Indonesia (Java, for example) in which simple (nuclear) family households (father, mother, unmarried children) are the usual type, and women's property rights are guaranteed not only by Islamic law but also by traditional local custom. About 85 per cent of the people of Indonesia are Moslems, but even so Javanese family structure has not been fundamentally altered, and Javanese women retain a great deal of the traditional freedom to engage in activities outside the home which we have come to expect from the previous examples of Burma and Thailand. The difference between Java and Pakistan in this respect is extreme. (Incidentally, it provides an excellent demonstration of our earlier argument in favour of the greater sociological significance of family structure than religion, while underlining also the astonishing durability of family structure in the face even of Islam.) Family structure and recent political history being what they have been in Java— the Dutch withdrawal in 1949 having been preceded by a long and bitter anti-colonial struggle in which women played a full part with men— the present situation as recorded in Table 9B follows our expectations.

The Philippines gives us the most striking example of rapid advance for women on all fronts. Here is a country where the traditional equality between the sexes that we have learnt to expect from the simple family system (and which Robert Fox also reports) was partially removed, though only for the upper classes, by 300 years of Spanish rule, only to emerge with great vigour in the last half-century under the United States Government's policy of equality of opportunity and free education. This last, which does not appear in our tables, was as we have seen, more widespread earlier than in any other country in our region, and there is no doubt it was crucial. Certainly the achievement of Filipino women in education, business, social welfare and the professions has been remarkable; they are in general well organized and politically aware—so much so that at the lower levels of political life, particularly during election campaigns, their voice is said to affect substantially the political climate of the whole nation.

If both recent government policy and traditional family structure have been favourable to women's emancipation in the Philippines, religion has been a conservative influence which probably most Filipino women have welcomed, at least as regards its refusal to countenance divorce. In the last resort, too, all forms of Christianity are committed to accepting the full equality of women with men. As for the training ground of long anti-colonial struggle, that too has not been lacking, for Filipino women took an active part in helping to overthrow Spanish rule, as well as against the United States occupation in its early days and in the resistance to the Japanese in the second world war. Thus from our present point of view women in the Philippines may be said to have had everything on their side—the only ones in our tables to have three 'plus' signs in the first series.

Perhaps we have already spent too long on what at this stage can only be a preliminary discussion of some of the factors which may have contributed towards the apparent ease and rapidity of the general political emancipation of women in South and South-East Asia over the last thirty years or so. If we have concentrated particularly upon family structure, upon the history of national independence and, though less strongly, upon religion, it is not because we believe that these are the only matters of significance, but because we do think them peculiarly important. This applies most especially to the first set of factors, family structure, and our readers are asked to look upon the analysis we have just been making as a kind of preliminary sketch for the fuller treatment of this subject which occupies the next section of this chapter.

But now, what of the second question we posed at the outset of this section? What are the practical results of women's participation in political life—we do not mean their 'success' or otherwise in the usual feminist sense, but the results in everyday life? What are the effects of their being in office, of exercising the right to vote?

As for women in office, or even in any kind of full-time or policy-making role in political life, it is frequently and correctly remarked how few they are in any country in the world. Our tables show a typical state of affairs. Even in the Philippines, since 1941 when the first woman entered the House of Representatives there has been but one woman chosen every election, and only one in the Senate. Even the situation in India may not be long-lived; indeed there is a curious set of facts from the analysis of the last general election in India[1] which shows that those areas and constituencies in which the standard of women's education was highest returned fewest women members, even produced fewest women candidates—but we need more study and much more comparative material to make sense of this phenomenon. The fact is that nowhere in the world are there many women in high political position.

This is, of course, in one sense nothing more than a reflection of the general paucity of women in the upper ranks of most other kinds of employment. It is probably to be explained largely in a similar way—that is, by the lack of equal educational opportunity, the inhibition of appropriate experience and inculcation of inappropriate attitudes, the practical difficulties of combining both domestic and outside responsibilities, and so on. But where posts which entail policy-making and the exercise of power are concerned, that is not all. Women do in fact remain at a disadvantage in appointment to leading and managing positions in almost all kinds of occupation (except those which employ solely female labour, and sometimes even there)—and in politics. As we have said, politics is in the last resort a matter of power, and, by and large, power remains a male prerogative. Despite the very great variations which undoubtedly exist between individual countries, we would expect Eastern and Western women to be in much the same predicament here. It is not for nothing that Mrs. Pandit

---

1. Published in *The Status of Women in South-East Asia,* Longmans, 1954.

—and she must know—has written of herself as a woman in a man's world.

In countries where the seclusion of women has been traditional, life is often exceedingly difficult for those few women who have emerged into this man's world. Even in those (rather few) Western countries where the free mingling of the sexes in social life is common, one often hears a woman of ambition and talent complaining of the difficulty of keeping abreast with her male colleagues into whose informal social life she cannot easily enter. And it is through informal social contacts that much significant professional and political business is conducted. An Indian or Pakistani woman may find this same situation far more difficult, the separation of the sexes having been traditionally so marked that there may at the outset appear to be virtually no respectable social patterns available for her and her male colleagues to model their professional relationships upon.

Professional women and women politicians in Asian countries without the tradition of seclusion are likely to find themselves in much the same situation as Western women, or perhaps rather more so, owing to the rather greater separation of the sexes in ordinary social intercourse. In many cases, as Daw Mi Mi Khaing and Daw Ni Ni make us understand so warmly, this is a situation which is accepted with grace, even welcomed. But it does not make for the advancement of women in new political roles.

But we must remember the distinction we drew at the beginning between holding political office and exercising the franchise. All the available evidence goes to show that enthusiasm for the role of voter is at present a characteristic of South and South-East Asian women in general. It would obviously be as unwise to assume that every illiterate village woman who casts her vote does so with complete understanding of all the issues at stake as to assume the same thing for every illiterate village man. Descriptions of the first national elections in India tell of some women who appeared to pay exactly the same reverences to the ballot boxes as to the Hindu altars in their own homes. But they voted. Indeed they flocked to the polls. Yet there was no compulsion. And in the towns at least there is evidence that their votes were often cast quite independently: women did not necessarily vote as their husbands did. They discharged their duties as citizens in their own right.

What are we to make of these things?

First, it is again obvious but necessary to point out that voting is not a full-time job. Occurring once and then not again for a matter of years, and taking the minimum of time to perform, voting in a national election creates no problems for domestic organization. Polling day can be, usually is, regarded as a holiday, a welcome break in daily routine, not an interruption. Reciprocally, the actual casting of the vote has virtually no effect upon traditional roles.

But what about its implications? We know already that wives do not always vote the same way as husbands even in the most conservative areas of our region, and even where patrilocal extended families with a 'patriarchal' type of organization have long been traditional. A vote is an individual matter. It cannot be doubted that this must have some effect—long term in most cases no doubt, and additional to many other modern influences, but nevertheless significant—upon the structure of families and the traditional roles of women in them.

But this is one of the topics of the next section of this present chapter, to which we must now direct our attention.

TRADITIONAL INSTITUTIONS: FAMILY ROLES AND THEIR MODIFICATION

Only two social tasks are everywhere inescapably sex-linked: the begetting and the bearing of children. Apart from these infinite variety is possible, though as far as we know all social systems do in fact make other sex linkages more or less rigidly. Men can make excellent child-minders, but in the absence of artificial feeding babies have to be suckled, so it is more convenient for child care to be a female occupation; cooking, cleaning and other domestic jobs can be done by people of either sex, but it is more economical to give them to those who are already anchored to the home by the small children. It is probable that such simple principles as these underlie the almost universal practice of handing over child care and household work to women. Further than this, as the well-known studies by Margaret Mead have demonstrated, generalizations about what are the 'right' or 'proper' or 'universal' or 'natural' roles of men and women simply will not take us. Variations exist even between the different social groups and classes of a single country, still more from one country to another. No matter how much it conflicts with popular belief, we have to agree that there was not a single traditional 'Oriental' conception of women's role and status any more than there was a single 'Western' one.

In this section of our essay we first suggest certain explanations for the differences which have long characterized the traditional interpretations of the roles of 'wife', 'mother' and 'daughter' in different parts of South and South-East Asia, and then consider some of the effects of modern innovations.

The significance of traditional kinship systems

We have several times referred to the significance of family structure, but we have not yet set out what we understand by this term. At the same time, it should have been quite clear that there are several different types of family structure to be found (and traditionally) in South and South-East Asia. In order to relate these differences to their sociological contexts, and to understand their significance for our subject matter, we must make a brief foray into the general theory of kin relationships.

Under 'kin relationships' or 'kinship' we include all social relationships which can be plotted on a family tree (genealogy, pedigree). These obviously include family relationships, relationships by marriage (affinal relationships), by descent, and so forth. Within the general category of kinsmen so defined there are nearly always certain particular groupings which are known in English as 'families'. We use this word to refer to a group of people related by marriage and descent (including adoption) who customarily live together and share a common household budget. The family, then, in our present usage, is simply the domestic unit of relatives, and we do not use the word in any other sense. Thus it refers to a hybrid concept, defined partly by genealogical relationship, partly by residence and partly by the economic criterion of shared consumption. All three criteria are essential.

The first, however, is elastic. Although groups of this general nature exist practically everywhere in the world, it is well known that the genealogical ties between their members are by no means always the same. So we can distinguish formally between the simple family (also known as the 'nuclear' family, the 'biological' family, etc.), which comprises father, mother and unmarried children, and various types of compound family. Compound families consist in effect of a number of simple families linked together either by the further marriages of (usually only one of) the spouses (polygamy), or by bringing in the spouses of adult children, or both. The first method gives rise to the polygynous family (father, mothers, unmarried children) or the polyandrous family (fathers, mother, unmarried children), which is rare; the second to various types of extended family (a three- (or more) generation family) of which the patrilocal version is the most common in our region. In the patrilocal extended family married sons stay with their fathers and bring their brides home to join them with the result that the group comes to include father, mother, unmarried daughters, sons, sons' wives, sons' children. Such a family may also be polygynous. Matrilocal extended families, in which brides stay with their mothers, though predominating locally in parts of Malaya and Indonesia (and elsewhere), are not widespread in our region.

The term 'joint family' does not appear in this classification. We find it more useful to restrict this to legal rather than sociological use. As a term which has special connotations wherever Indian legal codes apply, it is not strictly relevant elsewhere.

It seems likely that other things being equal the traditional status of women has often been rather higher and their roles often less restricted in simple than in compound forms of family structure. Within a simple family the wife is subordinate to no other woman, and because of the sexual division of labour her occupational status *vis-à-vis* her husband is likely to be complementary rather than inferior. Moreover, the hands to do all the necessary work being few, a wife is likely to have to take a part in management and policy-making for the group as a whole. This is especially probable in a subsistence economy, or among small-holding agriculturalists, or in cottage industries, where the family itself is the unit of production, or in small-scale family trading business. All our contributors are agreed that the traditional status of women within the family has been relatively higher, and their activity less restricted, in the lower socio-economic classes in, say, India, Pakistan, Ceylon or among the Chinese, than in the upper classes. People with lower incomes could not usually afford to build up large extended families or to maintain several wives, and their families were, therefore, usually of the simple type; at the same time they were likely to be gaining their livelihood in ways which required the wives' as well as the husbands' economic contribution.

The traditional ideal of the extended patrilocal family (often poly-gynous) which existed in these countries was, generally speaking, realized only by the relatively well-to-do. Among them virtually no adult married woman could avoid a period of subordination to her mother-in-law, and very many women (young widows, wives of younger sons, for example) could hardly have been able to look forward to attaining any sort of position of real authority in the home. At the same time the economic contribution which women made to the family's livelihood in the upper economic classes was negligible. The sharing of tasks and interests between the sexes was likely to be at a minimum. When to this was joined, as in all these countries it was, a set of values which required the more or less complete seclusion of a respectable man's female relatives, and their very early arranged marriage, it is obvious that these traditional extended family systems set narrow limits to the number and scope of the roles available to women, and often denied them power even at home. The traditional family structures of India, Pakistan, Ceylon and China thus present us with a paradox in that in certain senses women whose fortune it was to be poor enjoyed higher status than those who were rich.

In Burma, Thailand, the Philippines and most parts of Malaya and Indonesia this did not apply. There traditional families at all socio-economic levels were simple families. We have already noticed that these—especially the first three—are the countries in which pro-portionately more women have entered paid employment and received higher education. Can we assume that this is because of their simple family structure? We think that there is a close connexion, but that the argument is not quite so simple as that.

We earlier used the phrase 'other things being equal'. They seldom are. Family systems are subject to non-family pressures which may well be strong enough to modify their influence. We have already put forward some of our arguments against those writers on the position of women in Asia who have emphasized only the religious pressures, but we do not deny that the influence of religious and ideological systems can be very great. So, too, we must consider the influence of occupational systems and systems of stratification, of political and legal systems, and of the wider kinship systems in which families themselves are embedded. As we have already discussed religion and politics—and will have to mention them again—we will deal here mainly with socio-economic, kinship and legal matters.

We have just mentioned the significance of a family's means of livelihood. In simple families which are themselves units of production, a wife's (mother's) position is inevitably fairly strong. But this may be reversed if the source of livelihood is one which employs the husband separately and takes him away from home, as has been the tradition now for a long time in most parts of the West. If, further, as in the contemporary and nineteenth-century West, prestige is derived largely or even partly from economic achievement as such, there may be a tendency to denigrate domestic work at home—i.e., 'women's work'—which is not economically priced. At the same time domestic work, being a form of manual labour, has little prestige on its own account. The abundance of domestic servants which existed in nineteenth-century Europe made possible the emergence of the 'lady' whose freedom from domestic chores was regarded as an index of her husband's social and economic success, and not at all as an opportunity to gain education and enter the world of occupations outside the home, from which indeed the prevailing sexual division of labour long continued to exclude her.

In such circumstances the situation of middle- and upper-class women in Europe (the Americas and other areas of European settlement overseas had their special differences) was remarkably similar to that of their sisters in the patrilocal extended family systems of India, Pakistan, Ceylon and China.

Legally, too, their position was similar. A hundred years ago the status of a married woman in England was as stated by Blackstone: '. . . the very being and legal existence of the wife is suspended during marriage, or at least is incorporated in that of her husband. . . . But though our law in general considers man and wife as one person, yet there are some instances in which she is considered inferior to him and acting by his compulsion.' Only in 1882 were married English women given the full right to the enjoyment, management and disposition of their own property. In 1923 they were allowed to claim divorce on the same grounds as men, and in 1925 permitted equality at law with their husbands in the guardianship of their children. The doctrine that a man and his wife are one person and that person the husband is not dead even in the England of today.

There is an interesting study waiting to be made of the comparative influence of differing economic systems and legal codes upon family structure in the West, but this one example will have to suffice here to show the effect occupational and legal factors may have. By the nineteenth century—and for a considerable period previously—the simple family system of England was almost as strongly biased in favour of male dominance as any patrilocal extended family system.

We have already seen that this latter system where it existed in India, Pakistan, Ceylon or China, went with a division of occupation which kept family women at home. The legal status of wives, too, though not identical in each place, was compatible with their social inferiority. In all four countries women were traditionally regarded as perpetual legal minors, whose affairs must be conducted for them by others; divorce, if permitted at all, was harder for women to obtain than men; guardianship of children (except when they were very young) rested with the father and his male kinsmen; inheritance rights of daughters were either limited or non-existent. Our contributors from these countries give ample illustration of the practical effect of these limitations, and tell us as much again about the modern changes that are being made. To these we shall return.

What of the legal position in the simple family areas of Burma, Thailand, the Philippines, Malaya and Indonesia? Here daughters traditionally inherited equally with sons; guardianship of children was usually a matter for mutual convenience; divorce—though certainly easier for men in Moslem Malaya and Indonesia—could be initiated by either party; adult women—though with disabilities in Moslem areas—were not regarded as minors. The differences are striking indeed.

To try to explain them solely in terms of family structure, however, would be to beg the question. This is where we must look to the wider kinship system in which family structure itself is enmeshed, and with which local customary law is always closely connected. Setting aside the somewhat special case of Ceylon for the moment, we can state formally that the difference between the predominating kinship systems of India, Pakistan, Viet-Nam, China on the one hand, and Burma, Thailand, the Philippines, Laos, Cambodia, Malaya and the simple family areas of Indonesia (we have in mind mainly the Javanese) on the other, is that whereas the former are patrilineal the latter are what we shall call radial systems. In the next few paragraphs we explain what we mean by this difference and the ways in which we believe it to be crucial for our subject.

When an English-speaking person talks of 'my relatives' he has in mind all those who could be placed anywhere on his own family tree. Each kinsman and kinswoman in the total aggregate of relatives can be imagined as occupying a point on one of the circumferences of a series of concentric circles centred upon the speaker (to whom anthropological jargon usually gives the nickname 'Ego'. The only thing such points necessarily have in common is some kind of radial relationship with the centre of the circles—Ego. This radially reckoned collection of relatives on both sides and in all lines is usually termed Ego's kindred. His kindred includes, of course, his family, but whereas a family is by definition a corporate group (sharing at least residence and a common budget) a kindred is not. Membership of a kindred does not, therefore, entail responsibilities towards all the other members jointly, but simply connects one in a particular way (the way of kinship) with a series of individuals. Whether or not one uses these connexions is usually a matter for personal choice, but it is commonly found that people do make use of them for support in illness or other trouble, on ceremonial occasions (such as a family wedding or funeral), and for raising loans, making business contacts and so on.

Every people we know of reckons kinship radially like this. A very large number of peoples, including most Western and South-East Asian peoples, use no other method. The result is that for them families and kindreds, as we have defined them, are the only recognized aggregates of kinsfolk. Such kinship systems are usually termed 'bilateral' or 'non-unilineal'; in some ways the term 'radial' which we have used here is more useful. A pure type of radial system would give equal weighting to males and females, with the result that the monogamous simple family, living separately, would be usual and such kin-linked matters as rights of inheritance would be equally held by both sexes.

Equal balance of this kind does appear to exist in our region among the Iban and the Land Dayak peoples of Borneo, for example, aboriginal peoples whom we have not mentioned before. It is less in evidence among more sophisticated peoples, but very nearly exists among the Burmese, the Filipinos and some others. The kind of upper- and middle-class English system we have just discussed is today approaching the pure type of radial system after a prolonged period of weighting on the male side (probably to be ascribed partly to ecclesiastical and legal influences derived from the patrilineal systems of Judea and ancient Rome); there is some evidence that some lower-class English systems are, or have been, slightly biased towards the female side. The connexion between these differences on the one hand, and differences and changes in the distribution of various kinds of property and in mobility, occupational status, and political, legal and religious pressures on the other, requires much more detailed discussion than we can give it here.

But it certainly has a bearing on our subject matter; for it is obvious that the more nearly a radial system of kinship approaches to the pure type, the more equally balanced are the rights and duties, and with them the roles and statuses, of men and women. The countries of our region in which radial systems predominate are Burma, Thailand, Cambodia, Laos, the Philippines, Borneo (which we have not mentioned previously), Malaya and parts of Indonesia. These are, as we should now expect, the simple family areas, and we have already argued some of the consequences for women of this. We can now see that they are also likely to be the areas in which women have equal rights to inherit and own property. And this is so.

But not all these radial systems are of the pure type. The effect of Islam in Malaya and Indonesia, for example, has been to introduce a certain male bias; Robert Fox argues that more than three hundred years of Spanish rule had a somewhat similar effect upon the upper-class systems in the Philippines, now thrown off in so far as legal status is conceived, but lingering still in attitudes; where polygyny exists outside Islam, too, as to some extent, though decreasingly, among the Thais and, still less, the Burmese, an element of male bias is inevitable. (In Laos, on the other hand, the custom of living with or near the wife's parents may impart some female bias, such as has been suggested also for certain areas of working-class England; but a tendency to live nearer the wife's rather than the husband's kin if both are not equally nearby is also reported from Java and elsewhere. It seems likely to be more a matter of practical convenience than of basic family structure. But we shall return to this point again.)

A detailed working out of the various differences between these several radial kinship systems of South-East Asia and their influence upon the reciprocal status and respective roles of men and women in the family and beyond is outside the scope of this essay, but enough has been said to demonstrate their significance. The chapters which follow—particularly Daw Mi Mi Khaing's on Burma, the Hanks' on Thailand and Robert Fox's on the Philippines—provide ample illustration. A glance at the contrast presented by the predominantly patrilineal systems traditional in India, Pakistan and China will make the point even clearer.

In these countries, as in many others, the predominant kinship systems are somewhat more complicated. In addition to the radial reckoning of all relatives, there is the custom of emphasizing certain kinds of relatives—those linked by common descent in the male line—more than others. In most Western countries, there is a custom—historically fairly recent—of using surnames. Though there are variations in their employment, Western surnames are usually handed on from fathers to their sons and unmarried daughters. Women do not transmit surnames to their children. In other words, in so far as the surname in the West is inherited, it is inherited unilineally (i.e., through one parent only)—and indeed patrilineally (i.e., through fathers). It is likely that this fact has helped to introduce some of the male bias we have noted in Western radial systems. (It is noteworthy that there were no surnames in traditional Burma or Thailand, that the Filipino ones were introduced by the Spanish, and that the method of naming after the father used in Malaya and Indonesia is strictly Islamic.) But Western surnames, though they do mark off patrilineally related kin from others, are not in fact much more than useful identification marks. In traditional India, Pakistan, China, the principle of patrilineal descent was taken much further.

Above all, it was a framework for the formation of kin groups of a kind unknown to purely radial kin systems. This may be seen in its clearest form in traditional China. The Chinese use surnames patrilineally inherited by both sons and daughters (traditionally a Chinese woman did not take her husband's surname on marriage). But these were more than mere identification labels. Strictly speaking, it was held that all bearers of the same surname were ultimately descendants of the same distant common ancestor, and as such they were forbidden to marry one another. In its widest extension (stretching over more than 2,000 miles of territory and possibly several mutually unintelligible dialects) a Chinese surname group could contain many hundreds of thousands of individuals. They could clearly never form a fully corporate group, and indeed their only shared activity was the general interdiction on intermarriage; but even this goes far beyond the requirements of a 'surname group' in radial reckoning Europe. Locally, however, those who bore the same Chinese surname could recognize and trace the details of their common ancestry, and did in fact often form a close-knit corporate unit. In south-east China (the original homeland of most of the Overseas Chinese in our region) it was common to find a whole village occupied solely by members of one such local surname group (and their wives) who organized local surname temples, schools and so on, and regarded themselves as a largely self-contained unit against all the world. To such groups as these, gaining their membership by shared and traced unilineal descent from a single common known ancestor, social anthropologists give the name 'lineage'. (If, as in this case, descent is derived from fathers, the group is a patrilineage.) Unilineal reckoning does not supersede radial reckoning; it is merely additional to it; so a unilineal kinship system is also radial and can, therefore, form at least three different kinds of kin grouping: families (which may be of varying composition), kindreds and lineages. (The word 'clan' is usually reserved for wider unilineal groupings in which common descent is not actually traced but merely believed in. The widest Chinese surname groups we have just described would be examples.)

Now, in such a system as this, one overriding interest of the lineage is to perpetuate the male line. Daughters are inevitably less valued (though not necessarily less loved) than sons because they cannot help in this—worse, they leave on marriage to become active contributors to the growth of other lineages. Women in the local group are therefore either young unmarried girls or outsiders brought in as wives, essential for the production of new recruits for the lineage, but not themselves birthright members. It is not surprising that they should be regarded as of lower status than adult males who alone are full members. Obviously compatible with this state of affairs is the institution of polygyny—making the higher production of sons per father possible, but necessarily subordinating some women. Closely connected, too, is the ideal of building up a patrilocal extended family so that property, inherited by sons alone—daughters get a marriage portion which does not break up the estate, but no more— may be held together as long as possible. Again, it is only to be expected that in such a system divorce should be very difficult, if not impossible, and widows and their children should be under the control of the deceased husband's brothers or other male kin. All these things, which we have already noted, are documented in the articles by Ann Wee and Foong Wong below.

In traditional India (we are now writing of the days before the partition of the subcontinent between two separate States) the predominant types of kinship system were not altogether dissimilar from the Chinese. Without either the concept of the surname or the local single lineage villages of South China, most kinship reckoning in India nevertheless emphasized the male line and used it as the framework of family groupings. Like any other patrilocal extended family, the usual Indian 'joint family' (to give it its commonly used legal appellation) comprised in effect a small patrilineal core of males (which could be called a small patrilineage) together with their wives and children. On marriage the sons (full members) remained, the daughters moved out to make their contribution to the continuation of a different patriline. Property, especially if it consisted of real estate, was ideally kept undivided, being held jointly (not severally) by all male members of the group, relinquished rather than transmitted by those who died and entered into rather than inherited by those who were born. Women held rights to maintenance only.

Again it is obvious that such a system sets a premium on polygyny, and against divorce and the remarriage of widows, controlling women in the interests of the group—in effect, of the men—and denying them full property rights or the guardianship of children. In other words it necessarily places them in the position of minors.

It is interesting to note that whereas in the radial system of the Javanese (Indonesia) Islam appears to have imparted a male bias, in the patrilineal system of India it worked to some extent the other way. For under Islam a daughter is entitled to inherit property (though a lesser share than a son), polygyny is limited, and divorce and the remarriage of widows are permitted. Thus it was that upper-class Hindu women, who in many parts of India experienced the full influence of patrilineal kinship institutions backed, as Romila Tharpar shows us, by religious sanctions, were in several respects more restricted than their Moslem counterparts. (But, as we have already argued, Islam can impose a stronger control than Hinduism, and when modern changes began to flood in upon India, Hindu women often profited by them earlier than Moslems.) As for the radial systems of Java, the relatively slight male bias introduced by Islam seems to have been far less than the male dominance which existed in eighteenth- and nineteenth-century Europe, let alone in the patrilineal systems of India. Islam itself, of course, like Judaism, arose in a predominantly patrilineal area where the subordinate status of women was taken for granted.

We have now enough material to try to classify traditional (by which we mean, say, the eighteenth- and nineteenth-century) kinship systems of our area. We can place them in a graded series, stretching from the almost pure radial systems of aboriginal Borneo and traditional Burma through the slightly more male-biased radial systems of Laos, Cambodia, Thailand and the Philippines, and the Moslem-influenced radial systems of Malaya and Java to the more or less strictly male-dominated patrilineal systems of Moslem India, Hindu India, Viet-Nam and China. Though the exact order requires much more careful inquiry, we can set out the series tentatively as follows:

	Borneo
	Burma
	Laos
	Thailand
Radial	Cambodia
	Philippines
	Java
	Malaya
	Ceylon
	Moslem India
Patrilineal	Hindu India
	China

Ceylon, which we have so far omitted, occupies a kind of intermediate position. Traditional Ceylonese kinship was complex, but in general it appears to have been reckoned radially and to have allowed the inheritance of property by women. However, at least in areas where irrigated land was in short supply, a strong effort was made to meet the difficulties of land division which this would entail by restricting it in practice and building up extended patrilocal families, or, it seems, developing polyandry.

Our readers are invited to compare this graded list with the tables we have presented earlier, and to bear it in mind when reading the articles which follow. We believe that the facts recorded in our tables and the articles of our contributors together support our present hypothesis, which is, simply, that the reciprocal statuses of men and women are likely to be more nearly equal, and their respective roles less rigidly demarcated, among people who emphasize the radial rather than the unilineal reckoning of kin relationships.

Matrilineal reckoning requires fuller treatment than we can give it here. It occurs sporadically in our region, notably in Minangkabau (Sumatra, Indonesia) and Negri Sembilan (Malaya) and elsewhere, but is predominant in none of our countries. Briefly our argument would be that whereas a woman is likely to have a higher lineage status in a matrilineal system than in a patrilineal one, it does not follow that she has a higher status than a man. The point about matriliny is not that women are the recipients of inherited rights and positions (they often are not), but that these things can be transferred only through mothers. The analogy is with the genetic transmission of certain kinds of haemophilia (bleeding disease) which are found only in males but inherited only through females. Although the fact that her children are members of her own lineage group and not his may give a woman a certain measure of independence of her husband in a matrilineal system, her lineage status *vis-à-vis* her brothers may well be low and her roles relatively circumscribed. Our hypothesis is not affected.

Kinship and change

What of modern changes in traditional kinship? In general we see them tending in the direction of pure type radial systems. We have already remarked this tendency in the West, where, it is important to remember, eighteenth- and nineteenth-century systems of kinship, radial though they were, were much more male-biased than most South-East Asian ones. There is every reason to suppose that the essentially similar influences which are at work in the East will have similar effects.

One set of influences which we have not so far considered is the legal. Legal changes are discussed by many of our contributors, notably Romila Tharpar and Ann Wee. The ending of polygamy, the raising of the ages of consent and marriage, the granting of inheritance rights to widows and daughters, and so on—these and similar provisions are aimed directly at raising the status of women. They will have an indirect influence in the same direction too, for they are in effect attacks upon the principle of patrilineal descent and the patrilocal extended family. The degree to which legal changes are effective in practice is said to be small as yet. It is likely to grow.

It will grow because other changes are tending the same way. Anything which gives women the status of full adults in their own right before the law, allows them to own and manage property, gives them access to occupations and contacts outside the home is an attack on strict patriliny. Our contributors show us more than enough examples, and mention in their turn nearly all the innovations we have discussed earlier. We shall dwell upon only one: urbanization.

Professor Karim's is the most decided of our contributions on this subject. Women, he tells us, are much freer in the towns than in the villages of Pakistan. Why?

The reasons usually given are many. They include the contrast between the greater conservatism of villages, where everybody knows everybody else and no-one dares to break customary conventions, and the relative anonymity of city life; the break-up of extended family living which the shortage of housing often brings about; the greater opportunities for employment, education, 'Westernization' and so on. Most of these points are valid though their weighting must vary greatly from place to place. It is unfortunate that detailed studies of what really happens when, for example, the members of a strictly patrilineal type of family and kinship unit come to town are so few.

One of the fullest is Maurice Freedman's book on *Chinese Family and Marriage in Singapore* (London, 1957). This makes it quite clear that one of the most significant concomitants of living in Singapore has been the virtually complete loss of the southern Chinese lineage system and the almost complete disappearance of polygynous extended families of the traditional type. Stephen Morris (in an article in the *British Journal of Sociology,* 1958) has recorded the somewhat similar disappearance of the legal joint family organization among the Indian and Pakistani immigrants in the towns of East Africa. Can we take it that this kind of thing is typical not only of immigrant communities overseas—obviously cut off from their home ties—but also of modern urbanization in general? It is our suggestion that we can—and that the evidence of our contributors supports us.

We must first distinguish between two conceptually different things:

the custom of stressing the patrilineal line in reckoning kinship on the one hand, and the existence of exclusive corporate groups of patrilineal kinsmen on the other. What we wish to draw attention to is the effect upon these two things (in practice usually closely connected) of two particular aspects of modern urban life: first, economic relationships, and second, the legal and administrative framework in which they operate.

What a person in a modern town wants is a job, or a commercial or professional contact of some kind. To rely solely on one's patrikin for this would be as obviously foolish as to ignore them if they could be useful. One exploits any and every connexion, or better still series of connexions: one's acquaintances, friends, friends' friends, co-members in any and all sorts of organization, and, of course, all possible kinsmen. Neither in India nor China was it usual for people to rely on their relatives alone, even traditionally or even in the rural areas, and certainly not on their patrilineal relatives alone; but where matters of essential livelihood were concerned and income was derived from land they were usually more important. Where income is derived from employment in non-traditional occupations, from commerce, and the professions, as it is in a modern town, this is no longer so. There, radial linkages—in addition to non-kin ties, of course—are more valuable because they are more numerous and wide-spreading.

It is probable that commercial businesses and indeed any undertakings that require wide personal contacts (politics, for example) have always had this kind of effect for those who practise them. Be that as it may, we suggest here that in so far as the reckoning of kinship is concerned an economic system such as we find in most modern towns adds weight to radial rather than merely unilineal methods.

This might not necessarily weaken the use of patriliny for group formation, however, as the long continued existence of patrilocal extended families in many trading communities shows. A more direct attack upon patrilineal groupings appears to come from the legal and administration and the provision of certain social services—especially Ann Wee both have something to say on this topic, in addition to the points we have already raised. Our present comments are confined to economic matters.

The traditional South Chinese patrilineage never had much economic importance. Its practical *raison d'être* was closely bound up with the management of relationships with a particular form of local

89

administration and the provision of certain social services—especially education—for its members. Neither of these tasks is necessary in the modern city of Singapore, or, indeed, in any well-run modern city. Even the substitutes for local lineage organization which developed in the early days among Singapore Chinese are now largely redundant.

Different factors can lead to somewhat similar results for the traditional patrilocal joint family of India and Pakistan. It should be obvious that in writing of this we do not have in mind the poorer sections of the population but the rather better-off who in traditional times would have built up extended families based solidly on joint property. Their modern counterparts are the people who now go ahead in business, the professions and the higher salaried positions. But it is hardly possible for any of these occupations to be run as a joint family enterprise today.

It is true that a pair of brothers may be partners, or a father and his sons form a company, and that various forms of so-called 'nepotism' may be discerned in the allocation of salaried posts; but none of these things is necessarily an indication of the persistence of the joint family in the strict legal sense, or even of the custom of living together in extended families. After all, similar 'familial' links can be found in similar concerns throughout the world, including many places where there is no tradition of extended family living or joint family property at all. Moreover—and this is the point—the legal and administrative framework of modern economic institutions is a modern innovation, developed originally in the West, different in principle from that of the joint family. This is obvious for institutions employing salaried workers, but is no less true for partnerships or companies whose members hold shares (for shares are owned severally not jointly), and they can be withdrawn.

Thus, to use the distinction drawn by Maine, the modern relationship between partners is contractual, the traditional relationship between members of a joint family was one of status. Once this change has been made, and property is no longer jointly held, the peculiar legal structure of the joint family—which we insisted earlier was its distinguishing mark—is destroyed. What is left may well be some kind of extended family dwelling group, bound by strong ties of affection and feelings of mutual dependence and obligation, which find expression in mutual assistance of all kinds and also in continued co-participation in family ritual observances. But these things alone do not constitute a 'joint family' in the strict (i.e., legal) sense. Furthermore, as our contributors show us, once the element of legal jointness has been removed, the component units of an extended family often set up separate households, though, of course, there is continued visiting, mutual assistance, and sharing in family rituals and ceremonies (as, indeed, there is between related families in radial kinship systems which have never developed extended family organization at all). It is interesting to note too—as Morris did in East Africa—how often at the present time business partners are in fact not patrilineal kinsmen at all.

We conclude, then, that the economic, administrative, and legal systems of modern towns are such that while they lend weight to radial (and non-kin) linkages they also undermine the importance of patriliny as a principle in the formation of corporate groups. The full working out of these tendencies is likely to be a slow process; at present all stages of the change are still to be seen. Moreover, by no means all towns are 'modern' in the respects we have picked out, and even in truly modern towns traditional occupations continue to be organized along largely traditional lines. Nevertheless, we claim that the trend away from patriliny is plainly built in to modern urbanization.

Indeed we go further and suggest that it is built in to modern economic systems in general. It is only because in our region towns are in effect still the only centres of modern economic organization that this appears to be an urban phenomenon. It will spread.

It is likely, of course, that however rapid economic development proves to be pockets of traditional economic structure will linger for a very long time, much as small-holding ('peasant') farming and family trading businesses still continue in the modern West. As far as kinship organization is concerned, however, this will make little difference to our prediction, for, as we have already seen, such small-scale enterprises as these were not usually organized in extended family units anyway, nor did their members pay much attention to lineage organization where this existed, either. In any event, the majority of the population is likely to be caught up in the developing modern systems, and as these will also be those of the well-to-do they will set the standard.

What will this standard be? We have argued a general tendency in the direction of a pure type radial system of kinship. Our earlier argument leads us to expect two interrelated concomitants of this: first, the general appearance of simple ('nuclear') family units, and second, the more equal balance of status and role between the sexes.

But other modern developments are working in the same direction. Urban housing, the need for mobility of labour, 'Westernization'— all require the simple family; modern world opinion demands the raising of the status of women. So, too, does modern economic growth which probably depends, even more than on the increasing employment of women as well as men, upon an increasingly numerous and discriminating set of consumers. Because of their special position in the family, wives and mothers are potentially society's most active buyers; but as long as the status of women is relatively low, and their role relatively restricted, the full effect of this particular spur to economic growth will not be felt.

Our previous hypothesis was that the relative statuses of men and women were likely to be more equal and their respective roles less rigidly demarcated in societies which emphasized radial rather than unilineal methods of reckoning kinship. If we have now established that one of the particular effects of modern change in general is the strengthening of radial and the undermining of unilineal relationships, we can put forward the further hypothesis that modern socio-economic development favours the greater equality of the sexes—and not only in South and South-East Asia.

THE RELATIVE EASE OF CHANGE: THE QUESTION OF COMPATIBILITY

It will appear to many of our readers that we have left the most obviously important aspects of modern changes until last. If it is a fact that women everywhere spend most of their time on domestic tasks, then surely the things that really matter to them as individuals are the layout of their houses, their access to water supplies, their furnishings, pots and pans, and methods of cooking, the kinds of clothes they and their families wear and how these are made and mended and washed? And surely when a family moves to town, or a village improvement scheme gets under way, or imported cloth and processed foods replace the home-made varieties, these are just the matters that change most quickly and easily?

Of course this is largely true. We have touched upon it in our discussion of modern communications. If we do not describe it

92

further here it is because we do not feel it necessary to anticipate what our contributors can and do tell us so much more expertly from their own first-hand experience.

In any case, the extent to which such strictly technological changes, vitally important though they may be in affecting almost every aspect of daily life, lead actually to changes in the respective roles of men and women is problematical. Is the division of labour between the sexes affected by, say, the fact that cloth is now imported and no longer woven at home, or cooking done on a gas stove instead of a charcoal *chatti?*

Potentially much more important for role change than changes in the techniques of domestic work are changes in its organization. We have frequently referred to the indirect contribution to these which the 'enabling' nature of some technical innovations makes. Sometimes there is a direct connexion; the design of living accommodation in a tenement block in, say, Singapore, which makes impossible the traditional separation between the men's and the women's quarters of a Malay house is an example. Sometimes role changes are connected with the adoption of new medical or hygienic measures; for instance, Javanese husbands who traditionally played a responsible and important part at the birth of their babies are now shooed out of the way by modern medically trained midwives. More often, however, role changes within the family seem to stem from such changes in the family's own structure and organization, as we have been discussing in the previous section of this essay.

A simple family is a very different work group from an extended family. Because only one adult of each sex is present, even the most rigid traditional sexual division of labour cannot always be maintained. We have argued that this fact helps to raise the status of a wife and extend her activities; but there is another set of factors we have not considered.

Experience of the 'isolated' simple family in the West—removed from all kin, unable to rely on neighbours for help, and without domestic servants—shows it to be only barely a viable unit, especially if (as is usual) the husband is employed away from home. As long as all goes well, no-one is ill or incapacitated, and the children are fairly widely spaced out, this domestic unit can be self-contained—given hard work and sensible management on the part of the wife; but sickness, too many children too close to one another, the additional

93

work caused by the presence of, say, an invalid mother or an elderly father-in-law, any of these things can make it impossible to manage. The development of social services, the custom of putting old people into institutions, and the determination to control birth spacing and numbers in the West should be seen in the light of this organizational fact at least as much as in purely economic or psychological terms.

Moreover—and this is a point we wish to stress—there can be no doubt that one of the factors which today make further change in the respective roles of Western men and women difficult is the relative isolation of the simple family, for this necessarily creates a practical incompatibility between the role of wife-mother and the role of worker outside the home—at least during the years of child bearing and child rearing. Are we therefore faced with the paradox that the predictable spread of the simple family, which we have argued augers a less restricted set of social roles for women and their improved status, carries within itself also the denial of these things?

There are, in fact, various possible solutions. They include the widespread development of specialized domestic services, whether commercially or through governmental agencies, the employment of household servants, and, of course, the removal of 'isolation'. The first has hardly been fully worked out anywhere in the world as yet, though the social services in certain European countries go a long way towards it. It seems likely that if increasing economic growth makes increasing demands for women workers such services will be widely extended. At present they barely exist anywhere in the Orient.

In most parts of South and South-East Asia, however, household servants are still easily available, and the isolation of the simple family is also far from complete. In the traditional simple family areas of Burma, the Philippines, Indonesia and so on, it is usual for a couple to set up house after marriage near one or other (often both) of their parental homes, with the result that practical assistance is always at hand—as it is also for the so-called 'matrifocal' clusters of families found in many settled areas of, for example, working-class England. But we do not need to dwell on these matters. Our middle-class contributors are all well aware that in this respect changes of role are easier for them than for their Western counterparts today; they are also much concerned for the future of their daughters and grand-daughters in the coming years, when household servants may

94

well be hard to find and families may well be both simple and scattered.

Mrs. Subandrio's article is of particular interest in this connexion. A woman of great achievement outside the home, she is also the wife of Indonesia's Foreign Minister and a mother in a Javanese simple family. She has several ways of dealing with the practical business of organizing this apparently rather complicated series of roles. There are household servants; there are commercial suppliers of excellent cooked meals; there are close relatives nearby on whom she can rely but to whom she is not at all subordinate in the running of her own home. The result is that in fact her several roles are not incompatible.

She herself makes another point. Nowadays, she tells us, sons as well as daughters are being taught to take their share in domestic work. If this means that a Javanese man can, without loss of dignity, perform what are usually considered women's tasks it is of more than practical significance, for it implies a flexibility of attitude towards the sexual division of labour which is not found everywhere in our region—or in many parts of the West—and which where it exists must help to make some modern changes relatively easy. By contrast, a rigid sex-typing of occupations can make change difficult, for it may lead to such a close identification of occupation with sex that it becomes impossible for a man to perform 'women's work' without loss of 'manliness', or for a woman to perform 'men's work' without diminution of 'femininity'. These are usually not strictly practical but what we have earlier called ideological incompatibilities. Our previous argument might lead us to expect greater flexibility in this respect in the traditionally more purely radial—and simple family—kinship systems, of which Java's is certainly one. But there are other factors too.

It is sometimes suggested that it is relatively easier for women to enter paid occupations in the new nations of the world than in the West simply because most occupations there are too new to have been given any rigid sex-typing as yet. If there is no tradition of, for example, modern medicine at all, so the argument runs, then there can be no traditional sexual allocation of the role of doctor. Similarly, if women are prominent in pharmacy, for instance, as they are in Viet-Nam, this is because pharmacy is a new occupation without any traditional sex linkage.

95

There may be something in this argument, but it ignores the possible carry-over from traditional occupations which were similar if not identical with modern ones (after all, healing is not a new art), and fails to notice that the sexual division of labour in many a new nation often follows that current in the Western nation which has most influenced it. Pharmacy is popular among women in France as well as Viet-Nam; employees in textiles are predominantly female all over the world; transport and communications work is strikingly masculine in most parts of both East and West; the majority of pre-university teachers are women in the United States of America as well as in the Philippines. On the other hand there are important divergences from this pattern. Typists and secretaries, in the West so often female, are in our region predominantly male, and most countries of South and South-East Asia can show large numbers of women working in unskilled tasks on construction and road building which in the West are performed either by machines or exclusively by men.

These last two examples, however different from modern Western practices, are closely similar to those of the nineteenth century when, as in the modern East, secondary schooling—essential for office work—was still primarily for boys, and the harder manual work had not yet been legislated out of the hands of the poorer women. Fashions as to the belief in compatibility between certain occupations and the 'natural' physiological and personality characteristics of the two sexes vary historically as well as geographically.

There is one further problem of compatibility which is crucial to our subject matter. It arises from the family role of men, which despite our earlier protestations we have so far almost entirely neglected. In most of the countries of our region—probably most in the world—the chief nurturing role within the family is a female one. Men may take part in it, or not. But there are other roles equally necessary which are predominantly male. Two in particular, the roles of chief breadwinner and of holder of authority and power, are discussed very fully by our contributors below. Closely allied with them is a third: the role of status giver. Almost everywhere in the world a family's prestige and status are judged according to the prestige and status of its senior male members. This is probably because in most societies—and our region is no exception, as we have seen—men take a larger part in the occupational, political, religious and legal systems of society at large, and thus have the main responsibility for their families' relationship to it, and are seen as their representatives.

It appears to follow that a woman—certainly a married woman—is allotted the prestige and status of her husband (in a simple family; her father-in-law in an extended family). A social system which permits married women to participate in occupational, political, religious and legal roles outside the home may thus create considerable difficulties if such women are then allocated prestige and status in their own right. What if the status of husband and wife are incompatible? What if the wife stands higher than the husband—to whose status shall the family be allocated?

Social systems which do not permit women to compete with men at all certainly avoid this problem. In other words they obviate any possible incompatibility between the status of husband and wife (father-in-law and daughters-in-law) by postulating an absolute incompatibility between the roles of men and women. We have already argued that such rigid sex-typing as this makes change particularly difficult. We suggest that the social system traditional to Pakistan was of this kind. Other systems allow women to compete in certain occupations only—as actresses, for example, or in other kinds of entertainment in which they can have a prestige ranking in their own right, but at the expense of being altogether *déclassées* in the 'respectable' world of the regular (male) stratification system. Several Western countries have fallen into this category at certain periods of their history; so also, we suggest, did traditional China, Japan and probably India at certain periods. Change in such countries will not be easy, for women must face the charge of being not only unfeminine but also disreputable. (The example of Florence Nightingale comes to mind immediately.) Once fairly launched, however, women may well find change less difficult in such a system, for at least the walls have been partially breached.

A third method of dealing with the problem is to allow women to enter freely into most occupations, leaving questions of status and prestige to be settled in a different sphere altogether—as in Burma, for example, where men have prestige built in to their manhood and recognized in their superior religious status with which women by definition cannot compete. A rather similar system seems to obtain in Thailand, and probably also in Cambodia and Laos. Most occupational changes here are likely to be relatively painless, at least as long

97

as the religious system holds its prestige. But there is one exception. Because status (in our usage) is necessarily associated with power it can never in fact be a purely spiritual attribute. It is not an accident that, despite their long tradition of relatively unrestricted access to occupations outside the home, Burmese, Thai, Cambodian and Laotian women have not entered political life in any numbers or really competed for authority in any sphere.

Our contributors make it perfectly clear that this situation is gladly accepted along with the religion which entails it; it is a religion which also holds out prospects of future rebirth in masculine form and does nothing to limit the very wide choice of secular occupations in this life which the kinship systems of these countries permit. By contrast, the Republic of the Philippines, with a similar kinship system and a similarly wide choice of occupations outside the home, but with Roman Catholic Christianity instead of Theravāda Buddhism, is one of the few countries of our region which has produced a strong feminist movement.

It is not suggested that these three ways of trying to meet the problem of avoiding ambiguities in allocating family status exhaust the sociological possibilities, but they do illustrate the main differences in our region.

A complication enters the picture when a man's prestige (if not his status), and therefore the children's, depends in part upon his wife's assisting him in his career, especially in its public social aspects. Hitherto this has been largely a Western phenomenon. Dr. and Mrs. Hanks have interesting things to say about its adoption in Thailand, where women have up till now played roles in the secular and non-political world in their own right, and left questions of status largely to their husbands. The Hanks see this piece of 'Westernization' as a threat to women's personal independence, and predict a revulsion from it once Thai women fully appreciate what is happening. In other words, they see Western women as being considerably less independent than their Thai sisters.

The arguments we have put forward above prepare us not only to agree with this view, but to maintain that it holds good for several other aspects of the mutual roles and relationships of men and women and for several other parts of South and South-East Asia as well.

We shall not recapitulate the various points this essay has tried to raise. We have made some tentative sociological analyses in general terms, using mainly the concepts of role and status. We should, however, be the first to insist that role analysis alone cannot be exhaustive, and further, that even the fullest sociological analysis alone cannot give complete explanation. It is for our readers to decide, from the detailed studies of particular countries and the personal documents which follow, how far our present essay goes towards this desirable ideal.

PART II

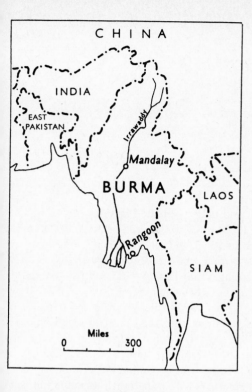

C H I N A

INDIA

EAST
PAKISTAN

Irrawaddy

Mandalay

BURMA

LAOS

Rangoon

SIAM

Miles

0   300

Burma

Area: 677,950 square kilometres.

Population: 20,662,000 (estimated 1960).[1]

Recent history: 1942-45—Japanese occupation; 1946—British Government transfers sovereignty to Union of Burma.

Citizenship: Men and women have equal rights.

Religion: Theravada (Hinayana) Buddhism; there are Moslem and Christian minorities; some hill tribes are pagan.

Inheritance and family patterns: Traditional Burmese rules of inheritance make no distinctions between the sexes; some non-Burmese groups practise patrilineal inheritance. Nuclear families predominate, the new home set up on marriage being usually not distant from the parents of at least one spouse. In patrilineal hill groups, patrilocal extended families are found.

---

1. Latest official estimate of population as published in *The U.N. Population and Vital Statistics Report, October 1960.*

103

Burma:
balance and harmony

by MI MI KHAING

Burma is a naturally rich and underpopulated country (area 261,000 square miles, population 19.24 million), situated between two gigantic nations with exploding populations. It presents certain contradictions to the casual observer: it is rich, yet a recent report in *The Times*[1] places it second lowest among South-East Asian countries as regards the life expectancy and standard of living of its people. Visitors, however, seldom fail to remark that the Burmese appear the happiest of Asian peoples. One likes to think that this cheerful atmosphere is derived from a peculiar native genius in the ordering of the relations between men and women which forms the subject of this article.

A word as to the term 'Burmese'. The Union of Burma consists of a fertile plain formed by great rivers running north to south and, surrounding this plain on all sides except the south, an arc of highland areas. There are about 16 million people on the plain who more or less follow the customs described here as 'Burmese', and over 2 million on the arc of highlands, some of whom have differing social customs. The official language of the country is Burmese, and the Buddhist religion, the spirit of which animates and moulds everything, has its chief sources of inspiration in the Burmese plains. I may therefore be forgiven if I write only about 'Burmese' customs, leaving to some other discussion the customs of minority races which do not conform. However, the descriptions of most Burmese customs are also applicable to important sections of the hill people, particularly because, though racially of different branches of Mongolian stock, the major races of Burma have a common culture inspired by Buddhism.

---

1. London, 9 February 1960.

The Buddhism of Burma is Theravāda Buddhism, its basis of belief being Gautama Buddha's recognition, about 2,500 years ago, of the fact that all existence is painful, that this is so because all living beings have desires and attachments, and that when they rid themselves of such attachments and recognize the illusory and transitory nature of existence, they will no longer suffer pain. The Burmese Buddhists believe that Gautama Buddha arrived at this great enlightenment after successive existences of the kind that every living being must go through, life after life, until, by following the path to enlightenment shown by him, it can rid itself of desire and the wrong acts consequent on desire and thus attain the absence of existence and pain which is called Nirvana. More about the ways in which Buddhist philosophy has influenced the Burmese people will appear in the course of this article; here it must suffice to say that Burmese Buddhists in their quest for Nirvana follow the ethics rather than the metaphysics of Buddhism, and that these ethics are based on five precepts prohibiting killing, lying, stealing, lust and intoxication.

BURMESE FAMILY AND KINSHIP

A discussion about men and women in Burma is best begun by examining what the family means in Burmese society. The words for 'family' in Burmese may be interesting in view of the fact that the language is a monosyllabic one and most words can be broken down into component meanings. A family is a *mi-tha-ta-su* or a *tha-ami-tha-aba,* that is, 'mother-children-one-group' or 'children-mother-children-father'. The emphasis is more strongly on the mother than on the father. It is also on the simple family of parents and children rather than on a compound or extended family of more numerous elements.

Although the simple family is the most common Burmese idea of a household, the presence of more kin than this living under one roof and as one 'family' is also very common, far more so than in the West. There is, however, no customary rule about which or how many other relations should be accepted. Ties of affection and convenience (accommodation, finances, personal situations) decide this. They decide whether a young couple will, on marriage, set up separate house for themselves, or whether one or more of his, rather than her, relatives will live with them. The ideas underlying the making of additions to the simple family are: that helping hands are often needed in the care of

105

children and house; that companionship over and above that given by a spouse is also needed; that elderly people are not left to live by themselves if it can be avoided; and that the more affluent kinsmen succour those less fortunate. These ideas are strongly felt through all types and strata of Burmese families.

Polyandrous families are never found; and polygynous families, with a man and more than one wife living under the same roof with their children, are extremely rare in the society called 'Burmese' in this country. They are rather more frequently found among hill peoples, such as the Shans, where polygamy is far more common and carries less social embarrassment, though the sanctions for it are the same among both Shans and Burmese.

Kinship beyond the immediate family is reckoned radially. To what extent outwards from himself Ego will proceed in his reckoning usually depends on affection and the accidents of propinquity. Affines are always included to the same degree as the corresponding 'blood' relations.

There is an interesting system of nomenclature for relationships among kinsmen but I must first point out two ideas running through Burmese Buddhist culture; the distinction between male and female and the distinction between age and youth. Fuller discussion of these two ideas will follow. Here, for the sake of underlining the nomenclature used for kin, it may be baldly noted that 'male' is spiritually superior to 'female'; and that age is always entitled to preferential treatment from youth, while older people have certain responsibilities towards the younger.

There is a separate term for each member of the simple family: father, mother, elder brother, elder sister, Ego, younger brother, younger sister being *abay, amay, ako, ama,* Ego, *nyi/ maung, nyima/ hnama* respectively. Ego refers to his elder brother and elder sister by the same term, whatever his or her own sex may be. But the terms are different for the younger siblings according to Ego's sex in relation to them: if of the same sex they are *nyi* and *nyima*, and if of a different sex from Ego they are *maung* and *hnama*. It is thought possible that this is because Ego's relation to an elder sibling is the same regardless of sex. It is one of respect and obedience, and in the parents' absence he will give to the elder sister the respect which is due to the mother, and to his elder brother that which is due to the father. When it comes to the younger siblings, the duties that Ego might be called on to perform in the parents' absence will be different according to which parent Ego represents.

When Ego marries and the spouse is brought in, the parents call the son-in-law *tha-met* (desired son); and the daughter-in-law they call *chway-ma* (the sweat-woman). In connexion with these terms, old sayings are sometimes recalled that a daughter's husband is of more help to the parents than even their own sons; and that a wife should tend her parents-in-law even more assiduously than their own daughter should. But, in fact, neither law nor custom enforces specific duties on the 'sweat-woman', and the sayings are probably based on the recognition of natural instincts or on bygone conditions. Both parents merit equal respect from the child-in-law; they are both termed *yaukama* (parent-in-law) regardless of sex.

After the spouse enters Ego's family, his or her relationship to Ego's siblings bears distinctive terms. Siblings of the same sex as the spouse are called *yaukpha* (male) or *yaukma* (female), no matter whether they are older or younger than Ego. But if of different sex from the spouse they are called according to the age level, or rather the position level, with regard to Ego. Thus, if the incoming spouse is a man, his elder sister-in-law is his *mayee* and his younger sister-in-law is his *khema*, whereas both his younger and his older brothers-in-law are *yaukhpa*. If the incoming spouse is a woman, her elder brother-in-law is her *khe-oh* and her younger brother-in-law is her *mut,* whereas both her sisters-in-law, younger and older, are *yaukma*. This differentiation may be due to the fact that a man does not marry his widowed elder sister-in-law; he may and often does marry his younger sister-in-law after his first wife's death.

When children are born to the couple they are all equally niece and nephew to Ego's siblings, but they call their uncles and aunts by different terms. An uncle older than one's father is *ba-gyi* (bigger father); one younger is *u-lay* or *ba-dwe* (younger father), which term is also used for stepfather. An aunt older than the mother is *gyi-gyi* (elder one); while an aunt younger than the mother is *a-daw*. No distinction is made as to whether these aunts and uncles are maternal or paternal.

Ego's parents do not divide his children into grandsons and granddaughters, but they themselves are termed grandfather and grandmother.

No further terms are used to describe the extension of the family. Relationship is assessed and termed collaterally, and a suffix is added to show the closeness or remoteness of the relationship. Cousins, for example, are referred to as 'brothers (or sisters) once-removed'. The children of one cousin are the 'nephews (or nieces) once-removed' of the other. Their children are 'brothers (or sisters) twice-removed', and so on.

What is the tie between a man and his kinsmen? There is no occasion in a person's life when only kinsmen may or must be present to the exclusion of other people. There are occasions, however, when only a small group of people needs to be assembled: an engagement ceremony, perhaps, which is private in contrast to the public marriage ceremony; or in a boy's initiation into the monkhood, the actual shaving of the head and donning of robes which for reasons of economy may be kept private, though the feasting is always public; or a second marriage of a widow or widower where a bigger ceremony might be considered embarrassing. On such occasions a husband and wife may marshal their brothers and sisters, their married children with spouses, and their grandchildren. But attendance is not compulsory nor essential to the proceedings, and along with these 'close relatives' there may be unrelated close friends or benefactors of the family.

Close relatives are expected to be at a kinsman's disposal for help with money, employment or accommodation when needed, but here again the amount of help given and the degree of kinship which makes requests for help legitimate rather than resented depend on no prescribed rule: the request and response depend solely on the ties of affection actually existing. But, like the additions to the simple family, requests of this kind are made and answered far more commonly than is usual in Western societies.

MARRIAGE

The laws which bind Burmese society belong to a corpus known as Burmese Buddhist law. This law is not actually a Buddhist one; it is so called because it is observed by the people of Burma who are Buddhists. From about the fifth century A.D. onwards, Indian Buddhists entered Burma, which they regarded as a golden land to settle in. With the Buddhist faith they brought also their modification of Hindu law. The religion was embraced by the people of Burma, and the law also, becoming further modified by the influence of the customary laws of the Burmese people, came to be the law of the land. The result is the

Burmese Buddhist law of the present day, the codes of which govern the marriage, inheritance and property rights of over 85 per cent of the people of Burma.

Marriage for such Burmese Buddhists has no religious character. It is a purely civil contract between two parties. For the marriage to be valid these two parties must, first of all, be of age. This means the man needs only to have attained puberty, but the woman, if she has not got the consent of her parents or guardians, must be 20 years old if she is a spinster. Below that age she must have the consent of parents or guardians. A widow or divorcee, however, may marry at any age. The two parties must also be mentally competent to contract; their kinship to each other must be such that their union does not offend the sentiment of the community; they must give their mutual and free consent to becoming man and wife; and there should be consummation. As for marriage gifts, Burmese tradition, still scrupulously adhered to in the rural and hill regions, requires the groom or his parents to offer gold, jewellery or a set of clothing when asking for the bride's hand. Burmese custom does not give its open sanction to the more modern custom of enhancing the attractiveness of the bride with property attached to her hand.

Though parental consent is necessary, a minor cannot be forced into a marriage against his or her will. This applies equally to bride and groom. Regarding prohibited degrees of relationship the old law books do not specify exactly, but leave the matter to the sentiment of the community. This sentiment as a rule frowns upon marriage between cousins born of two siblings of the same sex. Marriage between a man and his deceased wife's younger sister is common, but one with a deceased brother's widow or a deceased wife's elder sister is discountenanced.

Regarding a marriage ceremony, though in some cases a ceremony has been declared as not essential to the validity of marriage, it is customary between parties marrying for the first time to invite an assembly of elders and provide some sort of entertainment of friends as evidence of the wedding, which usually takes place in the bride's house. It is customary also for the married couple to visit pagodas together; to visit and receive friends together; and to live openly as man and wife. As for choice of residence, the law rules that when the husband is able to live separately from his parents the wife is not bound to live in the same house with them; convenience decides the rest.

Polyandry is never permitted, but polygyny is; that is to say, a Burmese Buddhist man may, during the lifetime of his wife, unite with another woman and give her the status of a wife. But though this right of the man alone is recognized by the old law books and still prevails here and there in Burma, there is a strong feeling against the practice. It can be said quite definitely that Burmese Buddhists are monogamous rather than polygamous.

In cases where more than one wife is taken, however, the law clarifies her position. A man who marries two or more women at the same time may given them equal status, and they will all then be known as superior wives or wives proper. He may on the other hand differentiate between them. In that case the wife who lives on terms of equality with him, who is endowed with proprietary and personal rights, and who takes part in the husband's business and contributes to the acquisition of property is considered to be a superior wife. A woman with whom this man enters into and keeps up conjugal relations but whose position falls short of the first wife's is considered an inferior wife. Clandestine relations do not constitute marriage. A marriage is established by reputation; and there must be some body of neighbours to witness that a man and his lesser wife live regularly together and in a manner leading the community to treat them as man and wife.

Having taken a second wife, a man cannot force his chief wife to live in the same house as the other. A woman who marries a man knowing that he already has a wife cannot, however, refuse to live with the chief wife. Actually it is extremely rare for two or more wives to live with the husband in the same house.

Marriage is easily dissolved between Burmese Buddhists if there is mutual consent to the dissolution. But it may be safely said that divorce is rarer in Burma than in many countries which try to impede it by laying down difficult conditions. A mutual-consent divorce must have some formal agreement or expression; angry letters and hasty rejoinders will not suffice to establish it.

If there is not mutual consent to a divorce, neither party can divorce unless the other has been guilty of some matrimonial fault, even if he or she is willing to surrender joint property or pay compensation. Matrimonial faults include misconduct, cruelty, desertion and misrepresentation. Misconduct usually means adultery. Adultery on a wife's part entitles a husband to sue for divorce, but does not in itself dissolve the marriage tie. Adultery by itself on a husband's part, however, does not entitle a wife to claim a divorce, but if he takes another wife without her consent she has a right, except in certain cases, to claim a divorce provided that she does so within a couple of months after her husband's new marriage. The exceptional cases when she cannot object in this way to her husband's second marriage are when she has produced no children after eight years of married life; when she has produced eight daughters in succession and no son; when her children always die in infancy; when she is suffering from certain severe diseases such as leprosy, insanity, epilepsy, etc.; and when she breaks the customary rules of conduct and shows no love for her husband. Cruelty as a ground for divorce includes mental as well as physical torture. The definition of desertion differs slightly for a man from that for a woman. A wife who has no affection for her husband and deserts him for one year, during which time she receives no maintenance from him, is considered to have deserted her husband. A man, however, must be shown to have deserted his wife for three years, during which he has not maintained her nor communicated with her, before she can sue him for desertion. But desertion by a chief wife on account of the husband's second marriage is not a matrimonial fault. Misrepresentation as grounds for divorce means that a man or girl has been induced by misrepresentation to marry.

MARRIAGE AND RIGHTS OVER PROPERTY

Something must now be said about the effect of marriage on property because in Burma it has for long ages been customary for the wife to take a great deal of trouble in the acquisition of property and so Burmese wives have definite property rights.

During the continued existence of a marriage, and while concord lasts, the property of a couple is regarded as belonging equally to both: husband and wife are joint owners as well as joint possessors, though the husband is deemed to be the manager of the estate. Names of husband and wife (the wife does not change her name on marriage) are often coupled together in business affairs; documents are often drawn up in their joint names; whenever there is an occasion to sue anybody, they sue jointly; and they are in turn often sued together by their adversaries. When a husband's and wife's wishes about the disposal of property do not coincide, however, or where there is question of the

111

marriage being dissolved, the question of the different types of property owned by the couple becomes important.

First, there is the *payin* or that property which belonged to either spouse individually before marriage. After marriage each continues to retain a vested interest in his or her own *payin* property. Neither spouse may in any circumstance dispose of the other's *payin* property without his or her consent; and though both may dispose of their own *payin* without this consent, a husband is debarred from giving it to his concubine. Second, there is *letterpwa,* or joint property which accrues from the exertions of one spouse alone or is inherited by one spouse alone after marriage. Of this, the spouse who acquires or inherits it is entitled to two-thirds and the other to one-third. Third, there is also *hnapazon,* or property which accrues during marriage by the common effort of the couple, or from the produce of property already held. This belongs equally to both, and neither party may alienate the share of the other without that other's consent, though each may give away his own share of it. Most property acquired in marriage is regarded as *hnapazon.*

When there is a divorce, the division of these three kinds of property is decided after the following factors have been taken into consideration: (a) whether divorce is by mutual consent or for some matrimonial fault; (b) whether the parties have both been married before (classified then as *eindaungyis*) or whether only one or neither has been married before (classified then as *nge-lin-nge-maya*); (c) whether the parties stand as supporter and dependant, by reason of one party having brought much property to the marriage and the other little or none, or by one alone acquiring or inheriting property during marriage.

When division is by mutual consent the husband and wife, whether *eindaungyis* or *nge-lin-nge-maya,* will, if they do not stand as supporter and dependant, each take back his or her *payin* property and divide the joint property equally. But when they stand as supporter and dependant, the supporter gets only two-thirds of his original *payin* property, the dependant getting one-third; and the same applies to the joint property acquired during marriage.

When there is a matrimonial fault on the part of one party, however, cases are judged on their merits, and the guilty spouse may either get the shares as above or may have to forfeit the share in joint property, or even his or her own original *payin* property.

The children in a divorce by mutual consent are generally given to

112

the parent of the same sex, but decisions are often modified to safeguard the interests of the children.

There is also the question of inheritance. A Burmese Buddhist cannot make a will. His property when he dies must be inherited according to the Burmese Buddhist laws. The general principle behind these laws is that inheritance shall not ascend when it can descend, and that the nearer by blood shall exclude the remoter. By following these principles the following order of priority of inheritance is obtained:

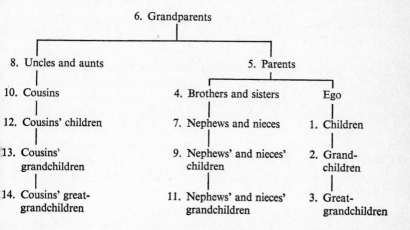

The table does not contain Ego's spouse. The spouse, if there are no children or if the children are all minors at the time of Ego's death, will succeed to the whole estate, including the right of the deceased Ego to a share in an undivided ancestral estate, whether that spouse be man or woman. This does not apply if there is among the children what the law calls an *orasa*. An *orasa* child is the first-born legitimate child who has attained majority and is competent to undertake the responsibilities of a parent of the same sex. This may be a son or a daughter. If the first-born dies or becomes incompetent before attaining his or her majority the next eldest, either son or daughter, becomes *orasa*. *Orasa*'s privilege is that he or she (no distinction) may, on the death of the parent of the same sex, claim a quarter-share of the parental estate from the surviving parent of the opposite sex. If *orasa* is of the same sex as the surviving parent, he or she cannot claim as long as that parent does not marry. On remarriage, however, this parent has to grant a vested right to one-quarter of the estate to *orasa*. When both parents are dead, all children get equal shares regardless of sex or age. An adopted child has claims if he or she can be shown on community evidence to have been adopted with a view to giving inheritance rights along with other care which parents usually show to their own children.

MEN AND WOMEN: DIFFERENTIATION OF ROLE AND STATUS

It will be seen from the foregoing accounts that a woman's place in life is not greatly differentiated from a man's by the laws which govern the conditions of her marriage, her property or her inheritance. These laws recognize her as an active member of the community, able to take a place equal to a man's in the acquisition of property and in the contribution to the community's social life. In spite of this real or near-equality, however, few visitors to Burma fail to see a differentiation in the cultural and social relationships between men and women.

This differentiation is, of course, based on the idea which every Burmese Buddhist holds firmly, that men are of a spiritually higher order than women. There is innate in men their *hpon* (glory), synonymous with their manhood, which they carry from their birth, and which is given a kind of enshrinement and recognition by their initiation, for a short or long period, into the Buddhist monkhood as soon as they reach an age when they are considered old or intelligent enough to grasp its significance. In every Burmese Buddhist's mind there is, ineradicably, a harmony about this whole conception and procedure: the young boy, the yellow robe, the example of his father before him, the good fortune of his mother who has achieved this in and for a son, all belong together. They belong with the golden vision which we all have of the first attainment of enlightenment by the Buddha. The Blessed One seated in the repose of understanding all; the dark shade of the leafy Bo tree; the glowing colour of his robe; the light of the early dawn, and in this morning freshness the woman Thusata who, having prepared a dish of milk and rice for her child, now sees the Buddha and offers him his first refreshment after his long night's struggle through darkness to enlightenment. Thus, in one of the best-loved scenes of the people's inspiration are the elements of the idea guiding their whole cultural life: man in a supreme spiritual moment

114

such as can never be attained in a woman's form, and woman the first to tend to his needs at that moment. It is to this potentiality of a spiritual ascension in a man that Burmese women subordinate themselves, and it is a subordination which does not need to touch their rights in the purely mundane life.

The superiority of men from a religious point of view does not set them apart in any rituals other than those attendant upon their symbolic entry into the monastic life. It is an idea which is accepted and carried out in simple terms. Watch the Burmese at any pagoda among the myriads dotted over the countryside. Whole families walk up the steps together. At the top of the climb it is the wife who hands out money for flowers, candles and incense sticks. The whole family performs the same acts of worship, kneeling with flowers in folded hands as they say their prayers, putting these flowers in the vases before the Image, lighting candles and incense sticks, perhaps slipping money into the boxes which are placed there for donations towards the upkeep of the pagoda, and striking a bell to denote the completion of their good work. All do this alike. But should the Image on its pedestal need special attention or cleaning, it is the man or his sons who draw close to do it, or who climb up the terraces of the spire to gild it or fix the crown of gold and jewels at its pinnacle.

On full-moon days our household visits, not the big monasteries in town, but a new one on the hill where the monk has just started to set up residence in a little wooden structure. The floor of this is rough cement and on festival days the crowds of peasants soon cover it with mud. The monk sits on a large platform at the inner end of the room, and this is covered with good mats. As we crowd in, the men make for this platform to take their place higher and closer to the monk. My driver Ba Khin has, the minute before, seen me out of the car in his usual respectful way. Unlike the majority of servants in Burma today, he bows when he hands us things and uses honorifics when he talks to us. On entering the monastery, however, he is in another world as he sails past me and my two daughters sitting on the muddy floor in our best clothes; he stoops to catch up my 5-year-old son with him, and steps up to the platform alongside his master, smiling assuredly at all around him.

Outside religious precincts this distinction is still seen in the general manners of women towards men. Women feel free to mix freely with men except at large gatherings, but they always show deference for those men who are their equals or near-equals in age, as they naturally do to all who are older. Even a 'Westernized' Burmese woman does not normally ask these men to get up or fetch and carry for her but would, instead, do it for them. She certainly would not obtrude her person or her clothes into their vicinity. With men who are clearly younger, her age gives her complete authority to order them around if she knows them well. There is no doubt of this; but still their physical persons are to be respected. She would not step over even a young male child, for example, and to her male servants she would not give tasks involving the handling of her clothes and slippers. To observe these manners which are expressive of a male superiority is not regarded as impairing a woman's independence in any way; to omit them would be an impairment of her feminine grace.

RELATIONSHIPS WITHIN THE FAMILY: THE DIVISION OF LABOUR

Having explained at some length this basic conception about male and female, a conception which has suffered no diminution at all with changes into modern life, we may turn to the specific relationships between members of the family: to begin with, that between husband and wife. Among current terms of address between a couple, the eldest and 'best' form is the one where the wife calls her husband *Maung* (younger brother), and he calls her *Khin* (beloved). In modern times personal names may be used, abbreviated and prefixed in the same way as between a brother and his younger sister. Sometimes a form considered suggestive of the films is used by the wife, which is *Ko Ko* (elder brother). These names set the relationship, which is that the husband chops firewood, and the wife carries it in small bundles to lined by the basic idea mentioned above) permits.

The equal relationship between the spouses is a complementary rather than a symmetrical one. In the acquisition of property, for example, though by tradition husband and wife are joint earners, the idea is that each should work according to his or her own special ability. Thus in agriculture the husband does the heavy ploughing and digging, and the wife takes an equal or greater share in transplanting, weeding, reaping and winnowing; in the resting season the husband chops firewood, and the wife carries it in small bundles to sell around the village. In trade he might do the travelling or transportation of goods, while she does the retail selling or accounts. In the case of a skilled craftsman or other type of worker whose work is self-sufficient, the wife does separate but casual work, or work which still does not bind her down to rigid hours, such as cigar-rolling, hawking of home-made sweets, brokerage of gems or sale of cloth pieces from house to house on spare afternoons. This was the traditional pattern, and it is still largely true.

With a small section of the urban population, however, it is becoming more common for the wife to seek a salaried job with regular hours, fixed pay and a status of its own, when extra earning is needed for the family. But even this intrusion of a more modern set-up disturbs the complementary relationship between man and wife very little. The principle of a woman earning money towards the upkeep of house and family has always been present in Burmese society and it is therefore a stable element, rather than a disturbing one; and because this economic importance of the wife has existed alongside the spiritually different relationship for centuries, the latter idea, continuing to be as strong as it was, still prevents the successful salaried woman from wanting and getting a social or personal 'promotion' which her husband does not want to give her. This is as true of the last of the four families described later as it is of the first three.

Division of work between man and wife in the home is as follows. In poorer families the wife does all the housework (care of children, cleaning, cooking, washing, fetching of water from the well). So she normally handles all the joint earnings because it is she who purchases the food and clothing. The husband works more at earning the livelihood, builds and repairs the house, and does the heavy garden work. He is never asked to cook, sweep or wash clothes. This remains true even where the wife goes out to a modern type of job with fixed and long hours. Help with the housework will then be given her by children, younger brothers and sisters, or older female relatives. The man is left free to sit, read or visit, with no suggestion that he fails to do his share. A change which has come with modern life is that the man no longer hands all his money over to the wife. Present-day conditions, with their tea-shops, cinemas and stores, make it necessary for him to handle money too.

Religious activity plays a large part in the life of the average family. Here again the complementary nature of male and female roles is seen. Traditionally the man pays long visits to the monastery, chats most with monks when they visit his house, collects donations for the activities of the neighbourhood, and says longer prayers if he wishes to. His wife's part is to tend the altar with its offerings and flowers, and to cook food for the monks and for this altar besides saying her prayers. Modern life, with its increased social activities, often whittles down a man's opportunities for religious activity, with the result that in many families religion has become the woman's business in a way foreign to the older society.

Parents and children

In the bringing up of children we have already made the brief observation that more emphasis is placed on the mother. This is seen not only in the word for 'family', but in the very word for parents (*mi-ba*), which means 'mother-father'. The mother is always placed first. A letter begins 'Beloved benefactors, beloved-mother, beloved-father', always in that order.

There is no doubt as to a mother's complete authority over her sons. They prostrate themselves to her in the *shikkho*, the roles being reversed in this act of respect only when they are temporarily in the yellow robe. She is free to chastise her sons equally with her daughters, remembering only not to insult their manhood in the manner of doing it. The father's role in the care of children is that of co-benefactor, but less intimately so. He works to feed them, he exercises a higher authority than his wife's when necessary, and he takes his share in the discharge of the five duties of parents towards children. These are to prevent them doing bad deeds, to guide them towards good deeds, to teach them good learning (or skill), to give them an inheritance when the time comes, and to settle them in marriage with a spouse of a suitable stock.

It will be seen that the authority of parents over their children extends to the arranging of marriages for them. It might be asked whether this authority has lessened with modern relaxations of conduct. There is no doubt that manners between parents and children have become more informal, that there is more acceptance of children going out with adolescent friends in parties, much less adult chaperonage of girls going out in groups, and much more money given for spending. But there is little change in the theories of relationship between children and parents. 'Love-fear-respect' is still the formula taught for

118

every child's attitude towards his parents; and any stand for independence which goes against it is still considered to be unfilial conduct. In actual practice, few parents force children into marriages; indeed, by no means all are active in the discharge of this duty, but when they are, their activities are invariably regarded as helpful by the child concerned.

Siblings

In the relationship between brothers and sisters, two things can be noted. The elder ones have a general duty of caring for the younger, but over and above this, the eldest boy or girl has the responsibility of performing the duties of his or her parent of the same sex in their absence, or of contributing towards this even during the parent's lifetime. This is laid down in the duties of an *orasa* child. The other noteworthy feature is the necessity of observing the spiritual difference alongside an equal status in all other respects. This necessity has brought about the only difference which existed in the upbringing of boy and girl children. Burma was said to have a 'one-sex literacy'. Of the literate population in 1931 only 20.6 per cent were women. This was the incidental effect of the fact that all schools in earlier days were in monasteries, and all boys had to go to them in preparation for their initiation, which necessitated learning to read and write. When secular schools were established in addition to the monasteries, the traditional principle of giving equal opportunities in secular fields was followed, and in the younger age groups when girls' interests are still separable from care of house and marriage, nearly as many girls went to school as boys. The importance of the monastic schools in unbalancing schooling opportunities is shown by the figures from the 1931 census in Table 1.

TABLE 1. Distribution of primary students

School	Male	Female
Public institutions (i.e., State (secular) schools)	165 649	136 558
Private institutions (nearly all monastic)	175 506	3 356

Secular schools have increased greatly over monastic schools since then, but in 1953 female literacy was still only 37.9 per cent of the total literate population; this is largely because in the main girls leave school earlier than boys. The present-day increase in education for women is due to changes in the circumstances of community welfare, rather than in the outlook adopted towards girls' privileges, and so no radical change has been brought about in the relationship between siblings of opposite sex as a result of girls going to school with their brothers. Age, rather than sex, had traditionally set the responsibility to succour, and this still stands.

Grandparents

A last note about family attitudes: grandparents occupy a special place in the household. They are expected to devote much of their time to prayers, telling of beads and, in the case of grandmothers, taking over the altar duties from her busy daughter. These are vital contributions to every house in a land where the hold of religion is so strong that not even the gayest young couple can feel easy when the daily rituals are neglected. The old people must also provide greater cultural and religious influences for the children of the house than the parents themselves can, out of the wisdom, greater leisure and inclination which their stage in life gives them.

Thus, three ages are marked out for a normal Burmese Buddhist life: the first, up till about 25, which is that of learning, with a receptive and obedient attitude towards all elders and teachers; the second, which must of necessity be spent by both men and women largely in securing property to make possible the discharge of their duties as parents and as adult Buddhists towards monasteries and pagodas; and the third, when one must cease from such preoccupation with acquisition, and give almost all one's time to religious work and meditation on the folly of attachment to the world which one is about to leave so soon.

WOMEN IN THE NATIONAL ECONOMY

To turn now to the role of men and women in the economic life of the community at large: it is not surprising to find that women have worked to some degree in all but a very few professions for a long time past. Nevertheless, as a total working force, they number far less than men. This is only to be expected everywhere. In Burma the factors responsible for the difference are that women have less time to take full-time jobs, and that their casual labour is not listed in the figures; their physical difference and weakness precludes them from a number of occupations; they have little urge towards making careers for themselves in the modern way because tradition, giving them a large measure of equality of rights with men, makes life satisfactory enough; thus they seek regular employment only when financial necessity drives them to do so, and when it does, they choose only occupations which entail the least physical or mental discomfort; furthermore, the belief in the innate spiritual superiority of men prevents women from seeking positions of prestige and authority in, for example, government and administration (though on occasion history has recorded a ruling queen, women chieftains and headwomen of villages).

These observations are borne out by figures from the last census of 1953 and 1954. The labour force for the total urban area showed only 25 per cent females.[1] Still, we find women present in all major divisions. But whereas most occupations showed a far greater preponderance of men, one or two showed nearly equal numbers of both sexes; and some branches of these major groups showed more women workers than men. In Table 2 the numbers of women and men present in these occupation groups have been worked out to show simple proportions. We may examine the 1953 (urban) figures first, before looking at the 1954 (rural).

Looking at the urban list first, we see the greatest disproportion in armed services and operation of transport, both physically 'male' rather than 'female' occupations; the next largest disproportion occurs in the managerial and administrative category, where posts carry authority and prestige. There is least disproportion in trade and related occupations where retail sellers, including hawkers, actually include more women than men, and men are mainly employed in wholesale trade. 'Crafts' show a comparatively small disproportion, and the separate heads under this title show more women in textiles, ceramics,

---

1. The Burmese by themselves showed a higher figure (31.5 per cent), but the presence of other indigenous races and foreign groups such as Indians and Pakistanis brought this figure down.

TABLE 2. Ratio of men to women in total labour force

Division	Urban (1953)		Rural (1954)	
	Male	Female	Male	Female
Total labour force	75%	25%	68.9%	31.1%
Professional, technical and related occupations	3.2	1	4.4	1
Managerial and administrative occupations	10.3	1	22.0	1
Trade and related occupations	1.1	1	1.0	2
Farming, hunting, fishing and forestry	3.6	1	2.6	1
Mining and quarrying	6.3	1	3.2	1
Operating transport	108.0	1	4.0	1
Crafts	2.1	1	1.3	1
Service occupations	6.0	1	2.2	1
Armed services	199.0	1	(not available to writer)	

food and tobacco processes, which are all light and fairly pleasant occupations, and many fewer women in pelts and hides, construction, metal or woodwork. There is only a medium amount of disproportion of men over women in the technical and related group, owing to the presence of women in teaching, medicine and nursing, though (higher) occupations relating to physical, biological and agricultural sciences still show no women in the sample taken. This fact emphasizes the indifference of women towards careers. A good marriage is still the first aim of every women, even among the university-educated groups, and women go on to higher fields only if marriage does not claim them on the way. The small number of women members of parliament in a country where women take such a noticeably active part in political campaigning and voting, for example, shows the unwillingness of Burmese women to subject themselves to a professional life with the potential discomforts of public censure and invective, as long as they can take a satisfactory share in it through their men.

A comparison between the urban and rural figures is interesting.

We see first of all that the percentage of women earning regular wages is higher in rural areas which are considered as still being more true to tradition; secondly, that women actually outnumber men in trade and related occupations; and thirdly, that there is less disproportion, especially in operating transport, for villages have animal rather than mechanical means of transport.

The censuses of twenty and thirty years ago showed much the same trends. The division of occupations did not always use the same headings as above, so a direct comparison of figures cannot be made easily, but a few figures will serve to confirm the trends governing women's part in the economic life of the country.

The proportion of male to female earners in all occupations was eight to three. A break-down by occupation is given in Table 3.

TABLE 3. Division by occupation

Occupation	Female earners per 100 males
Ordinary cultivation	409
Raising small animals	1 064
Mining	48
Textiles	22 794
Hides	197
Hotels and cafés	962
Hawkers of food	1 915

Independence from the British brought many changes in the economic life of the country. A large foreign labour force of Indian manual workers left conservancy jobs, porterage, roadwork, mines, etc. Changes in China also stopped large numbers of seasonal and all-year-round workers from coming to the roads and mines of the hill regions in the north. A great effort to put the control of the country's economy into indigenous hands, to make the country more self-sufficient in products, and to conserve the low exchequer holdings consequent upon the destructive effects of war and insurrection, also led to controls on foreign imports. The inspiration of Independence in itself was sufficient to make people more interested in doing things for themselves and more enterprising generally. All this has led the

123

Burmese, not only women, but men too, to enter occupations in which they took little part formerly, in mines and on roads, in shop-keeping, building and construction, small industries and large-scale commerce. In these changes women have been abreast of men. For example, in the government's scheme for starting large joint venture corporations with indigenous capital and management, to wrest the import trade from foreign firms, out of ten corporations, the one declaring the highest dividends for the year (1959) was the one with an all-women board of directors.

RELIGIOUS GROUPINGS

There is one more important walk of life for men and women in Burma, and that is in the religious orders. Of men 3.3 per cent become monks, and of women 0.4 per cent become nuns. The monasteries exist purely for the monks. Here they live either as novices or as ordained monks. The leading monastery in this town (Taung-gyi), for example, has about 100 inmates, of whom forty are novices and the rest full monks, with one abbot who has spent forty years in the yellow robe. There are also about forty boys from poor families who are being taught to read and write and learn the scriptures. They help in the cleaning of the monastery and its grounds and in the collection of food, and wait on the monks' needs.

The ordained monks observe over 200 rules of conduct, most of them small regulations to ensure chaste, restrained and ascetic behaviour, but the main basis of their daily regimen is the ten precepts which, in addition to the five observed by all Buddhists, enjoin them specially not to eat after noon, not to handle gold and money, to avoid ornamentation and soft beds. During the day the monks teach the monastery boys and novices; they also are taught by the abbot or the more renowned monks (with the aim of sitting for the Vinaya examinations which are held regularly under government sponsorship); they recite orisons, tell beads, meditate and help to keep the monastery a clean and pleasant place. Each morning they walk out to beg for food from householders who wish to acquire merit by offering cooked food in this way; or boys go out to collect it from pre-arranged donors; or cash and provisions are offered and received into the monastery stores to be used as needed. The monks' duties towards the public are to recite precepts and scriptures, and give sermons whenever people wish them to do so either in their homes or in the monastery. No request to do this or to partake of a meal at the correct times is ever refused. They are considered to exert an influence for stability and benefaction over the community by their example of a good life as well as by the opportunities they afford the people for donating their wealth towards the promotion and perpetuation of the Buddhist faith.

The nuns are totally subsidiary in this respect. They are usually recruited from young and growing girls who desire a quiet and religious life, or from elderly women who have been widowed or used badly by life. They usually live in a building adjacent to the monastery grounds. They observe the same general regimen as the monks, but they do not have so many small rules regulating behaviour. They do not have any duties towards the public, though they also are supported with food and stores; their role is purely to lead a blessed and sheltered existence and to show a good example to all women.

DAILY LIFE: FOUR EXAMPLES

We shall now give an account of an ordinary day in the life of four households. These were chosen as being available for inquiry and observation, and because they provided examples of a rural and an urban household, both from the lower-income brackets, and of a traditional and a modern household, both from the higher-income brackets.

Rural simplicity

U Lay Pe and Daw Hnin Ohn, a Burmese-speaking Mon-Karen couple, live in the village of Munkyi between Rangoon and Moulmain in the south of Burma. The village is reached by bus or side-car (cycle with side passenger seat) from the bigger village of Paung Kywegyan, which is on the railway. Munkyi is divided in two by the bus route. Beyond its hundred odd houses on both sides are paddy fields, and beyond these on the east begin the foothills of the Tenaseerim Yomas. U Lay Pe lives in a thatched-roof wood and bamboo house raised on posts about 6 feet above the ground, and standing in large grounds of about $1\frac{1}{2}$ acres. He also owns 6 acres of paddy land. The plan of the house is shown on the next page.

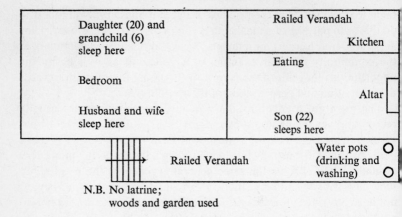

Daughter (20) and grandchild (6) sleep here	Railed Verandah
	Kitchen
Bedroom	Eating
	Altar
Husband and wife sleep here	Son (22) sleeps here

Railed Verandah — Water pots ○ (drinking and washing) ○

N.B. No latrine; woods and garden used

U Lay Pe is a practitioner of indigenous medicine. He married his wife in Paung and brought her to live with him and his brothers in this, his parents', house. His parents are now dead and his brothers moved away after marriage. The household at present consists of himself, his wife, their son Ngwe Tun, aged 22, and daughter Hla Myaing, aged 20, who have both passed the top class in the village primary school, and their grandchild, aged 6, born of their eldest daughter who died in child-birth and whose husband has since remarried and moved away. During three months in the year (June, July, August) the son and daughter live for most of the time in a hut in the paddy fields for the ploughing, sowing and transplanting. Then Daw Hnin Ohn has a busy time in the house, but during the rest of the year Hla Myaing, who left school six years ago, takes over the main burden of housework.

The day begins at 4.30 a.m. when son and daughter get up if they need to go 'on the hill' to collect firewood or chop bamboos. The mother then rises at 5 a.m. and puts the rice pot on the fire to be in time for the altar offering at dawn. While the rice cooks she washes and prepares fruit and palm sugar to offer with it. When all is ready she makes the offerings, changes votive water and flower vases if necessary and says her prayers. When Hla Myaing does not go 'on the hill' she sees to these duties and the mother attends only to her grandchild.

Meanwhile the husband has risen, and after washing he begins his prayers. At about 6.30 a.m. the brother and sister return. They and their mother eat a boiled bean salad bought from an early morning hawker, with green tea brewed by Hla Myaing, while the father continues his prayers. Then Hla Myaing begins the cooking; her mother may or may not join her in this. They have stores of rice, oil, onions, saltfish, etc., in the house, and on most mornings fish and vegetable sellers pass, from whom the mother makes necessary purchases. Hla Myaing does not take time off except for puffs at her cheroot. When there is a pause in the cooking, she sweeps the floor. Her mother, in the intervals of helping in the kitchen, sits on the verandah and chats to her grandchild as she smokes.

When U Lay Pe's long prayers are finished, he tells his beads, and then he also sits and smokes. At 9 a.m. the meal has been cooked; it consists of rice, vegetables and sometimes meat, fish or dried fish. They all eat together in the living-room round a low table. Some of the main dishes have already been set aside in small bowls on a covered lacquer tray, and after his meal the father dresses in good clothes and takes this to the monastery. His family will not see him till nearly 4 p.m. He will sit and chat to the monks, read religious books or talk to other lay visitors all day, and when a patient needs his services the villagers will go and call him from the monastery.

Meanwhile his wife and daughter wash up after the meal. After this the mother lies down for a rest of about an hour. Then she goes to the well, which is about two houses away, taking her grandchild with her, to have her bath, after which she may go visiting, or she may stay at home to roll her cheroots, or to sell the produce of her garden to those who come and buy. They have a few vegetables growing, as well as a great variety of shrubs and trees whose leaves, shoots, stems, buds, fruits, seed pods, etc., are all edible.

Hla Myaing, after tidying the kitchen, has taken the washing to the 'water spout' which is the end of a bamboo aqueduct leading from a spring at the foot of the hill. This is about 10 minutes' walk. There she chats to friends as she launders. On her return she takes water-cans and fetches water from the well for drinking and cooking. She returns to the well for her bath. The company there is always mixed. She dresses and powders herself and starts to cook the evening pot of rice and soup to be eaten with the food left over from the morning.

During the periods when her brother is not down in the fields with reapers, or taken away by the army to carry loads (from which task he brings back good pay), he clears the garden, plucks fruit and leaves, chops firewood and stacks it under the house, or just goes off to visit a friend for the afternoon.

When the father returns he also goes to the well and has his bath. Then at about 4 p.m. the family sits down to dinner. After this the mother washes up. Hla Myaing goes with her brother or with girl friends to the pagodas, where all the young people collect in the evenings to carry earth or dig in construction work. The parents may stroll along there later. At dusk they return to light a kerosene lamp. They light candles also and pray at the altar by turns. Then at about 8 p.m. they go to bed.

The money used by the family is all handled by the mother. Her husband's slight earnings are handed to her—either cash or rice and clothing. The annual crop of paddy brings in about 300 to 400 kyats, enough to last all the year when added to the other earnings.

At the time of writing, the brother and sister have come to Rangoon to visit their maternal elder aunt who left Paung six years ago to enter domestic service. She is trying through her employers to find Hla Myaing a similar position and for Ngwe Tun an office job as a peon, chiefly because the family fears that the army might take him portering into dangerous areas. If she is successful, their mother will again have to do all the housework herself, but the aunt considers her sister lucky to have a husband who owns enough modest property to enable him to spend his days so meritoriously at the monastery.

Urban working class

Ko Nyo and Ma Sein live in the servants' 'barracks' attached to one of the big houses kept for the senior staff of the port authorities of Rangoon. Both of them have taken to urban life in the last eleven years. Ko Nyo came to the city to drive the car of his old employer's married daughter, for whom Ma Sein was working as a maid. After two years of common service they got married and when the first child came Ma Sein left work. This was possible because Ko Nyo, then already in his thirties, had always been careful with his money and she also was a thrifty girl. This was eight years ago; meanwhile Ko Nyo was transferred to driving one of the port lorries and their old employer also moved house, so they now have only one room in the block of six, where they used to have two. They have two daughters, aged 8 and 6, and a boy of 13 months.

The plan which follows shows how this provident couple, with the goodwill of less hard-working neighbours, have made a pleasant set-

128

ting out of their cramped city accommodation. Ma Sein's kitchen and work routine also show that she has benefited from service in a well-run house.

				Monastery Grounds				
		Fence						
Banana trees				Platform built by Ko Nyo			Trees planted by Ko Nyo	
				Cooking and eating			Tap ♀	Tap ♀
Ko Nyo's private garden				Ko Nyo and Ma Sein	Neigh-bour		Lav.	Lav.

The day begins as early as in the country. Ma Sein gets up at 4.30 a.m. to start cooking her husband's morning meal which he must take to work in a tiered container. She washes her face, goes to the latrine, and then starts a little kerosene burner. She cooks rice, perhaps heats up a meat curry from the night before, and cooks one more dish of vegetables and fish. She then puts on a kettle for coffee. She offers a small part of the rice on the altar, puts her husband's share of the meal into the container and makes the coffee.

Her husband, meanwhile, has woken up at about 5 a.m. He performs his ablutions, says short prayers and dresses for work. Just before 6 a.m. he has coffee and rusks, then walks about 650 yards to catch the office bus to work where he clocks in at 7 a.m.

The children wake up as their father goes. Ma Sein attends to the baby's milk first, then washes the other two and gives them some coffee and rusks. Then, while the elder one is set to reading lessons she sweeps and tidies the room, putting away bedding and getting out clothes for the schoolchildren. This takes her only a short time if she is not interrupted by the baby. After this she takes the two girls to the tap and gives them their bath. She dresses the younger one and then sits them down to their meal. At about 8.30 a.m. she hands them over to her neighbour's 15-year-old sister to walk to their school together.

129

From now until about 3.30 p.m., when the children return, her programme is elastic. She may walk to the bazaar, a 12-minute walk each way, leaving her baby with a neighbour. She also has her bath, eats her meal and washes clothes. She feeds the baby when needed. She may sew clothes for the family on her sewing-machine, bought four years ago. She may just cuddle the baby and chat to her neighbour, but not for long. She does not smoke. Sometimes she goes across to visit her old mistress and chat to the maids there who come from her home village, but she visits nowhere else.

Meanwhile Ko Nyo has been driving the lorry for a four-hour shift. He drives to wherever the electricians need to examine or repair lines. Once he gets to the destination it may be a long stop and, if it is, he takes out his newspaper bought just outside the office and reads it carefully, as he is keenly interested in politics. He also smokes. If they park near a tea-shop he can have a cup of tea while waiting. At 11 a.m. he drives the lorry back near the wharves and, taking his food into one of the sheds, he eats together with a few others. He lies down on the floor there for about half-an-hour, and then resumes work at 12. The afternoon passes in exactly the same way. He knocks off at about 3.30 p.m., and catches the 4 p.m. ferry home.

Arriving home, he waters the garden and tends the trees; he also bathes and sits chatting and smoking, with his baby son in his arms, while his wife cooks the evening meal. They eat at 6 p.m. all together. Then Ko Nyo goes through the fence into the monastery which has a meditation cell, and says prayers and tells beads for one hour. Meanwhile his wife washes up and tends the children. She then says short prayers and they prepare to go to bed. The daughters sleep in the bed with father, and Ma Sein rolls out her bedding and sleeps on the floor with her son.

On a Saturday, Ko Nyo's half-day, he may take the family to the Shwe Dagon pagoda, but Ma Sein does not often wish to go. On rare Sundays they visit the only relatives that either has in Rangoon. They are happy to follow this routine. Ma Sein takes pride in her saving and her modest possessions. They are able to save because they lend out money at interest. This is done by Ko Nyo as he goes to work, but everything is handed to Ma Sein. She gives him enough for his cheroot and cups of tea. Everything else is bought by her, either when she goes with Ko Nyo in a side-car on a Saturday afternoon or with her former mistress's maids in a car.

Retired civil servant

U Po Hla and Daw Tin Tin are a couple in their late fifties. He has just retired from the post of Assistant Inspector of Schools in the Shan State, and lives in a house which he calls Ruby Lodge because they both come from Mogok where the famous ruby mines are. Their only son is married and lives with his wife's family. Daw Tin Tin's younger sister has always lived with them, and when in her mid-thirties she married a master-goldsmith, a little smithy was built in the back garden, and the younger couple with their family of four children are now part of the household.

Every morning at about 6 a.m., the maid at Ruby Lodge gets up and starts the fire for the rice pot. Daw Tin Tin gets up about this time too and, after a wash, begins to sweep the floors with a feather broom. When the rice is cooked she arranges the offerings for the altar. She goes into the garden if necessary to cut fresh flowers for this, and then says her prayers as she makes offerings and changes the votive water. Her sister, Ma Win, has also got up early, but all her time between now and 8 a.m. is taken up with the children.

When Daw Tin Tin has finished her prayers she goes into the kitchen to prepare her husband's breakfast tray for which the maid has got everything ready. She serves this in the sitting-room, though she and the rest of the family including her brother-in-law, a younger man, drink coffee in the kitchen at convenient moments. U Po Hla has got up at about 7.30 a.m. He spent his career in arduous travelling and his wife wishes him to take things easy now. After his wash and his breakfast he joins two friends in a regular morning walk of about three miles round the town. On this walk they constantly meet people who stop them to talk and thus they keep in touch with community news just as they did before retirement.

Meanwhile, with the elder children off to school and the goldsmith gone to his workshop or his shop, Ma Win and the maid get down to cooking the morning meal. In these parts there is a big market every five days which the congregation of market gardeners, cart-men with fish, lorry-men with foods from the plains, and potters and other artisans makes a festive occasion. Daw Tin Tin makes big purchases in the morning on market days, and also in the afternoons of the previous day when fresh produce begins to arrive. On other days, while her sister and maid are busy in the kitchen, she waters the flower beds, and when her husband returns from his walk at about 9.30, she goes into the kitchen to add the finishing touches to the cooking and to dish up the meal herself. Husband and wife sit down to eat shortly after 10 a.m.

After this the husband reads till he falls asleep, but the wife has her bath, dresses carefully and then sets out on her private business. She deals in gems from Mogok, selling rubies, sapphires and spinels of all shades. By now she has gained a sound reputation, and so people ask her to sell their diamond jewellery also. Sometimes her presence is requested in the workshop by her goldsmith brother-in-law, who wants her to talk to special customers or to advise about stones and settings. When there is no business she rests. Or she may be called out on community business, of which more later.

At about 3 p.m. she starts to supervise the cooking of the evening meal. Her sister and maid, after short rests following their meal, have washed the clothes. Her husband has got up from his midday rest, read the newspapers, had his bath, and is now playing with the younger children or doing a little writing. He is keenly interested in Burmese literature and Shan folk-lore and has published a few books.

Dinner is at 5 p.m., and this they all eat together. If the erratic water supply is good at this time Daw Tin Tin waters her flower beds again. They may be visited by neighbours or by their son and his family, or they may listen to the radio and go to bed at about 9 p.m. Upstairs, U Po Hla says short prayers, but his wife says much longer ones aloud, which she means for both of them, as she shares merit with him at the end.

This routine is often changed by the social duties incumbent on them, as they live in a thickly built-up area of the town. Outside of Lent they have to attend a great number of engagement ceremonies (when they themselves may be asked to speak for the groom in asking for the bride) and also marriages, initiation ceremonies, feasting of monks for various purposes, donation of robes, etc., and in some of these Daw Tin Tin must help in the necessary large-scale cooking. She herself 'books' two days a month with two big monasteries when she supplies meals to about forty monks. During Lent, U Po Hla fasts every full moon and new moon day, but the two sisters fast on quarter-days as well. In addition, Daw Tin Tin belongs to the Maternity and Infant Welfare Society's Executive Committee as a quiet but dependable member who attends monthly meetings, takes weekly turns to give out Unicef supplies and visits poor mothers twice a month. Her husband's pension is handed intact to her, and she provides him with all that he wants. She does not know English and considers her husband far above her in his Burmese learning as in his knowledge of English.

An educated young married couple

U Win Kyu is a young Sino-Burmese engineer who lives in Taung-gyi with his wife and three children, aged 6, 3 and 1. They have a large house with two servants as well as a gardener, and his wife's maternal aunt also lives with them. She accompanied her niece from the start when, as a bride of only 22 years, daughter of a senior government official in Rangoon, she had to come far into these Shan hills. Daw Khin Nyunt Yin is a science graduate and she has been teaching in a school called Kambawsa College for two years now. She is called 'Kitty' by her friends. Her husband also has an English name from his days in the local convent, but it is rarely used now.

A day in the life of this young couple usually begins with the servant rising about 6 a.m. to start the rice pot and sweep the house. The aunt, who is in her fifties, rises about this time too, and having had a wash attends to the baby if he wakes before the mother does. When the rice is cooked, the aunt makes the offerings. At 7 a.m. the husband and wife get up and start to wash and dress. By this time their children are running in and out of their room as the eldest gets ready for school. Just before 8 a.m., they have their breakfast downstairs with eggs, toast, butter, jam and fruit. Kitty goes into the kitchen after this to give instructions about the day's marketing and cooking. When they are ready, at about 8.30 a.m., U Win Kyu drives them in the jeep, dropping the child first, his wife next, and then himself going to his office, each place being only a few minutes from their house.

The wife as a senior teacher has shorter hours in school than her husband at his office. She works from 9 a.m. to 12 with a regular break of twenty minutes, and on some days a forty-minute period 'off'. She is considered very competent (also beautiful and gentle), has little trouble with discipline, and as some of the work is practical demonstration, it gives her a variety of activity. During the regular break she joins the rest of the staff for tea and a chat in the common room.

At noon U Win Kyu comes to fetch his wife. He has spent the morning partly at his desk with papers, partly interviewing or

133

discussing projects with people, and often going round in the jeep to the construction site. When the husband and wife get home, their daughter, whose lunch hour starts at 11.30, has already arrived and eaten with the aunt. Kitty has to be back at work by 1 p.m. on four of her five workings days, so they both drive off again after having a short time with the children. On free afternoons she sews or washes a few articles of finer clothing. On other days she gets back a bit earlier than her husband, at 3.30 p.m., and waits for him to come home, when they have tea together. After tea he goes regularly to play tennis or golf while she bathes, works in the garden or takes a stroll with the children. He comes home at 6.30 p.m. and has his bath. Then they dine with their aunt, after which both work and read till 9 p.m., when they say their prayers and go to bed.

On Saturday afternoons they both make cakes and biscuits as a treat for the children, or the husband does repair jobs round the house, or they drive out for a picnic. Very often they have guests staying in the house, either her relatives from the plains or their mutual friends from university days, all of whom regard Taung-gyi as a holiday resort. On these days Kitty is extremely busy preparing extra food and arranging sleeping accommodation in between her school hours. They have no more time for religious activity than this account shows, though they subscribe to and attend the main functions of the year. During Lent they go to the monastery on some full-moon days, as schools close on these days instead of Saturdays. They both attend official functions scrupulously, but the normal day of both, especially U Win Kyu's, is felt to include enough social contacts. Apart from an occasional trip to Rangoon, visits to U Win Kyu's brother and mother, dinners with a few intimate friends, and rare visits to the cinema, this is their routine throughout the year. Their financial circumstances are easy, and they share the decisions about expenditure quite amiably.

CONCLUSION

In reading this article, one cannot fail to notice the strong influences which religion exerts on the life of the people. It is not within the scope of the article to describe social activities themselves; otherwise it would be even clearer that almost all celebrations, meetings and feasting begin with an invitation to monks to eat and to preach, or rather, they really arise out of the host's wish to have the religious part enacted—guests simply being invited to share in the occasion and the merit ensuing therefrom. Not only is there this pervasive extension of religion over social activities: almost all customs, and attitudes between persons too, take their sanctions from religious ideas, or at the very least they are instinct with religious associations. It is, in other words, the ideas of Burmese Buddhism which hold the balance in Burmese society and provide its whole cohesive force.

When considering future trends in Burmese social development, therefore, it is natural to ask: how strongly entrenched is this religious influence, and what are the prospects of its steady continuance? The answer is, undoubtedly, that it has extremely strong roots in the minds of the people right up to the present time. Hardly any Buddhist questions the faith. There is only the question of how much time each individual can give to its social and private observance, and this depends on temperament or on the way of life followed; as, for example, the difference between U Lay Pe (the man in the rural family in the last section) and the men in the two later families (the engineer and the retired civil servant); or the difference between Daw Tin Tin and 'Kitty'. The conviction which exists is a firm faith not only in the underlying philosophy of Buddhism, but also in all its Burmese Buddhist appendages such as the forms of gaining merit, the daily observances, the sanctity of the male person, the steps in the ladder of existences, etc., which ideas set the patterns of good family and community behaviour.

A good deal has been said by now about the Buddhist faith. What of the non-Buddhist section of the population? The latest census gives the Moslems as the largest non-Buddhist group—8 per cent of the total (in urban areas). As the social pattern in Moslem countries differs greatly from much of the preceding descriptions, one naturally wonders what effect the Moslem faith has had on the life of its Burmese adherents. As far as civil law is concerned, they come of course under the Moslem codes, and at one time a Burmese Buddhist woman marrying a Moslem was at a disadvantage because, profession of the Moslem faith being necessary to make such a marriage valid by Moslem law, she also was brought under its terms. But the Buddhist Women's Special Marriage and Succession Act passed in 1939 enables her to retain her own Buddhist laws. As regards social life, it has often been remarked that nowhere do the sobering influences of Islam on women sit so lightly as on Burmese Moslem women. They do marry

135

within their sect; they do scrupulously avoid pork, they do observe their fasts, feasts and prayer times; but that is all that non-Moslem neighbours see of the differences. For the rest, they move about and take part in economic and professional life in the same way as Burmese Buddhist women do.

Christians constitute 2 per cent of the population. This includes an important Burmese and Karen group living in the main plains as well as Christian communities among the hill races. The latter have been converted largely from animistic tribal customs, those remaining unconverted to Christianity and still far from Buddhist influences being entered in the census as 'Animists'. One of the social effects of Christianity on the Burmese and Karens has been to lead the women, ahead of Buddhist women, into professions associated with Christian ideals of service such as nursing and teaching. There is little other difference to be observed except in those social practices which are associated with acts of worship, such as the Buddhist habit of paying respect to elders in the same form of obeisance as used at prayers. Though Christian women discard the idea of a man's spiritual difference, for example, their manners and deportment towards men are just as deferential as those of Buddhist women.

One might, as a closing thought, consider the possibilities of changes in the social system apart from religion—that is, though the social system as a whole seems at present to be inextricably bound up with the Buddhist religion, which in turn seems too strongly entrenched to be dislodged, yet might not other factors, which are inseparable from the modern development of a country, force their way in relentlessly? The urban conditions of crowded living, for example, which minimize neighbourhood festivities, or the increase in factory-type jobs which tend to upset the domestic balance provided by helpful dependent extra kin, or the inevitable 'Westernization' of manners which offsets the traditional attitude between a man and a woman, causing discord and a need for new adjustments. I may be wrong if I forecast no great or rapid change from such factors, for it is undoubtedly true that there is in the Burmese a conservatism about the adoption of the superficial aspects of other cultures. No nation with so few social taboos has been so slow to change its traditional dress, whether for men or women, or its system of individual names, for example, or been so truly indifferent towards 'Westernized' forms of recreation which are so much more obvious in other capital cities than in Rangoon. The great mass of the Burmese people continue to regard these foreign influences as alien, or irrelevant to their life; a smaller section, those who have become well acquainted with the intellectual ideas of the West, along with its speech, its standards of material comfort (up to a point) and professional attainment, have been known to embrace all of them, and then turn back, as if naturally, to their own traditions for the social relationships pertaining between men and women, young and old, without a moment's hesitation or uncertainty.

Patterns of social change in a Burmese family

by NI NI GYI

That her grand-daughter in short sleeves and high-heeled sandals should be at a cocktail party with a glass in her hand (even though it be orange or tomato juice) is hardly a picture that my grandmother Daw Mein Ka Lay would have imagined in her wildest dreams half a century ago. We have certainly come a long way since the *ya-hta-lone,* the Burmese horse and buggy days. In her time Ma Mein Ka Lay, as my grandmother was called, was dedicated to the home and spent all her time at household chores, and would never go out at night except maybe to a pagoda festival, and then only in the company of the whole family.

Thus it is evident that even the staid and conservative Burmese culture which had always boasted of being impervious to the influences of 'foreign matter' is showing signs of thawing. In order to analyse to what extent cultural and social change has affected the Burmese family from my grandmother's day to mine, I will treat my family as the centre of the discussion and may even have to write in a personal vein.

My family cannot be described as a typical Burmese family, as the typical Burmese family would live on a farm, be literate in Burmese only, be engaged in farming and maybe never get to the big cities except on a pilgrimage. My family can best be described as urban (we settled down in Rangoon when my father retired from government service) with the socio-economic status of a middle-class family, and we are staunch Buddhists. I do not remember my maternal grandparents so I will confine myself to writing about my paternal grandparents, the only ones I knew. My grandfather was an administrative officer in the government service and served in several towns in his day. My grandmother was descended from one of the *Myosa* (petty

138

lords) in the days of the Burmese kings. During my childhood she often told us about the days when she was a young girl in her teens and actually witnessed the unceremonious capture of King Thibaw and his Queen by the British, and how her family stood in line to bid their king and queen goodbye and to pay their last respects. It should thus be all the more interesting to find out the series of changes that have taken place from the days of my grandmother, who lived under the last reigning Burmese king, to mine, the post-Independence days. The span of time includes Burma under the rule of Burmese kings, the British régime, Japanese rule, re-occupation by the British and Independent Burma.

A closer analysis of social and cultural change affecting the Burmese family reveals that the pattern of change remained fairly constant during my grandmother's and mother's time. Then the pendulum swung a bit faster in my younger days, but it seems to swing radically now, for the generation that is coming up. In my childhood the family was made up of my grandmother, father, mother, my sisters, an aunt (my mother's cousin) and a cousin who was really a poor relative living with us. The family was mobile in the sense that it moved wherever my father was transferred (he was the principal of a high school) and he was posted in each town for a few years at a time. I am proud to say that it was a congenial family in spite of its size. My father's pay was not fabulous, but the family income was substantially complemented by the yearly proceeds from my grandfather's estate and paddy fields which were a good source of income in those days.

There was no doubt whatsoever that my grandmother was the recognized head of the household and this was by virtue of the fact that she was the oldest member of the family, and not because she was a contributor to the family's income. My father would do nothing without the approval and consent of my grandmother and it was always the same with my mother. In her case the devotion and respect shown exceeded all expectations, as she was a niece and daughter-in-law combined. I do not mean to imply that my grandmother was a despot, but she was treated with reverence at all times and she had the final say in all matters in the household. To give an example of how much my father abided by her decisions I would like to write about an incident which has always remained impressed on my mind since childhood. It was in the late thirties, when for the first time a small seaplane landed on the sandbanks of the riverine town where my father was stationed. The plane had brought a famous monk to preach sermons in the town, and since the plane was returning empty the town crier announced that it would take passengers back to Rangoon. My father was very thrilled with the idea, booked a seat with the pilot and came home to tell us the news. My grandmother greatly disapproved and asked my father to drop the idea for her sake. My father complied with her wish and cancelled the trip. Such was the extent of his obedience towards his mother.

The family system was very strong and absolute respect and obedience were shown all along the line. Even the children had to obey the next in line, according to their ages. The deep-seated belief is that one is to show respect for people even if they are one day older than you are. My grandmother, being oldest in the household, formed the apex of authority and respect and she was followed by father, mother, aunt and cousin down to the children, from the eldest to the youngest. Burmese children from childhood are instilled with the idea of absolute reverence for the following, in the order given: Lord Buddha, his teachings, the clergy, parents and teachers. This is the reason why implicit obedience is accorded the parents.

The attitude is somewhat changed now; the trend is towards more rational obedience, and relations between my mother and ourselves are on a more informal plane. I noticed as a child there was never any familiarity or outright friendliness between my grandmother and my father or mother; she was treated with too much awe to allow that. Whereas now, if my mother makes a certain decision, we are able to explain things to her and even disagree with her and she takes it in the best light. In fact, when I accompanied my husband on a world tour in 1955 my mother was very much against it, but I was able to make her understand my point of view and even got her blessing for the trip.

Servants were no problem in the days of my grandmother and mother and the family had two, one a male cook and the other a maid servant, both of whom cost not more than four dollars a month. Thus neither my grandmother nor my mother had to perform regular household chores; my grandmother did a lot of sewing for the grandchildren on her hand-operated sewing-machine, while my mother attended to the needs of the children.

In the bringing up of children, although she consulted the doctor in all matters, my mother never neglected my grandmother's advice. Thus

140

if one of the babies in the house had an attack of colic, she would get a digestive mixture from the doctor and at the same time follow the traditional pattern of rubbing a little sesamum oil on the baby's stomach. So long as the remedies were not too drastic my mother was willing to combine the traditional with the modern practices of bringing up children. Although in her day, my grandmother had her babies just with the aid of an untrained but experienced midwife, and shut herself up in a closed room and applied heated bricks to her body to retain its warmth, she conceded that my mother should have her babies delivered with the help of a doctor in the modern way. That certainly was a big concession on the part of my grandmother.

The problem of the size of family has never really worried the Burmese Government or the families concerned, as it does in China or India, and the Burmese family accepts any size philosophically. This is partly due to the economic reason that food is no real problem in Burma. Famine is practically unheard of and no bread-winner worries in terms of the number of mouths to feed. 'Family planning' is unheard of, too, except in the better educated and higher income brackets where the trend seems to be towards 'giving the best to a few' in these days of high cost of living. Although sons are more desired because of the strong belief that all Buddhist males may one day become a Buddha, daughters are by no means shown less affection or appreciation.

In the matter of giving names to children there is still much adherence to tradition. Every Burmese child's name depends on the day of birth. Since time immemorial, wise men have laid down a code making certain sounds synonymous with certain days of the week. To give myself as an example, as I was born on a Saturday my parents could only name me from one of the following sounds: 'ta', 'hta', 'da', 'na'. In other words, my name could begin with only the T, D or N sounds. Accordingly I was named Ni Ni. It is only a first name and has nothing to do with my father's, since in Burma we do not have family names. No strict Burmese family will have any other criterion for choosing a name for a baby. Thus in Burma it is quite easy to guess someone's day of birth once you hear the name. The only modern touch in the matter of names is that most modern families are beginning to realize the confusion caused by having only personal names and are beginning to add the father's name to the daughter's for purposes of identification. For example, just as Mary, daughter of Mr.

Smith, is Mary Smith, Ni Ni, daughter of U Maung Maung Gyi, is now called Ni Ni Gyi. Wives, too, are beginning to take on their husband's names in addition to their own, thus if I wanted to be modern I could call myself Ni Ni Nyunt, as my husband's name is U Hla Nyunt.

In the matter of education, my grandfather went to a monastery where he learned the three Rs but more of religious instruction. My grandmother went to a lay school where she studied the three Rs and scriptures as well. The reason for the girls going to a lay school was that it was not proper for the monks to teach girls. By the time my mother went to school, Rangoon could boast of a modern school called the Empress Victoria Buddhist Girls' School and my mother and aunt were proud to be its pupils and to learn English there. At that time my maternal grandmother's idea was to give them enough 'modern education' to enable them to read English newspapers and she made them leave school after middle grade. It was strongly felt that a full education was only for the men. At that time, since there were no motor-cars, the owning of a horse-drawn buggy was a yardstick for measuring the socio-economic status of a family, and my mother and aunt lifted their heads high as they drove in their buggy to the school with the English name. My father went to a high school run by Irish missionary fathers, after which he went to Rangoon College for higher education.

The philosophy with regard to education had greatly changed when we reached school age. My father, in particular, had a very practical philosophy. Since he had no sons he was determined to give his daughters the best education he could. He explained that the best legacy parents could give children was education, and often repeated the well-known cliché that education is a pot of gold that no one can steal. He thus sent us as boarders to a convent renowned for its high standard of education. The strain on the family budget was made easier through my grandfather contributing substantially towards our education. My grandfather was at first very much against the idea of our going to an English school where we wore only European clothes and were given English names. He could not for a long time resign himself to the idea that we were giving up our national dress (even though temporarily) and our own names for the sake of learning to speak English, but he finally gave way in favour of the cause of education. In our generation two of the daughters got the benefit of foreign education. One of my sisters went to study in England before the war. At that time the

142

[Photo: Unesco/Bowers]

Indian girl playing the 'tampura'

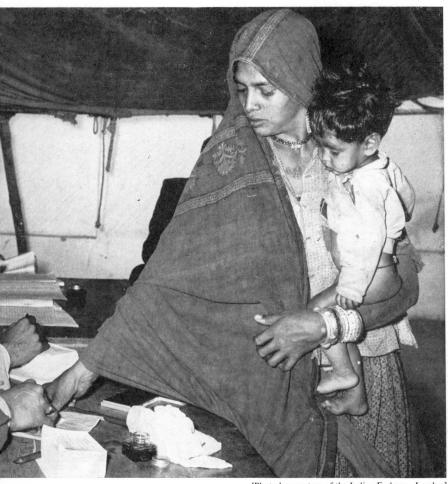

A woman at the polls in Delhi

At the Indian Conference of Social Work in New Delhi in 1961, women participated in the discussions

Children's corner in a public library in Delhi

A young mother student at the adult education class in Bombay ▶

[Photo: Unesco/Hunnar Publicity]

Young woman of Mysore

[Photo by courtesy of the Indonesian Embassy, London]

A tea picker

Javanese holding a bowl of Java's staple diet: fish and rice

usual reaction to the idea of a young unmarried girl going abroad was not very favourable. Quite a few of our elderly relatives criticized my parents for letting a young girl go alone to a strange country, where she might be exposed to the 'wild ways of Western civilization'. When I went to study in the United States as a State scholar a decade later opinion had changed considerably and my going abroad met with complete approval from everyone. At the present time every family takes pride in having a member going abroad to study. In fact things have reached the point where even elderly people would love to go abroad if 'they could only get the chance', at least on a pilgrimage. This is a clear indication of social change and changing attitudes towards travel and the lessening of suspicion of the West and what it has to offer.

Regarding the question of marriage, the marriages of my grandparents and parents were all arranged, in spite of which they were very successful. My parents' approach to the subject of marriage was very reasonable. They said they would leave the choice of a suitable partner to us, subject to their approval. In my own case I did an unconventional thing and have often joked about how my grandmother would have turned in her grave if she only knew about it. I met my husband while a student at Columbia University, New York. Coming from a conservative Burmese family, I must admit that I felt very guilty about making the decision while away from home and family, and wrote home about it full of sincere apologies for my lone decision. However, both families took the matter very well and chose an auspicious day to announce the engagement. While the Burmese Ambassador had a Western-style engagement party in New York, toasting the engaged couple with champagne, the elders at home made a formal announcement on a suitable day in the midst of both families and friends.

The trend of the present generation is to live in small family units. Soon after marriage, since our income was not too substantial, we lived for a time with my father-in-law, and my brother-in-law's family. We, who had been accustomed to independent living in the West for three years, found this combined family life very 'uncomfortable' in spite of the wonderful *esprit de corps* that existed, and we soon looked around for freer air. The scarcity of apartments or dwellings for rent has no doubt been responsible for large families living together under one roof. We were soon fortunate enough to be given excellent quarters at the University of Rangoon and we now live on our own with a couple of servants. We feel freer and more independent living this way, and we do not feel guilty of neglecting my mother because she has a house and is entirely on her own. The ties are still very strong and there are weekly visits to my mother's home. If, however, my mother were in poorer circumstances and had no house of her own, I would never think of letting her live alone or in any institution for the aged. I have already explained earlier the exalted position elders have in the Burmese family. The gregarious and family 'instinct' is very strong and this explains the absence of hotels and restaurants until recent times. If a relative was in town he was expected to board and eat with the 'family' or they would be greatly insulted.

Before marriage, in the matter of going out with boy friends or dating, the attitude of Burmese has remained almost unchanged from grandmama's day until my time. Up to the time I had met my husband and made my decision I considered dating taboo. Although I was the only Burmese girl student in New York City where there were a number of Burmese boys, all of them respected my wish to uphold the Burmese tradition of not dating. It may be called chauvinism or being ultra-sensitive of one's cultural heritage, but the Burmese as a people have always clung tenaciously to traditional ways and mores. Or it may be due to the fact that we have revelled so much in the glorious days of our civilization that we seem reluctant to veer off the traditional path. For instance, in the matter of clothing, Burma is one of the few countries in the world which has refused to adopt Western dress. It is almost unheard of for a Burmese woman to wear Western dress, and if she did, she would incur the censure of public opinion and be considered almost a traitor to Burmese civilization. In the matter of taking alcoholic drinks, too, for Burmese women time has had no effect whatsoever. It has always been taboo, and still remains so, and if there are a few exceptional ones who do drink alcohol, their mothers and grandmothers would sternly disapprove for it is our religion which prohibits drinking.

In the matter of entertaining, the post-war era has ushered in a series of Western-style parties. All the parties my mother and grandmother knew of were the traditional *soon-kywe* or feeding of monks, the *raya-ko-su* or nocturnal offerings to the nine gods to keep evil spirits away from the household, the *shin-pyu* or initiation into monkhood ceremony, the ear-boring ceremony, weddings, and pagoda festivals and fairs. Our generation now hears incessantly of open house parties, dances, cocktails, buffets and jam sessions. In fact, one thing that is frequently considered to be a hard blow at the core of Burmese civilization is the parties now thrown by teenagers. Their enjoyment of rock-and-roll and their birthday parties where they play modern games are beginning to worry some parents. Another modern innovation of the present generation is the holding of beauty contests. I am sure the grandmothers of all the contestants would blush to see their grandchildren parading before the judges and the public clad only in shorts or bikinis. I was called upon to be a judge in one of the beauty contests at the recent Independence celebrations, and as I watched the competitors I realized how strong a tide of change we had been swept up in, but I knew too that this change was inevitable according to the laws of social causation.

To return to the matter of dress: my grandmother wore white cotton jackets (almost Chinese style) complete with cloth buttons, fixed her hair up with one or several combs on the top and walked sedately so that not even her ankles showed. Her tight sleeves came down to her wrist and her *longyi* to her ankles. In my mother's time, the jacket was more loose but it still came down to her wrists, her *longyi* to her ankles, and her hair for formal occasions was done up like a cake on her head. The above style of dress still prevailed until the end of the war. However the post-war fashion is to wear short or three-quarter sleeves and now the present generation of teenagers and young girls go in for sleeveless jackets, brassières, short knee-length skirts and high-heeled sandals. The modern dress certainly helps to accentuate the better-developed bodies of the present-day girls and their physical measurements come up to accepted standards. In my grandmother's, mother's and my time, the female elders frowned upon developing bust-lines and unduly tight bodices were worn to suppress their development. This unhealthy restriction gradually lost its popularity after the war and the result is seen in the well-formed misses of today.

Another point of pride for the Burmese female is the hair, which is considered at its best when long and done up in a bun. It is only in this generation that a few girls have dared to cut their hair or have permanent waves.

I feel it is pertinent to write a few lines here about certain innate beliefs and mores that neither education nor modern times can shake off. In spite of the fact that the Burmese woman has 'gone modern' in more ways than one, it is almost paradoxical to see the way she sticks to certain of her ultra-traditional ways. Speaking for myself, I will never leave on a journey on the 'bad' days of the month and will invariably undertake major items like choosing the day for the wedding, shifting house, buying property, etc., only on the 'good' days, and these 'good' and 'bad' days are specified on each month of the Burmese calendar. To give another example, I would never bath or shampoo my hair while my husband was away on a journey unless I had definitively asked for permission to do so, prior to his departure, as washing one's hair when a member of the family is away is believed to bring ill-luck to the traveller. On the other hand, I fight with grim determination against the custom that one is not to cut one's hair or nails on a Friday, Monday or on the day you were born, and I do it any time the necessity arises. Nor do I adhere strictly to the mealtime custom of giving the first serving of every dish to the oldest or masculine member of the family. If a husband and wife are eating together, traditionally the wife is not supposed to help herself to anything until she has given a small spoonful to her husband first. This custom is fine in that it is a symbol of respect, but we find it more convenient to by-pass it and have done so by mutual agreement between ourselves. If, however, my mother or any elder is with us for a meal, both my husband and myself are prompt with the symbolic gesture.

One feature of our generation which was not common in the time of my mother and grandmother is the emergence of the career woman. Burmese women have always been noted for their shrewd business acumen and their ability to stand on their own as village chiefs, and have even sat on the throne at different stages of Burmese history, but their taking to regular careers is a new phenomenon. This phenomenon has its socio-economic explanations. The rising cost and standards of post-war living have made it necessary to have two incomes in order to live well. Although the husband's income may be sufficient for the basic needs of the family, any additional income contributed by the wife will afford the family the extra amenities of modern living. In addition to this economic reason, the modern educated woman feels a sense of independence in having her own career and is thus eager to make use of the excellent opportunities now offered to educated women. Besides, it certainly adds a touch of prestige to the family's reputation if both are bread-winners. In my grandmother's and mother's day, the position was reversed. The husband took pride in the fact that he was the sole 'rice-winner' and that his wife could afford the luxury of staying home. We find that the modern career woman-cum-housewife is heavily burdened with social obligations after office hours. In addition to her own professional social contacts, she is also expected to keep up with her husband's. We thus find her a busy socialite and this in great contrast with her mother's and grandmother's day, when a housewife was supposed to be home to tuck the children in bed or join in the family prayers or just sit around with the family till bedtime. Consequently, the woman who combines the roles of housewife and career woman has a full-time programme on her hands. Living between a full-time job, out-of-office-hours professional obligations, her evening social engagements, and the task of running a home, does take a great deal out of the modern woman.

The modern household where both the husband and wife have their own careers depends a great deal on reliable domestic help, which is proving to be a great problem these days. Servants cost at least five times as much as they did before the war and they have never been more mobile as a group as they shift from one household to another. I would attribute this so-called lack of loyalty and the resulting mobility to the general enlightenment of the servant class. They are being exposed to greater influences as they come into contact with various families and their outlook is broadened. They are also beginning to benefit from the system of free education in Burma. The current attitude seems to be, therefore, that they would rather work in factories and offices than as domestic servants at the master's beck and call for twenty-four hours a day. I am of the opinion that after several years servants will disappear as a class. Another factor is the rise of labour unions which aim at protecting their rights, resulting in friction between the master and servants. This uncertainty in the servant situation has paved the way towards electrification in the homes. I thus find myself indulging in the luxury of electrical appliances and labour-saving devices wherever I can, in spite of the high cost of electricity. My cook, like most others, still uses firewood and charcoal for cooking, but in case I am left to cook for myself I can always rely on my electrical appliances.

The Burmese woman has always had a distinct place in public life. Theoretically speaking, there is no social or legal barrier to her holding any position in the land. Throughout Burmese history, the position of Burmese women has always been on a par with that of men. Traditional law recognizes us equally with men and all through our history

147

we have had full inheritance rights. However, apart from the days when women ruled the country, the Burmese women have not taken any great interest in politics. There is no great political consciousness such as is to be found in some other countries. Accordingly, there is no Burmese counterpart of the political stature of Mrs. Pandit, Mrs. Sun Yat Sen or Mrs. Roosevelt. There are very few women in Burma who are active in politics or have the required sense of political consciousness. In fact I cannot think of a single member of our entire family who has taken any active part in politics.

This indifference to politics all along the line is noteworthy, especially with regard to present-day women. Never in any period of our history have we been so exposed to the '-isms' and never have words like 'democracy', 'communism', 'socialism', 'disarmament', been brandished about so freely. In spite of the constant exposure to the media of press, film and radio, we have managed to stay aloof from politics. If during the recent general elections the political fever seemed high, it was generally because people were interested in their respective political heroes, and not the '-isms' and ideologies they stood for. This apathy towards politics may be attributed to the general passive philosophy of the Burmese Buddhist mind.

To repeat for emphasis, we have certainly come a long way from the days of my grandmother. Summing up, we can say we have marched forward but with restraint. If in some ways the pendulum of social change has swung too fast, it has been because we were swept on by the inevitable chain of social causation.

Ceylon

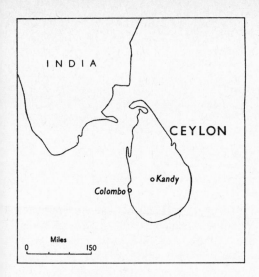

Area: 65,610 square kilometres.

Population: 9,612,000 (estimated 1959).[1]

Recent history: 1947—British Government transfers sovereignty; 1959—Election of world's first woman Prime Minister, Mrs. S. Bandaranaike.

Citizenship: Men and women have equal rights.

Religion: The Ceylonese (69 per cent of the total population) are predominantly Theravada (Hinayana) Buddhists; the Tamils (23 per cent) predominantly Hindus. There are also Moslem and Christian minorities.

Inheritance and family patterns: Customary rules of inheritance among the Ceylonese give daughters an equal share with sons, but, particularly among the well-to-do, the tendency is for real estate to be kept together for the sons. Small domestic units of the nuclear type are often, if not usually, absorbed into larger patrilocal extended families.

---

1. Latest official estimate of population as published in *The U.N. Population and Vital Statistics Report, October 1960.*

The life of Ceylon women

by B. S. SIRIWARDENA

The coming of the British to Ceylon in 1796 marked the start of a new era in the history of this country, which from then onwards began to undergo the many changes that paved the way for its present emergence as one of the leading countries in South-East Asia. Plantations of coffee, tea and rubber were introduced, and with them the economic development of the country began. With the introduction of British government the seeds of democracy were sown. With the improvement of the means of communications the country was opened up and became more closely knit. The traditional legal systems of the country were supplemented and modified to meet modern requirements. Health services began to be within the reach of everyone. Education began to be considered the right of all irrespective of sex, creed or ethnic group, and not as the privilege of a few. More than in anything else there opened a new chapter in the life of women in this country.

Traditionally, society in Ceylon was ordered strictly on a caste basis,[1] which roughly corresponded with a class basis. Those who belonged to the so-called higher caste were the rich upper class, who were landed proprietors and who held responsible posts in government. Until the country fell into the hands of the Portuguese, the Dutch and later the British, these posts ranged from those of ministers and commanders-in-chief down to village headmen, and after the British occupation, from *maha mudaliyar'* down to the village headman. All the paddy cultivators, too, belonged to this Goigama caste, although they were not rich. The rest of the people belonged

---

1. See Bryce Ryan, *Caste in Modern Ceylon.*

o the so-called lower castes, each with its traditional caste occupaion.[1]

Buddhism was the religion of the Ceylonese and Hinduism that of he Tamils, until Christianity obtained converts from both Ceylonese and Tamils. Moslems have always followed Islam. Religion was the basis of the culture and the way of life of the people.

In traditional Ceylon it was difficult to draw a hard and fast line between town and country. Even today three-quarters of the population consists of rural people, and the distinction between rural and urban society is something that has been developing only since the beginning of the twentieth century.

THE TRADITIONAL POSITION OF WOMEN

To be a good wife and mother was considered the ideal and the perfection of womanhood in all religions and caste groups from the earliest times and even after the coming of Christianity. Religion also fostered this ideal of the perfect wife-mother for the Ceylon woman. Careers were not meant for women. The only career women we hear of in ancient and mediaeval Ceylon are two queens (Anula and Lee-awathy, who reigned in their own right), female servants and attendants in royal and aristocratic households, and prostitutes who made a living by their trade. Any other kind of economically gainful employment for women was unheard of until the coming of the British. Girls had none of the opportunities open to boys to get a formal education in the *pirivena* schools run by the Buddhist monks or at the feet of Hindu Brahmin teachers. The few women who happened to be literate had been taught at home by their fathers, or elder brothers, or other elderly male relatives.

Women's position in Ceylon was far from favourable, and they 'have always been considered inferior to men in all aspects, and as a constant source of trouble and wickedness. They have been referred to as

---

. For example: Karava caste (fishermen), Berava (drummers), Salagama (cinnamon peelers), Vahumpora (toddy tappers), Durāva (minor arts and crafts), Rada (washermen), Navandanna (blacksmiths, silver and goldsmiths), Rodiyā (outcastes). The caste structure of the Tamils is very similar, but the Moslems have only a class structure. Connubium and commensality were taboo between the castes. Violation of caste rules in these matters resulted in the ostracism of the individual from his caste group.

151

the 'weaker sex' and the 'fair sex'. Even the Buddha is said to have at first refused to admit women to the Sasana (Buddhist clergy) because it was considered very difficult for a woman to lead the austere life of renunciation, since her mind is more prone to be fickle, unsteady and emotional than that of a man. It is the general belief among Buddhists that one must be a male to become a Buddha, and that *arahantship*[1] is more difficult for women to attain. To be born a female is itself considered the result of bad karma[2] in a past birth, and much merit has to be accumulated to be born a man. Hindus have the corresponding belief. It is these beliefs that moulded women's position in society

Woman was expected to be an affectionate and submissive helpmate to man. She was to be the responsible one in the domain of household duties, of bearing and rearing children, cooking and cleaning, sewing and mending, and ministering to the needs of the husband, parents and parents-in-law and children. It was contemptible for a woman to shirk these duties which had been assigned to her by birth itself. Recently the writer interviewed a young rural Ceylonese mother of 27 years. She said that her 5-year-old daughter sweeps the house and compound and looks after the baby, while the 7-year-old son does and is expected to do nothing of the sort because he is a boy. On the other hand women were not burdened with the need to earn a living or add to the family income.

Once past childhood, the two sexes were segregated, except in the case of brothers and sisters. Even cross-cousins[3] were not allowed to mix, because cross-cousins are eligible to marry each other and therefore premature developments are prevented. This segregation was imposed with the object of protecting the chastity of the girls until they are honourably given in marriage. Every woman was expected to remain a virgin until marriage, and no girl ever left home unescorted, not only before marriage but even until she become an old woman.

The age of 16 was considered a suitable age for marriage for both boys and girls, and girls sometimes married even as early as 12 o

---

1. *Arahantship* is the second highest state of 'enlightenment', according to Buddhism.
2. Karma is the consequence of a person's acts which fix his or her position in a future existence.
3. Cross-cousins are children of siblings of opposite sex. Thus the children of brother and sister are cross-cousins to each other, whereas children of two sisters or two brothers are parallel cousins.

13 years. Therefore, from the time a girl reached puberty she was considered a woman and was trained to shoulder the duties of a wife and mother. Only in royal and aristocratic and rich households was there a host of servants, male as well as female. In poorer families young girls were trained by their mothers, grandmothers and other female relatives to do all kinds of housework, ranging from cooking and bringing up children, to keeping the house and its surroundings clean and tidy, sewing, tending cattle and milking, working in the paddy fields, weaving reed mats and bags, cooking rice and curry and other foods, bringing water to the house, etc. She had also to wait on her father and brothers at mealtimes. Females did not take meals with or before the males except in the case of little girls. It was a woman's duty to see that the males were fed first. Robert Knox observed this feature among the Kandyan Ceylonese in the middle of the nineteenth century.

Marriage was arranged by parents with or without the consent of the bride and bridegroom-to-be. The girls had very little say in this, the most important event in their lives. Except in an exceptional case where love or any other factor had intervened, the matter was entirely in the hands of parents. Ariyapala[1] refers to a case where, when a girl was asked to marry a complete stranger, she said: 'Parents indeed desire the well-being of children and do not wish them ill. Therefore, if my parents give me away to someone I shall accept him as my husband.' Thus in a gradual process a girl learnt to play the role expected of her and to accept her position, which was inferior to that of men. This inferiority of position is well illustrated in a Ceylonese epic poem of the fifteenth century A.D., the *Kavyasekharaya*. Here a father advises his daughter on her wedding day thus: 'You must rise early, attend to all the housework and be the last to go to bed; when your husband returns home after a journey, you yourself must wash his feet.' The Tirukkuval of the first century B.C., which is an ethical code of the Hindus, conceives the ideal woman as being honourable, adoring her husband and never failing in domestic duties.

Not only was she inferior in position, but she was considered to be unclean too. This is because blood is associated with her during menstruation and child birth. Such periods are called unclean or *kili,* and traditionally a woman was expected to confine herself to one section or corner of the house until she was again clean after ablution. During

---

1. M. B. Ariyapala, *Society in Mediaeval Ceylon,* Colombo, 1956, p. 297.

153

this time she would not take part in religious activity or enter the precincts of a holy place.

In spite of her inferior position a woman was always secure under the protection and support of her male kinsmen. All her material needs were provided for. In the case of a wife, it was the duty of her husband, in the case of an old widow that of her sons, and in the case of unmarried girls in the absence of a father, her brothers or uncles saw to her needs, until she was given in marriage.

THE TRADITIONAL ROLE OF MEN

The traditional position of women in Ceylon may be better illustrated by comparison with that of the men. The male (whether he was father, husband, brother, son, uncle or grandfather) was expected to support and protect the females of his family. He was the bread-winner, the protector—the one who made the final decisions in important matters, the one who knew and had experience. A man was always believed to know more and better than a woman. It was contemptible and below the dignity of a man to perform any of the previously-mentioned tasks of women. At the same time it was equally contemptible for him to shirk his duties to the female members of the family. Thus, it was a dishonour for a father not to get his daughters married early, or for a brother to marry while his marriageable sisters were still unmarried.

Anything was permitted to males, whether in mode of dress, speech or action. But women were expected to act in an irreproachable and honourable way, being careful to preserve the dignity of themselves and their families. The saying was always: 'After all, he is a man. Therefore it is all right. A dog urinates at every bush.' Men were thus the rulers and women were the ruled, their only weapons consisting of submissiveness, affection and tears. Even when their menfolk shunned their duties towards them they had no other sanction. Thus, it could be his fancy to make her happy or unhappy, but it was always her duty as a good wife and mother to put up with mental and physical hardships, seeking only the happiness of her husband, children and others.

THE STRUCTURE OF SOCIETY IN MODERN CEYLON

Today, with the progress of compulsory education, cultural influence from the West and universal franchise, society itself has changed radi-

154

cally. Caste is less rigid and class less coincident with it. The acquisition of education and wealth has been responsible for a visible mobility in society resulting in the growth of a new middle class to which may belong people of any caste, creed or ethnic group. The majority of the middle class are clustered in the cities and towns. The quest for money and education has further resulted in the rise of a working class of skilled and unskilled labourers, also clustering in the towns except for these working on the tea and rubber estates. Thus, today's society can be roughly divided into rural and urban sectors. The rural category can be subdivided into the non-cultivator land-owning upper class and the working class engaged in small-scale paddy and other cultivation or in labour. The urban society can be divided into the *élite* upper class, educated and well-off, in important administrative positions or in business, the middle class, educated and moderately well-off in white-collar jobs, and the working class, performing skilled or unskilled labour, with or without a primary education, and poor. All the previously mentioned castes are represented in all these strata of urban and rural society in Ceylon.

WOMEN IN MODERN CEYLON

These and other changes in the structure of society in modern Ceylon have not been without their repercussions on the life of women. There are now equal opportunities for education from the primary school to the university for both men and women.

In 1957, English and vernacular schools totalled 8,188 of which there were 618 boys' schools, 540 for girls and 7,030 mixed. There were 986,333 boys and 846,741 girls attending school, and 1,990 boys and 728 girls at the University of Ceylon.[1]

Women now have equal opportunities for employment in any profession or occupation, excepting the Civil Service, and today women in Ceylon do have more chance of promotion. Through the cultural influences of the West which infiltrated into Ceylon through the spread of English education and Christian missionary activity, Ceylon's women themselves and men's attitudes towards them have changed. But at the same time it must be said that this still applies only to a few men, and relatively few women are actually able to avail themselves

---

1. Department of Census and Statistics, *Statistical Abstract of Ceylon, 1958.*

of the opportunities open to them. The position of women has changed but only for a few. The old ideal is still popularly accepted, that is that of getting married and being a successful wife and mother. Only a small percentage of women, and those especially in the urban areas have been able to add to their roles or change their position in comparison with men. But Ceylon is largely a rural country and the majority live in rural areas where change has hardly occurred at all.

The figures above illustrated that the proportion of girls attending schools is by no means small when compared with that of the boys. But the following analysis of the gainfully employed population shows how far the percentage of economically active females is below that of males.

In 1953 the economically active population (age group 10–65) numbered 2,991,738, being composed of 2,267,658 males and 724,080 females (53.1 and 18.9 per cent respectively). The gainfully employed population in the same year was 2,611,524, composed of 2,041,524 males and 570,000 females.[1]

These figures clearly illustrate that despite their having enjoyed equal educational opportunities with boys the majority of women still play the traditional role of wife and mother only. Though many women are anxious to do so, only a few in fact are playing the simultaneous roles of wife-and-mother and career woman, or even only the latter. Studies made by the writer show that adolescent girls, both urban and rural, do have vocational ambitions. Hardly any of them state that they do not want to do a job; but going out to work is not yet a popularly accepted pattern for Ceylonese women.

PRESENT ATTITUDES OF MEN TOWARDS WOMEN

Men of the upper and middle class, even those who have gone through a higher education course at the university or other institutions, prefer to marry stay-at-home wives with a dowry; not salary-earning, educated career women. They also feel that a woman with a higher education and a monthly salary would acquire a sense of independence and not be sufficiently submissive to their husbands. Such men often resent women going out to work or undertaking such activities as

---

1. R. M. Sunderam, V. R. Rao, S. Selvaratnam, *Manpower Resources in Ceylon 1956-1981*, National Planning Council, p. 10-11.

driving a motor-car or cycling. Thus, many highly educated career girls find it difficult to marry men of equal social and economic status and often continue to live as spinsters. Only a handful are fortunate enough to find husbands who demand neither old-fashioned submissiveness nor a dowry. It is true that working-class men and those of the lower middle class, where incomes are insufficient to make ends meet, do want their wives to add to the family income by going out to work, but once they become economically well-off they too would wish to keep them safe at home.

As a result, most fathers decide to give their girls only a secondary education and stop their schooling after that or even earlier. Instead, they wish to collect money for their daughters' future dowry and trousseau, and train them in household work. Rich parents want their girls to learn accomplishments like music and dancing, which are considered assets in getting a husband with social prestige—perhaps a doctor, a civil servant or a lawyer. But generally speaking, extra pains are not considered worth while in educating girls on equal terms with the boys.

CHANGES BROUGHT ABOUT BY MODERN EDUCATION

The grandmother of the present-day woman was a stay-at-home; a few mothers of the present day are career women engaged in such jobs as teaching. Most of the women of the present generation who are educated are asserting their rights silently, but effectively, and have found themselves in paths of employment which were never trod by women before. Thus, today we have women who are highly qualified teachers, university lecturers, doctors, lawyers, librarians and Members of Parliament and, until recently, even a woman Cabinet Minister.[1] During the year 1958, more women students than men entered the University of Ceylon. In the teaching profession, for the year 1957, there were 27,101 women, as against 28,309 men, and of these 890 were graduate women teachers. The nursing profession is entirely a woman's profession. Many more are employed as sales-girls, typists, stenographers and clerks.

All this is the result of education, especially the spread of English education. And the cost of living is so high that most husbands are beginning to feel that it would be a blessing to have an additional

---

1. In July 1960, Ceylon elected the first woman Prime Minister in the world.

income. Nevertheless, for various reasons according to surveys of the city of Colombo and two villages made by the writer, from 10 to 20 per cent of the children of school age today are not attending school. Thus, most girls are not in practice able to avail themselves of the opportunities theoretically open to them. Girls are today going to foreign universities at their own expense or through scholarships sponsored by Unesco and the International Federation of University Women, etc. They go for courses ranging from university academic courses to courses in home science, nursing and beauty culture. Many educated women are engaged in social service work, running crèches, female adult education, poor relief work, etc. The Lanka Mahila Samitiya is a women's association for such voluntary work.

There is many a working mother in every social class who, after the husband's death, has had to shoulder the burden of bringing up the family entirely alone.

THE STAGES IN THE SOCIALIZATION OF THE WOMEN OF CEYLON

Infancy

In Ceylon the majority of parents, urban and rural, prefer male offspring to female. To be saddled with a majority of girls or to have only female offspring is often considered to be the result of a bad karma. Ninety per cent of the parents interviewed by the writer recently in a Kandyan village admitted that they preferred sons to daughters. The reasons they gave were that bringing up sons cost less money and required less responsibility: whereas parents have to provide clothes and jewellery for girls no such expense is incurred for the boys, who instead earn and add to the family income. At the same time, there are some who believe that it is better for a daughter to be the first-born. Perhaps this is because she will be able to help her mother to look after the other children who will be born later.

Though this preference for male offspring is widespread, once a daughter is born she is cherished by all in the family and is brought up with the same affection as a son. All rural mothers and most of the working-class urban mothers breast-feed their babies, but most of the upper- and middle-class urban mothers resort to imported milk foods. Baby girls are weaned at 11 months or at any succeeding odd month (an even month being chosen for a son). At an auspicious moment the ears of the baby daughter are pierced by a woman who is experienced in the job or, in the case of the urban *élite* or middle class, by a doctor.

Childhood

Starting at an auspicious moment, the first letters are taught to the child before the age of 5 by a person considered 'lucky'. This occasion too is celebrated.

A girl is considered to be in her childhood until she attains puberty, which usually takes place during the age of 12 to 14 years. Till then she is allowed to play as freely with her brothers and others as if she were a boy. There is hardly any difference in the restrictions laid upon or the permissiveness allowed to girls and boys during this period. But even as early as the age of 5 most of the rural girls and those of the urban working class start their training for the role of wife-mother in the future. Thus, they are initiated into such duties as looking after the younger children, drawing water, sweeping the home and compound, washing crockery, running errands, soaping the washing, putting clothes out to dry and collecting them later. It is not seldom that the task of cooking a simple meal of rice and a curry falls on the shoulders of an 8- or 9-year-old girl in a working-class urban or rural home. As the child grows older she is expected to spend more and more time in these duties and she has hardly any time to play except at school. (This is why very often women of this class have told the present writer that it is no wonder that it is considered the result of a past sin to be born a female.)

The lot of the female child of the urban *élite* and middle class is a comparatively happy one. She is not burdened with the above-mentioned chores of her working-class sister. After school she spends her leisure as she desires, playing indoor and outdoor games with other children or entertaining herself at the cinema or at parties, hiking, bringing up pets or indulging in other hobbies. Some parents even go to the extent of directing their children's leisure so as to ensure a balance in school work and leisure. If it pleases the girl's fancy, she may dust the furniture or sweep the drawing-room and bedrooms or hold the baby for a short while, but she is neither expected nor compelled to do these things. She is petted and pampered by her parents and relatives and waited upon by female servants. Both girls and boys

159

of primary school age attending big schools in the cities are often chaperoned by *ayahs* or teenage servant boys and girls, who sometimes stay until school is over to bring them home again.

Adolescence

Although psychologists and educationists agree that the age between 14 and 19 years is the period of adolescence, most people in Ceylon consider a girl who has attained puberty or the first menstruation to be a woman. She is expected to shed her childish ways and learn to play the role of an adult woman, for she is now marriageable. The majority of the village girls of the last generation were married between the ages of 13 and 19, and a similar proportion would be found even today.

Parents never give their daughters approaching puberty any prior knowledge about the physiological changes they will experience; nor do they recognize that the child will have to cope with concomitant psychological problems. A girl who becomes legitimately inquisitive about her own self is looked down upon as 'too ripe' and a bad child. It follows that sometimes girls are totally ignorant of puberty or learn about it only secretly from female servants or girl friends who have already gone through the process.

All communities in Ceylon hold puberty ceremonies for the girl. In the case of the Ceylonese girl, as soon as signs of the first menstruation appear, the girl is secluded in a separate room. A female, young or old, very often a relative, keeps her company. She is never left alone even for a moment. The dhoby woman—washerwoman to the family—is sent for immediately. She provides the girl with newly laundered clothes brought by her. At the same time, an elder goes to consult the astrologer, who is told of the time and place where the event took place, and the colour of the dress the girl was wearing at the time. In the light of these facts he predicts her future in general and decides the auspicious moment for her to have her first post-menstrual bath. The astrologer is supposed to be able to predict whether she will be a flighty girl or a calm and modest one, whether her marriage will be happy or unhappy, and whether her stars will have a good or bad influence on members of her family. Until she is given her ceremonial bath she is kept on a light diet, free from oily and fried foods, meat and fish. An article made of iron, such as an areca nut cutter or large nail, is kept by the girl to ward off evil spirits. She is not allowed to speak to or see the face of any males, even members of her own family, because it is believed this would have a bad influence on them.

At the auspicious moment for the bath, which is after a few days, she is led by females to the place where it is to take place. She is first made to look at a tree from which milky sap oozes (e.g., a jak tree), and then the washerwoman pours seven potfuls of water, with a new earthen pot brought for the purpose, over her head. At the end of the bath the girl is asked to dash the pot on the ground. With the breaking of the pot all evil influences are supposed to be expelled. As she steps into the house after the bath, clad in new clothes, a husked coconut is placed on the doorstep and then split in two with a large knife. The half of the coconut with the three eyes is called the female side and the other the male. If the female half turns out to be bigger and facing upwards, the girl is supposed to be destined to beget more daughters than sons, and vice versa. If both halves are of equal size and facing upwards, an equal number of both sexes is believed to be the result, and if both face downwards, barrenness.

This ceremony is an occasion for much rejoicing. Therefore, milk rice and oil cakes (*kavun*) and ripe plantains are prepared, together with other foods. Close relatives and close friends of the family come and feast together and give the girl their blessings and presents. She worships her parents and close elderly relatives. The *rabana,* a one-sided circular drum, is played by women on this occasion, especially in the villages. The washerwoman is presented with money, food-stuffs and the ornaments and clothes the girl was wearing when she attained puberty. The degree of rejoicing on this occasion depends on the means of the parents.

Today there is a tendency among the more Westernized, upper-class, English-educated parents not to make this event an occasion of so much fuss. They keep the girl indoors during these few days and after the bath, which she takes alone, she resumes her old routine. But such parents are few. Many a parent even goes to the extent of incurring debts in order to celebrate the occasion, which is called the *kili magula.* Slight variations in the ceremonial procedure are made even in the same community in different localities and in different communities in the country.

Now the daughter is a young woman and no longer a child. It is the duty especially of the mother to look after her until she is honourably married. She is not allowed to leave the house unescorted, except perhaps to school provided the school is fairly close to the house. She should not freely talk with males who are not members of her family or close relatives. Mother, grandmother and elderly aunts use every opportunity to drive home to her how to behave herself in such a manner as to preserve the honour of herself and of her family. She is gradually taught to dress and walk modestly, talk softly and not do anything without the approval of her parents. She is expected to learn more about running a home by actually doing the work. It is not seldom that a mother reminds her daughter: 'It is not enough your going to school and learning your lessons. You must learn the work in the house. Otherwise you will regret it when you are married, and we shall be blamed.' (The writer's own experience.) Thus, as the girl grows older the number of duties in the home and the amount of time to be spent on them increase, in addition to her school work.

It is the village girl who is most hard hit, as has been observed by the writer. She has to take part in paddy cultivation, reaping and carrying bundles on her head, transplanting and weeding, as well as drawing water for the house, doing the family's washing, bathing younger children and looking after them, cooking meals, cleaning and sweeping, washing pots and pans, grinding curry stuffs, winnowing the paddy and a score of other things. Her urban sister of the working class would have all the housework, but nothing outside it—there being no land to cultivate.

A village girl is left with hardly any leisure. She seldom plays any outdoor games out of school, and indeed such activities are looked down upon. Gossiping seems to be the only usual recreation. This is done at the common well to which the girls go for water, or in the paddy field where they work in groups, or at the river or stream where they go to bathe. Adolescent village girls do enjoy themselves on festive occasions—the Vesak, and Ceylonese and Hindu New Year festivals. There they get together in one another's houses in groups and play the *rabana*, play on the swing to the rhythm of their own singing and play local indoor games. The sexes do not mix in these activities, and a country girl cannot afford the money or the time to attend to fashions in clothes.

The urban girl of the upper class would shudder at the thought of some of these activities (such as washing pots and pans, black with soot, or grinding curry stuffs or winnowing paddy) which would roughen her soft hands and spoil the beauty of her manicured finger

162

nails. Her time is all her own, unless she chooses to do some light
housework for a change. If she does any cooking, it will be on a kerosene or electric cooker and seldom on a smoky open fireplace, and
she will only do it to try out a new recipe. She knows and does more
and better sewing than the rural girl, because she herself desires the
greater quantity and variety of clothes such as are depicted in fashion
magazines, fashion shows and newspapers. She has time and her
parents' permission to go to the cinema with either parents or approved
friends and relatives, to go to parties, take part in outdoor and indoor
games of Western origin, and to go on shopping outings and have
hobbies of her fancy. There are servants to do the housework. Her
daily life is a more elaborate continuation of that of her childhood.
Often she is taught such accomplishments as music and dancing and
singing as additional assets in getting a desirable husband. Her con-
ribution to the work in the household could be compared to that of
a 5-year-old girl in the village.

The urban middle-class adolescent girl is more moderate and is a
greater help in the home than the upper-class one, but less than the
village girl or the urban working-class girl. She is directed by parents
to be more at her studies than anything else, so that she may get a
white-collar job.

At all social levels the adolescent girl is looked at with suspicion, as
one who cannot look after herself alone, apt to fall into a man's trap
and make an unwise marriage, and a burden to the family until she is
married. She is not expected to associate with any male or female
who is not approved by her parents as 'safe' or as one exerting a good
influence.

Girl's dress

When they are babies and up to the onset of puberty both urban and
rural girls wear frocks. Frocks continue to be worn by urban girls and
those in the rural areas in the low-country until they finish their school
careers, and at home even until they are married. They wear saris on
formal occasions before marriage and always after marriage. Cey-
onese Kandyan girls, both urban and rural, often give up wearing
frocks after puberty and wear saris but without the piece that falls
over one shoulder. After marriage the sari is the only form of dress.
Among Tamils and Moslems the adolescent girl usually wears a frock

163

to school or a long full skirt and blouse with another piece of cloth thrown diagonally across the chest over one shoulder.

MARRIAGE

We have already pointed out that marriage is invariably arranged by the parents and elders for both young men and women. Very few young people take the initiative in choosing their own partners by falling in love, as is customary in the West. Girls who get involved in love affairs are looked down upon with contempt, and called stubborn, badly brought up and immoral, sure not only to bring dishonour on their families but to make an unwise marriage with unfortunate repercussions even on their own children. But girls do fall in and out of love surreptitiously, both in the urban and rural areas, although few are able to carry the affair to the final end of marriage. A young girl's movements are always under observation, not only by the elders in her family but also by the whole neighbourhood, and frequently a girl's movements and associations outside the family circle are subject to much critical discussion. The aim of parents is to get daughters married as early as possible—between 18 and 25 years of age.

Either a professional marriage broker, a family friend or a relative brings to the notice of the girl's parents the names of eligible young men who may or may not be previously known to them. If the young man's caste and religion are the same as those of the girl, and if his economic and social status and age are considered suitable, their two horoscopes are compared by an astrologer. If the horoscopes are found to be agreeable to each other, a date is fixed for the young man to make a formal visit to the girl's house. A small party consisting of the young man and his parents and a relative or a friend goes to the girl's house at the appointed time. Special care is taken to make the house appear as presentable as possible. The girl, too, is dressed as for a formal occasion. The girl's people receive their visitors and chat with them for some time; then she is led out to meet them and serve them with refreshments and after that she sits down. It is only among the English educated families that she too takes part in the general conversation.

In the village family the girl offers the young man a tray of betel and disappears from the scene. It is with a moment's observation that her future marriage is decided. After the visit, if the young man i satisfied with the young girl's appearance, the manners of her people and the terms of the dowry, the marriage is decided upon. The girl's consent may or may not be given consideration, according to the enlightenment or otherwise of her parents. Priority is given to the man's consent. Frequently a girl's plainness, or poor health or insufficient education, are overlooked provided that there is compensation in the shape of a good dowry. At the same time, the same drawbacks and even the age of a man may be overlooked by the parents of a good-looking young girl if he has a job with prestige value and does not demand a dowry. Today, whether because of the influence of Western education and Western values or because of their own personal convictions, there exist both men and women who think such factors as mutual love, education, health, appearance and temperament are essential considerations too, but such persons are in a minority even among those who have had a university education. Among the ordinary villagers the question of dowry is not given as much significance as in the upper classes, whether rural or urban. Villagers give prominence to the girl's physique, which is an index of her ability to work hard, and her knowledge of all aspects of household work and work in the fields, as well as her reputation and that of her family.

After the parents of the two parties have agreed to marry their son and daughter together, it is the duty of the man's parents to consult the astrologer once again and decide the auspicious dates and times for the engagement and wedding ceremonies, and notify the other party about these. A report written in pompous style in Ceylonese is sent to the girl's parents.

The engagement takes place at the appropriate favourable time at the girl's house, and in the presence of a few close relatives on both sides and the registrar of marriages. Rings are exchanged and the bridegroom fastens a necklace round his bride's neck. A part (or sometimes even the full amount) of the dowry, consisting of money only or with deeds of gifts of immovable property, is formally presented to the bridegroom. A formal lunch is given and after that the bridegroom and his party leave. From the time when the marriage is decided upon up to the very date of the marriage itself the young couple seldom get a few moments together alone. The fiancé can see his betrothed only at her home. A few parents in the cities may allow an engaged couple to go out together occasionally, but this is looked down upon by society in general. In the rural areas they hardly speak to each other till they are married. Indeed, most Moslem girls actually see their bridegrooms for the first time only on their wedding day.

Among the rich and middle classes in the urban areas the wedding takes place in a public hall or big hotel, more or less in the Western fashion, except for the orthodox *poruva* ceremony among the Ceylonese Buddhists and the *thali* (necklace tying) ceremony among the Tamil Hindus, and a somewhat similar ceremony among the Moslems. Others hold wedding ceremonies in their own houses and put up decorated temporary structures called *magul-maduwa* (literally: 'wedding hall').

The *poruva* is a dais prepared and decorated according to the means and taste of the bride's party. It is lit up and colourfully finished. Rice is strewn on its floor and four new earthen pots, with the inflorescence of a coconut tree and a coconut oil lamp on each, are placed on the four corners of the *poruva*.

The bride is beautifully dressed in a white sari either in Indian or Kandyan style, decked with head, ear and hand ornaments, and she carries a bouquet. Christian, Moslem and some of the low-country Buddhist brides wear the veil. Kandyan Ceylonese Buddhists and Hindu brides never wear the veil as it is a foreign Western custom. All brides wear flowers on their hair which is traditionally tied in a large knot at the back of the head. Today, with the emphasis given to women's fashions, especially in cities, various hair styles are worn.

The bride and bridegroom are led on to the *poruva* by an uncle of each of them. The bride stands on the left of the groom. They exchange presents of two suits of clothes. Then the bridegroom presents his mother-in-law with a 40-yard length of white cloth and the father-in-law with a suit of clothes. Betel is presented by the couple to their very close elderly relatives. After the chanting of a blessing by an elder, the couple's two right thumbs are tied with a silken thread and a little water is poured over them by the bride's maternal uncle. This is the traditional, customary way of giving the bride away to the groom. A small group of little girls over the age of about 10 years, dressed in white in festive array, chant a set of verses in Pali (*Jayamangala gāthā*) as a blessing. Then the registrar conducts the legal registration of the marriage.

If the ceremony is held at the home, all then sit down to a nuptial lunch and if elsewhere, other refreshments are served to the guests. According to orthodox Ceylonese or Tamil custom, at a suitable time

166

after the lunch the newly-married couple leaves for the groom's house accompanied by both their relatives. Others follow the Western custom of going away on a honeymoon. Whether the couple stay at the groom's house or go on a honeymoon, the bride's virginity must be proved by showing the bloodstains on a cloth from the nuptial bed. This is a cause for much rejoicing and the affectionate acceptance of the girl by her parents-in-law, while her own parents gain respect for having brought their daughter up with care and honour. If there is no such visible proof of her virginity she is despised, and both she and her parents are looked down upon with contempt. This custom does not prevail among the Kandyan Ceylonese.

A spinster is despised, for marriage is held to be the right goal for women. The parents, or in their absence the brothers, of a spinster are blamed for not arranging her marriage. She herself is blamed as a stubborn girl who did not consent to proposals brought by her parents or for her immoral character and flightiness or bad looks which have resulted in the lack of suitors. Any girl who is past the age of 25 and still unmarried will frequently have to answer two questions: 'Why don't you marry?', 'What is going to happen to you once your parents are gone?' She will be told: 'You can't live with money or a salary. There must be someone to look after you.' Problems of this nature are a nuisance to a working girl who has chosen to stay single for her own reasons. It is said that parents cannot breathe their last in peace while there are still unmarried daughters. Though parents have to arrange their sons' marriages too, yet this is not felt as such a burden on their minds as to have unmarried but marriageable daughters. Permanent spinsterhood is attributed to the consequence of an unfavourable karma.

Barrenness is attributed to eating or destroying eggs or taking another's life in a past incarnation. It is considered unlucky to meet a barren woman when one sets out on a journey, or for a girl to see such a woman on her first ablution after puberty, or for a bride to see her as the first person once she dons the bridal clothes. A barren woman is often a disagreeable sight to the mother-in-law especially.

Early widowhood is attributed to a bad karma in the past. Among the Ceylonese there is no ban on the remarriage of widows. But if those over 40 marry it is looked down upon. It is only in the case of young widows that parents arrange the next marriage; others find their own husbands. Hindu widows do not remarry.

167

Monogamy is the rule and those deviating from it, especially females, are adversely criticized. Among the Kandyans it was traditionally legal for several brothers to cohabit with one wife, and traces of such polyandry may still be found in the Kandyan villages.

THE DIVISION OF LABOUR IN THE HOME

In urban areas the newly-married couple often set up a new home, but in the rural areas they usually continue to live in the home of the husband's parents, though sometimes with the wife's parents. When children arrive it is easy to care for them in these extended families, for there is help ready to hand in the shape of the wife's mother or mother-in-law or other female relatives in the home. The wife's lot in the house is easier too. Even if she has to go out to work it is convenient, for the children can be looked after by those at home. In the case of the newly-established home, all the responsibilities of the household fall on the wife. Servants were cheap and easily available until quite recently, and the middle-class urban wife had an easy time, even in these circumstances, but now servants are expensive and difficult to find. Professional women, such as teachers and doctors and nurses, whose own mothers are not available to look after their houses and children, are compelled to leave them to the mercy of servants. Working women engaged in manual labour cannot ever afford servants, and if no female relatives are available to look after the home, they often keep the elder daughter away from school to attend to this work.

As for the division of labour between the sexes, a man may fondle a baby or play with children to please himself, but seldom in order to help his wife. Sewing, cooking, child-rearing, cleaning, entertaining visitors, washing clothes or home utensils are all women's work today just as they were in the past. A man would lose his dignity among other men if he descended to doing these things, and would risk being called a henpecked husband. A man expects even a glass of water to be brought to him, his bed made and folded, his clothes arranged, and so on. Even if the wife is a working woman, she still has to perform these same duties when she returns to her home. Except in the case of the rich upper class, women rest only when they are asleep, for they have such an array of duties in the house. But the man is usually the one to make decisions on important matters such as directing the child-

168

ren's education, settling the older children's quarrels, arranging the marriage of a child, not to mention planning the family budget and holding the purse strings. Women have a say in these things, it is true, but usually subject to the husband's decision, though there are exceptions, in all classes.

Although living with the husband's parents is convenient where bringing up children and running the house is concerned, most women find it difficult to please their mothers-in-law who are often very exacting. Thus the wife has not only to wait on her husband and children, but on the parents-in-law too, or life would be very difficult for her. Women interviewed by the writer expressed the view that the only ideal daughter-in-law is one who is hard-working, obedient, industrious and thrifty, willing to wait on her husband and parents-in-law as if they were her own parents.

MY PERSONAL EXPERIENCE

I was born on 12 December 1928 in a township called Bope in the southern province of Ceylon. My father hailed from a village in Kalutara district and my mother from another village in the Matara district, both low-country villages. They both belong to families of the Goigama caste doing paddy cultivation as an occupation.

My father's parents were both illiterate but well-to-do farmers, and father was the youngest child in a family of thirteen. He was educated in the *pirivena* schools at the feet of Buddhist monks and was successful in the Cambridge examinations through his own efforts. He acquired a government scholarship to the University of Oxford, where he received his B.Litt. in Western Classics. From there he proceeded to Berlin University, where he did further linguistic studies and to Queen's College, Benares, for a further course in Sanskrit. He was Head of the Department of Indo-Aryan Languages at the University of Ceylon for some time.

My mother's parents were both literate, and were also rather well-to-do farmers. She was the fifth in a family of eight children. She was an uncertificated Ceylonese teacher when she was given in marriage at the age of 24 to my father, who was in his forties at the time. No dowry had been asked or given. The parents had decided for her and she had simply to consent. My father did not wish her to go out to work, and with reluctance she had to give up her job. Within one year after marriage I was born (they had no preference for either a son or a daughter). My grandmother and my mother's elder sister helped to bring me up as a baby. After two years my brother was born, and when he was 2 years old a sister also arrived.

We lived in a country house surrounded by a large garden and paddy fields, with the tributary of the Kalu Ganga flowing past on one side. Our childhood was a very happy one until my father died of a heart attack when I was just 11 years old. It was a very great shock to me at that time. My father was strict but, unlike most fathers, he was also a lovable companion. He used to play with us indoors and out-doors and take us bathing in the river, and he helped me in my studies. He did not make me read books all the time. He took me out for walks and made me observe the surroundings, and recounted incidents about his travels abroad. He instilled in me, a young child, what a long, un-ending, but happy process, learning is. He took me out on visits to the 'Sunday Fair', to the city of Colombo, and to my paternal relations in the village, who were all illiterate, hardworking and simple farmer folk. (It is through associating with them that I have developed a deep interest in the rural people of this country.) It was he who read me the first letters at the auspicious moment.

My father never for a moment forgot or belittled his native village or even the areas around it. As a lasting monument of his love for all the villagers, he founded an English school for them with his savings, the first and the only such school for miles around, at that time in the early 1930s. Very low fees were levied and he was the principal. This school was handed over to the government one year before he died in 1939. My brother and sister were too small to be so much influenced by him at the time.

My mother was always affectionate, discreet and very able. Al-though she had servants, she personally attended to my father and to us children and we were made very comfortable. She never did any-thing without asking father. Never did they argue or quarrel on any matter as far as I can remember, and we were really a happy family. My maternal grandmother lived with us too, and she often entertained us with folk-tales.

On my father's death the burden of bringing up the family fell on my mother's shoulders. More than anything else she strove to meet my father's last wish on his death bed—to give us children a good educa-tion. This was too much for her alone with a slender income and no

170

man at the helm, and after two years she married a relative of my father's who has ever since been a second father to us in every respect. The other important influence in our lives has been my maternal uncle, who is a Buddhist monk engaged for the last twenty-five years in missionary work in Penang (Federation of Malaya). He has been my spiritual guide ever since the death of my father, and even now we seek his advice on all important matters.

By the time I was 14 my mother had trained me to cook and sew and look after the younger ones. We were all also sent to both Christian and Buddhist English schools in the cities of Panadura and Colombo. Later my brother and I both graduated at the University of Ceylon, but my sister gave up school after a few years. She was petted too much and preferred staying at home and not going to school at all.

I went through the traditional puberty and marriage ceremonies described earlier. I was given in marriage in 1956 at the age of 27 to my husband, who was 30 at the time. The marriage was arranged by my parents, but subject to my consent. My husband is a Food and Drugs Inspector, educated in Ceylon and England. Dowry was not asked or given at our marriage. which was an orthodox Ceylonese Buddhist ceremony but for the fact that it was held at a public hall. We are of the same caste and religion.

We live with my own mother and her family in Kandy, an arrangement which is very convenient for me as our baby daughter, who was born within a year after our marriage, can stay happily at home— where she is everyone's pet—while I continue with my university work.

Immediately after graduation I took to the teaching profession, the vocation I had chosen ever since I was a little pupil under my great father; and I acquired the diploma in education at the University of Ceylon three years after graduation and on the eve of my marriage. My husband soon understood my desire to continue to learn and, as he was convinced that I would not assume undue independence, he allowed, and indeed encouraged, me to start reading for the M.A. in Education. This I am now doing. I travel daily to the university in my own car, which I drive myself. My husband takes pride in my work, even in the face of some criticism from his colleagues. I have not seen a husband more interested in his wife's continuing to study, even denying for himself much of the attention traditionally due from a wife.

But although I have a certain amount of independence which most

171

women in Ceylon do not enjoy, this does not mean that I have deviated much from the ideal pattern of the wife and mother. My position at home follows very much the traditional pattern. My husband decides all important matters, and often it is acceptable to me. He commands and I obey. Except on scholarly matters it is not for me to argue with him. I have to accept the fact that he knows best and that this is all for my own good. I never go out or do anything outside the precincts of the home without his permission. But we do discuss important matters together, although the tendency is for him to decide finally. I feel quite happy and secure in this manner.

We have no special preference for either sons or daughters, and when our daughter was born we were both happy. She is given the comforts that we can afford, by way of food, clothing, toys and attention. As a rule once we are back home for the day after work, we give her our company and it is seldom that we leave her to go out for an evening. We should feel sorry to deprive her of our company then. She loves to play and talk to us. I feel very proud that I breast-fed my daughter for ten full months, just as my mother did for me.

We hope to give her the best education available in this country, and later even in England if she turns out to be enterprising and interested. We shall leave it to her whether or not to choose a career or what career to choose. Whether she has a career or not, we wish to see her happily married to an intelligent, educated, good-natured, well-mannered and understanding Ceylonese Buddhist. Provided these characteristics are there we do not mind her making the choice of the young man without allowing us to arrange her marriage.

India

Area: 3,288,876 square kilometres.

Population: 407,900,000 (estimated 1960).[1]

Recent history: 1947—British Government transfers sovereignty to new State of India; 1949—Indian Constitution adopted; Republican status promulgated.

Citizenship: Men and women have equal rights.

Religion: Hinduism; there are substantial Moslem and Sikh minorities, and also groups of Christians, Parsis, Buddhists and others, including pagan hill tribes.

Inheritance and family patterns: Traditional inheritance rules are bound up with the existence of the 'joint family'. This is generally a patrilocal extended family corporation in which all male members are co-parceners, females having rights of maintenance. Nuclear families also exist; their number is said to be increasing. Recent (1955, 1956) legislation gives equal inheritance rights to sons and daughters in cases of intestacy.

---

1. Latest official estimate of population as published in *The U.N. Population and Vital Statistics Report, October 1960.*

Men's and women's roles in India: a sociological review

by S. C. DUBE

THE SOCIOLOGICAL SETTING

India is a land of great cultural variety and many striking contrasts. It has a population of approximately 438 million people, an overwhelming majority living in small village communities scattered all over the subcontinent.[1] The numerically small tribal group constitutes a culturally significant element in village India. Differences in the tribal, rural and urban ways of life are many and significant. The multiplicity of religions, sects and castes, and the great variation in local customs and regional traditions add to the complexity of the Indian cultural scene. Differentials in the rate of acceptance of elements from the modern Western tradition, as well as from the emergent national tradition of India, have contributed further to the cultural diversity of the land, and today a wide gulf separates the small *élite* from the large section of the population comprising the rural and urban masses. In thinking about contemporary Indian society, we have not only to take account of regional, religious and caste differences in the tribal, rural and urban sections of the population, but also to consider the differentials in adherence to old traditions and in the acceptance of new ways of life and thought at different levels.

It is naturally difficult to write with accuracy and precision about family and kinship in India as a whole, and to make any unqualified generalizations regarding the different roles and statuses of men and

---

1. The population figure refers to the provisional estimate of India's population in the 1961 census. According to the 1951 census, nearly 96 per cent of the people lived in villages, 5.36 per cent being returned as 'tribes'.

women in Indian society. The difficulty is lessened by the invisible thread of value-orientation provided by the country's classical traditions, which make the identification of a broad all-India pattern possible. The evolution of a largely common criminal and civil code for the country as a whole has also contributed towards fostering a national uniformity. This trend has been strengthened by India's increasing association with and participation in contemporary world movements, and scientific and technological progress. It is nevertheless necessary to emphasize that tradition and progress co-exist peacefully in many aspects of Indian life, and underestimating the meaning or significance of any of the cultural differences can lead to grossly erroneous generalizations. Against the background of the changing canvas of life in contemporary India, an attempt can be made, however, to present a general picture of the role and status of men and women in a somewhat broad and impressionistic sweep.

THE MEANING OF CASTE

Hindu society is caste-structured. The impact of caste is evident even in some sections of the non-Hindu communities of India. As the structure of family and kinship and the nature of interpersonal relations in the intrafamily setting are governed by caste to an appreciable extent, some comprehension of this system is necessary.

Caste is a troublesome and misleading word, but in any discussion of Indian society its use cannot be avoided. An improper or inadequate appreciation of its meaning has resulted in a great deal of confusion regarding the social system of India. For those uninitiated into the sociological intricacies of Hindu social structure, it calls for an explanation.

Hindu society is split into a large number of segmentary divisions called *jati* or castes. These segments, in relation to one another, are characterized by an ascribed system of status evaluation. In other words, the ritual status of a person depends upon the fact of his birth into a caste. Each caste maintains its special status by certain observances that are calculated to preserve its purity by avoiding all polluting contacts with other castes. Marriages are confined within the caste; while interdining may be permitted among castes with more or less similar ritual status. Less intimate physical contacts, such as touch, may be extended to a still wider group; but a member of a 'clean' caste must avoid the physical proximity of one of an 'unclean' caste whose accidental touch is believed to have a polluting effect. As occupations are also classified into the broad categories of 'clean', 'unclean' and 'polluting' occupations—with numerous minute intermediate shades—caste hierarchy closely follows the occupational hierarchy. Thus, alongside several 'open occupations', there are distinct 'caste occupations' also, which run in specified castes from generation to generation. With its individual norms a caste functions as an isolable culture-bearing unit. These segments (*jati*) are graded vertically in five levels: at the top the Brahman (priest), then the Kshatriya (warrior), the Vaisya (trader), the Sudra (artisans and workers), and finally the Untouchables. These levels do no more than indicate roughly the more or less equal ritual status of the castes (*jati*) placed on them, for each level has a large number of castes, each with its own hierarchy and permissive and prohibitive norms.

In the caste system the primary emphasis is on status evaluation on the ritual plane. Ritual status has always been distinguished from economic and political status, and its supreme significance has been generally recognized. A Kshatriya king may be powerful and a Vaisya trader may be rich, but their ritual status will be rated lower than that of the poorest Brahman. Although there is some historical evidence of vertical mobility of castes from a lower to a higher ritual status, in the well-developed scheme of caste organization instances of successful upward movement are not many. The structure has been able to maintain itself because of the strong hold of the twin concepts of karma and dharma on the Hindu mind. These concepts are fundamental to Hinduism. The karma theory, taking for granted the phenomena of transmigration of souls and rebirth, holds that the quality of one's actions in the past life determines one's present life, and that actions in the present life will determine the character of one's future life. The present is thus governed largely by the past; one must accept it as inevitable. While the past cannot be undone, the future can be ensured by pursuing the path of dharma—the prescribed way of life for one's station in life. The prescribed way for each level in the caste hierarchy is different. The ideal scheme of life recommended by the Scriptures recognizes the necessity and interdependence of economic pursuits, bodily satisfactions, worship and ritual, and the quest for salvation, and prescribes appropriate approaches to them separately for each level of castes. One must follow the path appropriate to one's own station in life, and should constantly endeavour to avoid *pap* (sin) and earn *punya* (merit). This alone can ensure a better future. The unquestioning acceptance of pre-ordained fate is further aided by the view that the material world and its manifestations are in the final analysis an illusion (*maya*) and not a reality.

Family and kinship

The family is the chosen vehicle through which the multifarious goals of life are to be realized. It carries forward the prescribed economic pursuits and offers the only recognized outlets for the satisfaction of human passions. While it thus caters to the material and animal needs of man, as a ritual unit it also looks after his spiritual needs and is expected to pave the way for the ultimate goal of salvation. Because the prescribed way differs for the different levels of castes, the general ethos of families at different levels is also necessarily different. The organization and value-orientations of the families are thus largely governed by their caste.

India is regarded, especially in the West, as the classic example of a society with large extended families, often referred to as 'joint families'. This impression, although not wholly erroneous, greatly exaggerates the actual situation. Large extended families are mostly an urban phenomenon, confined mostly to upper-caste groups in traditional small towns. In the rural areas they are to be found mainly among land-owning groups who also invariably belong to upper castes.

The traditional typology of simple, compound and extended family does not accurately fit the forms of family organization met with in India. At one point of time, the size and actual composition of a family often denotes only a particular stage in its developmental cycle. Simple families grow into extended families and then break up into simple families again. A simple family emerging out of this process may retain some adhesion or adhesions from the former extended family. Aged parents may later attach themselves to one of their sons who had broken away from them earlier to set up an independent household. The changes from simple to extended and from extended to simple families are fairly frequent. Perfect three-generation extended families are rare, and not many simple families can remain technically simple for a long period. Polygynous compound families are found among the tribal groups, Hindus and Moslems alike, but taking India as a whole into consideration, the number of such families is not very large.

177

Polyandrous compound families are found only among the Khasas of the Cis-Himalayan region of North India and among the Todas of the Nilgiri Hills in South India.

With a few insignificant exceptions confined to small tribal groups, the descent systems are unilineal. The Nayars of Malabar and a few tribal groups in southern and eastern India are matrilineal; the rest of the society is patrilineal. By and large residence after marriage follows the descent systems. Most brides first take up residence with the parents of their husbands. Although testamentary will of 'self-earned property' is legally possible, inheritance is largely customary. In the matrilineal society property invariably passes on from the mother to the daughters, and in the large majority of the patrilineal groups it goes from the father to the sons. There is great local and regional variation in regard to the property rights of women, but for Hindu society as a whole it could be said that they were entitled only to maintenance and to property acquired as gifts specifically given to them. Recent legislation has changed the situation materially.

Kinship and certain aspects of the so-called 'joint family' can be considered together.

Kinship systems in India have wide regional and local differences; in fact, even individual castes have certain special characteristics in this field. However, they have one common feature—kinship is lineally reckoned. Most identifiable lineages have a depth of four to five generations; but in communities served by professional genealogists reckoning may go back even to the mythical founder of the caste. Traditional rules of descent govern identification of individuals and families, emphasizing either the patriline or the matriline. A person identifies himself with one of these lines; the ties with the other are recognized, but its separateness is emphasized and there is often a marked degree of ambivalence towards it. Within the lineage itself 'near' and 'distant' kin are separately identified, and formal obligation for each of these categories are different.

The near kin either constitute an extended family or they may live in separate households as closely allied families. The term 'joint family', although it is widely used, can best be regarded as representing a legal entity in the context of ownership of property rather than as symbolizing a sociological concept.

Iravati Karve describes the northern patrilineal 'joint families' as follows: 'The joint family is a group of people who generally live under one roof, who eat food cooked at one hearth, who hold property in common, who participate in common family worship and are related to each other as some particular type of kindred. The joint family has a seat, a locus, and is made up of certain kin. The kin group of the patrilineal families is made up of men who trace their descent from a common male ancestor. With them are associated women who are brought as brides by these males with the young unmarried girls born in the family. Thus, there are three or four generations of males related to a male Ego as grandfather, and his brothers, father and his brothers, brothers and cousins, sons and nephews and wives of all these male relatives, plus the Ego's own unmarried sisters and daughters. Sometimes a father's sister may come back as a widow, but that is rare, and in the case of castes which allow widow remarriage, such residence is but temporary.'[1]

A similar institution is found also among the matrilineal groups. The Nayar *tharwad*, a form of matrilineal 'joint family', has been described by Karve as follows: 'From the point of view of the male Ego, the members of the family are: the grandmother (mother's mother) and her sisters and brothers, and the mother and her sisters and brothers, own brothers and sisters and the mother's sisters' sons and daughters and the children of Ego's sisters. In this family there are no relations by marriage. The wives of the males are with their own mothers and the children of the males also with their mothers. The husbands of the womenfolk live in the house of their own mothers, and are only occasional visitors of their wives and children.'[2]

These units cannot endure indefinitely. Speaking about the break-up of the patrilineal 'joint family', Karve says: 'The northern family breaks at the death of the man who first founded the family. When such a split occurs, it almost never splits into as many units as there are individual families, but into smaller joint families, consisting of a man, his wife, their children and his sons' children. . . . In one city or a village, there may be even ten or twelve houses, each sheltering a joint family, and all together acknowledging common descent and capable of showing relationships through one male line. Very often in such cases one house is known as the ancient house and called the "great house". It may still shelter the family gods, and all the people

1. Iravati Karve, *Kinship Organization in India*, Poona, 1953, p. 10 and 11.
2. ibid, p. 11.

of the other houses may have to go to the great house once in a while for certain occasions of common worship. In time even these ties may be broken, and offshoots may establish their own family gods in their own house.'[1]

The situation is somewhat different in the matrilineal families. Again, to quote Karve: 'In the matrilineal families, the group did not break into several fragments simultaneously as did the northern joint family, but when a house became too small for its inhabitants, one of the women together with her elder brother, or one of her mother's brothers was asked to separate. Land would be allotted to her and a new house built, and she would then be the founder of a new *thar-wad*.'[1]

It will be evident that a 'joint family' can mean many different things. It may mean a three- or four-generation extended family in which all members live together. It may also signify a sizeable part of such an extended family living together, and other parts living separately as independent households. It can also mean the joint living together of several families, all sharing joint legal ownership of ancestral property, but each having separate hearths and separate management of their share of the still legally undivided property. Finally, it may also mean the separate living of lineally related families who are joint owners of ancestral property in legal terms. To avoid confusion, a more sociological typology has been used in this paper throughout; the reference to 'joint family' has been added only to explain this widely used but not-too-clearly understood term.

Marriage

Family life represents a necessary and essential stage in the life cycle of an individual. Beginning with the stage of celibate life, the cycle must be completed through three other stages: the stage of family life, the stage of resignation from worldly goals and pursuits, and the stage of renunciation of all worldly connexions. Family life is not possible without marriage. As no-one can discharge his formal worldly obligations without entering this stage, marriage is considered to be a biological, social, economic and religious necessity.

According to Hindu ideals, marriage is a sacrament. It is a union

1. ibid, p. 11.

180

not for one life only, but for eternity. Ideally it is irrevocable; divorce and widow remarriage are, therefore, out of the question. But these ideals were applied more strictly only to the three upper levels (or 'clean') castes: the Brahman, the Kshatriya and the Vaisya. The Sudras and the Untouchables were always regarded as more worldly, and as such they were exempted not only from the requirements of the stages of resignation and renunciation, but were also permitted divorce and remarriage.

Three considerations govern Hindu marriage. Marriage must be within the caste, unions with certain specified categories of kin should be avoided, and no marital ties should be established within the same *gotra* or clan. As a general rule caste endogamy has been respected, although certain hypergamous unions across caste lines have been permitted and eventually recognized. There is considerable variation in regard to the rules permitting marriage between certain specified categories of kin. Among the Hindus of North India cross-cousin marriages as well as uncle-niece marriages (those between a woman and her mother's brother only) are not permitted. Cross-cousin marriages are the general rule in the tribal communities and are allowed among both the upper and lower castes in western and southern India. Moslems permit parallel cousin marriages also. Among certain groups of the Hindus and Andhra Pradesh and Karnatak in South India maternal-uncle and niece marriages are preferred, as they involve a cyclic change of hands in regard to substantial property. A man can marry a younger sister of his wife, but not her elder sister. Where widow remarriage is allowed a man may marry the widow of his deceased elder brother but not that of a younger brother. As a general rule marriages between *sapindas* (near kin who make ritual offering of balls made with flour to common ancestors) and between two persons of the same *gotra* (clan) are prohibited. Recent legislation has permitted marriage between certain categories of relations in these two groups, having the prescribed genealogical distance between them, but such marriages are to be regarded as exceptions rather than the rule.

In a large part of Hindu society pre-puberty marriages are regarded as ideal. Virginity is considered to be the most desired quality in a bride. Most marriages are arranged, individuals having little freedom in the choice of a mate. Arranging the marriage of a daughter causes considerable concern and anxiety to the parents, for sizeable gifts in cash and kind have to be given by the brides' parents as a part of the marriage agreement. These are the respectable norms of the upper castes; the tribes and the lower castes on the one hand, and the urban *élite* on the other, are not rigorously governed by them. The tribes and the lower castes permit considerable freedom to the girls before marriage, some of them even recognizing pre-marital sexual freedom formally or tacitly. In many such communities girls are married well past the age of puberty. Educated urban families are also generally tending to accept post-puberty marriages. Only among the tribes and the urban-educated is a measure of freedom permitted in the choice of a mate; in some families of the upper strata of the urban *élite*, the freedom allowed is very considerable indeed. But it is one of the paradoxes of modern India that many educated young men and their families still expect the bride's people to hand over substantial gifts and presents, which are negotiated with a combination of great tact and firmness in order to strike the most favourable bargain.

In the following section an attempt will be made to present a brief historical survey of the changing position of women in Indian society, and in this context some of the factors and forces of change will be analysed. At this stage it is necessary to emphasize that tradition still has a very considerable hold on Indian society, and even the Western-educated have shown great selectivity in accepting norms and values from the modern Western model. The structural base of the society is still largely founded on tradition; although the changes brought about in its fabric during the last hundred years, particularly the second half of them, are by no means insignificant.

A word of apology is due here. This study is mainly focused upon rural and urban patrilineal Hindu society. This limitation was necessary in view of the range of the author's field experience, and also for practical considerations of space. To arrive at any satisfactory presentation it was essential to cut through the bewildering maze of ethnographic detail and concentrate on the dominant section of the society. In consequence, several religious and cultural minorities have received very little or no consideration, and a wide range of minor variations in custom have been ignored. Hindu society is by no means Indian society, but the complexity of this part alone is so great that a balanced presentation of it involves several insurmountable difficulties. Let us remember that India is a subcontinent with traditions dating back to the hoary past. It has been a veritable melting-pot of ethnic groups and cultures, each of whom has made some significant contribution to the emergent pattern of the society. Within the construct of what we are calling 'Indian society' we are really dealing here not with a society but with a number of societies.

THE HISTORICAL SETTING

The analysis of the traditional and contemporary roles of men and women in Indian society may be appropriately prefaced by a brief historical survey of the changing position of women. Scanty references scattered in the classical texts form the basis of this account. According to the age of these texts, it will be convenient to consider the changing position of women in four different periods of the evolution of Indian society: the age of the Vedas (2500 to 1500 B.C.), the age of the Brahmanas (1500 to 500 B.C.), the age of Sutras and Epics (500 B.C. to A.D. 500), and the age of later Smritis (A.D. 500 to 1800).[1] It is necessary to point out that the accounts relating to the first two ages refer primarily to the position of women in Indo-Aryan society, rather than to Indian society in general. The later ages refer to the emergent pattern of society in which fusion between Aryans and non-Aryans was taking place at a rapid pace. As many of the contemporary attitudes towards men and women are rooted in the past, this synoptic historical survey is neither irrelevant nor unnecessary.

2500 to 1500 B.C.

At the dawn of the Vedic age in India women had considerable freedom. Girls were educated like boys and had to pass through a period of *brahmacharya* (celibate life). The marriage of girls used to take place at the age of 16 or 17 years. Educated brides of this age had naturally an effective voice in the selection of their partners in life. Occasional love marriages, which eventually enjoyed the blessings of the parents, are also noted. Women moved freely in society, often even in the company of their lovers. In social and religious gatherings they occupied a prominent position. Women had absolute equality with men in the eyes of religion; they could perform ritual sacrifices independently and were not regarded as an impediment to religious

1. The Vedas, Brahmanas, Sutras, Epics such as the *Mahabharata,* and the Smritis form the most important part of the corpus of ancient India's religious literature.

pursuits. Marriage was a religious necessity to both the man and the woman, since neither could reach heaven without being accompanied by the duly married consort. The position of the wife was an honoured one in the family. There were instances of polygamy, but ordinarily monogamy was the rule. Widow remarriage was permitted, but this was usually within the family. The preference was first for a younger brother of the deceased husband, then for any other eligible member of the family. Actually, this was not a remarriage, for an actual marriage was allowed only if the woman was a maiden or if marriage was started but not ceremoniously completed. Women could neither hold nor inherit property.

1500 to 500 B.C.

The changes which took place during this period in the position of women were gradual. According to Altekar: 'In the higher sections of society the sacred initiation (*upanayana*) of girls was common, and they subsequently used to go through a course of education. Some attained distinction in the realm of theology and philosophy, and a considerable number of women used to follow the teaching career. However, in this period the system of sending out girls to famous teachers or centres of education came to be discouraged. It was laid down that only near relations like the father, the brother or uncle should teach them at home. Therefore, religious and secular training became possible only in the case of the girls of rich and cultured families and a tendency arose to curtail the religious rights and privileges of the average woman; many functions in the religious sacrifices which formerly could be performed by the wife alone, now came to be assigned to male substitutes. Some sacrifices continued to be performed by women alone, and when the husband was out the service of the sacrificial fire continued to be entrusted to the wife. In cultured families women used to recite their Vedic prayers morning and evening, and perform sacrifices on their husband's behalf when they were otherwise preoccupied.'[1]

In further describing the customs of this period, Altekar states that the age of marriage for the girls continued to be about 16; in practice

---

1. A. S. Altekar, *The Position of Women in Hindu Civilization*, Benares, 1938, p. 410-11.

if not in theory, girls had some voice in the selection of their life partners. Ideals of marriage and the mutual relations of the husband and wife continued to be more or less the same as they were in the earlier age. Divorce was permitted to the wife, though the permission was not extensively utilized. Widow remarriage was still permitted, but women had ceased to attend public meetings.

The relative freedom allowed to women in these two periods can be attributed to political and religious causes. Altekar goes on to say: 'The general freedom and better status which women enjoyed in the Vedic age was largely due to men being engrossed in the work of conquest and consolidation. Women used to take an active part in agriculture and the manufacture of cloth, bows and arrows, and other war materials. They were thus useful members of society, and could not be treated with an air of patronage and contempt. . . .

'Asceticism was at a discount in the Vedic age. Maidens and bachelors had no admission to heaven; gods accepted no oblations offered by the unmarried. It was essential to offer the ordained sacrifices to gods for procuring happiness and prosperity both here and hereafter and they could be properly performed by the husband and wife officiating together. The wife was not an impediment but an absolute necessity in the religious service. This circumstance helped to raise her status.'[1]

In order to enable her to perform these religious rites, proper training and education were considered essential. Such training required at least six years to complete, and as a result early marriages were not practicable. Therefore, the age of marriage remained at 16 or 17, and such young women were permitted to express their likes and dislikes at the time of marriage. Since they moved freely in society and remained unmarried to such an age, some love marriages were inevitable. Women occupied an honoured position in the household, could move freely in family and society and took an intelligent part in public affairs.

500 B.C. to 500 A.D.

The position of women changed considerably in this period. The introduction of the non-Aryan wife into the Aryan household was largely responsible for this change. Aryan rule had now become established

---

1. ibid, p. 413 and 414.

over the greater part of India. The indigenous population was incorporated into the social structure of the conquerors as the fourth, or Sudra, level, and provided a huge semi-servile population. In some parts of India, however, where the Aryans could not completely wipe out the indigenous civilization, they merely imposed sovereignty over it. When the two ethnic groups proceeded to live together peacefully, intermarriages became inevitable. In the beginning, there seemed to be no objection to an Aryan marrying a Sudra woman provided he had another Aryan wife. Later this procedure was interdicted. However, the non-Aryan wife with her ignorance of the Sanskrit language and Hindu religion could not enjoy the same religious privileges as the Aryan consort. Instances where the husband attempted to associate the non-Aryan wife with his religious sacrifices led to the priests declaring that the non-Aryan wife was unfit for such religious rituals. When this rule was defied, the final solution to the problem was to declare all women unfit for Vedic studies and religious duties.

The growing complexity of the rituals connected with the Vedic sacrifices also contributed to the deterioration of women's status. The time involved in learning now meant that their marriages must be delayed until the age or 22 or 24. Certain forces in society began to clamour for early marriages. In the easy and luxurious life after their conquests, the Aryans settled down in a rich and prosperous country and their political supremacy was unquestioned. Now the procreation of a son became a religious rather than a secular necessity; he alone could discharge certain ritual obligations to the ancestors.

These causes contributed to the lowering of the age of marriage for girls and, as a consequence, their education was discontinued and their religious status in the family was lowered. Finally, by about A.D. 200, it was declared that marriage was the substitute for sacred initiation (*upnayana*) in the case of girls. Since *upnayana* was usually performed at about the age of 9 or 10, the same age now came to be regarded as the ideal age for marriage for girls. Such young brides without any education ceased to have any effective voice in the settlement of their marriage. Marriage now became irrevocable as far as the wife was concerned, although the husband could discard his wife for the offence of not being sufficiently submissive. Widow remarriage was opposed and was finally interdicted by about A.D. 500. Eventually the dictum 'the wife ought to revere her husband as a god, even if he were vicious and void of any merit' was accepted as applying to all women.

186

Political reverses, war atrocities and the decline of population and prosperity in this period produced a wave of despondency in society and facilitated the spread of the ideal of renunciation. This affected the position of widows—although the Vedas stipulated that a son was necessary for securing heaven, the childless widow was now forced by custom to seek the higher salvation (*mukti*) and not the lower one, heaven (*svarga*). This she could attain by burning herself alive on the funeral pyre of her husband. This practice, known as suttee, gradually spread and by A.D. 700 had become a religious duty. The practice was voluntary, but instances are cited which indicate that social pressures forced many women to follow it. Many of those who decided upon this course probably did so out of genuine love and devotion to their husband whom they revered as a god, convinced that this was in the best spiritual interest of both themselves and their husband. There are no statistics available, but one writer estimates that possibly only one widow in a thousand went to the pyre with her husband when this custom was commonest. When the custom was made illegal in British India in 1829 through the efforts of Lord William Bentinck, the law was welcomed by enlightened Hindu public opinion, although it was not without opposition from the orthodox.

The one improvement in this period was in the area of property rights. With widow remarriage discouraged, there began to arise a class of childless widows. Society had to devise an honourable means of enabling them to maintain themselves. Up until 300 B.C., the right of the widow to inherit her husband's property was not recognized by any jurist. Now some felt that the widow should be assigned a definite share in the family property; others were inclined to assign to her only the right to maintenance. In time different regional customs were evolved allowing varying degrees of proprietary rights to women.

The theory of the perpetual tutelage of woman was clearly formulated and expressed during this age. Manu, the supreme law-giver of Hindu society, ordained that the father should protect her while she was a maiden, the husband when she was married, and the son when her husband was no more; at no stage was she to be left unprotected. Intended perhaps to afford women additional protection rather than deny them freedom, the practice served to increase further in women their sense of inferiority. Gradually it was assumed that a women deserved no independence; she ought not to do anything on her own responsibility in childhood, or youth, or even in old age.

The position of women continued to change in this period. From the theological point of view women came to be regarded as of the same status as the Sudras. The proper age of marriage for girls was lowered still further. They were now to be married before puberty; the age of 8 was regarded as ideal. Brides of 8 or 9 could naturally have no choice or voice in the settlement of their marriages. Early marriage was followed by early maternity which increased the mortality among women. Widowers of 25 to 30 were then married to girls of only 9 or 10.

Although widow remarriage had generally become taboo, child widows were allowed to remarry up to A.D. 500. This permission was then gradually withdrawn. Permissive legislation was passed in 1856, but by this time prejudice against widow remarriage was so deep-rooted that the legislation had no appreciable effect on the situation for more than half a century.

As by A.D. 500 women were totally denied the opportunities of education, a new type of religious literature was prepared to meet their needs. This was the remodelled Puranic literature. It enunciated the principles of Hinduism in story form, in a homely, easy and attractive manner. Pious people made provision for the exposition of these stories to public audiences, and women became well grounded in the traditional culture by habitually listening to this literature. Faith, almost blind faith, was thus developed in women to the detriment of rationalism.

Down to the twelfth century A.D. there existed staunch opposition to the custom of *purdah* (keeping the whole body, including the face, covered). During this period, however, the influence of the Moslem conquerors began to be felt, and their customs and manners were gradually imitated. The custom of *purdah* began to spread among the higher classes in northern India, but was not followed in southern India. Another reason for the adoption of this custom was the additional protection it offered to the women, and there is some evidence that women themselves welcomed the custom at the time.

Many rich and cultured Hindu families were ruined by the Moslem conquest. They could no longer make special arrangements for the education of their daughters, and the number of women who could read and write further dwindled. At the beginning of British rule, female education had practically disappeared from Hindu communities.

Mention was made earlier of the right of a widow to inherit her husband's property when there were no sons. In Bengal, the widow's position was further improved now by conceding her the right even when her husband had not separated from the joint family prior to his death, and the scope of *stridhana*[1] was further extended by including in it property acquired even by inheritance and partition.

With these changes in the status of women, it was inevitable that their character and personalities should also be affected. Uneducated, considered on a level with the Sudras, married before their characters were fully developed, transferred from the loving and sympathetic atmosphere of the parents' house to the house of the parents-in-law where an atmosphere of awe prevailed, apprehensive of suppression, frequently forced to drag on a miserable existence in an interminable widowhood, their character suffered from forced repression in some directions and unnatural stimulation in others. They had no status in society; none in their own estimation. They were more like puppets which move when someone else pulls the strings than individual human beings with minds of their own.

During the British rule in India legislation was used to bring about significant modifications in the structure of society. Most of these measures had the support of progressive opinion in India, although they were viewed by the orthodox as undesirable and unnecessary interference on the part of an alien government. The British were naturally very slow and cautious in respect of these reforms; rather than attempt to force any profound changes upon the whole society, they made it possible for those who wanted change to adopt an alternative way of life within the framework of the new social legislation. Reference has been made to the abolition of suttee. Subsequent legislation recognized inter-caste marriages, as also widow remarriage. The age of marriage was raised, and divorce was permitted under certain conditions. Special facilities were provided for women to acquire modern education. They were also provided with increasing employment opportunities in certain selected spheres. Advantage of these measures was taken only by a small fraction of society in the first instance, but the process they initiated was indeed significant.

---

1. *Stridhana* means woman's personal property, usually ornaments and jewellery and moveable property given by relatives upon marriage or after marriage by her husband and intended for her alone.

Free India has carried forward the process to a point where legally at least man and woman are equal. Marriage and divorce laws have been modified, ensuring a greater measure of equality to women. Women now have a legal share in ancestral property. Educational and employment opportunities for them have been extended, and today they can enter the higher civil services and the professions without any legal discrimination. They have an equal right to vote. Many of them have entered the legislative bodies, and some of them even occupy important positions in the government.

Inadequate as the above survey is, it nevertheless gives some idea of the changing position of women in the different epochs of the evolution of Indian society. As subsequent discussion will show, many of the present-day attitudes have been influenced by factors of historical development.

CONTEMPORARY ATTITUDES

We can now proceed to consider some of the basic cultural orientations towards men and women in contemporary Indian society. These have been shaped by the authority of classical texts, teachings of religion, factors of historical development and the persistence of regional and local traditions. Contemporary developments have brought about some modifications in them, but the covert norms have not changed to any appreciable extent.

The contradictory attitudes expressed about women in classical texts persist in contemporary society. On the one hand they are regarded as the highest embodiment of purity and power—a symbol of religiousness and spirituality; on the other they are viewed essentially as weak and dependent creatures requiring constant guarding and protection. While the former view occasionally gets overt expression, covert norms defining her actual position are essentially determined by the latter.

Viewed empirically, two themes appear to be basic in the general area of attitudes covering the relative statuses of men and women. They are: (a) the male is more desirable than the female; and (b) the male is qualitatively superior to the female.

While girls are also considered necessary, the birth of a boy is undoubtedly considered more desirable. Ritual considerations materially add to the desirability of the male. In the traditional scheme of Hindu

190

life the attainment of salvation occupies the place of highest importance. For this it is absolutely necessary to complete all the rites and ceremonies of the life cycle prescribed by dharma. In the patrilineal Hindu society only a male heir can offer water to the spirits of the deceased ancestors; a son alone can perform the essential rites ensuring passage to heaven or attainment of salvation. This makes a male offspring very desirable. Besides, the possession of sons offers many other advantages. Parents can depend upon them for support in old age. They are expected to continue to live with the family, unlike the daughters, and are also looked upon as potential builders of family prestige and prosperity. Daughters, on the contrary, are regarded as birds of passage. Their upbringing is all worry and work for the parents; when they grow up and get married their loyalties are changed. As a popular saying goes: 'Bringing up a son is like manuring and watering a plant in your own courtyard, for when it grows up it will give you shade and fruit; but bringing up a daughter is like manuring and watering a plant in someone else's courtyard, for her services and affections are destined for others.' While her qualities of affection and tenderness are recognized, a daughter by herself can neither complete a household nor can she effectively take the place of a son. The difficulties and expenses involved in her upbringing and marriage further detract from her desirability. Even today in a large number of Hindu households the birth of a son is an occasion for rejoicing; the birth of a daughter is a cause for anxiety and sorrow.

The 'superiority of the male' theme has many latent and manifest dimensions. Woman is regarded as more susceptible to pollution; her defilement is easy, purification is difficult. Man on the contrary is not so easily defiled, and when defiled the removal of his pollution is not as difficult as it is in the case of a woman. In a pollution-purity conscious society, the significance of this view is crucial indeed. It is perhaps at the root of the prevailing double standards of morality; one set of principles governing the male and another governing the female. Because man is relatively pollution-resistant he is allowed certain freedoms which are denied to the woman. Implicit in this conception of the superiority of the male are the assumptions that 'Man is strong and woman is weak', or 'Man is capable of looking after himself, but the best security for a woman is in dependence'. This assumption regarding the strength of the male has built up the ideas of male dominance and female dependence. Outdoor activities and most of the major decision-making roles are thus the domain of man. Under the protection of man and in the security of the home, the sphere of woman has been strictly limited. In the traditionally-oriented groups the stereotype suggesting the desirability of life-long protection to a woman—in childhood by father, in youth by husband and in old age by son—is still seriously believed.

Norms for the division of labour

These attitudes are reflected largely in the contemporary definitions and delimitations of a woman's role, particularly in respect of the division of labour and responsibility.

Man must justify his masculine virtues in his day-to-day responsibilities. Being strong he has to assume full responsibility for the protection and support of the members of his family. Any inadequacy or his part in this respect is bound to be viewed critically; a man depending on women and children for support in the prime of his life or even in his middle age is likely to be regarded as something less than a man. He must also assert his superiority on the family scene by being able to control and keep under discipline the women and children of the household. While he has consciously to strive to build up an atmosphere of goodwill, understanding and co-operation within the family he is answerable to the community for all lapses on the part of women and children under his charge. On the other hand, since taking up any role or function which is culturally defined as 'feminine' will bring only social scorn and ridicule on him, he has to leave women relatively free in their own sphere.

Woman tacitly assumes her complementary role in which the superiority and dominance of the male is often taken for granted. Earning and giving economic support to the family are not her primary responsibilities; she undertakes them only if she has to and then she has the sympathy of the community with her. In respect of control over family affairs also, particularly over the conduct of the younger members of the family, her role is complementary. However, in the domestic sphere she is relatively free and can legitimately protest if her autonomy is unreasonably infringed upon.

The patterns of intrafamily relationships are governed by three major considerations: acceptance of the assumptions regarding separate male-female roles and spheres of responsibility, age, and position in the scale of kinship. In the context of the family itself, most of the relationships are complementary; relatively few being symmetrical. In the web of kinship extending beyond the immediate family, a large number of relationships are of the reciprocal type. Husband-wife relationships are definitely complementary; so are the relationships between parents and children. Time may modify some of the more formal aspects of the husband-wife relationship, but they continue essentially complementary in nature. The relationships between father, mother and sons also belong to this category although time reverses some of their roles. When the children are young the father is expected to support and protect them, but when they grow old this responsibility is taken up by the sons. The position of the daughter is somewhat different. She is never regarded as a full member of her parents' family. Before marriage she must be kept under discipline and trained well in domestic arts and crafts. A blot on her character would injure the reputation of the parents' family. Inadequacies in her training will also lower the prestige of the family in the critical estimation of her in-laws. After marriage, when she returns to her parental home for brief intervals, she is always treated as a guest and kept free as far as possible from domestic chores. It is realized that she has constantly to work hard for her in-laws, and so her brief sojourns in her parental home are regarded as a period of rest and recreation. The position of the daughter-in-law, on the contrary, is one of subordination; complementary in relation to both her husband and her mother-in-law. As years pass, much of the *de facto* control of household affairs is taken over by the daughter-in-law, but because of her higher place in the scale of kinship and age the mother-in-law continues to occupy a place of respect in the family. The relationships between brothers, as also between sisters, are complementary if the differences in their age are considerable, and more or less symmetrical if these differences are not very great. They may start as complementary relationships and gradually develop into symmetrical or even reciprocal type of relationships. Brother-sister relationships are in some ways complementary and in other ways symmetrical; after a sister has been married for some years they tend to become reciprocal. Finally, the relationships between two or more daughters-in-law in a family are partly complementary and partly symmetrical. In the first few years of her marriage a daughter-in-law behaves in a complementary way in relation to the other senior daughters-in-law in the family, but

193

as time passes more symmetrical and reciprocal patterns are estab lished.

These norms of interpersonal relations within the family may b regarded as valid for Hindu society in general, but adherence to them is perhaps most marked among the upper-strata rural families and among the traditionally-oriented urban families. These are the group that symbolize traditional respectability in India. Lower-strata village families (both tribal and non-tribal) and the *élite* urban families deviate considerably from them in their day-to-day life. Among them the com plementary phase of relationships is relatively short, and even when the relationships are of this nature, the actual expectations within their framework tend to be specific rather than diffused. While these rela tionships continue to be complementary in theory, they increasingly acquire symmetrical and reciprocal overtones. The lower-strata fami lies are too low anyway to bother about traditionally respectable pat terns of behaviour; the *élite* groups operate in a different scheme o values, where the adoption of modern Western attitudes and ways c life has greater prestige than the traditional attitudes and life-ways.

In this section the discussion has been focused more on the level c verbalized norms than on the level of empirical realities. In the deve lopment of actual relationships the traditions of a particular family an the personality factors of its members play a significant part and deter mine the degree of adherence to or deviation from the norms. A con siderate husband allows much greater freedom to his wife than a les considerate one; a wife with a strong personality and character ca establish herself in a domineering position. Within the general frame work of the traditional norms, wide variation in the patterns of in dividual relationships is thus possible and can actually be seen in dif ferent families.

The acceptance of these norms is by no means universal, althoug only a very small fraction of the population has been able to reje them in both theory and practice. Increasing association with th values of modern science and thought has brought about considerabl change in the thinking of the educated sections about the position c woman. Educated women can assert their claims for equality and gai at least partial acceptance for them. Prejudice against women enterin the professions and the services still persists, but many in the urba areas are beginning to recognize it as inevitable. This trend toward the relative economic independence of women is viewed with a degre of ambivalence by many men—even some of them Western-educated. A working wife is economically advantageous; if she works in a responsible position she is also a distinct social asset. But her having to mix with others, especially with other men, is not favourably viewed. Her preoccupation with an outside job often results in some neglect of her traditional domestic responsibilities, and this is almost always commented upon adversely. Working women themselves find it difficult to carry on their two roles together, and some of them are not altogether happy regarding some 'masculine' aspects of their new role.

Educational opportunities for women, particularly those of higher education, are available only on a limited scale. Girls from villages and from the lower strata of urban communities rarely get any education extending beyond the fourth or the sixth grade, but the significance of even this much of education in widening their mental horizons and changing their self-image cannot be minimized. Higher education, available only to the few, makes a stronger impact, and is a recognizable force in modifying the social conception of woman's place in society.

A COMPARISON OF TYPE FAMILIES

Variations in the form of family organization in India are so great, and they involve so many different patterns of division of authority, responsibility and labour, that it is practically impossible to evolve a typology representative of all of them. Three main types will be considered here: tribal, and lower-strata rural and urban families; upper-strata rural families and traditional upper-strata urban families; and progressive urban families.

It is necessary to emphasize that none of these types is exclusive. A sizable section of tribal peasantry has adopted many of the social norms of upper-caste Hindus. Upper castes on the lower economic strata, as a general rule, tend to observe these norms more than the lower castes on the same economic level. Families of the second type, depending upon their economic, educational and occupational status, often have certain progressive elements also in them. The same is true, but in reverse, of families of the third type; except for the most sophisticated and highly Westernized urban *élite*, they have certain orthodox and conservative elements in them.

To ensure comparability, the discussion in regard to the division of

195

labour and authority between men and women in each of these types will be focused on spheres of activity, responsibility and initiative, authority and decision-making, rest and recreation, and participation in community and national life.

Tribal and lower strata rural and urban families

Spheres of activity. Separate spheres of activity for men and women are not clearly distinguished. Recognizing the different biological make-up and functions of women, relatively less strenuous indoor and outdoor tasks are considered proper for them. However, both men and women work and earn to provide for the needs of the family. Management of the home and care of the children is primarily the responsibility of women, but in addition they participate in economic, social and religious activities both inside and outside the family.

Responsibility and initiative. Men have to undertake a greater share in earning and providing for the family, but women are also expected to work and contribute their share to the family budget. In the villages women may work for daily wages as agricultural labourers, collect fuel, cut grass, or share a part of the traditional craft of the family. If the family has any agricultural land, they assist the men in the less exhausting but nevertheless important aspects of the routine. In towns, they take up domestic employment or have a well-defined share in the traditional calling of the family.

Management of the household is primarily their responsibility. The daily routine includes: sweeping and cleaning the house, removing cow-dung and providing fodder for the cattle, fetching water for domestic consumption from the well, tank or river, cooking and serving food for the men and children, scrubbing the utensils, washing their own clothes as well as those of the men and children, and looking after the storage of provisions. Men help in these functions only when women are sick or otherwise physically not in a condition to work.

The care of children is also the responsibility of women. Depending upon their age they must be fed, bathed and put to bed. Their soiled clothes are changed and washed by women. Older children and men help by taking charge of the babies when the women have to be away for work out of doors.

Families on this level have to be self-sufficient, for they cannot afford to hire any domestic help. In periods of sickness and difficulty, relatives and neighbours help one another; ordinarily work has to be shared by the members of the family themselves.

Except in the early phase of their daughter-in-law role, women participate equally in the social and religious life of the community. A close watch on their activities is neither possible nor considered necessary. Their behaviour will, however, be watched when they are suspected of sexual lapses.

The stereotyped routine of the family offers little opportunity to any member for an unusual type of initiative.

Authority and decision-making. Authority is very much a matter of age and kinship status. As most families on this level are of the simple type, authority is jointly shared by the husband and wife, the former being regarded by tradition as superior. Most males doubtless assert their dominance by occasionally scolding and even beating the women, but the latter can resist by arguing, quarrelling and, in extreme cases, even by hitting back in retaliation. Not bound by the norms of respectability, they can always threaten to go back to their parents. Older children exercise considerable authority over their younger siblings. Minor day-to-day decisions are taken by the husband and wife individually; the more important decisions must be taken by them together. It is considered good form to consult with the elders of the kin-group (even if they are outside the immediate family group) in such matters as disposal of substantial property (especially land, houses or livestock), negotiation of marriages, holding of large feasts, etc.

Rest and recreation. Both men and women have a hard day during which there are only a few pauses for rest. Brief periods of rest after principal meals are considered desirable. Approximately eight hours of sleep are regarded as necessary for adults. The average day begins at or a little before dawn and ends around 9 p.m.

Except in some of the tribal groups, who have community dancing several evenings a week, there are few organized opportunities for recreation. Most of the recreation must be found in gossip and watching people quarrel. Women go out to answer the calls of nature and to bathe in small groups. The village well or tank provides another opportunity for their groups to gather together. These occasions are utilized for gossip and the exchange of news. Weekly or bi-weekly visits to country markets or occasional visits to fairs and towns provide some diversion. Religious festivals, marriages, performances of folk-drama and the narration of mythical tales by professional story-tellers occasionally help to break the monotony of their daily routine.

Participation in community and national life. The participation of both men and women is restricted to family, kin, caste and village affairs in that order. As women work out of doors and contribute economically to the family, there are not many restrictions on their equal participation in these spheres. They participate in state and national elections, but very few of them have any comprehension of their meaning and significance.

Upper-strata rural families and traditional upper-strata urban families

Spheres of activity. Separate spheres of activity for men and women are clearly distinguished; men are not expected to undertake women's work, nor are women expected to assume any masculine roles. Out-door work is man's domain; management of the home is woman's responsibility. Women are at least partially secluded, and opportunities for them to meet others outside the family and kingroup are limited.

Responsibility and initiative. Working, earning and providing for the family is men's work. Land, business and property are managed by them. Older women may be consulted, but this is not considered essential unless some of the property is being disposed of.

Management of the home and care of children are principally within the jurisdiction of women's responsibility. In these spheres the work of women is almost the same as described for families of the first type, with the exception that work requiring their going out of doors or involving undue physical strain may be done by hired domestic help. A servant may be engaged for drawing and bringing water and also for scrubbing utensils.

For outdoor work and responsibilities men have considerable initiative; women are left relatively undisturbed in regard to the internal affairs of the household. The economic sphere is controlled mostly by men; so are the external contacts of the family, but in respect of intra-kin and intra-caste social and religious affairs women enjoy considerable autonomy.

Authority and decision-making. Male dominance is most pronounced on this level, but in practice division of authority and decision-making is determined by age and kinship status as well as sex.

In respect of the management of land, business and property, men have the final authority, although as mentioned earlier they do not generally take any major decisions in regard to them without also consulting the women, especially the old and experienced female members of the family. The internal affairs of the family are managed by women, men occasionally exercising some supervisory powers.

In the women's sphere, kinship status contributes materially to the authority and functions of individuals. The mother-in-law enjoys considerable authority over the daughter-in-law, and definitely has the upper hand in decision-making. Unmarried daughters work more for their own training than as a part of their fixed domestic responsibility. Married daughters visiting their parents briefly are treated as guests and are not expected to work. Over the years the supervision of daughters-in-law is considerably relaxed, and they come to acquire definite decision-making powers. However, the position of the mother-in-law continues to be important until she becomes so very old as to be incapable of any effective interference in domestic affairs.

Norms of respectability enjoin almost complete submission on the part of daughters-in-law in particular and women in general. Men can scold their women and even hit them, depending upon their age and kinship status. Women similarly control the children and their daughters-in-law, although they rarely hit grown-up children. The mother-in-law keeps a watchful eye open, and whenever the daughters-in-law make any mistakes they are treated with scornful taunts.

Rest and recreation. Freedom from outdoor work and some availability of domestic help make the work of women in this category less strenuous, although their domestic chores are still considerable. Periods of rest and leisure are definitely longer for them compared with those of women in families of the first type, but they are denied many of the outdoor relaxations. Educated women may occasionally read story magazines; in urban areas they may go to the cinema once in a while. On the whole, their freedom to go out is severely limited, and when they do so they are almost always accompanied by a responsible male.

Participation in community and national life. Men are increasingly participating in community and national life, but women are still largely confined to the domestic sphere.

Progressive urban families

Spheres of activity. On this level, again, the spheres of men and women are less strictly demarcated. Families inclined towards traditional ideals emphasize the domestic role of women, allowing them at the same time considerable latitude for participation in community and national life. On the other hand, the sophisticated and Western-oriented segment of the urban *élite* recognizes the principle of equal participation of women. The distinction between the spheres of men and women gets blurred as the families go up in the scale of sophistication.

Responsibility and initiative. The responsibility for working and earning is still mainly that of men, but women may also work for economic gain. At the lower economic levels, women's share of earnings materially improves the budget of progressive families; at the upper levels they may work only for prestige or for providing for their personal creative satisfaction. Where women do not work to earn, they may take up some voluntary social work.

Management of the home and care of the children are women's responsibility, but their actual share of work depends largely upon the economic status of the family. At the lower economic levels, domestic help is limited and time-and-labour-saving gadgets are fewer. Thus, women have to do part of the work themselves, though partly they simply supervise the work done by others in these spheres. Men occasionally lend a hand, but their participation is often nominal. Women's burden in respect of certain domestic chores, such as cleaning the house, washing clothes and scrubbing utensils, etc., is very substantially reduced by the presence of domestic servants. For example, they never have to do all the cooking by themselves. Nevertheless, while their burden is thus reduced, they have to take up certain additional responsibilities in other spheres. Home decoration, social obligations and a certain amount of voluntary work come to occupy a substantial part of their time. Social visits to and from their circle of friends increase in frequency as the economic level is raised. Where women have professional interests or an independent job they have to divide their time carefully between their family and professional obligations.

Authority and decision-making. Authority is shared more or less equally by the two sexes. Day-to-day decisions and control over the purse are vested in both, minor decisions being taken independently and the more important ones being taken by consultation and discussion. On the upper levels there are few overt signs of authority. Men, women and even children have considerable freedom of action and decision. Only when there are any blatant breaches of norms by any one is there any interference on the part of others.

Rest and recreation. Periods of rest increase in their frequency and duration on this level. Even on lower economic levels families of this type can afford some newspapers, magazines and books. The radio provides a relatively inexpensive and constant source of recreation. Visits to cinemas are more frequent. Most families of this type have provison for some indoor games; on the upper levels women join with men at card games such as bridge. Other games popular with the women are table tennis, badminton and lawn tennis. Social occasions, such as formal teas, lunches and dinners, can also be viewed as opportunities for recreation. Men and women from this group eat out more frequently than those from other groups, a cup of coffee or tea with a snack being a necessary part of every shopping expedition or evening stroll. The 'smart set', especially its younger members, are fond of Western music and dancing, and frequent restaurants providing services for dining and dancing. People of this class also take vacations, both in the country—in centres of historical and cultural interest or at hill stations—and abroad, if they can afford them.

Participation in community and national life. Families of this type have contributed most to the social, cultural and political life of the country. Women entering the higher professions and services have mostly been from this group. Those known in the fields of the arts, literature and music have also come up from these groups. Women leaders thrown up by this level are guiding the formulation of policies and plans which will have a far-reaching impact upon the status of women in India as a whole.

It is interesting to observe that families of the first type look up to families of the second as a model, and families of the second type in their turn look up to families of the third. Among the third-type families there is a constant effort to fight conservatism and orthodoxy, and to secure for women a position of equality consistent with the ideals and spirit of the republican constitution of India. Families of the second type are also being slowly infected with their zeal and objectives.

There are unmistakable signs that the traditional conceptions regarding the place and role of women are slowly changing in contemporary Indian society. The process has been generated and aided by a variety of factors which are operating almost simultaneously. Increasing opportunities for modern education, greater geographical and occupational mobility, and the emergence of new economic patterns are in the main responsible for this trend.

The acceptance of some of the values of modern science and technology has resulted in the weakening of the ritual theme in Indian life, and consequently there has been a noticeable shift in the emphasis of life from the sacred to the secular. The traditional premises of family and kinship organization have thus come to be questioned. Ever-widening opportunities of education and employment, especially those for women, have reinforced the trend. Together with certain economic forces, these factors have contributed towards weakening the bonds of kinship. Land can no longer support even a fair proportion of the population, which is increasing at an alarming rate. In consequence, land-bound subsidiary occupations are also naturally becoming uneconomic. Many of the traditional arts and crafts have been fighting a losing battle against modern technology, resulting in an increasing drift of people from traditional to new occupations. Increased geographical and occupational mobility has significantly modified the size and composition of large extended families; couples migrating from villages in search of new urban occupations continue to maintain contacts with the parent families, but their relative independence and contact with urban values result in their increasing individualization. Beside their traditional kin- and caste-orientation, they develop an interest-orientation also. They often do not completely discard tradition, but they do nevertheless take significant and irretraceable steps in the direction of a new way of life. With the weakening of the hold of kin and caste, simple families can assert their independence more; complementary types of relationship are increasingly being replaced by symmetrical and reciprocal relationships, and even where the break-up is not complete, the expectation system in intra-kin relationships tends to be defined in more specific terms gradually overshadowing the diffused expectation system latent in the traditional norms. There are reasons to believe that on the level of the sophisticated urban *élite* the kinship system, while superficially retaining a lineal character, is becoming radial in content.

The hold of tradition over a large part of Indian society is still strong, but the trend towards change appears to be irresistible. Economic and social forces in the India of today lend a character of inevitability to this trend. Naturally the transition cannot be rapid in a society that has been tradition-directed for several centuries, but there are signs that the resistance of orthodoxy is gradually weakening. New horizons are opening up for Indian women. The changes are most apparent today on the level of the sophisticated urban *élite*, but the compulsions of a competitive economy and a growing democratic society will increasingly bring women from other urban segments of society into more active and direct participation in community and national life. Increasing urbanization will gradually draw village women also into the trend. The *élite* formulation of the economic and social goals of national policy definitely point towards this direction.

Our changing life in India

by SUSHILLA NAYER

India has seen unprecedented changes, political and social, during the last thirty to forty years. We are conscious of the political change, and attach great importance to it, but the social changes are taken for granted. However, they have a most important bearing on the life of any nation today and tomorrow. These social changes can be brought out vividly by looking at the changing pattern of life of one family during this period, with special reference to the life and thinking of women, stretching over four generations.

My paternal grandfather was a highly respected village landlord. He earned his living from the land, though he did not till the land with his own hands. He was also an able practitioner of the indigenous system of medicine, and in my childhood I used to see rows of patients sitting in front of his door waiting to get his famous malaria powders, three doses of which were supposed to control the fever which came on alternate days. He never charged a penny for his services or for the medicine. His knowledge consisted of a few tried prescriptions handed from father to son, and was used as a sacred trust in the service of humanity. My grandmother was always plying the spinning-wheel. She had five sons, three of whom came to occupy important positions in government service. Nevertheless, she did all her household work with her own hands, and in her spare time spun enough yarn to get cloth woven by the village weaver which she had dyed and embroidered for the trousseaux of the grand-daughters.

My grandfather had a big house in which he had given separate portions to each of the sons to lead their own lives with their wives and children. My grandfather and grandmother had their own portion where they lived close to their children and grandchildren. Theirs had been an arranged marriage, but they were devoted to one another. My grandfather was a tall, handsome man with a white beard which I loved to play with. At the age of 80 he could walk ten miles, but then my father passed away as a result of high blood pressure and cerebral haemorrhage; this broke the old man's heart and he became bed-ridden and died within five years of his bereavement. My grandmother, who was married as a little girl not 10 years of age, was a year or two older than he. Her mind could not withstand the loss of her husband. She could not accept the fact that he was no more. She had been spinning by his bedside when he passed away in his sleep. She had taken his morning cup of Sanatogen to him, but he would not wake up. Her mental faculties broke down. My mother often brought her over to our house (my father had built a separate big house next door to his father's), but after staying with us for a day or two, she would insist on going back. 'I must be at home when your father-in-law returns from the fields', she would say, and go back to her own room in grandfather's house. Nothing could make her accept the fact that grandfather was dead and would never return. She was normal in every other way, but this one delusion she clung to as the prop which helped her to bear her loss. My mother, my uncles and aunts were unhappy that she should live alone in her old age, but she insisted on occupying the room she had occupied with her husband on the first floor, and always kept his bed ready for his return. One evening, at the age of 90, on walking out of her room, she mistook the window for the door, stepped out, fell on the street, fractured her skull and passed away during the same night.

My maternal grandfather was a timber merchant and lived in a city where my father was a district official. He led a gay life, was fond of drink, kept a mistress, and left the business worries to his servants. My father was heard to remark in a half-serious, half-joking manner that he wondered when the business of such a master would go into liquidation. Ultimately he was cheated by his partner and servants. There was a fire believed to have been engineered by the guilty parties, and he became a man without means for the type of life that he was used to.

My maternal grandmother had one son and one daughter, and lived by herself from the time that her husband had taken a mistress. She was too proud to live under the same roof with her. She sold her jewellery to bring up her children. From time to time my grandfather would visit her in a drunken state and demand money or jewellery.

On her refusal, he would beat her and snatch what he could from her. My mother remembers several occasions when her own mother sat with a heated brick wrapped in cloth fomenting her aching body after the husband had beaten her and gone away with what money she had. Tears would flow from her eyes but from her lips came words of prayer: 'Oh, Lord, my husband is the only son of his parents. Please protect him and help him.' She was the now almost extinct traditional Hindu wife who looked upon her husband as her god, put up with all his vagaries, and never complained. Her son became a first-class railway guard, a job which was generally reserved for an Englishman or an Anglo-Indian in those days. Her daughter was married at the age of 13 to my father, a government officer, who was almost three times her age.

Previously my father had been married as a young boy at the age of 10 or 12 to a little girl who was later found to be mentally defective and given to peculiar behaviour which could not be controlled. My father never lived with her. She stayed alternately with my grandparents and her own parents. My father devoted himself to his official duties and read books in his spare time. He was a religious man, brought up with a very strict moral and ethical code which embraced his private and public life. He was about 40 when his parents and his friends coaxed him into a second marriage. They told him they had announced his engagement to a nice girl and if he did not get married to her it would bring her a bad name in society. He was too chivalrous a man to injure a girl's reputation and so he was married to my mother. From my mother's talk I gather they were very happy in their marriage. The young wife did everything she could to please her husband and fall in line with his wishes. He in his turn gave her all his love and protection and provided her with every comfort.

My father believed that a woman's place was in the home and my mother was kept in *purdah*. She never did any household work and never went out except in a closed carriage. When she had to undertake a train journey to accompany my father on transfer from one town to another or to pay a visit to her mother, she was carried in a closed palanquin from the house to the closed horse carriage and from it to the railway compartment. Soon after the marriage of my father, his youngest brother, who was my father's favourite brother and generally stayed with him, was married. His wife was an educated woman with progressive ideas. She taught my mother and other girls in the family how to read and write and they started a school in my father's house to which other girls from the village could also come for education. Thus my aunt became the pioneer in girls' education in our family and in our village. She had come under the influence of Arya Samaj, a reform movement in Hinduism, similar to Protestantism in Christianity. She was a vegetarian, and under her influence my mother also became a vegetarian and brought up her children as vegetarians.

My mother had ten pregnancies during the twenty years or so of her married life, and has three living children, two boys and one girl (myself). I never came to know my father. He died soon after my birth. He was in his fifties and had high blood pressure. He was of athletic habits, ignored the warning symptoms and died of a fatal stroke.

My eldest brother, Shri Pyarelal, was studying in a boarding school at Lahore at the time of my father's death. My second brother was taken away by my uncle soon afterwards, and I grew up as a lonely child with my mother in our village home. My brothers came home during their vacations, but there was almost a decade between each, and in childhood years appear much longer than in adult life, with the result that there was hardly any companionship between us.

I was sent to the village primary school for girls. I was fond of reading story books. Many of the novels in the house were taboo for children which made me all the more eager to read them and thus I got into the habit of reading in the lavatory.

My eldest brother was about to complete his college studies when he came under the influence of Mahatma Gandhi in the early twenties. The massacre of Jallianwala Bagh had affected him deeply. He had seen Mahatma Gandhi and found in him a master whom he could gladly follow and at whose feet he could sit and serve.

He announced his decision in a letter to my mother. She was very upset. He was to enter the Indian Civil Service after getting his master's degree, and my mother had hoped that he would look after the younger brother and sister. His decision to choose a stormy future for himself shattered her hopes. The day my brother said goodbye to her in his new attire of coarse home-spun cloth, she sobbed the whole night. I was very small and used to sleep with her. I cried because she cried though I could not understand the reason for her grief.

Shortly after my brother joined Mahatma Gandhi, my second brother, who was with my uncle at Rohtak, fell ill and my mother went there to look after him. One day there was news that Mahatma Gandhi was to visit Rohtak and would address a women's meeting. Women of our family were not expected to go to public meetings. It was considered a sign of aristocracy that they should not be seen in public and my uncle, who was a junior district judge, was anxious to keep up the standards adopted by my father in this respect. My mother, however, decided to attend the meeting and, while my uncle was at the district courts, she quietly wrapped herself in a big shawl and went out. I ran after her and she took me along. I have a vague recollection that it was a very noisy meeting and Mahatma Gandhi, finding it impossible to get a hearing, started collecting funds for his work. Women took off their gold ornaments and presented them to him. My mother elbowed her way through the crowd to reach the dais on which Mahatma Gandhi was standing. She introduced herself to the Mahatma and asked for an appointment. He gave her an appointment at Lahore a few weeks later. Her object in going to see him was to ask him to send back her son, who was her only hope, a widow with two fatherless children to be educated and looked after, but she was so much overpowered by his personality that she told him that he could keep her son for three or four years, but he should send him back in the end.

The years that followed were filled with the stormy struggle for independence. In the early thirties my brother was able to persuade my mother to send me to Gandhi's Ashram during my summer vacation. I came back impressed with the Ashram life, and this did not please her. She did not want any more of her children to follow the stormy and precarious life chosen by my eldest brother.

In 1931 Gandhi was to attend the second Round-Table Conference in London. My brother was going with him. I had gone to the Ashram and went to Bombay to see them off. A few months later, when they returned, my mother decided to go and meet them. The political atmosphere had deteriorated during Gandhi's absence from India. Leaders like Pandit Jawaharlal Nehru were already in prison and Gandhi expected to be arrested before long. After three or four days with him at Bombay, my mother went to take leave of him. The Mahatma joked with her: 'How can you go away like this! See us off to gaol and then follow us yourself!' This, to my mother, was something new, unheard of, but she was not going to let the Mahatma's words go in vain. She stayed on; Gandhi was arrested. She went about with other women workers for a few weeks, picketing foreign cloth and liquor shops. Those in charge of the movement were afraid to send her to jail because she was altogether unused to rough life. But she insisted on courting imprisonment. She was arrested in Bombay and taken to Yarawda prison, the Bastille of India, and sentenced to six month's imprisonment as a class 'C' prisoner. She, who could not step out of her door unescorted, was suddenly transformed into a soldier of freedom, a Satyagrahi, ready to face hardships of all kinds, court imprisonment, even beating and bayonets, if necessary.

After completing studies in the village primary school, I started studying at home. No one could even think of sending me to the boys' school, and the village had nothing more than a primary school for girls. I passed the middle and then the high school examination as a private student. Being a lonely child, I spend most of my time in studies and secured a place among the top ten successful candidates in matriculation. This entitled me to a merit scholarship and an easy admission to college. We had moved to Lahore by this time. I took up the pre-medical course and was ready to go to medical college at the age of about 14. The age for admission to medical college was 18. I had, however, secured a position among the top three successful candidates in the whole state and was admitted to the girls' medical college in Delhi.

I was socially backward, and extremely shy. I blushed to the roots of my ears every time I tried to speak to any one in college. I was helped to make an adjustment by one or two older girls who later became my lifelong friends. I was the first girl from the family and from our village to go to college, and I felt it my responsibility to prove worthy of the opportunity, do well in my studies and not break any of the conventions of proper upbringing, one of which was to avoid all social contacts with boys.

In the summer vacation, both my brother and my mother being in gaol, I had no home to go to. It was not permitted to stay in the hostel during the vacation. I was invited by a family friend to spend the holiday with his family at Dalhousie. Before the end of the vacation it was time for my mother's release from prison and I and my second brother went to Poona. My mother had already been released and was at the house of Dr. Trivedi, a very kind friend of all those engaged in the freedom struggle. She had lost 40 lb. in weight during her imprisonment.

We went to see my brother in the Yarawda prison. He was dressed in convict clothes, had a beard, and had become very thin. The walls of Yarawda prison looked so grim and terrifying that I felt deeply depressed. The warder insisted that my brother should talk to his mother in English. He refused to do so. It was most unnatural for him to talk to his mother in any other tongue except his mother tongue, Punjabi. Moreover, my mother did not know English. We, therefore, sat there for fifteen minutes in silence. Then the warder relented and we talked for fifteen minutes. The gaol authorities would not allow him the use of his own razor; he did not wish to be shaved by the prison barber, and so had grown a beard. There had been trouble in the prison and they had put him in solitary confinement. On being deprived of his religious books when he was put in solitary confinement he had gone on hunger strike, and was reduced to skin and bone. I came back feeling very depressed.

Soon after our return to Delhi I went back to college and my mother again offered Satyagraha and was arrested in Delhi and sent to prison at Lahore. She was put in the same yard as Mrs. Sarojini Naidu. This time she was treated as a 'B' class prisoner and given facilities to cook her own food. Her culinary skill was greatly appreciated by Mrs. Naidu and her other fellow-prisoners.

My mother had been brought up as an orthodox Hindu who would not eat anything touched by a Moslem, a Christian or an Untouchable. Her resistance broke to some extent when I started bringing home my Moslem and Christian college friends. They would walk into the kitchen with me and my mother served us our meals with a mother's affection. But she still would not eat anything cooked by Moslems, nor would she mix with Untouchables. Even this resistance wore off in prison and she became practically free from caste prejudices.

In the midst of the freedom struggle I became a doctor. I had often felt moved to give up my studies and join the movement. But my mother's insistence that I must not interrupt my studies, and the realization that if I once gave them up I might never get a chance to complete them (for in those days girls' education was not given much importance, as a rule) prevented me from taking such a step.

On 8 August 1942, the All-India Congress Committee passed the 'Quit India' resolution at Bombay and the final phase of the non-violent struggle for India's independence began. I had just taken my M.D. and had come on a week's leave from Lady Hardinge Medical

College, New Delhi, where I was working as a medical registrar, to Bombay to see Gandhi and others. Early in the morning of 9 August 1942, Mahatma Gandhi was arrested. It was decided that in his absence Kasturba Gandhi should address the public meeting that Mahatma Gandhi was to have addressed that afternoon. She was arrested as she was proceeding to the car that was to take her to the meeting. She was ailing and weak, and it was felt that she should not be allowed to court imprisonment all by herself. Whoever addressed the public meeting was expected to be arrested, and it was decided that I should do so and so court imprisonment in order to be with her. Thus, on the afternoon of 9 August 1942, Kasturba Gandhi, I and my eldest brother, Pyarelal, were arrested and taken to Arthur Road prison, Bombay. From there two days later Kasturba and I were removed to the Aga Khan Palace detention camp, at Poona, to be with Mahatma Gandhi. My brother was brought to the Aga Khan Palace detention camp about two months later after the death of Gandhi's secretary, Shri Mahadev Desai, who passed away after a week in the detention camp.

Our life in the detention camp was interesting and strenuous. I had to look after Kasturba and Gandhi himself, and also Mrs. Sarojini Naidu and Mirabehn (Miss Slade), who were semi-invalids, as well as the seventy-odd convict prisoners who were brought from Yarawda prison every day to attend to the various duties at the Aga Khan Palace.

The sudden death of Mahadev Desai at the end of the first week of our life in prison was followed, six months later, by Gandhi's twenty-one-day fast. Then Mrs. Sarojini Naidu fell ill and was released on health grounds. Kasturba's failing health grew worse and worse and at last she passed away in February 1944 in prison. This was followed by Gandhi himself going down with a severe attack of malaria which ultimately resulted in the release of all of us after twenty-one months of detention.

In November 1945 I met a young man who had been brought up in Gandhi's Ashram, had later gone abroad and had just returned after completing his studies, and we became engaged to be married. But the days that followed were full of hectic activity for Gandhi. There were pre-partition communal riots. I accompanied him to riot-affected Noakhali and was posted alone in a village, like other members of Gandhi's party. The plan was to infuse courage into the minority and to make the majority see their duty towards the minority. The medium of establishing contact in my case was my medical skill and knowledge. It was most successful. While each of us stayed in one village, Gandhi went on foot from village to village rousing the conscience of the people. I was terribly afraid to be by myself in a village from which most of the Hindus had fled to save their lives and where their houses lay in ruins. I overcame the fear by serving and trusting the Moslems, which in turn roused their better instincts.

In July 1947, I went with Gandhi to Kashmir. On his way back he left me in a refugee camp at Wah, near Rawalpindi in West Punjab, to reassure some 15,000 Hindus and Sikhs who had been brought there from their villages as a result of communal atrocities. They were convinced that as soon as the partition took place on 15 August, they would be butchered. They wanted to be evacuated to India. Gandhi said to them: 'Sushila will die before a hair of your heads is touched', and he left me to look after them. At first they treated it as a joke. But as danger came close, they clung to me. My only contribution was that I was not afraid, and courage, like cowardice, is infectious. I worked in the hospital in the day, and in the evening played with the children and talked with the adults. One day I was awakened and given the news that the camp was about to be attacked. I was very tired and had gone to bed early. I told them, they should let me know when the attacking mob arrived. Some one came and shook me: 'Look, women and children in the barracks are crying. You must go and comfort them.' I got up, but by the time I reached them, they had quietened down, thinking that if I was so unconcerned, there could be no real danger. There was no attack on our camp. If it had occurred, God only knows what my courage would have availed us.

I was in that camp on 15 August 1947, when India became free at the painful price of partition. Communal passions were unabated, but the butchery just before and after partition took every one by surprise. Gandhi had hoped the residents of Wah camp could be able to go back and settle in their own villages. Instead, they and millions of others had to be evacuated and a gigantic exchange of populations took place. After seeing the first train of evacuees from the camp leave, I was allowed to return to India.

I must cut short the narrative by omitting the story of the setting up of the new Indian government. Gandhi's Calcutta fast with its miraculous effect, when in the words of Lord Mountbatten 'our one man boundary force' did more to check the outbreak of communal riots in Calcutta than 50,000 troops in East Punjab. I must also skip Gandhi's fast in Delhi which purged many hearts of bitterness and communal hatred, his sending me to another 'lion's den' in Bahawalpur in Pakistan, and his assassination while I was on my way back from that assignment.

Lady Mountbatten was engaged in the recovery of abducted women at that time. I had done a lot of work for the Moslem refugees in the camps in Delhi. Lady Mountbatten put me in charge of the recovery of Moslem women abducted from East Punjab, while Mridula Sarabhai was put in charge of the recovery of Hindu and Sikh women abducted from the West Punjab. It was interesting work, but I must not take time over it.

After Gandhi's death, I felt I had to make a new beginning with life, and decided to go abroad for higher studies. Delay in my marriage owing to the various happenings mentioned above had led to an estrangement between me and my fiancé. My fiancé accused me of being attracted by the reflected glory around Mahatma Gandhi. I felt deeply hurt. The engagement was broken. In June 1948 I left for the United States on a United Nations fellowship to study maternal and child health and welfare services for six months. I visited Johns Hopkins University, and decided to take up a longer course of studies there on a WHO fellowship. I obtained a doctorate in public health early in 1950 in maternal and child health and welfare. I also studied pediatrics and problems of mental health.

After getting my doctorate, I spent three months on a speaking trip for the American Friends Service Committee. I was impressed by the deep interest of Quakers and other peace groups in the United States in Gandhi's teachings.

On my way back from the United States I spent about three months in visiting different medical centres in England and Scandinavian countries. I also visited Germany, France, the Netherlands, Switzerland and Italy, and participated in work camps and conferences of young people interested in the ideology of non-violence.

I returned to India on 1 October 1950, after two-and-a-half years abroad. Apart from refreshing my medical knowledge, the experience had enabled me to look inwards and become more truthful with myself, more humble and more tolerant.

I was made honorary secretary of the Leprosy Board of the Gandhi

Memorial Trust. I was already the honorary secretary of the medical section of the Kasturba Gandhi National Memorial Trust, and I travelled all over India in connexion with the work of these two trusts. In December 1950 I took over as the Chief Medical Officer at Farida-bad Refugee Township, and started working out a pattern of integrated preventive and curative medical service for the new township and the surrounding villages. In 1952 we had the first general elections. I was persuaded to stand for election to the Delhi State Assembly and on 17 March 1952 was sworn in as the Minister for Health, Rehabilitation and Transport in the state of Delhi.

Early in 1955 there were changes in the political set-up in Delhi. The Speaker of the Delhi Legislative Assembly was elected to be leader of his party and became the Chief Minister. I was elected to be Speaker, and functioned as such till Delhi State became a Union Territory, towards the end of 1956, in pursuance of the recommendations of the States Reorganization Commission.

In 1957 I was elected to Parliament from Jhansi. The Rani of Jhansi had played a leading role in the 1857 war of independence, and it was decided that the centenary of that legendary figure's death in battle should be commemorated by selecting a woman to represent Jhansi in the Indian Parliament. My special fields of interest are health, education, social welfare and external affairs. I work about twelve hours a day, dividing my time almost equally between Parliament, medicine and social service. I am a practising physician, and am president of several welfare organizations, three of which are All-India organizations.

I live with my mother and second brother and his family. My eldest brother married a Bengali schoolteacher, who had become a widow in her childhood, in 1951, and lives separately. In his early youth he had wanted to marry a niece of my aunt, but was not permitted to do so because of some caste difficulties. Twenty-five years later the social pattern had changed so radically that an interprovincial and inter-caste marriage with a widow was accepted without public comment. My second brother lost his first wife in 1943, while we were all in prison, as a result of her first child-birth. The baby girl was brought up by my mother. In 1947, he married for the second time a highly educated lady who was the headmistress of a girls' high school, and she gave birth to a boy on 6 February 1948, a week after Gandhi's death.

214

Thus, my grandfather had five sons; my father left two sons and one daughter; the progeny of these are the two children of my second brother. The girl goes to a Hindu college, and is studying in the pre-medical class with boys. No one has ever thought of objecting to co-education in her case, as they did when I was ready to go to college. Imperceptibly but surely a tremendous revolutionary change has come about in the thinking of the family and the social pattern of our life. Gone is the absolute obedience and the worshipful attitude of the wife towards her husband, good or bad. It is interesting to note how afraid my brother is to take an unannounced guest home for dinner. His wife insists on prior warning. Gone are *purdah* and protective confinement to the home as the sole sphere of activity for women, who are now taking their due place in public life without losing their sense of responsibility towards the home. Marriage is no longer indissoluble. Two of my cousins, a man and a woman, have had to seek divorce for very valid reasons. Gone is the prejudice based on caste and creed. We often have guests of all religions, communities and nationalities. My eldest brother had a woman sweeper belonging to the lowest caste of Untouchables as a cook, and I have had an excellent Moslem cook in my house. My mother no longer objects to these things. Gone are the ideas of segregation of sexes. Men and women are working together in all fields, and all over India co-education is being accepted as necessary and desirable. All avenues have been thrown open to women for education and for jobs.

The pace of life is becoming more and more hectic. I have written these lines on the plane and in the train. What the result of it all will be is difficult to say. We are already noticing an increased number of cases requiring mental health and hygiene facilities. Will the Indian woman be able to retain a balance between old values and new? This is a vital question. On that will depend the future of Indian culture, and I may add, of the Indian nation.

Three generations
in my Calcutta family

by JYOTIRMOYEE SARMA

My family has been settled in the city for four generations. We keep no ties with the village of our origin. My great-grandfather came to settle in north Calcutta in the middle of the nineteenth century. Calcutta as a city developed under the administration of the East India Company. At that time the European residents congregated near the administrative sections in the centre of the city, and the Indian population mostly resided in the northern sections. My great-grandfather was a man learned in the classical Sanskrit language, according to our caste profession, and taught in the Sanskrit College of Calcutta. He died when my grandfather, an only child, was only two years old. My great-grandmother was a very capable woman, and we have heard of the odds she conquered in bringing up grandfather. They had relatives living nearabouts, who had not given them as much care as could be expected of them in our society, and so my grandfather had little to do with them when he grew up. He availed himself of the formal school education of that time, learned the Sanskrit language, and studied Ayurvedha, the traditional science of Indian medicine. In time he became a renowned physician, and a prosperous householder. When he had fully established himself he severed all claims on the ancestral property in the village, leaving his share to go to his kinsmen. As a result, none of his descendants has ever seen the original village home.

My grandfather married in his late teens, and my grandmother was then about 10 years old. In those days child marriage was customary in our country. It was believed that a girl made good adjustments with her husband's relatives if she came to his house as a child. After the marriage ceremony she continued to live in her parental home until she came of age, but her in-law relations were decided for her before she developed the power of discrimination. My grandmother was a village girl. Her parental village was only thirty miles from Calcutta, but at that time the difference between the village and the city was so great that she was greatly awed at marrying into the city. Her feeling of love and respect for the city lasted throughout her life.

My grandparents had a large family characteristic of that time. They had eleven children, six girls and five boys. The house in north Calcutta was too small for the growing family so my grandfather built a house on the southern fringe of the city. This area has now been drawn into the greater Calcutta region. For a long time the family lived in both places. Since schools and colleges were far from the new house, a part of the family, particularly the boys attending schools and colleges, stayed in the north Calcutta house most of the time.

My grandmother took great pride in the size of her family and the number of kin relations that grew through their marriages. The older girls were married as children, and the younger girls were married in their teens according to the changing standards of the day. The boys brought in their wives one after another to fill the emptiness left by the girls. All these marriages were arranged by parents or other relatives of both sides. After marriage a girl was brought into a house filled with all her husband's kinfolk. After the first seven days' stay, most of which time was spent in the performance of rituals, the girl was returned to her parents' house. If she was under age it was expected that she would stay there for some years. But even after a girl became properly established in her husband's house and had many children, she went back to her parents' house periodically for some days or weeks as a rest from her duties in her husband's house. My grandmother's daughters used to come for these periodic visits with their children, so that our house was never without some of them as long as she lived. As the family grew, few rooms were left vacant, and my aunts were expected to alternate their visits.

The sons' wives were brought in one after another, according to their order of seniority. The older sons were married in their teens and the younger ones in their twenties. My father was the third son in the family and was married at 18 years of age, my mother being then 13. The age of marriage for both the sexes has been increasing steadily in our society until today no definite limit exists for the marriageable age. My brother married last year at the age of 30 and his

217

bride was then 21 years old. My grandfather felt obligated to provide for his sons and their wives as long as he was able to do so, and the occupational ability of the sons was not considered when the marriage was arranged. My father and two of my older uncles were college students when they married. My grandfather's status and prosperity were taken into account by the girl's parents when they negotiated the marriages, and the health and appearance of the boys and their future prospects were also considered.

My grandmother could read and write in the vernacular, and in her younger days spent much time in reading the sacred books. In later years she liked having others read to her. When I was a child she used to ask me to read to her during the noon recess, and I thereby went through the epics of the *Ramayana* and the *Mahabharata* with her at a very early age. When my grandmother's daughters were growing up, much disparity remained between the education of boys and girls in our society. While the boys received training in English in the schools and colleges, and expected to enter any of the modern professions, the girls received only rudimentary vernacular education in schools or at home. How much education it was proper for women to receive was the subject of much discussion in those days. My mother had completed the full course at the middle school near her father's house before she was married. In her day, although many high schools for girls existed in the city, the difficulty of transportation permitted only those living nearest the schools to attend them. Moreover, it was not expected that girls should complete high school and enter college. Girls were expected to devote their whole time to housework right after their marriage. The other daughters-in-law of my grandmother had formal education to a level similar to that of my mother.

In my generation the expectations concerning female education changed greatly. The possibility of going to college was held up to me as an ideal. It is now expected that girls should have some years of college education before they marry. My brother's wife had finished college when she was married. Before the second world war few girls were expected to make careers for themselves, and the education given to them was simply to prepare them for a better life. Education for the sake of education was the ideal, and families that could afford to do so were expected to give their girls the opportunities for acquiring as much knowledge as they had the intelligence and the desire to acquire. The advantages of having well-informed daughters and mothers were

218

much discussed. But after the war another great change came in our society in the role of the working women. With the partition of India, which caused thousands of men and women to leave their homes in search of new ones, and the increasing prices which came as the aftermath of war, many families found that they could no longer give their women the protection and security which had long been their due. The refugee girls groped their way into any occupation for which they were fitted. Since the new Constitution of India guaranteed equality of opportunity to both the sexes, many women of stable families also found it advantageous to increase their family income by applying for and attaining occupations suited to their educational levels. Teaching, which had always been open to women, is still the favourite for educated women of the upper- and middle-class groups. Office work, which does not carry as much prestige value as the academic field, is nonetheless now also employing a great number of women. And many women have now acquired distinction in professional and administrative capacities. Whereas fifteen years ago a family would be ashamed to let a girl go to work and supplement the family income, working women now arouse much admiration from general society. Women working before their marriages often keep their jobs even after they marry, and their kinfolk try to help with their household duties or look after their children so as to make their life easier. Obviously, married women working cannot give much time to their homes or raise many children.

The trend towards small families is most apparent in the educated levels of our society today, even when their women are not working. Whereas my grandparents had eleven children, my parents and their respective brothers had one to three children each. This change is associated with many factors. Upper- and middle-class people are conscious of the disadvantages of a high birth-rate, and openly discuss the situation. The responsibility of bringing up children is taken more seriously by the parents now than in the time of my grandfather. Children are expected to attain certain goals or fulfil certain wishes of their parents, and they are trained from their childhood to develop qualities suitable for the performance of certain selected occupations. In my grandfather's time, if a man had some property or a business he felt that he had made sufficient provision for the maintenance of his children, and that the older children would look after the younger ones. But now parents feel that equal attention needs to be given to each

219

child, and the emphasis on occupations based on many years of formal education has increased greatly. Moreover, even from my mother's time, women in our society have expressed the feeling that looking after children in their early years is very hard work, and they do not want to repeat the experience too often. Two or three children were thought to be sufficient, and when they came to a responsible age, the mothers expected to have some time for other interests. This feeling, that rearing children is very hard work and therefore it is not desirable to have too many of them, prevails among the young mothers of my time even when they have no other occupational pursuits.

My grandmother kept the full responsibility for the management of our household as long as she was alive. She would rise early in the morning and worship the household deity. In most Hindu houses there is a shrine where the image of a deity is kept and worshipped by members of the family. In our house the image of Shiva was installed by my great-grandmother. Usually the worshipping is done by some older person of the house, either male or female. It is compulsory for worship to be performed every day, and if no member of the family is competent to carry out this religious act, a priest may be employed instead. In our house, after my great-grandmother died, my grandmother performed the daily worship, and after her my father, but now we have a daily priest.

Women are expected to perform certain religious rituals on certain days throughout the year. Some are of lesser and others of greater importance. Some rituals are meant for married women, some for the unmarried, and some for widows. Again, many perform them spontaneously, and many may have to be prompted to do so. Since my grandmother was a religious person she performed as many of these rituals as she could, and inspired her daughters-in-law to do so. The performance of all sacred acts calls for fasting until the ceremony is over, and grandmother was much used to self-discipline.

We have religious days of greater or lesser significance throughout the year. Only one or two of these annual ceremonies were held in our house. Preparation for these ceremonies is expected to be made by the women, and knowledge of such preparations is expected of a good housewife. My grandmother was used to such work and taught her daughters-in-law to carry out these religious duties properly. After the women prepare the settings for the ceremonies, priests of higher orders perform and complete the religious rituals. Since religiousness

220

is on the decrease in most households in our society, the annual ceremonies have been stopped in our house. Even the ceremonies of lesser
significance are performed less and less, but whenever they do take
place we still talk about the way grandmother used to have them
done.

After her religious duties, my grandmother used to manage the kitchen. With so many people in the house, the preparation of household
meals was difficult and complicated. Shopping was done by servants
or by the male members of the household, as the housewives never
went to the market-places. My grandfather was very particular about
his food, and so he had the habit of going to the market himself whenever he could spare the time.

The house was cleaned by servants. They would go about their work
in a routine manner. My grandmother and later her daughters-in-law
would be busy first in planning the menu and then in directing the
cook. In a household as large as ours, different persons had different
likings for food, and often special dishes were prepared for particular
persons. An early lunch needed to be prepared for those going to
schools and colleges. After them the rest of the children would be
seated together and given their separate dishes. My grandfather would
have a special sitting for himself, and my grandmother and the other
women members would serve him with great care. After him the other
adult sons would take their food. In the last batch my grandmother
with her daughters and daughters-in-law sat together and would be
served by the cook. They would take a great deal of time to chat over
their food as all their work for the morning had ended. The dishes were
always cleaned by the servants, and the ladies and the children now
had their noon rest.

This noon recess was spent by the womenfolk in reading or sewing
or just sleeping. The summer noons are hot and drowsy, and the noon
break has long been a habit with our people. Modern working hours
do not permit the offices or the big stores to close during the day, but
many small shops remain closed at noon and open again in the afternoons and in the evenings. In my grandmother's time womenfolk did
their visiting in the late afternoons and the early evenings before the
work for the evening meal began. Then women were not expected to
go much farther than their immediate neighbourhood for their social
calls. Nowadays women are free to move about and are used to riding
in public vehicles, and their range of social contacts has increased.

221

They may go out or visit at any time suitable to themselves and do not simply regulate their outside social life to suit the routine of a large household.

My grandmother's evenings were spent again in directing the kitchen. Since all the daughters and the daughters-in-law helped, the occasion provided opportunities for entertainment as well as for work. The kitchen verandah used to take on the appearance of a ladies' club where, along with the kneading of bread, peeling of vegetables and preparation of sweet dishes, there was much merriment and laughter. This was the time when my grandmother was in her most jovial mood. Since the cooking proper was done by a paid cook, the women members did not go near the fireplace except when they wanted to prepare a special dish or cook something quickly. In most joint households the evening work is thus done in a pleasant atmosphere. This is lacking in the small nuclear families where the housewife looks on housework as a chore or lets the work be done by paid servants. When we were children, in order to keep their eyes on us, our mothers or grandmother used to ask us to sit near them and study or do our needlework, or provide them with some entertainment. We sat there until we had our meals, since as children we had the right to be first served.

The harmony of our joint household was best maintained while grandmother was alive. With so many persons in the same house discords were apt to arise. My grandmother had the personality to make amicable settlements. She died ten years before my grandfather, and with her death great changes occurred in the house. We all continued to live together, but the feeling of unity which prevailed at the time of my grandmother began to weaken. It takes time in every household for another female member to take the position of leadership. Usually the eldest of the daughters-in-law should now be the leader, but much depends on her personality. Subordination to her may not be as completely accepted by the others as it is to the mother-in-law, especially since with the latter's death the possibility of separate households comes in view. But as long as the male head of the house lives, the household needs to be kept together, and ours remained so with varying changes that came with marriages and deaths, and the children growing up, until the demise of my grandfather.

In our society each son has an equal right to his father's property unless the father deliberately denies him a share of it. Since with us wealth is maintained mostly in the form of land and houses, the division of property becomes a difficult affair. If the household has a common source of income then the members will continue to take their meals together as long as it is possible to do so amicably. The division of the income and property takes place gradually. This period of transition may continue for several years, and is the hardest in any household. In our house five years after the death of my grandfather the household was divided into four separate units. It should have been divided into five units, but the eldest of my uncles had settled elsewhere, and died without any children. So the four units were for each of the succeeding sons of my grandfather and their respective children.

Our meals are now cooked separately, and the rooms are so divided as to give the appearance of four separate apartments. But the house is still common property, and the kinship bonds prevail strongly. On ceremonial occasions, such as weddings, all members help one another. The feeling that the members should continue to hold the house together, and that the present generation of sons should bring their wives into the house, continues to hold sway. When my brother was married, the invitation cards were sent out in the name of my father's younger brother who is now the most senior male member in the house. All members participated in the rituals and the festivities that accompanied the wedding, and the new bride was accepted as a member of the entire house. I have two other male cousins, and it is expected that when they marry they will marry in the house in the same manner as my brother. With each succeeding generation the relationship between the members becomes more distant. There is no general rule on how many generations are needed to require that a house be held together. It depends entirely on the convenience and the wishes of the inhabitants.

A subject which I have not yet discussed is that of caste. Our society is divided into several groups which are ranked in higher and lower levels. The most basic feature of caste is marriage within the caste. My family belongs to the Brahman caste, and our boys and girls are expected to marry only into Brahman families. Occupation is also associated with caste. Thus, the traditional occupation of the Brahmans is to be engaged in learning and worshipping, and therefore the Brahman caste has the tradition of being superior to all other castes. The traditions regarding occupation are not necessarily maintained, nor is the superiority of the Brahmans acknowledged by the other castes in

223

the secular spheres of life. There are other castes in our society which rank high in secular status, and the members of several castes combine to form the secular upper class in our society. In the beginning of this article I have mentioned that my great-grandfather was a man learned in Sanskrit and taught Sanskrit, and this was in keeping with his caste profession. But my grandfather became a physician. My father became a physician of the modern school, and so did my brother. My uncles were and are all engaged in some modern profession. No sentiment pertaining to caste is felt in the selection of an occupation. In my family it is expected that everybody should be educated to a certain standard and maintain the professional level of the family. For marriage, however, the feeling still prevails that one should not marry outside of the Brahman caste.

In my grandmother's time marriages between members of different castes were not at all recognized. When my grandmother was a little girl intercaste marriage was introduced in a new sect of the Hindus called the Brahmo Samaj. Some of the educated people of that time revolted against the inequalities of the caste system. Basing themselves on a re-interpretation of the Hindu religion, they attempted to form a casteless society by promoting intercaste marriage and other social changes. Since marriages between castes were not tolerated at all in the traditional society, a secular marriage act was passed in 1872. By this act marriage necessitated a statement by the marrying parties that they did not belong to any of the existing religious faiths. Since caste was still a significant part of the Hindu social order, such secular marriages between castes made those who contracted them suffer from social ostracism, and the Brahmo Samaj became a distinct group on its own.

One of the greatest changes between my grandmother's time and mine is the acceptance of intercaste marriage in Hindu society at large. Until 1954 intercaste marriages could be performed only under the act of 1872. As women became free to attain higher education and entered the occupational fields in greater numbers, they were thrown more and more into contact with men. It was normal that many of them would want to marry the men they met, and in many instances the men would be of other castes. Such marriages were never accepted by their families with enthusiasm, but the greater independence of women and the greater frequency of such marriages began to force the issue. At the time of the marriage a formal renunciation of all

224

religions was made, in accordance with the provision of the act of 1872, but it was taken very lightly, and the marrying parties did not consider themselves to be non-Hindus. As the greater Hindu society began to treat intercaste marriages with less and less prejudice, the sects which were founded with the purpose of encouraging such marriages, such as the Brahmo Samaj, gradually lost significance. Finally, in 1955, the Hindu Code Bill was passed by the Union Government. This bill gave recognition to intercaste marriage among Hindus. In secular marriages the declaration of having no religion was no longer necessary, and marriages performed with sacred rituals in the traditional manner but between members of different castes were held legal. Formerly the priests used to refuse to solemnize intercaste marriages. Even now the greater number of priests may object to doing so, but whenever such a marriage is planned someone can always be found who is willing to perform the ceremony.

Intercaste marriage with religious ceremonies takes place only when the families of both the parties are agreeable to the marriage, as the religious ceremonies demand that certain acts be performed by certain family members. Unless the families are willing to participate only secular marriages are possible, and the pair may have to suffer some difficulties until the families are reconciled to the situation. These days everybody expects that after the marriage the families will be at some time reconciled. In my household no intercaste marriage has as yet taken place, but in my mother's house one such marriage took place recently. Although it was known that the young couple were marrying of their own volition, arrangements were made as if it were a negotiated marriage, and invitations were sent out accordingly. Only members of three families did not come as against members of fifty or so other families who did come. Most of these guests did not want their children to marry in other castes, but they admitted that since such marriages have now become common in our society they had no objection to witnessing them.

Another great change that has been introduced in our society since 1955 concerns women's inheritance. In my grandmother's time, and even before that, women were expected to lead dependent lives. A woman who had many relations to look after her held herself to be fortunate. Parents expressed their concern for her by giving her in marriage to a family with the means of keeping her well. Since sons inherited their father's property, girls inherited only when they had no

225

brothers. Marriage offered complete security to a girl, and as her formal ties with her parents were broken at marriage it was customary to give her a dowry including clothes, jewellery and money. The amount of the dowry depended on the ability of the parents. The jewellery was completely her personal property, and her husband had no right over it unless she gave it to him. Much value was, therefore, put on the possession of valuable jewellery by the women, as it could be exchanged for ready money in times of need. It is much easier to sell jewellery than it is to sell land or any other property.

The equality of women in educational and occupational fields brought about the feeling that the property rules should also be changed. In the new India, where adult franchise for both the sexes was ensured in the constitution, discrimination in the rights of inheritance could not be tolerated. The new code passed in 1955 gave girls the right to some share of their father's property. The high valuation given to the integrity of the joint household in our country, however, produced a dilemma. In the joint household the property is maintained by a group of brothers. If the sisters take out certain portions of property belonging to a joint household, the institution would naturally be disrupted. Certain clauses are, therefore, added in the new code giving preferential rights to male heirs if the property is maintained as a joint household.

The effects of the new laws are still to be seen. Girls generally desire a share of their father's property only when their husbands are not as well-off as their parents. Otherwise a married woman may ask what she would do with a room in her father's house when she has so much of her own. Sentiment for the maintenance of ancestral dwellings is so great that under ordinary circumstances a family would not like to sell a house and divide the cash only to give the girls their share of the property's value. On the other hand, the giving of valuable jewellery to a girl at the time of her marriage is so much a part of the ceremony that up to now no family would think of denying a girl such gifts with the feeling that she would inherit some share of the joint household property instead. Jewellery completes the bride's wedding costume and it is not only given by the parents, but by all relations and friends and from members of the family that she is being married into, as jewellery is meant to convey good wishes at the time of marriage. Married last year, my brother's wife received as much jewellery as my grandmother or my mother received in their time. In the long run therefore, if girls are to inherit equally, the giving of dowries would become a problem, for girls would have a double advantage. Legislation to stop dowries and expensive gifts at the time of marriage was lately being considered in the Indian Parliament, but as there was much doubt as to how to execute such a law, the matter has been put aside for the present. Actually, such changes can come about only when the people themselves introduce the changes, and not by the passing of laws. So even though laws have been passed to give women rights to their father's property, I would say that not much change has taken place in this field between my grandmother's time and mine, although my mother and I can vote whereas my grandmother could not.

This short sketch may help to show certain major changes that have taken place in our society in the last one hundred years. The nature of our joint household was much the same as that of other households in our society, and the changes we faced were experienced by all. I may point out again that the greatest changes have come about in the political, educational and occupational spheres, less in marriage and family relations, and the least in property inheritance.

All social changes are interrelated, and it is to be expected that changes in one element of society would necessarily be accompanied by changes in the other elements. Changes come most easily in matters which are least sentimentally evaluated by the society. The voting rights of women are accepted without any hesitation. The attainment of higher education by girls was easier than their entrance into occupational fields where they come into contact and competition with men. Yet the undertaking of careers by women was more easily accepted than their selection of their own husbands and their taking the initiative for their own marriage. Even now individuals marrying of their own choice try to make it look as if their families negotiated the marriage for them, and a girl marrying of her own will does not normally expect to live away from her husband's kinfolk. As a matter of fact, it is because she passes so completely into her husband's family that the need for equal rights of inheritance has not been as hardly pressed as it would have been otherwise. A woman still gets a great deal of protection from her husband's family members if she becomes a widow. And then if she has no one to look after her in her husband's house, she can come to live in her father's house as in the past. In the past it has often been that if a woman inherited property, because she had no brothers, she looked on it as belonging to her sons rather than to herself, and she may still feel like this even now if she inherits through the new laws. The security of property rights is needed mainly when a women has to make her place in the world all alone. In the past it has been the lot—and the good fortune—of the Indian woman to have a great many kin relations; what she may have to face in the future we can only wait and see.

Indonesia

Area: 1,491,562 square kilometres.

Population: 89,600,00 (estimated 1959).[1]

Recent history: 1942-45—Japanese occupation; 1945—Independence proclaimed; 1949—Netherlands Government transfers sovereignty to the Republic of Indonesia.

Citizenship: Men and women have equal rights.

Religion: Islam; there are also over 4 million Christians, smaller groups of Hindus (especially on Bali) and Buddhists, and a number of pagan tribes.

Inheritance and family patterns: Customary rules of patrilineal and matrilineal inheritance are both found in different parts of Indonesia, but the predominant form of traditional inheritance does not discriminate between the sexes. Patrilocal and matrilocal extended families are found in the patrilineal and matrilineal areas respectively; elsewhere—and predominantly—nuclear families are usual. Islamic law gives a man's daughters the right to inherit property to half the value of a son's inheritance, and secures a life interest of one-third to widows.

---

1. Latest official estimate of population as published in *The U.N. Population and Vital Statistics Report, October 1960.*

The respective roles
of men and women in Indonesia

by Hurustiati Subandrio

INTRODUCTION

Undoubtedly there have been marked changes in the relative roles of men and women in Indonesia during the past three generations. For lack of space I shall have to limit myself in my account to the situation in Java, taking my own family as an example. I shall relate my grandmother's, my mother's and my own life, bearing in mind that there are thousands like ourselves in Java.

I cannot go beyond the island of Java, for family systems in the other islands of our multi-island country are very different. Even in one island there are found totally different social structures, family set-ups and religions, appertaining to different geographical areas. For instance, in the island of Sumatra we have the matrilineal Moslem Minangkabau community in Central Sumatra, the patrilineal Christian Batak community in some parts of North Sumatra and the patrilineal Moslems in South Sumatra and in Acheh in the north. Although in Java there are some 2 million Christians and Catholics among its population of about 60 million, these followers of the Christian faith live scattered amongst the rest of the population. Social conditions are very much alike among all religious groups in Java, except for the people of foreign origin, as for instance Chinese and Eurasians.

As for my own relatives, I am not able to say that they give a picture typical of the life of the millions in Java, as they belong to the upper strata. Political and economic changes have affected them as much as they have all layers of the population. The main change has been the emancipation of Indonesia from colonial status into an independent nation.

My grandmother's life was based on ideas of education and social behaviour which prevailed at the end of the last century, the most glorious period of Dutch colonization. Although she lived two-thirds of her life in the twentieth century, she was a product of her upbringing, and her ideas belonged to a period before our modern times. My mother's upbringing was that of an enlightened colonial period of the years before and during the first world war. My own youth coincided with a period of tremendous Westernization in the twenties and thirties. During this period the nationalist movement gained more and more ground. Political parties, labour, youth and women's organizations sprang up in rapid succession in spite of the acts of repression on the part of the colonial government. The first Indonesian political party was founded in 1908, clearly with the ultimate aim of the country's independence. About that time, too, started the other movements and organizations, gaining maturity in the twenties and thirties.

Major social upheavals were the result of these movements, governing the lives of the individuals of my grandmother's, my mother's and my own generation. Clearly the three generations belong to periods with quite different sets of ideas. The upbringing and education of each of them illustrate this statement. However, the family systems have not been affected in a drastic way, although some influences are discernable. The main reason is that in Java for many centuries the system of the simple family has been the rule. Here there is no question of breaking up large families into smaller units as in so many other areas. In such a simple family the specific roles of men and women are not tremendously affected by the changes of time.

Nevertheless, there are changes in the ideas governing these roles, which only insiders can explain and expound upon.

EDUCATION CHANGES

My mother's mother was a daughter of the chief judge of a province in East Java and she was therefore essentially a townswoman. Her early youth was in the seventies when practically no girls were sent to school, only boys. Sons of the gentry attended governmental schools to provide for the need of personnel in the civil service of the Netherlands East Indies Government. Whatever education a girl had at that time had to be given in the home as it was not considered proper for

231

a girl of the upper classes to leave the house before marriage. She should stay indoors and not be seen in the street. Very rarely my grandmother and her sisters were allowed to go out, and then very elaborate preparation had to be made as they were only allowed to leave the house in a carriage and accompanied by older women and servants.

My grandmother was not taught the Latin script, but the Arabic, which went together with the art of reading and reciting the Koran. A religious teacher came every afternoon to teach the daughters and sons of the chief judge. In the morning when my great-uncles went to school, my grandmother and her sisters learned housekeeping, cooking, dressmaking and sewing. These were considered essential to make the girls good housewives. It seemed at that time that only one career was open to girls, that of becoming a married woman. Apart from these first subjects, my grandmother was also taught fine needlework, crochet, knitting, tapestry and, above all, *batik* (wax drawing on cloth). She had to go through all the elaborate procedures of preparing the cloth or *batik* until it was a finished dyed product with beautiful traditional designs, ready to be worn by men and women as an ankle-length skirt. For all these fine arts and handicrafts several teachers were engaged, who visited the girls every day in my great-grandfather's home.

The girls married before they were 20. Grandmother's first husband died and, as a young widow with more freedom than an unmarried girl, she began to enjoy economic independence for the first time, as she started quite a *batik* business of her own. She employed women who prepared the cloth for her and she earned a good living from the sale of the finished products. Later she remarried, and gave birth to my mother at the beginning of the twentieth century. Her second husband was thus my grandfather. A district commissioner in the East Indies Government, he introduced new ideas regarding the education of girls as he actually sent my mother every day to school. He changed my grandmother's life in that she now had to perform her duties as wife of a district chief. She had to deal with local people, with townspeople, amongst whom were my grandfather's superiors, and also with Dutch officials who admired her skill in cooking European food.

My mother's schooling marked a new era in the life of the women of my family; it was the beginning of the modern era, in which girls were required to read books, magazines and newspapers in order to keep informed of the trend of society and the world in general. My mother was also taught a foreign language—Dutch, as she went to a Dutch school. It was expected that even more than her mother she would have to deal with foreigners—Dutch in those days. The advantage of the foreign language was that there were Dutch books in abundance, which in the Malay or Javanese language was not the case.

Clearly the ideal for girls in those days was still marriage, but a marriage in which husband and wife would share responsibilities in the home and in society. The wife's part was no longer limited to household duties; she would take a greater part in public life, but still simply as a wife. For that purpose my mother's education was arranged. She married at quite an early age, when the first world war was still raging over Europe. Already in those days she was thinking of studying for a career, she wanted to become a doctor, but the ties of custom and tradition were too strong for her and she had to consent to the early marriage.

For my mother's daughters, however, the road was free for them to choose any career they wished. My education and schooling were the full preparation of a career woman. Marriage was neither encouraged nor discouraged. My two sisters chose marriage, and broke off their studies before reaching the university, but I had an education both for a profession and for marriage. I married three years before I finished my training as a doctor and graduated after the birth of my son. As a young girl I had to learn household duties as well, but not as a principal item, only additionally. I have some knowledge of cooking, dressmaking and needlework. I was told then that I had to prepare myself for a meagre income and for not having any servants. As it was, I considered my training as a doctor of the first importance, although everyone, including myself, was pleased when I became engaged to be married to a medical man. The next step was to prepare myself for a career as a married woman. It did not occur to any of the family that I should give up my career for marriage. Everybody was interested to see how I would manage all my duties, but no one expected that I should drop any one of them.

In my own education, as also in my husband's, the most important new factor was entering the university. University life was largely responsible for our development into political leaders. A great deal of our thinking was spent on political issues, on the national independence movement, on social progress and development, and so forth. I joined students' organizations, students' movements and took part

233

in political debates and discussions. I visualized a scope of life which was entirely strange to my mother. Her world was still her family and her life was devoted to her family. Beyond that, though she knew of it by reading the newspapers, by the wireless and by what was told to her by others, life held no interest for her. She took no part in organizations or movements, and had no other ties with her fellow countrymen apart from the ties of blood relationship and friendship, besides being the wife of a high-ranking official. She had no ties which could be called ideological bonds.

In my family the latter element was only introduced by the generation which was young in the late thirties, when I was at the medical school. There was then a general trend in Indonesian society towards national unity and even beyond that. It coincided with international interests, when the sons and daughters of Indonesia tried to find their country a place in the international world. The development into nationhood went together with defining Indonesia's place internationally. There was a growing sense of unity among the different ethnic groups of the country, with the object of gaining national independence by the strength of unity. University life gave an excellent opportunity for students from different areas to mix and mingle in a friendly atmosphere. It was also the opportunity to know each other's culture. Bonds of friendship were established between many ethnical groups, a feature that was not known in my mother's youth and upbringing.

In short, my own education, as compared to my mother's, gave scope to my development into a married career woman with national and international aspirations. On the other hand, my mother's life and education ensured the best service a married woman could give to her family, her husband, who needed an understanding wife in his own career, and her children, who needed her understanding for their own education and development.

My uncles and parents-in-law also have given an education to both sons and daughters to prepare themselves for a profession. The general idea has been that women as well as men can go to work to earn their living, and that marriage should be entirely a voluntary matter. Amongst my cousins and sisters-in-law it is not frowned upon if any of them remains unmarried because she prefers the life of a career woman to that of a married woman. This was not so when my mother and aunts were young; they were expected to be married in any case.

234

The development has been favourable to women, as nowadays in advanced circles girls are given equal educational opportunities with boys. They also enjoy a fair competition with boys. During my school-days, however, when a family had limited means the boys were chosen in preference to the girls to be sent away to school, even when the girls showed greater ability. Even today, as recent university attendance figures show, in a great many families it is still regarded as more essential to prepare boys for the better jobs than girls. Girls' attendance in any branch of the university rarely exceeds 25 per cent, and figures between 10 and 15 per cent are fairly common. It can be said of the women graduates, however, that a very high percentage amongst them take up a job and continue to work after marriage. If some leave their jobs for marriage, they make themselves useful by joining and leading women's or youth organizations or doing other voluntary work.

MOTIVATIONS OF EDUCATIONAL CHANGES

It is obvious that educational changes have been brought about so as to suit the changed role of women in the family. My grandmother was entirely a housewife. She was wife, mother and grandmother; and the role assigned to her in the three capacities was mainly that of chief of the household. My grandfather was completely free from household duties, and in many ways ignorant of them. His main duty was to earn for the family and to perform duties in public life. When my grand-mother attended a public function, it was in the capacity of wife of my grandfather, and in most cases they arrived together. Later in life she very often went alone, especially to family gatherings such as wedding parties and funerals. In the house, however, she supervised all the work to such an extent that she even put out my grandfather's clothes to change daily. He never saw the inside of the wardrobe.

As for my mother, these duties were performed to even greater per-fection. My mother was impressed with what grandmother taught her, and took her as an example. Besides, she went to a Javanese and later to a Dutch school, so she knew a great deal more of the world. The result was that in household affairs my father was even more ignorant than my grandfather and also more dependent on mother's assistance. For instance, he does not put the food on his own plate at table, but mother gives him the best bits and pieces. In my grandmother's day, as she could not read the Roman script, grandfather paid the household

235

bills, but this duty now is also left to my mother, as she went to school and can read perfectly.

My mother's public functions are not confined to family gatherings, but also extend to civic receptions and public meetings. Before my father's retirement my mother, who was the first lady of some half-a-million people—my father held the post of chief administrator in a regency or county—had also to perform the role of women's leader in the area. For a few years she had to preside at women's meetings, especially during the war under the Japanese occupation. As for the education of the children, she had to look after them when they were small, and when they went away to school she had to look after all their needs and comply with their wishes. She sent postal orders for paying school fees and for board and lodging for the children, and ordered books for them. In short, my mother's duties as wife, mother and head of the household were carried out in the best possible way. One thing, however, she never did, and that was to earn money. That part was left entirely to my father.

As for the younger generation, the change in women's role in the family has been fundamental. The duties and rights of men and women, of boys and girls in the family, have been drawn closer to each other and made nearly equal. I say 'nearly' as differences still remain, although they are not fundamental. The bulk of household duties still remains with the women as does the main money-earning duty with the men. But husband and wife can do the same tasks. No more, for instance, does the wife keep the husband's wardrobe. She sees that clothes are cleaned and mended, but she does not look after the daily change of clothes. The kitchen is still the wife's department. Although her husband is kept out of it, yet the boys enter it freely and in many cases have to prepare their own breakfast, though not their midday meal. Boys as well as girls are taught to set the table and to attend to visitors. After lunch or dinner, they are taught to help in putting plates and dishes away. They are both taught to look after their own clothes, as for instance to give them to the washerwoman, and to make their own beds. In short, boys and girls are taught to share household duties and to help their parents in the house. Sometimes they have to play with little brothers or sisters and keep them busy. Formerly, when both my grandmother and my mother were young, only girls were taught all that.

When my husband was young, although girls were already allowed

236

to study for a career, the boys were still kept away from household duties and lessons. Therefore, my husband and my sisters' husbands can help very little. While the wives also go out to work, the responsibility for the house and family still remains mainly with them. But we are training our sons to share all the duties with our daughters so that they can be of greater assistance to us and to their future wives.

In Indonesian society today more and more women are taking up positions not only in the towns but also in the countryside. In many families it is a necessity, for the salary they earn is badly needed. Women continue to work after marriage, most of them to keep their income, but in many cases for the work itself because being simply a housewife is not interesting enough. Equal pay for equal work in all government services and in most of the business houses helps a lot.

A job, combined with the mounting difficulty of obtaining good servants, makes life very busy for the working mother. This is why all the children, boys as well as girls, are trained to help in the household. It is still possible, however, for the average family to get servants, although the number is limited. As apart from a job there are a great many outside activities in which a woman can take part, the household tends to become more simplified than a generation or so ago. Time spent on cooking is limited and many families order their food from caterers. From three to five different dishes are sent home every day. The rice which is cooked at home does not take long and does not need elaborate preparations. This arrangement saves labour and the time spent in shopping, cooking and washing up.

A woman with a good income of her own is regarded as a good match in marriage. This is shown, for instance, in the popularity enjoyed by trained midwives who are licensed to have a private practice. The government is having difficulty in their appointment as they soon get married and are allowed to follow their husbands wherever they are placed.

But Indonesia is still essentially a man's world. For all the growing desire on the part of women to take part in all aspects of public life and public service, men still play the most important roles outside the home. The most important jobs are still occupied by men, although the number of women in high posts is growing. The idea prevails that if a man is of high position his wife enjoys the same status, but a woman of position does not raise her husband's status. This shows that in fact there is still no true equality between men's and women's rights.

237

Equality will only finally come after years of experience of women in public service.

It will certainly come, since the equality of girls and boys is now impressed on the mind of youth from early childhood. Husbands and wives, men and women, will develop comradeship and an understanding between themselves, so that differences in the social status of the sexes will become vaguer and vaguer. In the end, the idea that the husband should head the family and not the wife, will go by the board. When more and more mothers earn the income of the family, more and more the idea will gain ground that the wife's position may also be decisive in raising her husband's status in public life.

CHANGE IN SIZE AND LOCATION OF THE FAMILY

I mentioned before that the simple family system prevails in Java. Married sons and daughters live in their own houses and rarely stay together with either the wife's or the husband's parents. Widows, as did my grandmother, return to their parental homes, especially when they are still considered eligible for remarriage. Although my grandmother had an independent income from her *batik* business, as a widow she stayed in her parents' home together with her two young children. At present, however, widows or divorced women often prefer to stay in their own houses with their children if they have an income of their own.

In many cases the size of the family is today slightly reduced, at the wish of the wives. It is obvious that with so many duties a modern wife is most reluctant to bear many children. Family planning is known to and practised only amongst the most advanced families. My grandmother had only two sons and one daughter on account of her prolonged widowhood. Her sons and daughter, already in the twenties, went to see the doctor about family planning methods. But, as mentioned above, only very few families even knew about the possibility of family planning, still less practised it at that time. At present, most advanced families practise family planning in the big cities where the means are more easily available.

With a single exception none of my first cousins, brothers and sisters has more than five children. By contrast, one of my mother's two brothers had six children and the other seven, while my mother also bore seven. Another reason for the younger generation's smaller

238

families is that the age of marriage of both men and women has gone up recently because of longer studies, the fashion for girls to take up a job and for other economic reasons. One and two children are considered 'too few', three are 'comfortable', four just 'nice' and five are already 'a great many'. There is no doubt that with women going out to work, and with the spread of education, the development of industrialization and urban areas, family planning is now practised in ever-growing circles.

As for the location of the family, all my grandmother's sisters and brothers got married and stayed with their families in the same town, in East Java—Pasuruan—which was my father's regency capital. They are all dead now and are all buried in the same family graveyard belonging to the old chief judge, their father. My father was married into the family and came from a nearby town as a young official of the civil service. Now, however, as a retired regent, he and my mother with my two young brothers have settled in Bandung, a town in West Java, some 600 miles away from Pasuruan. It so happened that the widow of one of my two uncles settled in Bandung also. My grandmother's children and grandchildren have all left Pasuruan and most of the grandchildren have now settled in West Java, in Djakarta and Bandung. I can count in Djakarta five of my grandmother's grandchildren, all married to men and women from different parts of Java, and even from Sumatra. In Bandung two grandchildren are studying at the university, while my two young brothers are there also at the senior high school. One of my two sisters, herself a mother of five boys, followed her husband when he was appointed to the Bandung area, where she also made sure of getting a place herself as a teacher in one or two high schools. That makes a total of ten out of my grandmother's fifteen grandchildren who are still alive. The other five grandchildren remain in East Java and are not likely to move out of the area. It can be said that the main reason for the trek to West Java of my parents, my aunts, my cousins, my brothers, my sisters and myself has been because my generation has been called upon to serve in the central government in Djakarta. Because of that both my parents and aunt have settled in Bandung so as to be near us. Without Independence and the setting up of the national government, it is likely that my mother's and my own generation would have stayed in East Java, where our roots are stronger.

However, the removal has not affected my brothers, sister, cousins and myself in any serious way at all. My generation and the generation after mine have become very 'Indonesian' in our way of life, in our ideas and contacts with people, and we have left a great many of our more parochial East Javanese characteristics behind. We mix with a great many people from many different parts of the country, and come in close contact with customs and ways of life which are typical of different parts of Indonesia, and often very different from those of our own original locality. In fact we also intermarry with other groups. For my parents and my aunt, who have settled in Bandung where a different language is spoken from their own, the adaptation to local conditions has taken much longer. In the beginning they felt lonely and missed their friends in East Java very much. But in a few years this difficulty was overcome, as their outlook became wider and they made new friends.

It is quite clear from my family's records that it is my generation that has taken the leading and also the stabilizing part in the country's political upheaval towards independence and full nationhood. My generation has to look both backwards and forwards. Not only must we take care of the generation before, reassuring them and helping them to adjust, but we have also to educate the young so as to prepare them for their future tasks. In all this women are making a great contribution, for they can make many things smooth and easy, in the home as well as in public life and service.

THE LEGAL STATUS OF WOMAN: THEIR RIGHTS IN MARRIAGE
ACCORDING TO CUSTOM AND RELIGION

Today Indonesian women enjoy full political and educational rights according to the Constitution of the Republic of Indonesia. They can vote and are eligible for the various organs of the State. In 1955 the first general elections were held for Parliament and the Constituent Assembly. Quite a large number of women were elected for both Houses, and a great number turned up at the polls, even more than the number of men.

Educational rights are made good use of. The only restrictions are, as I explained before, economic restrictions, when a family is not able to pay for the education of the girls. Governmental and other grants are helpful. In general, girls are judged by their ability to learn and to work and not by their sex.

240

In local elections there is also great enthusiasm on the part of the women. The main governmental bodies include women members as, for instance, the Parliament, the People's Consultative Assembly, the National Planning Council, the Supreme Advisory Council. In many cases the percentage of women members is high in comparison with Western standards. For instance, there are 30 women members in Parliament out of a total membership of 270.

The civil rights of women are not yet embodied in a civil code, although many women leaders have pressed for this. Great difficulties have yet to be overcome in establishing such a code because Indonesia consists of so many different ethnic groups, each with its own set of laws and customs. In Java, civil rights are still governed by Moslem law (except for the Christian and other groupings who do not adhere to the Moslem faith). Women leaders have pressed for at least a marriage law, in which the rights and dutes of both partners in marriage would be laid down. The fact that, in the absence of a progressive marriage law and a civil code which sufficiently protect their rights, the Moslem law prevails, is disliked by many women.

The reasons for this are several. In the first place Moslem law allows polygynous marriages up to a maximum of four wives. Polygyny of this kind still exists in Java, but it is not important in educated circles. In my family, for example, there has been no case of polygyny since at least the time of my great-grandmother (of the generations before that I have no information). But that it still exists at all is very hard for most of our women leaders to accept. Another factor is that the right of inheritance according to Moslem law is not the same for boys as for girls. Boys inherit twice as much as girls. Yet another is that Moslem law gives greater powers to husbands in repudiating their wives than to wives in divorcing their husbands. Yet in spite of these disadvantages, Javanese women do enjoy certain rights in marriage which are not always even now accepted in the West. In the case of divorce, for instance, each of the separating parties takes his or her own property which they brought to the marriage, while what they have acquired together during the marriage they share equally. The custody of the children in such cases is discussed together by the separating parties; as a rule sons go with the father and daughters with the mother. These advantages are ascribable to local Javanese custom rather than to Moslem law itself. But even Moslem law holds one advantage over some Western codes, for a wife is permitted to own property and engage in financial dealings of her own without let or hindrance of any kind. Nevertheless, many of our leaders today are looking forward to the passing of a truly progressive marriage law as at least a preliminary to the establishment of a civil code for the country as a whole.

This would, too, be in keeping with the general secularizing of life in Indonesia today. In general, it can be said that with the introduction of modern school education, religious instruction is now very much neglected, at least in very many families. My grandmother, for example, had to study with a religious teacher, and for a short time my mother also, but my generation has had no or at most very little religious teaching. The rites, are, however, still observed carefully at the main events of one's life: at circumcision for boys, at marriages, at funerals; and in addition there are also local ceremonies to be observed at child-birth, marriage and death. Secularization has not meant the disappearance of religion, but certainly it no longer dominates our education, and most of our women leaders look forward to the day when it will no longer dominate our marriage laws either.

Laos

Area: 236,800 square kilometres.

Population: 2,000,000 (1955 estimate).

Recent history: 1954—Complete independence from French Union established.

Citizenship: Men and women have equal rights.

Religion: Theravada (Hinayana) Buddhism; there are small groups of others and a number of pagan hill tribes.

Inheritance and family patterns: Customary rules of inheritance do not discriminate between the sexes. Nuclear families predominate, the new home being set up near the bride's parents.

243

Yesterday and today in Laos:
a girl's autobiographical notes

by BANYEN PHIMMASONE LÉVY

I never had the happiness of knowing my paternal grandparents or my maternal grandmother, nor do I remember very much about my maternal grandfather. He was born in Vientiane, of one of the oldest and most distinguished families; I remember him as an old man with a shaven head, always dressed in white,[1] and bent double over his stick when he moved about, either to go to the temple, or to visit his many children and grandchildren. I had the greatest respect for him and credited him with the possession of unusual powers.

In this connexion I have a very clear memory of him which goes back to a particular experience of my childhood. I must have been 7 or 8 years old at the time; I went about barefoot as did all my brothers and sisters, and indeed all the people of Laos.[2] Our house, in the Inpèng district, was built on piles, but my father had built a num-

---

1. White is the usual mourning dress which women, in particular, wear for a short period—three days, a week or a month. It is also worn by 'white ladies'—women, generally no longer young, often widows, who have vowed themselves to the Buddhist religious life. Some old people dress in white even while continuing to live in their own homes, as a sign of religious fervour.

2. Most Laotians, and especially children, commonly go barefoot. Some priests of a certain rank may wear sandals, but do not always do so. Princes and princesses, when adult, and high officials wear shoes. In our home, only my father wore shoes to go to his office, for the official dress was the *sampot* (sarong) of the traditional colour, a white shirt and shoes. My mother, like some other wives of officials, had a pair of black heel-less slippers, and I have seen her wear another pair, imported from Cambodia, of red velvet embroidered with gold thread. Nowadays, although many Laotions still go barefoot, and children always do, most of the younger men and women in the towns wear shoes out of doors.

ber of stone houses which he let to Chinese and Vietnamese people who were not used to living in the Laotian style of house.[1] There were some of these at the back of our house, two of which were let to a Chinese family who used them for distilling and marketing rice alcohol. These apartments opened on to a covered concrete verandah. A footbridge gave access to it from the road, for all the roads in Vientiane have gutters at their sides to carry off the rain-water. One evening, just at nightfall, I was hopping about on this verandah. I used to play a game while I walked, which was to look on the ground and step on anything I saw, such as fallen leaves, bits of wood, pebbles, etc. That evening, as I was hopping along, I saw in the shadow a black stick and quickly put my foot on this unexpected object. The thing forthwith nipped my foot, and I shrieked with pain as the centipede's venom penetrated the wound. My young servant Pion (she later became the mistress of a French administrator) picked me up and carried me back to the house. I screamed for my grandfather as if he were the only person who could give me relief from this awful agony. They sent a message to his house on the other side of the Inpèng temple, and after a few minutes—they seemed endless to me—he came, bent over his stick and painfully climbing the stairs. At the sight of him I felt that I was saved and could bear the pain. He took my hands, blew[2] on my injured foot and told the servants to give it a steam bath. I don't know exactly what was in the pan, the steam from which was to cure my foot, but I remember that they put in a lot of sand. My grandfather stayed with me till I fell asleep, and the next day, though my foot was still very much swollen, the pain was much less severe. My grandfather came to see me again and the sight of him was a great comfort to me.

I have no other memories of him. I know that he was a merchant and dealt in elephants, and that he had been very wealthy. He had seven children, four daughters and three sons. My mother's eldest sister, the only one still living besides her younger brother, used to

---

1. Laotian houses, even those built of stone or concrete, are raised on piles. But of recent years, in the towns, European-style houses and even flats have been built, and houses on piles are gradually going out of use except in the country districts.

2. Healers blow on a sick person, or on the affected part, if there is one, while uttering, almost inaudibly, the appropriate magic formula. Most men know some of these formulae, at least the simpler ones. There are very few women healers.

245

tell us that in her father's house they never bothered to count their money, for the storehouse[1] was so full of it that they measured it by basketfuls. I think myself that it was cowrie shells that were counted in that way, for the currency at that time consisted of silver and copper bars, coins, and also cowries. Personally, I have no recollection of such abundance.

My aunts and uncles lived very simply in their separate houses grouped around my grandfather, and they saw each other almost every day, and often helped each other in case of need. My grandfather owned several plots of land, and as his children married he gave a plot to each one.[2]

I never knew a really wealthy Laotian; everyone lived in a quiet way with his own house and storehouse, and his own rice plantation which he cultivated with the help of his children. Those who were better off might have two or three rice-fields and employ peasants to cultivate them, but they did not make large incomes. They also owned tenements which they let to Chinese who, with a few Vietnamese people, had almost a complete monopoly of local trade: grocery, hardware, drugs, drapery, etc., as well as butchers' shops and restaurants. Nowadays many Laotians engage in business of all kinds, but it was not so in my young days, except for the Laotian women (never men), who always used to bring their produce or their stock to sell in the market—rice, chickens, eggs, some vegetables and fruit as well as betel nuts, lime, areca nuts, salt, pickled and fresh fish, bamboo shoots, etc. Each family was self-supporting, and all ate the same kind of food—sticky rice,[3] fish, chicken, meat and home-grown vegetables.

The only things which distinguished those who were better off were their larger and better houses and the gold ear-rings, bracelets and necklaces which the girls wore on high days and holidays. For such

---

1. In Laos, the storehouse, or granary, where the unhusked rice is stored, is built on piles, close to but separate from the dwelling-house.
2. The custom in Laos is for the young husband to live with his wife's parents. If the wife is the only daughter, he stays with them permanently and brings up his own family there. If there are several daughters, the first one to marry moves away with her children to another house when the second daughter marries, in order to make room for the newly married pair, or simply when the house becomes too crowded.
3. Laotians, unlike other Asiatic peoples, cultivate and eat only this kind of rice, which is richer in gluten than ordinary rice. They cook it by steaming.

occasions even the poorest people would have a silk dress or skirt. There was indeed very little difference between rich and poor, for no one was either very rich or very poor. Beggars were very seldom seen in the towns, and I never remember meeting one in the villages or in the countryside.

All the women worked in their homes, alike in the country and in the towns; and every Laotian woman had to know how to turn over the layers of rice while it was cooking,[1] how to winnow it[2] and how to weave. Everyone, in fact, used to spin cotton or silk, and tie and dye the threads so as to make various patterns,[3] and all could weave their own skirts or scarves on large looms, generally kept under the house.

Until our own times women in Laos never went to school. There were indeed no schools: some children learned to read and write from the priests for whom they worked as house-boys. A good many men acquired some education during their stay in the temple, for every man before he married had to spend a period of initiation in the temple, in order to be cleansed from the sins he had committed against

---

1. The rice is steeped overnight in an earthenware bowl and early the next morning is put into a slightly conical-shaped basket of woven bamboo to drain. The basket is then placed in the neck of a large earthenware cooking pot on top of the stove. When the steam from the boiling water begins to pass through the rice, the bottom layer is nearly cooked. Then the rice in the basket has to be turned over two or three times without letting it stick to the sides or allowing any grains to fall outside the basket. Thus the upper layer gets cooked by putting it underneath the rest. This trick of the hand, which all Laotian women have to acquire, is comparable to that with which Europeans turn their pancakes.
2. Although hand mills were sometimes used, paddy is more commonly husked in a large mortar worked by the foot. The rice is then winnowed by hand; this is quite a skilled operation and is always done by women.
3. It is the tying of the silk that makes the pattern in Laotian weaving. The threads of silk, unbroken and of equal thickness, are wound round a frame and tied at regular places with banana fibres. When the first tying has been made, all the threads are removed from the frame, the ends are fastened together and the whole bunch is dipped in a bath of dye. Only the untied portions take the colour. The silk is then dried, the threads all replaced on the same frame in the same order and a second tying is effected. Then the dyeing is repeated with a deeper colour, and so on till the desired pattern and colours are obtained. After being dried for the last time all the ties are undone, and the silk is wound on bobbins made of pieces of thin bamboo; these are placed in a shuttle shaped like a small narrow canoe. As the shuttle passes across the weft of the loom the varied colours of the silk form the desired pattern.

his mother. Some women learned to read from the inscriptions—mostly legends—written on palm-leaf sheets bound together by a couple of threads,[1] which were read aloud in a peculiar sing-song voice, especially during the vigils kept at a woman's confinement, or beside a dead person.

There was a precise division of labour according to sex. Men ploughed or harrowed the rice-fields, while women or children, following behind the men, fished with the *kheung*[2] for the eels and small fishes which abounded in the furrows. Men usually sowed the seed, as well as harvesting and threshing the crop, but thinning and pricking out the seedlings were generally done by women.

Hunting was exclusively a man's occupation, and so was the felling and lopping of trees. Men did every kind of work with bamboo and cane: making slats, ropes, baskets, fishing tackle and musical instruments. All building and furniture making, all carving and engraving, turnery, pottery, as well as goldsmiths' work were reserved to men. (My uncle's second wife, however, was noted for her skill in making jewellery, but she came from the Siamese side of the border, and when she settled in Vientiane she ceased to practise her craft, not because she was forbidden to—on the contrary, everyone urged her to carry on—but being now comfortably off she did not want to go on working.) Fishing with drag or bow nets and with lines was men's work, while fishing with the *kheung* was done by women. It was rare for women to play musical instruments for they had less leisure than men. Indeed, besides working in the rice-fields (there is only one rice crop a year in Laos; cultivation starts in May and the crop is harvested in November), women husk the rice, do the housekeeping and the cooking, look after the children and the stock (cattle, pigs and fowls), fetch water from the well or spring, do the weaving and all the attendant processes (rearing silkworms, spinning, dyeing, etc.), as well as making and washing clothing.

Such is in general the Laotian way of life, for the country people

---

1. Writing on sheets of palm leaf (*borassus*) is done with a dry metal point, after which a piece of charcoal is rubbed lightly over the leaves. The marks are thus blackened and become legible while the smooth surface remains clean.

2. The *kheung* is a fishing implement consisting of a semi-spherical sieve woven of thin slats of bamboo; it is held in the hand when fishing from the shore, in small streams, lakes or rice-fields.

nd for many townsfolk, even in some aristocratic and well-to-do families. It would be true to say that many of the wives of ministers nd prime ministers today have known what it is to work hard, especially carrying water[1] and husking rice.

Personally I was fortunate in being the daughter of a father who, in my eyes, is quite exceptional; the only Laotian I know who has witnessed and experienced so many changes and developments in the course of his life. All his colleagues are dead, and he is the only one to have lived to take part in the present war which is dividing the normally peaceful people of Laos. I propose to speak of him at some length here, first because he deserves a tribute, and second because his life is a key to the understanding of a whole people.

He comes of a peasant family living in Ban Hat Siên on the upper Nam Ngüm (a tributary of the Mékong), about 100 kilometres from Vientiane, and he has lived the life of a peasant. He has driven a plough, harrowed the rice-field, cut and threshed rice. He can drive an ox cart, ride a horse, row and punt a boat, is skilled at navigating a canoe or a raft, can shoot with bow and gun. So lively and inquiring is his mind that he can turn his hand to any man's job. He can make ropes and nets, he is highly skilled at basket-work from the simplest

---

1. There was no piped water supply except in some large towns and in European houses. I have seen drinking-fountains in Vientiane and Savannakhet, but no Laotion family had piped water, probably because the cost of connecting up the supply would be too high. Public wells in the towns are generally in the temples. Water is drawn up in an egg-shaped basket, woven of bamboo slats and coated with resin to make it watertight. The basket is let down into the well by a rope attached to its handle, and when filled is drawn up again, hand over hand and often at great speed. The water is then emptied into two other baskets also woven of bamboo and coated with resin, but of a special shape, rounded at the top and square at the base, standing on four feet. When full, these baskets are hung from a yoke and carried thus on the shoulders. In the house the water is emptied into large earthenware jars; women have to make several journeys a day in order to fill the jars. The labour of drawing up the water from the well and carrying it back to the house is very heavy—each load weighs at least 20 or 25 kilograms—and this task always falls on women. The Vietnamese use petrol or oil cans instead of the Laotian square-based baskets; these are lighter but they also have greater capacity, for each holds 40 litres. Laotians, who find their own loads heavy enough, feel sorry for the Vietnamese—often children 10 or 12 years old—who carry these great cans on their shoulders. Many Vietnamese and a very few Laotian men work as water carriers in order to earn some money.

to the most elaborate forms, he handles cane, bamboo and wood expertly. He is an artist who can invent as well as copy. In Vientiane he was well known and greatly admired as a decorator of catafalques. He also used to make musical instruments, particularly a type of violin known as *so*, the sound box of which was constructed from a coconut which he carved himself, or from a piece of bamboo covered with snake skin. The strings were made from the fibres of the grass-cloth plant. He was equally proficient at playing the *khene*, the xylophone and the *so* violin. I remember musical evenings in which my uncle (the husband of my mother's eldest sister, who came from Luangprabang) my father and a neighbouring friend of his, used to take part; they met in turn in one another's houses and, after a meal of *lap*,[2] used to play trios till far into the night.

As well as being an instrumentalist, my father sang beautifully, and his voice was the envy of professional singers. His singing was greatly

---

1. These are used at funerals. The open coffin is placed inside another chest the catafalque, which has a steeply sloping lid like the high-pitched roof of a little house. The dead body, dressed in all its finery, is put into the coffin with its face uncovered. The coffin is then placed inside the catafalque, which is covered all over with designs cut out of tinsel paper representing scenes from the life of Buddha, flowers, animals, etc. The coffin with its catafalque is always laid across the house—at right angles to the direction in which the living always lie when sleeping. My father was often asked to decorate catafalques, and he would readily offer to do so of his own accord when i was for someone to whom he wished to pay his respects. Indeed, twenty years ago the people of Vientiane were one large family, where all knew each other and all services were given freely without any recompense except a feast. On the day of the burial, or rather the cremation, for the dead are nearly always cremated (except for certain prohibitions, as, for example women who have died in pregnancy), the catafalque and its contents are taken to the cemetery and placed on a funeral pyre, which has been prepared beforehand, and publicly burned; three days afterwards the ashes are collected and put in a little jar. Later on a *that* (a monument in the form of a pyramid) will be placed over it either in the cemetery or in the temple precincts (the Buddhist *stupa*).

2. *Lap* is a favourite national dish among the Laotians; it is made of minced raw meat or fish seasoned with pimentos, limes, garlic, finely chopped onions rice ground and toasted, etc. Contrary to the usual custom, the preparation of this dish, particularly the mincing of the meat and the final seasoning, is done by men; my father would never eat a *lap* unless he did the final mixing himself, for it was the last touches, so it was said, which ensured the success of this epicure's dish.

dmired by his friends and the gayer spirits of his day, who often made him sing at parties and festivals. He would refuse on the pretext hat he was too old and that it was unsuitable to his age and position. But sometimes he would let himself be persuaded because, like all Laotians, he enjoyed laughter and gaiety. I remember once meeting an old peasant woman in a village of Nam Ngüm who said to me: 'It is easy to understand why I remember your father! He had an unforgettable voice: every night when he was coming back after visiting some girl,[1] if I heard him singing as he crossed the rice-fields, I used to get up so that I could hear him better. I have never heard anyone sing as he did.' She might, of course, have said this to please me, but even so I could well believe her. He was especially good at singing the songs of Nám Ngüm, which have a peculiarly lilting melody, greatly admired by the Vientiane people.

He entered a Buddhist order[2] when quite young and left it when he was 30 years of age with the title of Chan Khou.[3] His long residence in the temple was a very fruitful experience for him. There he learned to read and write the Laotian and the Pali languages, and was instructed in the Buddhist faith and traditions.

In his youth as a merchant he had travelled a good deal on the rivers Nam Ngüm, Nam San (another tributary of the Mékong), and the Mékong). Then, being naturally ambitious, he came to Vientiane to look for better employment. There he made the acquaintance of my mother and married her. By virtue of his gifts and education he ob-

---

1. In Laos young girls would spent the evenings at home, either alone or more often several together, chatting, rolling cigarettes or spinning, while young men, either alone or in groups, would come to pay court or exchange jokes with them.

2. Buddhist religious orders do not require their members to take vows for life, but allow them to return to the world at any time. A novice may enter at a very early age if his parents so desire or, very often, after the death of a near relative. When a member of a family dies, one or more of the young men (sons or nephews of the dead man) shave their heads and put on the yellow gown in order to take part, with the monks, in the funeral procession. Afterwards they live with the priests in the temple for at least three months, often much longer. Women wear white mourning robes, as do those who enter religious orders, but do not shave their heads.

3. A priest who returns to the world is given a title according to the grade which he has attained in the temple, and this is ceremonially conferred. Chan Khou is the most honourable title, and is conferred on those who are considered to be thoroughly versed in the Buddhist religion and the Pali language.

251

tained the position of *samiène*[1] in the Laotian civil service. He gradually progressed through the higher grades and became, together with
four or five others, one of the most important and respected people in
Vientiane.

Apart from his official duties, he also practised, unofficially, the art of
healing—a profession very highly thought of by the Vientiane people
for the Laotians at that time still set great store by traditional local
medicine. His friend and colleague Phasi, with whom he used to play
the violin, also had the same gift. My father had a little bag of flowered
red and yellow cotton material in which he kept the dried roots of
certain medicinal plants which he used to rub on a small piece of
silicaceous stone kept for the purpose in the same bag. When anyone
came to ask for his services, he would go off with his bag and, after
examining the patient, would choose the appropriate root, soak the
end in a bowl of water and, holding the piece of stone against the
inside of the bowl, he would rub the wet root against it, from time to
time washing both stone and wet root in the water until he thought the
mixture was right. He proceeded thus with several different roots according to the nature of the illness. The juice from the roots, diluted
with the water, was then poured off and the patient had to drink
prescribed doses of it. Then, in a low voice, my father would utter the
appropriate magic formulae and breathe on the sick person, from his
head down to his feet, in order to drive out the disease.

My father had learnt all there was to be known about the art of
healing, including how to approach the *p'i* (spirits, often maleficent)
for if the treatment with medicinal plants fails to effect a cure it is because the *p'i* are angry. If anyone falls ill, it is because his soul has left
his body and is lost. That is the reason why, when the patient is beginning to recover, a twist of white cotton is tied to his wrist in order
to recall the soul and invite it to re-enter the body. My father also knew
how to exorcise *phipôp*.[2] The village of Ban Kéum in Nam Ngüm,
about 100 kilometres from Vientiane, is well known to abound in

1. *Samiène* is the first grade in the Laotian civil service.
2. A person who is believed to be able to 'possess' other people by means of a
   spirit whom he worships for one reason or another, and very often because
   the spirit endows him with a certain power—known as *môn*. If the man who
   possesses *môn* does not observe its laws or its cult, the *môn* turns against
   him and causes him to become a *phipôp*, that is to say, he will possess another person and speak in his name.

phipôp. I think that today, especially among the younger people, this reputation has almost, if not quite, disappeared. But in those days there was a one-armed beggar, a Siamese, in Vientiane who was said to be a *phipôp,* and no one dared refuse him alms for fear of his possible vengeance. N.I., one of the women traders, a Sino-Siamese, enjoyed a similar reputation. She had small, very bright eyes, and people said that she could not look you straight in the face for long in case you might see in her eyes your own image lying recumbent—for the eyes of a *phipôp* always reflect an image lying down instead of upright as the eyes of normal people do.

One evening my father was sent for. We were no longer living in the house on piles, which had been pulled down, but in part of the block of apartments which he had built. A woman of our acquaintance, related to my mother, was possessed by a female *phipôp*. I was all eyes and ears, for I had long wanted to see a *phipôp* in action. I waited for my father to go, and as soon as he had left the house I went out too; my mother did not notice me because there were so many of us. I followed my father stealthily, but not too far behind him, for I was frightened of ghosts and phantoms. We crossed the Inpèng temple precincts and took a narrow road which led to the Mékong; the patient lived almost at the end of the road. My father, quite unaware of my presence, went straight to the patient's side. There was a small group of people round her, and a certain atmosphere of excitement. She was lying in bed, covering her face with her hands and tossing from side to side. My father asked her, in a stern voice, what was the matter and why she was hiding her face. She did not answer. My father threatened to beat her, at which she begged him not to do so, and said that she was hiding her face for shame, and that she would go away. He asked her who she was, but she made no reply. Then they brought my father some pepper and he took her hands away from her face and threw the pepper in her eyes. She began to cry out and beseech him, and said that she would submit. Again he asked her who she was, and she answered that she was N.I. and that she would go away and would never return. Suddenly the patient sat up. Her eyes were still red from weeping, and she complained of pain in her stomach. She no longer hid her face, but rubbed her eyes. My father uttered certain formulae, breathed on her, and the pain disappeared. The *phipôp* had departed, for it is said that when a *phipôp* leaves a person its departure is always signalized by a painful spot, sometimes a painful swelling, which soon passes off. The patient had now become quite normal again and talked as if nothing had happened.

My father had not seen me among those who were present, but when he was about to leave I rather timidly approached him. He did not scold me, but took me home without speaking. I was glad to have seen a *phipôp* in action at last, but disappointed at not having seen the whole thing. For I had been told that one of the most notable methods of exorcising was to shave the *phipôp*. This was done by putting a coconut shell on the patient's head and shaving the coconut. This is one of the most effective ways of exorcising the *phipôp* because, if he is made to undergo this operation, his head will really be shaved, and he will no longer venture out of his house for shame. I have also heard it said that some *phipôp,* fortunately not many, can cause very severe illness and even death, without being recognized. For this reason *phipôp* are greatly feared and, if they are recognized, are hunted from village to village. These stories are told, but anyone may believe them or not, as he will.

My father, for all his medical treatments and his beliefs, had, none the less, a great respect for European medicine, and when we had attacks of malaria he was quick to give us quinine. But his own remedies were also efficacious, particularly his laxative suppositories, cut from the tuber of a plant (*van phay*) of the saffron family and rubbed with dried bear's gall which he kept in his own pocket. These acted almost instantaneously. He also treated colic, particularly in new-born infants, with the juice from pineapple leaves which had been dried in the smoke of a burning resinous torch.[1] I think myself that the deposit from this heavy smoke acted like a piece of charcoal in absorbing the intestinal gases, assisted no doubt by the soothing properties of the pineapple-leaf juice.

My father's many-sided gifts were so widely known that his advice and help were sought on many occasions, and it often happened that he was asked to do something he had never done before. For example, he was asked once to make crowns for a company of amateur dancers. With the help of my eldest brother, and entirely from memory, he made exact reproductions of the traditional crowns, rising by tiers to

---

1. A torch about 40 or 35 centimetres long is made of a mixture of dust and fragments of rotted wood, dried and mixed with resin and wrapped round with palm leaves. Because of its cheapness it is the most usual means of lighting in country districts where there is no electricity and oil is expensive.

their pointed tops, with glittering flowers hanging from their stalks, all painted and gilded. They had one defect, however, they were much too heavy! This amused him very much when he put them on his head.

He had an insatiable curiosity, and always wanted to be the first to know what was being said or done. Thus, when he was quite young he had all the lower part of his body, to halfway down the thighs, tattooed, for tattooing was considered to be a sign of courage and virility.[1]

Having a mind naturally receptive to knowledge and progress, he readily embraced and adapted himself to new ideas. His small official salary was not sufficient to support his large family (he had nine children) and maintain a few servants. He therefore was always seeking means to meet his current needs. Thus, by borrowing from the Bishop of Vientiane, as did four or five of his well-known colleagues in the town, he built his tenements with a view to letting them. Then he employed Vietnamese workmen to convert a Citroën touring car, which he had bought cheap from a French dealer, into a van suitable for public transport, with a handsome body of polished wood, a roof, seats for passengers, doors, footboards, etc. I may mention, incidentally, that all these Vietnamese workmen had a great respect for him, mixed with fear, for they found that he knew how to give orders.[2]

On one occasion my eldest brother, who had learnt at college how soap was manufactured, offered to teach my father. He was full of enthusiasm and admiration and, no doubt already seeing himself at the head of a large-scale soap factory, eagerly got to work. But the result was disastrous: the soap smelt disgustingly of beef fat. They had many a good laugh about their failure!

Though he was fundamentally a traditionalist, my father's mind was always directed towards progress. His one great regret was that he knew no French.

---

1. Tattooing is regarded as evidence of courage because the process is extremely painful. But it also has a magical significance, and people who have been tattooed are believed to have acquired more-than-ordinary powers, according to the formulae uttered and the ceremony performed before the operation; in particular, they become immune to snake bites.
2. Twenty years ago the Vietnamese in Laos looked down on the Laotians whom they considered inefficient, and the Laotians, on their part, hated and despised the Vietnamese, regarding them as vulgar people with the souls of slaves. I think that nowadays this outlook has changed on both sides and, as understanding has increased and prejudice diminished, relations have become more friendly.

My mother, though she was a townswoman, did not much relish change and, if it had been left to her, would never have sent my sister and me to school. She liked a quiet life and, like all Laotian women, chewed betel incessantly.[1] My impression is that, being the youngest of her father's daughters—his Benjamin as it were—she didn't have to work so hard as her older sisters. All the same, she was a good cook, and could weave and also winnow rice. But we always had servants, and I have never seen my mother husking rice, far less carrying water. Even if she had wanted to, she would never have been able to do it, poor thing, for as a young woman all her life was spent in having babies and bringing up her children.

My mother always had her babies at home, as was the Laotian custom, because in her time nobody went into hospital. An old native midwife used to come and look after her, and my father himself would assist. He would cut the cord with a sliver of bamboo, the end of which had been sharpened and held in the fire. The way in which the cord was cut was regarded as very important, for the character of the child depended on it and it was necessary to go about it in the right way. If a child had a bad disposition, there was much jesting at the expense of the person who had cut the cord at its birth.

The birth normally takes place in the kitchen which, in Laotian houses, is generally fairly large. If, however, it is too small, a fireplace is built in another room, for there is always a fire on the hearth where a birth is to take place. The hearth, about 15 centimetres high, is placed flush with the floor and filled with earth; three bricks are put in the middle, and a wood fire is kept burning continuously till the confinement is ended. Beside the hearth a couch, made of a single layer of woven bamboo raised on four bricks and covered with a soft mat, is placed for the mother. She lies thus night and day in the warmth of the fire, screened by a clothes-horse made of bamboo on which the baby's garments are dried. This régime should be followed for at

---

1. A quid is made from the bark of a tree mixed with lime, betel and areca nut; when chewed it produces a red juice which reddens the lips but, in course of time, blackens the teeth. Originally, I think, chewing was indulged in simply from affectation and flirtatiousness, but it became a habit, probably owing to the mild intoxication it produced, and some women cannot do without it. In my youth I sometimes chewed betel for coquettishness, but not enough to acquire a taste for it. Modern women today do not go in for it; they use rouge for their lips and keep their teeth white.

least two weeks (or three in the case of a first confinement). The mother generally spends most of this time lying down, but sits up to suckle the infant and to drink copious infusions of herbs from a rectangular bowl; this bowl is made from the sheath of areca-flower clusters, and is at once solid, supple and watertight. These infusions, taken very hot and in considerable quantity, are said to promote lactation; she also has to take douches, as hot as she can bear them. Once a day, and after every douche, she has to stand up for a few minutes with legs apart, over the glowing embers of the fire to toast herself.

The infant is placed either in a cradle hung from the ceiling by a rope or in a hammock within reach of the mother. During all this time the mother must not eat any sauces or pickles, any meat or fat. She eats rice with dried fish, galanga root and salt.

During this period of karma, neighbours, friends or acquaintances, especially young people, come to 'watch' through the night. There is reading aloud and card-playing; the young men pay court to the girls, whose favourite occupation at these times is rolling cigarettes. The period of karma ends with an intimate little family ceremony. The mother gradually returns to ordinary life, without any sudden change. This routine is always followed in country districts. In the towns the hearth with the wood fire is now being superseded by a brazier placed under the bed, even though the confinement is conducted by a midwife trained in European methods. The dietary rules are much less strict, and are being more and more relaxed.

As the wife of a mandarin, my mother would not be expected to do heavy work. When she had any leisure she occupied it in weaving. She was much younger than my father, but they got on very well together, and she had the greatest respect and admiration for him.[1] My father was a gentle person and never beat us, but nevertheless he was

---

[1]. Laotian women have to treat their husbands with great respect. A wife must never touch her husband's head, or the head of any other adult man. She must never lie on a bed higher than that of her husband or than that of any other man who is older or of superior status. She must not walk in front of a man who is seated, and if she wants to reach something above a man's head she must ask permission. A man similarly must ask leave of any person, man or woman, to whom he owes respect. This is part of the rules of behaviour in Laos. A Laotian woman may never come too near to a priest, or touch his body or his gown. A Laotian woman is, by definition, inferior to a man and must therefore always take a lower place in any circumstances. A man always goes before a woman.

the master and always took the initiative and shouldered all responsibility. My mother could indeed speak her mind and, as with all women, her word certainly had weight; but if there was any discussion she could not sustain her point for very long, for she wept easily, and when my father saw great tears welling up in her eyes he would drop the argument.

My mother had had nine children in all, and I was the third. She was not a very strong personality and preferred life to be uneventful. She had learnt to read the inscriptions, but had in course of time forgotten almost everything, for she had little leisure for reading and preferred to be read to. She did not consider that women needed to be educated, but she let my father send my sister and me to school after we had run wild during our early years.[1] We were placed at the temple of Vat Tiane with an old Maha, a wonderful man with children, who taught us the rudiments of Laotian writing. There were about fifteen of us, the first girls in Vientiane, with a few Sino-Siamese.

I do not remember exactly how old I was when I started school, but I know that after Vat Tiane we went to Miss Berthe Tafforin's school where we met three other Laotian girls from the southern district of the town, and some Vietnamese. My sister and I were the only ones from the northern district, for my father was the only person in that area to send his daughters to school. There were fifteen or more children in the school, which included infant, preparatory and primary classes. My sister and I began to learn the French alphabet. Miss Berthe was a tall, thin woman, not disagreeable, though she had favourites among the Vietnamese girls. These girls used to tease us by tapping us on the head with thimbles on their fingers.

I don't know whether I learned anything at that school, but after that we were put in a proper school which was started about then

---

1. Laotian children have plenty of freedom; they play among themselves and go wherever they like, except that if they want to go any distance they ask their parents' permission. Their parents do not worry about them very much. When I was young I went about all over the place to my aunts' or uncles' houses, where I always found some cousins to play with. We did not have toys because there were none, but we played at housekeeping or shops, we sang and danced, making ourselves crowns of banana leaves decorated with red hibiscus flowers. Our parents seldom beat us, our father never did. My mother sometimes did so, because my sister and I quarrelled a lot and my sister, being stronger, was often rough with me so, as I was rather delicate, my mother protected me more.

where our teacher was a real French-speaking Laotian princess, Sèng Souritiane, known as Augusta, grand-daughter of Augustus Pavie himself. She, with another princess, had been the first Laotian woman to be sent to Bangkok to study French with the nuns. With Princess Augusta our studies were more serious, and other colleagues of my father sent their young daughters there, as well as some other Laotians of lower rank. This school provided a real education. There were about forty girls; Princess Augusta taught the preparatory and elementary classes, while another princess taught the infants in the next room. Our mistress was extremely capable, gay and well liked, but she was able to discipline us, making us stand in front of her desk while she struck us on the palms of our hands with her ruler, not harshly, but often with a smile, so many strokes for so many faults. With her I really learned to read French. When we left the elementary class we had to sit for the Laotian certificate of elementary studies, which certified that we were proficient in reading, writing and arithmetic.

After that we went on to the first-year middle course, but many of my companions left school then to do household tasks. My sister and I went on and were placed with Vietnamese, for in the first-year middle course all the instruction was given in French, with two or three hours a week for studying the local language, Laotian or Vietnamese, as the case might be. In the higher course the instructors were French and all very good teachers.

If one succeeded in gaining the certificate of primary studies, one could go on to the college which had been founded some years previously for boys, or one could become a teacher. Two of the Laotian girls, older than I, who had begun their education at Miss Berthe's school, had gained their certificates before I did and had become teachers like Princess Augusta. But although I was a year older than the date given on my birth certificate, I was not old enough, when I got my certificate, to become a teacher. I was therefore admitted, together with Douang, a girl from Luangprabang, and two Vietnamese girls, to the college. We were the first women students. My sister, who got her certificate a year after I did, was appointed a teacher.

The young men who had entered college generally began to adopt European dress and to wear shoes. For some years past I had worn wooden-soled slippers or sandals to go to school, although I often went barefoot. At college I always wore sandals. Douang was the first to start wearing European-style shoes, and I followed her example;

we were the first women to wear shoes, except for princesses who considered this mark of superiority suitable only for themselves.

My mother did not see any reason why I should waste four more years at college when I might have made myself useful at home and learnt to cook and weave. My eldest brother had already been sent to Hanoi to work for his bachelor's degree, so my father still had to support all the children, and this my mother thought all wrong. However, since my sister was able to earn her own living, and since the diploma which I should get at the end of my four years at college would enable me to find a better position, my mother resigned herself to waiting four years longer. It is true that I was not much use in the house; I always had the excuse that I had work to do for my classes, so it fell to my eldest sister to help my mother in the kitchen. All the same, I could winnow the rice, for when I was younger I had often helped the servants to husk the paddy, not that I was made to do so but because it amused me, and also because I used to tell myself stories of ghosts and phantoms which enthralled me even while I was almost dying of fright. Sometimes also I had spent my holidays in the rice-fields, pulling up the plants, looking for crabs or fishing. Occasionally I helped to prick out seedlings, but never for very long for I had a horror of leeches, and the very thought of finding one on my leg was enough to make me come out of the water.

When I received my diploma at the end of my college course, my father had recently been posted to Kèng Kok. I did not want to be a teacher, but I very much wanted to do as the men students did and go abroad to take the bachelor's degree. I was even more ambitious: I wanted to become a doctor, and in some small way to enhance the reputation of my country. But I did not think that my mother, or even my father, would ever consent to my going on with my studies for ten more years, when there were six younger brothers and sisters at home.

I went to see Mr. Boulé, then Director of Education in Vientiane, who promised to help me and, thanks to him, my father was persuaded to agree; I obtained a bursary for Cambodia.

My hand was still swollen from another centipede bite when I embarked one morning with my cousin D. and five or six of my fellow students on a launch belonging to the company which ran a regular service on the river Mékong. We travelled on deck, for all the cabins were reserved for first-class passengers, French for the most part. We carried our own bedding; my friends each had a mat and a small mattress, but I had a folding bed which raised me higher than the others. This drew from one of them the remark: 'We shall see something indeed! Now women sleep above men!' To which I replied: 'You will see more thàn that, my friends.'

At Phnom Penh I was hospitably received by Mr. Boulanger, whose wife was a relative of my mother. He and Mrs. Boulanger had three daughters, with whom I got on very well, and two young sons. Mrs. Boulanger pursued her own life and had very little to do with other European families. She spent most of her time on the plantations, supervising the coolies in the cultivation and harvesting maize and kapok. At the home of the Boulangers I had my first experience of a European house and its conveniences—the W.C. with its automatic flushing and the bidet. Mrs. Boulanger was regarded with some awe by all who came in contact with her, and by her servants and her children. So when she came into the house they vied with each other in helping her in the kitchen, for she prepared her own meals and very well she did it. From her I learned to make *khaopoun*[1] and other Laotian dishes.

I spent two happy years with my cousins; Mr. and Mrs. Boulanger indulged me as if I were their own daughter, and my bursary could be used as pocket-money. In the holidays I went back to my parents at Kèng Kok where I showed off my new culinary skill. My mother, placid as always, showed no surprise but simply said that with my increasing age my skill had probably increased of itself. On the other hand she was anxious to teach me weaving, and since I did not know how to do it and couldn't get hold of any books, I readily set to work to learn that art. But I never became really skilful at it. As for French rules of good manners, I learned them from books, not from my cousins.

At the end of two years at Cisowath College I passed the first part of the bachelor's degree. The Boulanger family were then going to France for the long vacation, so I applied for a bursary to enable me to go to Saigon, where there was a boarding house for young women.

---

1. Another Laotian dish, very popular especially with women. It consists of a rich soup of chicken, fish, pork and other ingredients with coconut milk, and is eaten with vermicelli, shredded raw vegetables, such as sprouting beans, banana flowers, cucumber, banana shoots, water convolvulus, green paw-paw and other highly aromatic plants such as Chinese parsley, mint, basil, etc.

But I had a good deal of difficulty in getting a bursary which would admit me to the Chasseloup-Laubat College in Saigon, which was reserved for French students, for the bursary required was much larger and the boarding house for French girls was also more expensive; in fact, in order to get admitted to the college it was necessary to dress in the French style and be a boarder at a French girl's school. I did get the bursary, but only with difficulty and after many applications. I spent a year at Saigon and passed the second part of the bachelor's degree there. After that, as my eldest brother was able to give my father some little assistance, I fought another battle to secure a bursary and a supplementary grant to begin my medical studies at Hanoi. Since I was the first Laotian woman student, I was given the additional grant, but I had to live with six others in a rather uncomfortable students' hostel where I suffered very much from the cold.

While at Hanoi I met my husband, and we were married during the first year of my medical course. I gave up my studies to follow my husband, who was posted to Laos.

Here then is a brief account of the progress of a woman of Laos. There are many other memories of my childhood that I could write about, but time and space are not unlimited. My experience is that of hundreds of others, except that Laotian women today, even the older ones, take an interest in politics, particularly in the area occupied by Pathet Lao, where groups of partisans instruct and train them. For my part, I had never been interested in political questions and I am grateful to my husband for having enlightened me.

In Laos, although women play a leading part in the household, the husband is always the master, and the responsibility for all major decisions is always his. A Laotian woman, even if she has an official position (and these are as yet very few), is still a housewife, submissive towards her husband and dependent on him; I believe this explains, to some extent, why women have shown little desire to continue their studies with a view to acquiring a profession and becoming independent. They are quite content to be married and to let themselves be supported and directed by their husbands. Nowadays almost all the women in the towns go to school, but leave when they have learned to read and write and do arithmetic. Most of them understand or can speak French fairly fluently, especially those who have had an opportunity of visiting France. But in spite of the right to vote, and in spite of differences of opinion, family relationships have not changed;

women remain under the protection of men even when they are fighting side by side in the zone of resistance.[1]

When considering the occupations of women today, exception must be made of those modern town-dwellers, wives of high officials who have become wealthy, who are glad to leave all domestic duties to their servants in order to devote their energies to dress, parties, card-playing and entertainments in European style. The less well-to-do townswomen and the peasants, as well as those who share in the political activities of men and the resistance to Pathet Lao, pursue the same avocations as in the past: rising early to husk the rice before the sun is too hot; cooking the rice which has been soaking all night in order to contribute to the alms offered to the priests;[2] for the countrywomen, leading the stock into the pasture, letting the fowls out of the henhouse, doing the housework, fetching water and cooking; in the afternoon, according to the season and the time available, going into the forest to look for bamboo shoots or mushrooms, or doing the weaving. And then in the evening, when dinner is over and everyone has gone to bed, one must always remember to put the rice in water to soak for tomorrow.

Weaving is still done, not so widely in the towns, where it tends to be concentrated in fewer hands, but extensively in the country, especially in the Pathet Lao zone where, like agriculture, stock-raising and other small industries, it has become the subject of competitive production.

Laotian women, even those who have acquired some education and some contact with modern ideas, are still much more conservative in their dress than Chinese or even Vietnamese women. The traditional

---

1. Nevertheless Laotian women have equal rights in inheritance. Usually the property is evaluated and shared equally among both sons and daughters, except that where real property is limited it is more likely to go to the sons, the daughters taking an equal value in jewellery. When there are several parcels of land, the daughters inherit them equally. Even when details of the partition have not already been decided by the parents before their death, they are usually settled amicably between the children under the general direction of the eldest.
2. Every morning the priests go in procession to certain fixed spots to take up their daily collection of alms. Women wait at these points, and as they pass, offer a handful of cooked rice to each priest, who receives it in a large, round, black lacquer bowl. After each collection the priests say a prayer aloud while the women listen, their hands clasped above their heads.

native skirt is still indispensable,[1] and so is the traditional style of hair-dressing—long hair drawn loosely up into a chignon at the top of the head. In Viet-Nam short waved hair is quite common, but not in Laos.

Marriages are still arranged in the old way and according to the old rites, and the husband still comes to live in his wife's home. When a young man is ready to marry, whether it is a love match or an arranged marriage, one of his close relatives—often an aunt of mature years—goes to call upon the bride's parents. Usually they are already unofficially aware of what is afoot. The date of the wedding is decided upon and the marriage conditions arranged—for the young man has to provide a certain sum of money (the amount fixed by the girl's relatives) as well as symbolic gifts consisting of a sleeping mat, a mattress and a pillow.

On the appointed day, the bride is dressed in her very best clothes and decked with every jewel she possesses (often these are borrowed from friends and relatives for the occasion), and at the appointed hour the groom arrives. He is dressed simply but attractively in a bright silk sarong (red, orange, purple, royal blue, green or bright pink) and a white shirt. He is supported by a friend holding an open parasol over his head, and escorted by a host of friends and relations, all announcing his arrival with loud shouts of the local equivalent of 'Hurrah'. In front of the entrance to the bride's new house they clash with the bride's supporters and a struggle takes place—the bride's party attempting to prevent their entry. Finally, however, to the accompaniment of joyful shouting from both sides, they make their way in and up to the door of the house. There a young relative of the bride washes the bridegroom's feet. Nowadays this is merely a symbolic action, but the youngster still claims a good tip for his pains.

---

1. The Laotian skirt is made in three sections, each woven separately; the main (middle) portion consists of a wide band of dark coloured material, generally having an unobtrusive pattern of vertical lines (in some areas the patterns are bolder and in brighter colours); secondly, a narrower band, reaching from the waist to the thigh, made of gold or silver thread with small vertical stripes of bright coloured silk; and lastly, a third band, still narrower, at the bottom of the skirt, woven of gold or silver thread in horizontal stripes, with a red hem at the lower edge. The skirt, which is quite straight, is worn with a wide concealed fold in front and is held at the waist by a separate belt of twisted silver.

Then the groom advances to seat himself beside his bride, who has been waiting in front of a mountain of flowers and candles, surrounded by her friends and close relatives. The ceremony follows. It is purely secular, no Buddhist monks taking any part at all. There are prayers, the expression of good wishes, the tying of white thread around the wrists of bride and groom, obeisance to relatives and aged friends. Once the ceremony is over, a 'matron of honour'—often one who is the mother of a large family—leads the groom by the hand to the bridal chamber where the bride joins him a little later on.

The extended family of the past has given place to a smaller grouping, as young couples prefer to set up their homes apart from their elders, owing to a taste for independence or for modern housing. Where circumstances allow, young people still settle in the same district near their parents, but this is not always possible in the towns owing to the development of urban life. The conditions of modern life often require young couples to move away from their families, but if they go to live in another town they cherish the secret hope of returning to the neighbourhood of their parents or brothers and sisters. Of course, some couples live wherever they please; but family ties are not thereby weakened. Mutual help is still practised; on occasions such as serious illness or a funeral, members of a family will still come together, if means permit, just as they do in Europe.

My own family, for example, is scattered at present, but our hope is that one day we shall be reunited and, though our political opinions may not always be in agreement, we still have the same affection for each other. This sense of fellowship is not confined to brothers and sisters, but unites all Laotians.

Malaya

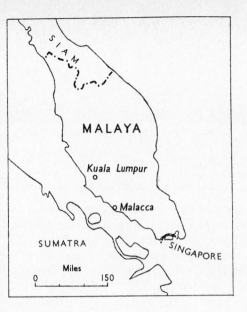

Area: 131,287 square kilometres.

Population: 6,698,000 (1959 estimate).[1]

Recent history: 1942-45—Japanese occupation; 1956—British Government transfers sovereignty.

Citizenship: Men and woman have equal rights.

Religion: Malays (50 per cent of the total population) are Moslems; among the Chinese (37 per cent) Confucian, Taoist, Mahayana Buddhist and local cultic beliefs are all to be found; Indians (11 per cent) are mainly Hindus. There are also Christian, pagan and other (i.e., non-Malay) Islamic groups.

Inheritance and family patterns: With the exception of the state of Negri Sembilan, where matrilineal inheritance obtains, Malay customary rules of inheritance do not differentiate between the sexes. Matrilocal extended families are found in Negri Sembilan; elsewhere, nuclear families are the usual type, the new home set up after marriage being situated near to the parents of both spouses if possible. (For Chinese and Indian patterns see accompanying articles on Singapore and India respectively.)

---

1. Latest official estimate of population as published in *The U.N. Population and Vital Statistics Report, October 1960.*

Men and women
in Malay society

by MICHAEL SWIFT

The people I am going to discuss in this article form about half[1] of the population of the Federation of Malaya. The largest other group is the Chinese, recent immigrants and descendants of the great numbers of Chinese who have come to Malaya to make their fortunes since the nineteenth century.[2] In addition, there are many other races settled in Malaya, especially Indians from south India.

Malaya is what has been termed a plural society. This term is used to refer to a country whose population is made up of diverse racial groups which, despite their close geographical proximity and daily contact in the economic field, live in almost complete social and cultural isolation from each other. This distance between the races means that cultural differences between them persist, with very little movement towards the formation of a typical national culture, in this case a Malayan culture, and indeed, the differences between them may increase as each group stresses what it feels to be special to its own culture as a means of maintaining its identity. For this reason it is impossible to make generalizations about Malayan society as a whole which have any depth. Answering questions about Malaya one has to qualify continually, stating which ethnic group is intended and pointing out how the answer would not apply to another group.

Even the Malay group is very diverse. The present Malay population has been made up from many sources, including large-scale recent

---

1. Cf. T. E. Smith, *Population Growth in Malaya,* London, 1952. An excellent discussion on the demography of race relations. This work is based on the 1947 census. Results of the 1957 census are not yet available.
2. Cf. the contribution by Foong Wong in this volume.

immigration from Indonesia, and over the centuries has been exposed to various important cultural influences. Of these the most powerful were Hinduism, traces of which are still very evident in most Malaysian cultures, and Islam, the present religion of all Malays and the vast majority of the population of Indonesia. The diversity arising from origin and history is further reinforced by ecology and differential exposure to modern influences in contemporary Malaya.

Because of this variety I am going to base my discussion on the type of Malay society that I have intensively studied myself. There is sufficient unity in Malay society and culture to make this a valid procedure, the principles governing the relations between the sexes being the same, although the particular expression which they receive varies with local conditions. Where there is a clear instance of important variation I will draw the reader's attention to it, without however claiming to cover all such variation. Until much more field work has been carried out in Malay society no one can know for sure the precise details of internal variation in Malay culture.

MARRIAGE AND DIVORCE

Malays marry young. Although not precise (and exactness about age is not important to Malays), 15 may be taken as the usual age for a girl to be married, while a man, although marrying later, will usually be married before he is 20.

Most marriages are arranged. Parents and kin choose spouses and make the arrangements to carry out the wedding. A kind parent will endeavour to follow his children's wishes in this matter, should he know what they are and feel that they are suitable. But having preferences (falling in love) depends on having opportunity to meet the opposite sex, and this is not available to most Malay adolescents. Marriageable girls are very restricted in their movements and contacts, ideally being confined to the house and closely watched even there. Although youths are not so closely controlled, they are still without opportunities to get to know potential brides through any form of courting, not even mixing freely with their marriageable cousins, although before adolescence these girls were their 'sisters'. This makes it easier for choice to be left to parents, for the potential bride and groom know that they will have to marry someone, and they will have no very strong personal preferences. A youth has some choice,

269

however. Informants often remarked, when discussing marriages, that you cannot force a man to marry if he does not want to (implying that you can a woman). Parents may ask their son whether he has any suggestions or, as he will probably be too shy, he will ask someone to inform his parents of his preference. Perhaps unduly frequent visits to the house of a particular relative or friend may show that he has special interests there. Most frequently, a youth's parents will suggest so-and-so; he will then endeavour to find out something about the girl, and steal a look at her, before informing his parents of his decision.

Most girls do not have even this limited freedom. Modesty does not accept the idea of a girl having a wish to marry a particular man, nor is she felt to know enough about it to make a wise choice. What is felt to be a good choice is made for her, and great pressure may be put on her to induce her to accept it. There is likely to be a continuous barrage of praise for the prospective groom, pleading that she value the trouble her parents have taken for her and respect their wishes, abuse for an ungrateful and stupid daughter, even pinching and slapping—this last particularly if the girl becomes reluctant after the arrangements have been made.

In selecting a spouse, parents seek for the highest possible status, and a near relative. For the traditional aristocracy status is primarily a matter of descent, as it is with Malays of Arab extraction, especially the Syeds, and this can outweigh all other factors in seeking a son-in-law, but for the ordinary Malay wealth, the regard with which a family is held in the village, the official position of the bride's or groom's father if he be a wage-earner, the economic prospects and education of the groom and the education of the bride, all play a part. Malay society generally traces descent through both parents (bilaterally), and marriage choice is restricted only by the Islamic version of the universal incest taboo, so that all cousins are potential spouses and, *ceteris paribus*, more desirable than any other choice. An exception is found amongst the people of the state of Negri Sembilan[1] where descent is unilineal, traced through the mother, giving membership in clans and sub-clans. Here marriage between close matrilineal kin, say between the children of two sisters, is regarded as a form of incest, and strongly forbidden by the morals of the people, although nowadays.

---

1. Cf. M. G. Swift, 'A Note on the Durability of Malay Marriages', *Man*, October 1958.

when custom is in decline, there is no formal punishment for the few who break this rule beyond the force of public abhorrence. In this area the most desirable marriage is between cross-cousins, the children of siblings of opposite sex.

The first step in arranging a wedding is an indirect questioning, so that a refusal will hurt no one's pride. If these first informal overtures are successful, then some female relatives of the man will go and formally ask for the girl, and should these direct negotiations proceed satisfactorily this visit will be followed by a formal engagement.

The marriage itself is composed of two elements: first there is the marriage agreement between the groom and the guardian (*wali*) of the bride. While he is alive this will be her father or his representative; should he be dead then the nearest patrilineal relative becomes *wali* according to Moslem rules. This agreement must be made in the presence of two witnesses, who should also satisfy themselves of the willingness of the bride, failure to refuse being regarded as a modest way of showing acceptance. It is now that the marriage payment (*emas kahwin* or *mahr*) changes hands or, if it is to be owed, then the quantity is formally stated. Custom fixes the proper sum in some areas, for example 24 Malayan dollars for a first marriage, and 12 dollars for any subsequent marriages, in the area where I worked; but there are also areas where it is open to discussion and varies with the standing of the parties. In any case, it is rarely a large sum, and it is always the property of the bride herself, and not of her father or any other kin.

But the expenses a groom faces are not confined to the marriage payment. There are also 'marriage expenses' paid to the father of the bride towards the cost of the wedding celebrations. This is a much larger payment than the *emas kahwin*, a matter of hundreds or thousands of dollars, depending on the wealth and standing of the parties, and is very much a matter of competition, for the reported amounts general in the various areas seem to be rising continually. I have even read complaints in the Malay press that in Singapore these expenses are now so great that young men cannot afford to get married. This, however, is difficult to credit, for the fathers of girls are generally even more anxious to see them settled with a husband than most men are to get married. In some parts of Malaya the money of the marriage expenses is disposed of completely at the discretion of the bride's father, while he probably has to add money of his own to achieve the magnificence of celebration he desires, but in areas of Johore it is

271

customary that the money be used to provide household essentials for the newly-married couple.

Once the marriage agreement has been completed in the presence of witnesses it must be registered, and it is usual for a representative of the religious authorities to attend and do this on the spot, although this is not essential. Once the marriage has been registered the couple are man and wife as far as both Moslem and administrative law are concerned, but for the people it is essential that further customary ceremonies be carried out before they may live together as man and wife.

It is these customary celebrations which are expensive. The Moslem rites are simple, marked only by a small feast and the presence of the mosque *Imam* to read a sermon of advice. The details of the wedding according to custom vary very markedly, but the constant feature is the *bersanding* ceremony. For this the young couple are placed on an elaborate dais where they can be seen by all visitors to the ceremony; the ritual itself is simple, but the dais always shows great ingenuity and expense. The desire for economy of time or money may lead to any of the other customary rites being cut, but never the *bersanding*. The celebration of a wedding according to custom is reserved for a girl's first wedding. (For any subsequent weddings the religious rite alone suffices.)

Despite the ceremony and expense with which they are celebrated, Malay marriages are fragile. The general tenor of the figures occasionally announced by the Religious Affairs Departments of the various states is that for any one year the total of divorces registered amounts to more or less half of the total of registered marriages in the same period.[1]

For divorce all that is required is that the husband should inform his wife, verbally or in writing, of his intention to divorce her. This is known as a *talak*. Should he only say so once then this is merely a one *talak* divorce, which can be revoked by mutual consent during the hundred days period of the *edah,* during which a divorced woman is forbidden to remarry. Revoking a divorce is known as *rojok,* and this practice weakens the reliability of the divorce statistics, as it cannot be known with certainty how many hasty divorces are promptly revoked without being registered, and also what proportion of the marriages and

---

1. Cf. J. Djamour, *Malay Kinship and Marriage in Singapore*, London 1959, p. 135-6.

divorces represents *rojok* and remarriage after *rojok*. Precise or not, there can be no doubt that the frequency of divorce is extremely high.

A triple *talak* divorce cannot be revoked, neither can even a single *talak* divorce after the expiry of the *edah*. Should the couple then desire to marry again, the wife must first have a (consummated) marriage with another man. The rigour of this rule is evaded with the connivance of a man who marries the woman for payment, agreeing to divorce her the next day. Such a man is known as a *muhallil* or *chinabuta,* and naturally figures as a comic figure in Malay humour. An example of this type of humour, in this case to the advantage of the *muhallil,* is the tale of a *chinabuta* who broke his bargain to divorce the woman, while she, in turn, preferred him to her previous husband! Three one *talak* divorces add up to a triple *talak* divorce, that is to say, the last divorce is irrevocable. But in village practice, at any rate, there is a certain amount of elasticity about this rule, in that people may simply count wrong if they wish to revoke their third divorce. At least, I have come across cases where everyone except the principals was convinced that this is what had happened.

Stated baldly, the rules of divorce seem to leave everything to the husband's discretion. There are, to be sure, certain conditions under which a woman may make an independent approach to the religious judge (*kadthi*), but women rarely venture to do so unless aided by a male relative, and in any case *kadthis* as a whole tend to emphasize a husband's rights. This tendency probably derives from their greater exposure to the spirit of old-fashioned Islam, which advocates a greater inferiority of women than is generally the case, even in traditionalist Malay society.

But should a woman desire divorce and her husband not, there are ways in which she can induce him to divorce her, even though she cannot directly divorce him. For a start she can obviously make life very unpleasant for him within the household until he accepts her view that the marriage has lasted long enough. A more serious pressure still is to complain and nag him where other people can overhear, so exposing him to the shame (*malu*), fear of which is so important to the Malay. A man should be ashamed to hold on to a woman who no longer wants him, for 'there are plenty of other women'. What the woman must be careful not to do is to exasperate her husband so much that he simply leaves her, still married but without support, while he marries again. This is called 'leaving her hanging'. To 'leave a woman hanging' without good cause is also criticized, and another cause of shame. A man and wife should stay together as long as they want to and then, should they wish to part, this should be done without recrimination and fuss. If a wife has treated a husband particularly badly, then there will be a feeling that 'leaving her hanging' is simply what she deserves, but even then society will begin to complain if the man does not divorce her after allowing a reasonable time for his bitterness to abate.

There is no need for the participation of any official, religious or otherwise, in a divorce. There is, however, a legal obligation on the husband to register it, paying a small fee. This requirement of registration is an administrative addition to the Moslem code and, through the fee, a source of income to the *kadthi* or assistant *kadthi* who registers it. (This gives rise to the suspicion that some of them are less whole-hearted than they might be in carrying out their obligation to act as mediators.)

In Malay society divorce is just as 'normal' as marriage. Not at all evil, it is at the most unfortunate, and often not even that. Two people agreed to get married, now they no longer wish it, and that's that. It is true that nowadays speeches and articles in the Press express disquiet at the high rate of divorce, but this is partly at least due to the feeling that divorce lowers the Malay community and the Moslem religion in the eyes of the modern world.[1]

Divorce often presents a wife with great problems, especially if she has young children to rear. If there are only a few children these are normally left with their mother. Cases coming to the attention of social workers reveal women left in a desperate situation. In the towns a man can divorce his wife and leave her unsupported with his children in a way that would not be possible in the village situation. Moreover, if she is living amongst relatives there is also a limit to the hardship that a woman will have to bear. Her situation may be unpleasant and hard, until she can remarry, but as long as her relatives have food themselves she should never starve. The desperate situation of the town divorcees makes them a primary source of recruitment of prostitutes and 'bar-waitresses'. If a woman applies to the Court she can hope to

---

1. W. Cantwell-Smith, *Islam in the Modern World,* Cornell, 1958. Although not concerned with Malaya it contains a revealing discussion of the importance of 'apologetics' in contemporary Islamic thought and writing.

get a maintenance order made against her former husband. Low wages and unemployment make this a rather slender hope, even when the husband can be traced, and even when the woman is familiar enough with the correct procedure to have recourse to the Courts.

The system produces victims who are worthy of every sympathy and help that can be given, but their plight should not be generalized into too desperate a picture of the lot of Malay women as a whole. A man who divorces one wife will marry another, and the chances are that this will be someone else's divorcee. As far as children are concerned, the elementary family cannot of course have the same stability as in a society where divorce is rare; but the adverse effects are mitigated, first, by the practice of not separating the children from their mother, and, second, by the way in which a Malay can accept and care for his step-children with almost the same affection as he shows to his own children. Society expects him to do so, and watches for discrimination, say in clothing or education. On the other hand, Malay society expects a step-mother to be cruel, a view not only expressed in conversation but enshrined in songs and literature. A step-mother has a greater chance to be cruel when the children are at their most defenceless, and society's expectations are an important reason for the practice of leaving children with their mother even when the father would rather take them with him.

The customary rule is that property acquired during a marriage is regarded as joint property, and divided if there be a divorce, or at the death of either partner. If there is bad feeling at the time of divorce this rule is often hard to enforce, with each partner simply keeping whatever he or she can get hold of. Thus the wife will keep all her jewellery (and jewellery is one of the most important forms of village saving), plus whatever property the husband may have registered in her name. A more laudable course of action, and one which men sometimes follow, is simply to leave all the property that has been acquired during a marriage with their wives to provide for the support of the children. For many peasants there is not a great problem here, in that the only valuable fixed asset that they possess is their house, and this is almost certain to be left with the wife while the former husband goes elsewhere. It is difficult to pass from the formal rule of division of the property to an empirical generalization about what actually occurs.

The Islamic rules of inheritance give a greater share to male than female relatives. Thus, of a man's property one-eighth is his wife's

275

share, while the remainder is divided amongst his children so that a son receives two shares for every share received by a daughter. Should there be no son, the wife still retains one-eighth, while daughters share a half of what remains, and the other half is divided amongst the dead man's patrilineal kin.[1] Normally in the Malay family a wife's share will not be important; if she and her husband were aged, it is quite probable that they had already begun to divest themselves of their property in order to assist their children in raising their respective families, and a woman with adult children will normally expect to live with them when her husband dies. If, on the other hand, her children are still young, then she will retain control of all the property on behalf of her children.

The precise rules laid down by the religious code are not, however, always followed. There is another ideal which sees justice in equal shares for all children, regardless of their sex, and even in greater shares for those in greater need. In addition, quarrelling about inheritance shares is very much frowned upon, although not always avoided, and there is a tendency to follow the rule of 'more or less' in the interests of harmony. The religious rules stand as a last resort for occasions when some other agreement is not reached, for example, when there are no close kin, and the property has to be divided amongst a number of not very closely related people, or when some personal bitterness has disrupted the unity of the family.

In respect of inheritance, the state of Negri Sembilan is once more a special case. Traditionally, all fixed property, especially land, the main property in a peasant society, was regarded as clan property, although held individually by the women of the clan. From them it passed to their daughters on inheritance, or, failing daughters, to the daughters of the owner's sisters. This land law was maintained by the British administration with an important proviso. Lands already occupied and owned by women under the clan law were registered as ancestral property, and were to continue to devolve in tail entail female. On the other hand, land newly cleared and planted did not, unless the owner specifically registered it as 'ancestral' land. In the

---

1. Cf. A. A. Fyzee, *Outline of Mohammedan Law,* 2nd ed., Oxford, 1954. This is a convenient English language source on Moslem law. It is, however, written according to the Hanafi school (while the Malay follow Shafii) and is influenced by legal practice in British India.

traditional economy the most important forms of land were rice-fields and the 'homestead' (*tanah kampong*) used for house sites and fruit trees. The relative economic importance of these was soon dwarfed by the adoption of rubber as the main peasant crop, planted on land that was previously jungle, and so outside the current jurisdiction of the customary law. Even so, this land code is not without importance in terms of our interest here. Together with other aspects of the matrilineal system, such as the extended family and matrilocality in marriage, the ownership by women of riceland and homestead land in Negri Sembilan gives them an additional measure of security over that enjoyed by Malay women elsewhere.

THE FAMILY AND HOUSEHOLD

The nuclear family of husband, wife and children is the most important unit in everyday Malay life. Within the family it is the relations between husband and wife which are most relevant to our concern here.

As might be expected from our discussion of marriage choice, there is no notion of love in the Malay conception of the relations between husband and wife. Given that the partner's personality is tolerable, the emphasis is all on the performance of objective requirements. A wife's primary task is the performance of domestic duties, cooking, running the household, and caring for the children. If she can perform these duties well, and without nagging, then she is a good wife. The husband, on the other hand, is primarily the provider for the family. Above all, he is the provider of cash income. Most Malays, although peasants, are firmly involved in a market economy, and need a continuous supply of purchased goods to meet their ordinary daily requirements. Thus, in the area where I carried out my field research, this meant that only men worked tapping rubber. Women made a contribution to the household (apart from their domestic work) by collecting wild vegetables and rice-field fish. They also bore the major burden of cultivating the rice-fields, which here was a subsistence rather than a market activity. But they were not expected to find money for the things that needed to be bought. A wife does not even do the shopping. The husband wishes to retain control of the financial side of household management and, what is more, going to the shops or the market exposes a woman to too free a contact with the public.

The details of this pattern cannot be generalized for the country as a whole. For example, in Johore it is common for all able members of the family to take part in rubber tapping, and this cannot be solely explained by a greater poverty in Johore. Perhaps the diligence of the Javanese (who make up much of the Johore population) is a more important explanatory factor. As regards the control and disposal of income, on the other hand, in the fishing communities of the east coast[1] the wife acts as family banker, partly at least because the men are away at sea a great deal of the time, and in the markets of the east coast women form a majority of the sellers.

Although the division of labour by sex is clearly marked, it is not rigid. Should necessity require it men cheerfully undertake work that their wives would normally do, and vice versa. Thus men very rarely wash clothes. Indeed, as washing is made a social occasion by the village women, a man could hardly join them, but should his wife be ill a man carries on with good grace, although not as far as possible drawing attention to his situation. In the long run a man who has to do his own domestic work will usually look for another wife but, in the short run at any rate, there is nothing like the same emotional definition of men's work and women's work as is found, for example, amongst London's East Enders. Similarly, a single woman in need may undertake share tapping on a holding near the village without exciting adverse comment. Most divorcees and widows try to manage without doing so, but what restrains them is more a desire to hide that they are worse off than their fellows who do not need to do this work.

There is no question but that in the Malay's image of their society the husband is regarded as the dominant partner in a marriage. Not only do they maintan that this should be so, but also seem to believe that it is so. And the shy submissive bearing expected of Malay women serves to support this image. If a male visitor comes to the house he will be received on the verandah, separate from the family's living quarters, and the women of the household will not appear. When village affairs have to be settled at a meeting, it is the husband who attends representing his family, a situation which is reinforced by the use of religious buildings for meetings. Even at kin gatherings, where at least the senior women are not so restrained, since many of the men are their sons or nephews, they still play a very minor role.

Thus, according to public appearances, the women are in the posi-

---

1. Cf. Rosemary Firth, *Housekeeping among Malay Peasants,* London, 1943.

tion of having decisions made for them by the men, and the question that arises is, to what extent does this appearance coincide with the reality of the situation?

It has first to be admitted that a woman's interests are more limited than those of a man. On a question affecting religion it is probable that she will have no opinion at all if, for example, there is a proposal to reform ritual. But where her interests are concerned woman has an opinion, expresses it and can often carry the day for her views.

If a man announces his intention to build a new house it is very probable that he has reached this decision only after careful discussion with his wife, and it may well have been she who initiated the proposal. Choosing a son- or daughter-in-law is also a question where I have seen the wishes of the mother predominate. But perhaps it will seem natural that a woman should decide these domestic matters. Even in economic matters, however, it may well be the wife's views which are important. I worked in an area where it was customary to plant rice seedlings on the edge of the jungle where they relied on stream water. From there they would later be transplanted to the irrigated rice-fields. Planted in this way the seedlings are very exposed to drought and in 1954, when the planting season was very dry, most of the seedlings died and the people were only able to plant their irrigated fields with seedlings acquired from the Department of Agriculture. This provided an opportunity for the Department to increase and repeat its propaganda that rice-nurseries should be made in the irrigated fields, and because of their recent painful experience it seemed as though the villagers had finally been convinced of the wisdom of this advice. However, when the next planting season came round people proceeded just as they had done previously. Surprised by this, I investigated, and discovered that all the men who had previously seemed committed to the new scheme said that their wives had not liked it, and that since women had to do the transplanting that was sufficient. Even in matters concerning rubber cultivation, which is not women's work at all, they have views and influence, for this affects the property and income of the family. I do not wish to seek to go from one extreme view of the subservient Asian wife to the opposite picture of the wife as the dominant member of the family. It is just that it must be realized that the Malay family, and the relations between husband and wife, are much more egalitarian than at first sight they appear, and than the people themselves say they are.

279

The identification by husband and wife of their individual interests with that of the family as a unit is limited. The wife, particularly, places great importance on her membership of a group of kin which excludes her husband and, because of this, occasionally finds herself phrasing her relations with him in terms of 'we' and 'you'. This is probably common to many if not all societies, but it assumes greater importance in a society where divorce is so common. The ease with which divorce can be obtained means that the Malay wife can never be completely secure in the permanence of her relationship with her husband and, should she and her husband separate, it is to her kin that she must turn for assistance. These ideas are most clearly formulated in Negri Sembilan where organization into exogamous unilineal corporate groups underlines the situation, but it is not only confined to that state.

This limited commitment to the family and the marriage not only affects the personal loyalties between husband and wife, but also the operation of the family as an economic unity. Each partner, but especially the wife, for it is she who has the greater fear of being left unsupported, is concerned with the improvement of the economic position not only of the family as a unit, but also of his or her own individual position within it. Malays, in any case, place greater emphasis on present consumption than on present abstinence with the goal of accumulation and enjoyment of a greater income in the distant future. This tendency is increased by the fear that any sacrifice made may be for the benefit of someone else. If a wife helps her husband to get rich, how can she be sure that he will not use this money to attract another younger and prettier wife, or that they will not quarrel and she herself be divorced? If a husband spends a great deal of money on a fine house, how can he be sure that he will not divorce his wife later on and so enable some other man to enjoy the house he made?

A wife wishes to see as much as possible of the resources of the family invested in a secure form, even if this yields a very small return. Jewellery can be used as family savings, bringing no return but ready always to be her security if she be divorced. If not jewellery then land, registered in her own name, or in the name of her children, can play the same part. If the husband, in his role of cash-provider, should wish to undertake a project that will require investment, a wife will resist the use of resources over which she has control for this purpose, and will generally tend to use her considerable influence, which I have discussed above, to dissuade her husband from risking the family's capital. This is a strand in the relations between husband and wife, not a complete picture. Wives may devote all their resources, even raising more from their kin, and may bear great discomfort, for the furtherance of their husbands' ends, but as marriage is defined in Malay society they are not required, or even expected, to do so.

This matter relates closely to the part affection plays in husband-wife relations. Given the way spouses are acquired, it follows that people are not expected to love each other before they are married. But neither are they expected to grow to do so. A display of affection between husband and wife would be regarded as comical. If a husband shows that he is very fond of his wife gossip discusses the possibility that she has bewitched him. Showing grief (*meratab*) is frowned upon in Islam, but men may show great grief at the loss of a parent or a child, even at the loss of a great friend, and women are even freer in this respect, but open grief is not shown at the loss of a spouse. People speak as if the relationship were a purely practical and calculating one. If a wife is unhappy because she feels her husband is unfaithful, she may want a divorce, but the advice she will get will hinge on whether he is a good provider or not. If he is, then she will be told to be thankful. A husband who complains about his wife will be told to look for another. And yet here, too, there is a discrepancy between appearance and reality. Affection is an important tie between husband and wife. It will not be shown openly; indeed, since this is a society which does not make a demonstration of its affections at all except with very small children, a couple may be shy of plainly showing affection, even privately. But it is impossible to live in close contact with Malay families without realizing that affection is, in fact, a very important factor in the relations between husband and wife, and therefore in this important focus for relations between the sexes.

PARENT-CHILD AND SIBLING RELATIONS

There is very little specific to be said about parent-child relations, or sibling relations with regard to the question of relations between the sexes. They may be generalized by saying that towards the young the elder, whether parent or sibling, gives affection, guidance and author-ity, while the young show affection and respect towards their elders.

While the children are young it is the mother who carries the main

281

responsibility for their discipline and care. A father may spend a great deal of time playing with his children, but he functions more as a place of appeal against the discipline of the mother than as a support for her authority.

As the children grow older the position of the parents with respect to discipline alters. The daughter, helping her mother about the house, is naturally still very much under her control, but a son will expect to be spoilt by his mother, and to get her support in managing his relations with his father. For the father attempts to become a disciplinarian controlling his son as the boy grows to adolescence.

Elder siblings supplement parents in providing authority and guidance. An older brother watches over his sisters' relations with their husbands, showing no obvious concern when all appears well, but ready to come to her assistance if she should seem to need it. An older sister, too, is often an important influence for reasonableness and right conduct amongst her younger siblings. I feel that criticism from an elder sister has great weight with a man, whereas he would resent and resist as interference advice from other sources, even from a brother.

Relations between siblings are not, however, precisely defined as to content; their general nature is quite clear, but we do not find, as in many other societies where kinship is important, specific rights and duties institutionalized.

WOMAN IN THE WIDER SOCIETY

So far we have considered the Malay woman within her family, the group comprising herself, her husband and children, and occasionally another relative without a family of his own, which forms the main economic and social unit of peasant society.

For the vast majority of Malay women a discussion of their place in the family exhausts the topic of their place in society, for there are very few other spheres of society where women can have a place. The village does not engage in a great deal of co-activity, and in what there is men play the major part. There is, for example, no place for women in village Islam. Women have religious duties, but these provide no opportunities for them to hold public positions, or to participate in public worship.

Politics, which are becoming increasingly important nowadays, do provide an opportunity for the woman who feels too restricted within he confines of her home. Within organizations such as Kaum Ibu, the women's section of the United Malay National Organization, women have an opportunity to act as leaders not open to them elsewhere. However, as we shall discuss further below, village women rarely play a part in such organizations, for they conflict with their view of the proper activities for women.

Village girls do go to school. This may be the only opportunity they have of freedom before they are married, when the limitations on them will relax somewhat. But for village girls there will only be vernacular education, and as soon as they reach their early teens they will be taken out of school, 'for it's not proper, and they are too big'. But should a girl's father allow her to carry through her vernacular education to completion, there is one hope for her to achieve some other ambition than being a housewife. She may be able to proceed with her education and become a teacher in a village school. All other employment opportunities require an English education, and almost by definition a village girl will not receive such teaching—after all, very few village boys do so, and they are not restricted by values concerning modesty.

THE TYPICALITY OF VILLAGE PATTERNS

The vast majority of Malays are peasant villagers. It is to them that the generalizations I have advanced above are meant to apply. The picture is different if we turn our attention to two other important, but small, sub-groups within the society.

Malay society is stratified into classes. The lowest and largest class consists of the peasantry. Above them in traditional society was to be found an aristocracy recruited by descent. This traditional aristocracy was able to carry out more closely the ideal concerning the position of women held by the whole society. For the peasant, the seclusion of women is a luxury that he cannot afford. Because of the importance of woman's economic contribution to the household she cannot be secluded, nor is it easy to subordinate her. For the aristocracy, on the other hand, there is no occasion for their wives and daughters to go to the rice-fields to work, nor to go with the washing to the public bathing-place every day. The economic ability to afford seclusion is reinforced by a pride of descent and concern for appearances not so highly developed amongst ordinary people. Thus, the traditional aristocracy deviates from the peasant pattern towards the 'classical' picture of *purdah*, modified to some extent by that respect for the individuality of women and relative freedom which has characterized all Indonesian cultures from the remote past.

Today the traditional upper class has lost its former pre-eminence in Malay society. With the exception of the rulers themselves, only those descendants of the traditional aristocracy who have managed to adjust themselves to the new situation have retained a high status position. The new Malay *élite* consists of Western-educated government servants. Malays have played little part in the economic development of modern Malaya, which has been mainly a Chinese preserve. But the creation of a modern administration has opened up wide employment opportunities within the administration and here many Malays have achieved good positions. The key to a government post is possession of the necessary educational qualifications, and this means a modern education through the medium of the English language. It is perhaps not surprising then that this class deviates from village Malay patterns towards Western ideas about the proper relations between the sexes and the correct place of women in society.

The process of inculcating Western values is started by their education itself. After that, in employment, Western standards are associated with senior rank, or were so associated at least until Independence in 1957. Social relations outside working hours also naturally involve contact with Westernized fellow administrators, and open up opportunities for the acculturation of the administrator's wife as well. If another Malay pays a visit with his wife, they will know how to behave whether their host receives them in the old or the modern style. But if the visitor is a European, he will think it odd if he is not introduced to his host's wife, and if accompanied by his own wife she will not expect to go through to the back of the house where the women are.

The official is not only exposed to Western values, but he is drawn to adopt them as a clear symbol of his status and his differentiation from the rest of his people. There is, of course, a vast difference between the adoption of the external features of another culture and the adoption of their values at points where these impinge seriously on cherished native values. An official who seems completely Westernized may nevertheless wish to bring up his daughter according to traditional propriety. But this is difficult for him to do. In the first place, status considerations require that she be given an education in keeping with his position. In the second place, if he does not send her to a modern school there is very little chance of her making a good match when the time comes for her to marry.

What a girl of the official class will be allowed to do will depend on her parents, and to some extent on where they are living. Free conduct on Western lines will seem a great deal more natural in a large town than in a small one where the Westernized *élite* are only a small group. There the pressure to maintain traditional practices will be much greater.

All modern fathers, then, want their daughters to be educated. Most of them will be glad if they can take up employment when their education is finished. But they may insist that their daughters attend a convent school because they feel that there their morals will be most closely guarded. They may allow their daughters to take any job that they can get, or they may feel that being a teacher in a girls' school is all that is suitable. Some fathers try to restrain their daughters out of school hours completely, allowing them only girl friends and insisting that even these come to the house. Other fathers allow their daughters a little freedom, on the understanding that they only go about with other girls of respectable families. At the farthest extreme some girls are even allowed to be friendly with boys, and accompany them to the cinema, at least in a large party. Standards are now in flux, but there is no doubt that it is the modern Western values which are winning. Moderate freedom for daughters is now an acceptable norm, and it is the old-fashioned parent who is increasingly on the defensive.

Modern Western notions about freedom are confined to only a small section of society, but it is an important section, and one which, by its high status position, defines the desirable style of life for all others seeking higher status. The farther one moves away from the Western-educated official class, the less these values are found, whether along a rural urban continuum or an educational one.

In the upper ranks of Malay society qualified women can occupy positions of prominence. Some women are political leaders whose speeches regularly make the newspapers; women also practise as doctors and lawyers, although admittedly these are mainly from the other Malayan communities, Chinese, or Indians, for example. For the qualified woman who wishes for prominence, conditions are very favourable in that the country is so short of educated leaders that there is no bar because of sex. Old-fashioned ideas in the home may prevent girls getting as high educational qualifications as sons, but society is prepared to receive those who do.

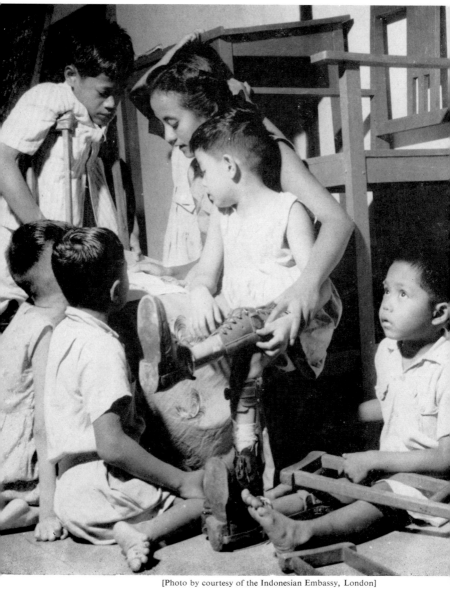

The care of crippled children at the rehabilitation centre in Java

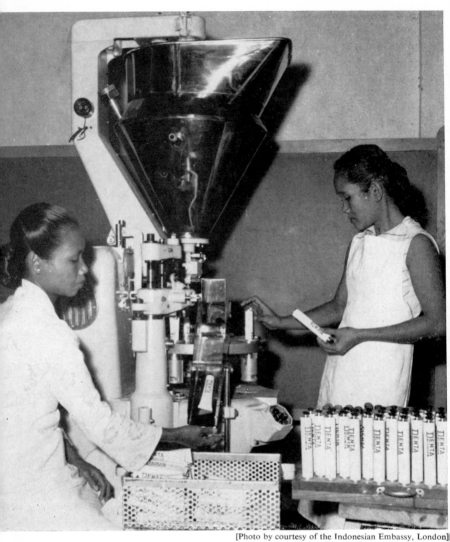

Young women working in the first dental paste factory in Djakarta

Lahore townswomen knitting for refugee children

[Photo by courtesy of the Office of the High Commissioner for Pakistan, London]

This girl is throwing the discus in an athletic competition at the Dacca Stadium

[Photo: United Nations]

Mother and child

Warping strands at a textile factory in Manila

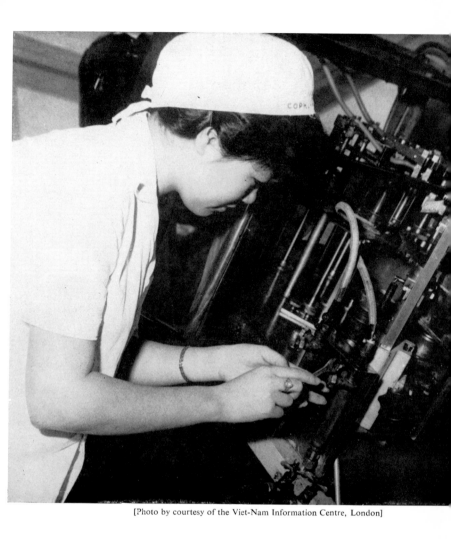

[Photo by courtesy of the Viet-Nam Information Centre, London]

Viet-Namese woman working in a pharmaceutical laboratory

[Photo: Unesco/Aubert de la Rüe]

Woman from a rice-growing village

Changes in the position of Malay women

by HASHIMAH ROOSE

An attempt to evaluate the impact on the Malay social structure and cultural values of Western education and social values is certainly an undertaking for a team of social anthropologists. In the remarks below I merely touch upon the outward manifestations of the changes in respect of the position of Malay women as a whole. First I give a brief picture of both contemporary and non-contemporary social structure, and then turn to a generalized account of the phenomena of change as I have observed them in my own and the neighbouring families.

In the urban centres of Malaya, outward indications of changes are most dramatically evident. Here an *élite* of government servants, the bureaucrats, still highly conscious of social prerequisite and prestige symbols, find themselves constantly attempting to better their mode of living, while increasingly adopting a social pattern barely distinguishable from that of the European community with which they have increasingly fraternized. They inhabit new houses in the suburbs, own and drive cars and purchase essential domestic utensils once considered luxuries. Mixed sports, occupations and even cocktail parties are replacing the traditional family-and-friends-only gatherings, with their strict segregation of the sexes. Both men and women, in ever-increasing number, are becoming members of clubs, societies and associations based on Western traditions. The children are attending high schools and universities for higher and professional qualifications. The younger women are often preoccupied with charm schools, the latest fashions, cinema stars, etc., while a number of them are preoccupied with public and civic works and women's rights. Among the schoolgirls, 'dating', picnicking and dancing are now common, and a source of worry and annoyance to religious leaders and conservative parents.

To complete this general picture of the changes that have taken place during the last three or four decades I may mention here that the older women do retain their traditional costume, that is, their sarongs and *bajus*; whilst the younger generation is not averse to wearing and adopting Western costumes. However, on formal occasions most of them appear in the traditional dress.

This somewhat generalized picture indicates the substantial changes which have occurred generally in Malay institutions and social structure. Using this as a comparison, it may be seen later that the position and status of Malay women in society has undergone a gradual but almost complete change.

Now let us examine the development that has taken place since the turn of the twentieth century, as I think the position of women then could be considered the traditional one in the sense that it was largely unaltered; women were then mere chattels, and confined largely to their homes and their numerous progeny, and were isolated in every respect. I shall begin by explaining the position of women in matters relating to marriage, and from there go on to education, employment, social activities and aspirations.

The traditional position of Malay women in matters relating to marriage is well illustrated by the following saying: 'Untong si-laki-laki di-tanya-tanyakan Untong si-perempuan di di-nanti-nantikan.' I am afraid it is rather difficult to render this saying into English since a translation fails to indicate its hidden meaning and intention. It is necessary, therefore, to explain the saying as follows: it was the custom among Malay men when they wished to settle down to go about looking for suitable girls for their brides; on the other hand marriageable girls, for obvious reasons, would have to wait for their would-be husbands to approach their parents for their hands. In other words, the women had no choice in the selection of their life partners, the decision lying solely with their parents. Thus, Malay girls were usually married by their parents with or without their consent while still young in age. The question of the women consenting to their parents' choice would not arise because of the formal and rigid structure of family relationship between parents and their children, which applied especially to daughters; that is, respect for parents and passive acquiescence on the part of the unmarried daughters was strictly observed. This situation, however, no longer obtains, and at present girls do have a considerable amount of say in the matter of choosing their husbands.

288

As regards the boy-girl relationship: in the Malay *kampongs* (villages) they were allowed to mix freely up to the age of 13 or so, but as soon as a girl reached puberty she was kept under strict surveillance. She would seldom be allowed out of the house, and on the few occasions when she was allowed to go out she was carefully chaperoned. If she should encounter a childhood boy friend she had to show no sign of recognition, but modestly avert her eyes. The small shawl which all women had to wear then served a good purpose. But the strictness of the old folk was tempered by sound rustic commonsense and the realization that small safety valves can do much to avert rebellious explosions. The elders occasionally allowed the young some small release of their passions through the *bertandung,* that is, courting a girl with *pantuns*, one of the traditional verse forms of the Malay people. If the boy were to win the *pantun* contest he would be invited to eat with the girl of his choice, but if he lost he would leave hungry and might never see her again.

If a girl were to be married before she had reached the age of puberty—a practice common in the olden days—she would not be allowed during the first year or so to live with the husband as man and wife, for reasons obvious enough as they both would be too young. In such cases the girl would either stay with her in-laws or continue to stay with her parents, during which time she would be taught the rudiments of home-craft and, above, all, how to look after the husband. This in-training period would vary in length depending on the age of the girl on marriage. If she was 12, she would probably be allowed to assume her married life when she was 13 or 14. Should the couple then have a child, they would not be allowed to bring up and look after the baby as they would be inexperienced. Instead, the wife's parents would care for the baby, and this would provide another training period for the young wife.

When the couple was considered old enough in age and experience, they would then be allowed to set up a home for themselves on a plot of land near the parents' house. If they were unfortunate in having poor parents, they would not have the pleasure of setting up home so early. In these circumstances, they would continue to remain with either of their parents until such time as circumstances would permit them to do otherwise. Even then they would not be free from parental influence on many matters, especially those relating to family life and social obligations.

289

The division of labour and responsibility between man and wife was definite: the man was the sole bread-winner, the woman must look after the home. The woman would thus be confined to the kitchen and the children. It was the man's responsibility also to obtain and attend to the marketing and selling of foodstuffs, etc., and to purchase household utensils and family clothing. In this connexion the woman would be asked for advice and invited to indicate the materials required. She would, however, be in no position to object to or criticize the decision of the man.

In the circumstances it is obvious that women would not as a rule need to hold or acquire money as everything was bought for them, nor would they find any opportunity to use the money if they did possess some. On the occasions when financial position warranted it, the husband or the father would purchase clothes and jewellery for the wife and the children. Thus, in traditional times, the woman would have no occasion for indulging in shopping sprees which the present-day women enjoy so much that many husbands are annoyed.

Tradition had also made it a matter of course that when a Malay couple went out for a walk in the *kampongs* or in town, or went on a visit, the woman would invariably walk a few steps behind the man, and would never walk abreast as such a practice was considered highly improper. On the other hand, no woman would act as a hostess should male friends of her husband pay them a visit unless the visitors were close relations. If there were ladies among the guests the chances were that the men would form one group and the women another in another part of the house away from the men. The women would not dare even to dream of joining in the conversation of their menfolk, other than to inquire, as custom demanded, the state of their health when first they met and greeted one another. Thus, the separation between the sexes was rigidly observed in all respects.

In spite of the fact that her place was rightly in the home, a wife had no power whatsoever over matters affecting the family as a whole. The man would lay down the rules and make all the decisions without the advice of his wife, whose role could then be said to be 'not to reason why', but 'to do and die'!

At dinner, the men would invariably eat first and alone. As customs deemed it courteous, they would be served by their wives with choice morsels. The wives in this case would sit opposite the men. They would only take their meals together with the children in the kitchen after the men had had theirs, and often their food would be the left-overs in the sense that the best food had been enjoyed by the men earlier. This may sound rather harsh but in actual fact the family as a whole shared whatever food they had for that day without discrimination as to quality and quantity to be consumed individually.

Thus in a Malay home of seven decades ago the man was indeed the absolute master in all respects. He would be the one who arranged the life of the family, and his words were law. This was made possible because the children were not given any education, nor were they allowed to hold views different from their elders. However, with the passing years the sons were sent to schools to learn the rudiments of education (reading, writing and arithmetic) thereby making them literate to some extent. It was not until the latter part of the twenties that girls were allowed to be educated together with the boys. Until then, girl children were educated only in the sense that they could read the Koran, say their daily prayers and knew their household duties.

The process of emancipation of Malay women was thus put in motion when the educated Malays relaxed their strict application of traditions and customary laws and allowed their daughters to be educated, first in very small numbers and in Malay schools only. This process moved very slowly indeed and even today we find many Malays still refusing to educate their daughters and abiding by the old saying: 'It is better to let your children die than allow traditions and customs to lapse.' On the other hand, those who had had the benefit of English education had, by the mid-twenties, begun to send their children—boys and girls—to be educated in English schools, either in government or mission schools. However, as regards the latter, the old prejudices against and fear for the possible conversion of their children to Christianity still prevail, with the result that the number of Malay girls taking advantage of English education in mission schools remains comparatively small to this day.

As a precaution, girls were at first not allowed to go to school on their own. They were escorted or chaperoned by old men each morning and afternoon to and from their schools. This practice was eventually allowed to lapse with the improvement in the transport system of the country, and the increasing improvement in the economic position of the Malays generally. Nowadays girls are allowed to go to school either on foot, by bus or car or even by cycle—much to the

291

annoyance and disgust of their elders. Twenty years ago a girl cycling to school was unheard of!

A ready-made reply to any question why parents would not wish their daughters to be English educated was that such an education would be of no use to them other than to enable them to write love letters or arrange for trysts with young men leading to possible elopement later. This sort of reasoning or argument was justified then, as there was no intention on the parents' part to let their daughters complete their education. This was due to the fact that English education takes a number of years to be completed. Thus, more often than not, parents would terminate their daughters' education after a few years for fear that they would be old maids by the time they had completed their studies. Their chances of getting 'good' husbands would by then be slim. Furthermore, it was also considered improper to let young girls of 15 or 16 be seen in public unattended. Also, we must remember the fact that the parents of unmarried daughters would not dream of letting their girls seek employment. Hence it was rarely that Malay girls, before the second world war, were allowed to continue their education to colleges or the universities to obtain professional qualifications.

Nowadays, the number of Malay girls at the university, locally or abroad, is increasing yearly. There is now a tendency to encourage daughters, whenever possible, to be as highly educated as the boys. There seems to be developing a sense of family and racial pride when a Malay girl is able to continue her education at the university: this sort of pride was previously reserved only for achievement by the parents of the boys. This certainly augurs well for the future position of Malay women as a whole.

In spite of its brevity the education they received twenty or so years ago was more than sufficient to change the women's attitude to life. Thus, on being married they would no longer accept their subservient and relatively minor role in the home with equanimity. This rebellious attitude of the women against customs and tradition is widespread nowadays, and is heightened by the increasing contacts they have had with women of other nationalities and the outside world through magazines and other types of publication. This attitude is also encouraged in a way by the men themselves who are now no longer so anxious to exercise their superiority. This is, I think, mainly due to the influence of Western philosophies and ideas regarding the equality of the sexes.

The change in the status of women towards more equality and greater freedom of movement was accelerated during the forties when political awakening was beginning. It was feared that the nationalist movement towards independence would not be successful unless the women were to support it. The women were, therefore, encouraged to take an active part in all political as well as all social activities aiming at national awakening and nation building. Furthermore, during the Japanese occupation of this country when conditions were so unsettled and difficult, the women shared the responsibility of looking after the welfare of the family. They were then almost encouraged to work to supplement the income of their husbands or fathers in the face of scarcity of food and high prices. Consequently, a large number of them found employment in numerous types of work ranging from rubber-tapping to teaching, etc. They continued to remain in employment after the end of the war. Thus, it is not surprising to find many Malay women now working either with the government or with commercial firms. Therefore, when political organizations were being established the women began to take an active part in political activities, nor were they lacking in organizational ability. Today we find them heading influential social organizations and sitting as members of governmental bodies and boards, etc.

Thus, it was not surprising that when the first general election was held in 1955 we found a Malay woman candidate elected for the first time as a member of the then Malayan Legislative Council. At present there are four of them in the Lower House of Parliament, and several more have been elected members of various State Executive Councils.

One can, therefore, conclude that social, economic and political activities have by now become important factors in the daily life of Malay women. No longer are most of them satisfied with their traditional role of wife and mother, for they are now capable of becoming community and national leaders. We often find them out of their homes in the evenings, or even during the day, attending social or political meetings or even public lectures.

Thus, Malay women have indeed come a long way from their habitual domain in the home several decades ago to their present position beside their men in the important role of nation building. Once they were looked upon with condescending pity or outright contempt. Much that their older sisters regarded as sacred, their modern counterparts regard as superstition or even trivial. Their modes of life, their intellectual curiosities and satisfactions seem now to rival those of men. There is a closer affinity between the sexes for, added to the traditional relationship between man and wife, there is now a mutual understanding of their respective roles in life.

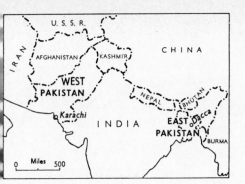

Pakistan

Area: 944,824 square kilometres.

Population: 86,823,000 (unofficial estimate, 1959).[1]

Recent history: 1947—British Government transfers sovereignty to new State of Pakistan, previously part of Empire of India; 1956—Republican status promulgated.

Citizenship: Men and women have equal rights.

Religion: Islam; there is also a substantial Hindu minority, and smaller groups of Christians, Parsis, Buddhists and others, including pagans.

Inheritance and family patterns: Primarily patrilineal inheritance in which, following Islamic law, daughters also take part (a daughter inheriting half the value of a son's share). The patrilocal extended family is the usual type; nuclear families also exist and are said to be increasing in numbers.

---

1. Latest official estimate of population as published in *The U.N. Population and Vital Statistics Report, October 1960.*

Changing patterns of an East Pakistan family [1]

by A. K. NAZMUL KARIM

The establishment of British rule in Bengal in 1757 set in train a significant series of changes which ultimately were to affect profoundly every stratum of Bengali Moslem society. Before that time the life of the people centred around the village and the village community. As the villages were more or less self-sufficient, the villagers did not have to look much beyond their frontiers to meet their daily needs, and therefore their thinking was confined to the village and its surroundings. This rural-centred life began to break up with developed means of communication and the money economy introduced by British rule. As a result, profound changes took place in the older types of institutions and social relations.

We propose to discuss in this article some aspects of these changes, especially as they have affected family life during the past few generations. As an illustration we shall take the family of the present writer. To comprehend the proper nature of the change that has taken place within my family during the past century we must understand two aspects of the social background in which the family lived, worked and survived. In the first place, we should remember that although by the middle of the nineteenth century the last vestiges of feudal social structure and feudal attitudes had almost disappeared from Bengali Hindu society, they continued to exist, though in a moribund state, in

1. This paper has been prepared in collaboration with my colleague, Mr. Muhammed Badrudduza, of the Department of Sociology, Dacca University. Professor John E. Owen of the Department of Sociology, Dacca University, has also given me substantial help by reviewing and correcting the article in the manuscript stage. I thank him heartily for his kind co-operation.

Bengali Moslem society.[1] In the second place, it was not only in the urban areas that Western ideas and Western institutions had made some headway; they had also in places penetrated to the rural areas.

The old world began to break up under the impact of the new education, the new legal system, the new State administration and, above all, the new ideas and institutions brought in by British rule. For the purpose of illustrating these profound changes I have, as I have said, taken my own family as an example, but it should be remembered that my family cannot be taken as an 'average' or a 'typical' Bengali Moslem family. Despite the remoteness of our ancestral home, the impact of the West was manifest quite early in our family, and therefore it has undergone a greater degree of change than other similar families. Nevertheless, a discussion of the changes which have occurred in my family will help us to understand the nature of the changes which generally take place in an old-world feudalism under the impact of colonial capitalism. We shall study in particular the changes which have occurred in the structure of the family, in the attitudes, roles, statuses and expectations of its various members, and in the relation of the family to its immediate surroundings and the world at large.

SOCIAL BACKGROUND OF THE FAMILY

The ancestral home of my family was until recently in the village of Falgunkara, in Tippera district in the eastern part of East Pakistan. With the establishment of British rule, Calcutta became the centre of British capitalist enterprise, and it was from Calcutta that the new ideas of the new age began to disseminate. My ancestral home, being far from the industrial and commercial zone in and around Calcutta, was therefore affected much later by the dissemination of the new ideas.

Changes had already begun in that old society; yet even so around the middle of the nineteenth century we find remnants of the old-world feudalism in the district of Tippera. This old-world feudalism had been characterized by a high degree of social stratification. Owing to various

---

1. By 'feudal' we mean the pre-capitalist society where land holding is the basis of economic and political power. Needless to say, by the use of this term we do not wish to convey all notions which are associated with the characteristic features of the land tenure system of feudal Europe, and which are very different from the land tenure system of pre-capitalist Indian society.

political and economic vicissitudes which we need not discuss here the small landed Moslem feudal class had by the nineteenth century lost its former grip on society. Nevertheless, it continued to enjoy considerable social prestige.

My family belongs to a traditional teacher class. So far as the information is available, my ancestors all belonged to the teaching profession, as I do myself. It is well known that the Brahman class and the teaching profession enjoyed a high status in the Indian situation, quite disproportionate to their income level or power position. It is therefore to be expected that our family enjoyed a high social standing in the old-world milieu a century ago. To illustrate the nature of this kind of social standing, we must say a few words about some of the feudal families of the locality, especially that of Nawab Faizunnessa Choudhurani of Poshchimgaon near Laksam (at present an important railway junction in East Pakistan), sixteen miles away from my ancestral home.

It may seem strange that as far back as the second half of the nineteenth century a Moslem lady, Nawab Faizunnessa Choudhurani, should have risen to literary and cultural eminence in the then Moslem Bengal. She personally looked after the management of her *zamindari* (rent-receiving) estates, and maintained a feudal court where bards, poets and men of letters of the locality were honoured and entertained. She herself was a poetess, authoress of *Rupjalal,* a book of poetry written in blank verse. This lady was a great patron of art and letters, and a number of the educational and charitable institutions of Tippera also owe their origin to her philanthropy. In recognition of her merit and services, the Government of India conferred on her the title of 'Nawab' in 1889, an unusual distinction for a lady in those days. (It may appear that there was more subjection of women at that time than there is now. But the Moslem lady of the feudal harem at times used to enjoy high prestige and wield considerable power in the management of her own and even her husband's estates. This is probably because, according to Moslem law (unlike Hindu law), daughters also inherit a share of the father's property along with brothers and other co-inheritors, and in the feudal families large landed estates were often inherited by female descendants. This fact will also help to explain the relative role of men and women in East Pakistani Moslem society today.)

My grandfather, Munshi Kamruddin Ahmed, who died in 1907 at

298

about 60 years of age, would at times visit the feudal court of Nawab Faizunnessa, and used to be well received by her. He also moved in the social circle of other Moslem feudal families of the locality. It was this kind of association, and not the possession of wealth and landed estates, which gave him and his ancestors their social standing.

STRUCTURE OF THE FAMILY

The modern age is characterized by the emergence of the individual. He was previously submerged in the clan, tribe, community, and, ultimately, the family. From the following discussion it will be clear how the individual was an inseparable part of the family and, again, how the family was, in its turn, an integral part of the community.

During the time of my grandfather my family lived completely in the countryside. It is further to be noted that in these rural surroundings all the neighbours were taken as if they were kinsfolk, whether they really were so or not. The neighbours would call each other by the various relationship terms, and in their day-to-day dealings they would behave as if they were actual blood relations, notwithstanding the fact that they differed in social status and attainments, sometimes very widely. They shared their joys and sorrows as if they were members of the same family. In any kind of misfortune, for example when a house had been burnt by fire or blown away by a storm, all would share it as if it were their own. They would gather together to help the victim in the reconstruction of the house. In a similar way, they would help each other with labour and implements at the time of sowing and harvest and in similar economic matters. For instance, neighbours would gather together for organizing fishing expeditions, and afterwards would share out the catch. The rural market, which was located about one mile away from my village, used to meet twice a week during the time of my grandfather. I have heard that when my grandfather went on his weekly shopping expeditions he used to go around the houses of his neighbours and ask them, especially the older female members, whether they required anything from the market. He would then buy those things for them. At social functions and festivities, particularly the various ceremonies connected with birth, marriage and death, the neighbours would be treated as if they were members of the same kinship grouping.

This type of honorary 'familial' relationship with the neighbours continued almost undisturbed until the time of my father, and even after he had to leave the village and work in semi-urbanized places. In my childhood I used at times to visit the rural home, and I used to be asked by my elders to call our neighbours not by their personal names but by the appropriate customary kinship terms. But as we grew up we gradually discarded the use of these kin terms, until now we treat our neighbours at best as 'good neighbours', and nothing more than that. During my father's lifetime, neighbours from my ancestral home occasionally visited him at his place of work, and when they did so they used to be cordially received and entertained exactly like our true relations. Today, however, it is unthinkable that such neighbours should visit my house in Dacca city and stay with me overnight.

We shall find that the family which we are studying has undergone radical change in its structure during the past century. The joint family with its deep ties in the rural community, has transformed itself into a nuclear type, and today individualism has become increasingly manifest in familial relationships.

It is interesting to study first the changes in the size of the family. Actual near relations who lived within the family household during the time of my grandfather and great-grandfather were but few. My grandfather had one sister and no brothers. After being widowed in her middle age, his sister came back and lived with him. The household consisted, therefore, of my grandfather, grandmother, their children and the widowed sister of my grandfather. During the time of my father the situation was different.

My father, Moulvi Abu Rashid (c.1876 to 1954), was an officer of the Education Department of the government and worked as sub-inspector of schools. He had two sisters and, again, no brother. The elder sister, Umdatunnessa, with her eight children, lived in our rural house under the same roof with my father, who himself shouldered the task of educating the children. This he did by taking those who were of school age to stay with him at his place of work. In a similar way the school-age children of his other sister (although she was not living under the same roof) also lived with my father. Some of my maternal cousins, too, used to live with him for purposes of education. Then of course, there were his own children, my siblings; we numbered altogether seven brothers and one sister. However, the size of the family was not actually at any one time as big as it may appear from this account. As soon as my cousins became earning members, they left my

300

father's household, though they used to render pecuniary assistance to him in defraying the educational expenses of their younger brothers, and would pay their courtesy visits off and on, especially at marriage festivities which were generally held at our rural home. In this way my cousins, both from my father's and mother's side, were constantly coming, staying in our household and ultimately leaving it during the time when we, the seven brothers and one sister, were growing up.

It has to be noted here that the household did not consist only of these relations. There were also the domestic servants who, during my father's time, were looked upon as part and parcel of our household, almost family members themselves. The male servants used to be paid a nominal wage, but in addition they received food and shelter within the family household. It was thought to be derogatory for the maid-servants to demand any wage above their board and keep. Of the many servants and maid-servants who came and went, a few became greatly attached to the family—as witness one of the old maid-servants (now about 60) of my father's time who is still living with a brother of mine to this day, not now as a maid-servant, however, but rather as a full member of the household.

As my cousins one by one left my father's household on obtaining employment in various occupations and professions, so we brothers also left our parents, and our sister too left when she married. Thus, although in my father's time it was a large 'extended family', it is surprising to note that within a single generation the families of all my brothers have become of the nuclear type. On the other hand, it is to be noted here also that my eldest brother had to help my father substantially in defraying the cost of the college and university education of my brothers. Although today his family is just a nuclear type, in the earlier stages of his career some of us used at times to stay with him during our schooling. The eldest son of the family in this part of the world had to play a much greater role in family matters than the other children. Even today, when we have lost our moorings in rural life and modernism is manifest in all familial relationships, my eldest brother has to attend upon and entertain our relations whenever they come to the city of Dacca. We, being the younger brothers of the family, are not expected to perform these duties.

We thus find that the break-up of the former extended families has been going on for some time. Since the second world war, inflation, increasing urbanization and expanding industrialization have further

301

accelerated the process. The former extended family has now been replaced by a number of nuclear families. Again, in recent times, they in their turn have been growing smaller in size. Married couples are having fewer children. This fall in the number of children in the family tends to be a very recent phenomenon, probably because birth-control techniques were not known and, if they were known, contraceptives were not easily available. Further, if the practice of birth control became known, it was frowned upon. Parents were also in favour of large families. During the second world war, however, middle-class families began to experience great hardship, and it became difficult for them to provide for two good meals a day for themselves and their children. It was keenly felt that it was not prudent to have a large number of children. Nevertheless, along with the hardship which war and inflation brought, came opportunities for men of enterprise and initiative. The partition of Bengal in 1947 opened up new avenues to the growing Moslem middle class of East Pakistan. In such circumstances, the idea of family planning could not make much headway. But as conditions are now being stabilized after partition, and as middle-class families are finding it more and more difficult to maintain themselves economically, they are beginning to think in terms of birth control and family planning. Recent attempts on the part of the government to popularize family planning have removed the social taboo from it, and it is likely that educated families in East Pakistan will increasingly resort to birth-control devices and that nuclear families in the future will shrink yet further in size.

RELATIONS BETWEEN DIFFERENT MEMBERS OF THE FAMILY

Modernism has not only affected the size of the family, but it has also profoundly affected the role and attitudes of the different members of the family. We shall discuss how the relationships between husband and wife, parents and children, brothers and sisters have been affected by the modern age.

Husband and wife and their in-laws

The wife was not thought of as a chattel, but soon after marriage she had to become an integral part of the husband's family, and had to perform all household duties. This was the prevalent notion till my parents' days. My mother came from a decadent feudal family where she was not accustomed to hard labour because there was a large number of traditional and hereditary servants. In her husband's house she adapted herself to the new situation, and assumed full responsibility for managing a big family. She had to lose all her own identity in the family of my father and, moreover, be responsible for the children of my father's sister as well. This meant a great sacrifice on her part even in terms of the standards of those days. (The normal assumption was that the relations from my mother's side would not live with my father, but visit us as guests. In the later years of my father's career, however, some of my maternal cousins did live with us for education, etc., but the family remained essentially that of my father.)

In family matters my father would be guided by his sister, Umdatunnessa, who was older than he, and it was expected that my mother would fall in line and that the other members of the family in turn would enjoy status according to their age and seniority. Although my father would consult my mother in family matters, she was expected to agree with him in everything, especially where his relations with his kinsmen were involved. And in fact she would be wise enough not to disagree in any such matters even though she might have harboured differing opinions. This type of strong tie holding together a patriarchal family continued unabated until my parental cousins became independent and got married. So long as the authority of my father and that of my paternal aunt and mother remained unchallenged, the unity of the family was preserved. With the coming of the new female members as brides who were not accustomed or willing to accept such authority, the former harmony within the family was greatly shaken. In the latter period of her life my mother also began to assert herself more and more. She used to say that as others were looking towards the interests of their children, she would fail in her duty if she did not look after the interests of her own children. My father tried his best to maintain the unity of the family up to the last moment of his life, but he found himself increasingly in a desperate situation.

In my generation, as I have noted earlier, families have taken a nuclear pattern, and so no conflict of this nature arises. In the new pattern the husband and wife exist for each other and they together exist for their children and nobody else. There has been a considerable change in the attitude and role of the husband and wife. The wife no longed silently acquiesces in things in the husband's family. Although

303

the family is still looked upon predominantly as the husband's, it is in fact being more and more built up around the wife.

The prevalent idea in preceding generations was that for a woman heaven lay at the feet of the husband. This notion has been gradually discarded in favour of a more egalitarian view of the role of men and women. It was a practice in the past that after the marriage ritual the wife would ceremonially salute the husband by touching his feet. Even a generation ago, in my childhood, I heard from some elders of the family that in order to inculcate the habit of obedience a female newcomer (a new bride) was taught to salute her husband by touching his feet every morning before he went to work. This outward demonstration of obedience to the husband is no longer a marked feature. Nevertheless, today it is still expected of the wife that she should be obedient and respectful in her behaviour towards her husband. A woman without a husband has no social status, so to speak. A woman disloyal to the husband is looked down upon. As we have observed earlier, the wife used to demonstrate her loyalty in her day-to-day life. Now she is not expected to demonstrate her loyalty in this fashion in public. However, she will at times show her loyalty secretly to her husband, for example, by touching his feet on the occasion of marriage, *Eid* festivals, etc. This seems to be rather an expression of her dependence on her husband than a demonstration of her loyalty, and a private matter between the couple, not an obligatory formal requirement.

It is significant that the mode of address has also been altogether changed. My mother would never utter my father's name. If another person's name in the household happened to be similar to that of my father, she would call that person by some other name. When she wanted to refer to my father, she would do it using the third person pronoun or some circumlocutory term or phrase. My father also addressed her in a similar way, although he was not so punctilious as she. It may be asked here, what was the reason for such a mode of address? We have said earlier that the nuclear family was non-existent at that period. Husband and wife owed allegiance to a much bigger unit, and therefore they were not expected to demonstrate their affection towards each other by the use of terms of endearment. If any loyalty and affection had to be shown by the husband in public, it was to the larger unit, the 'extended family'. The wife was, of course, required to show loyalty to the husband, but she was required to show no less loyalty to her in-laws. A new bride was not even expected to converse with her husband in the presence of her older in-laws.

In the present generation, modes of address have greatly changed. Husband and wife often call and refer to each other by name. Reference to the husband by the third person pronoun is, of course, still found, especially when the wife speaks in the presence of members of the older generations. But the wife is no longer expected to avoid the male in-laws who are senior to her. It is not even unusual for the bride to participate in humorous and light discussion in their presence.

Parents and children

My father was a liberal-minded man possessing many modern ideas, but in matters of family discipline he was a patriarch of the old style. For the maintenance of the cohesiveness of the large extended family of which he was the head, it was required that he should be so, although domination of others was not the main motive force in him. All children in the family must obey their parents without question. He would often quote the Sanskrit verse which delineates the attitude parents should take towards children:

> Laloyet panchabarshani
> Dashabarshani tarayet.
> Prapteshe shoreshebarshe,
> Putramitra badacharet.

This may be translated:

> Show affection and love to the baby up to the age of 5.
> Then up to the age of 10, 'to spare the rod is to spoil the child'.
> After the age of 16, he has attained manhood,
> He should therefore be treated as a friend.

My father would generally expect all to obey their parents and elders in matters of family discipline. When they grew older my father would no doubt consult them and often accept their opinion. If, however, he fundamentally disagreed with them, he would say: 'I do not object if you have your way, but I must also have my way.' Although he was a strict disciplinarian, it was not possible in his old age for him to maintain the unity of the family.

In the present generation the autocratic patriarch is not to be found, as he is no longer needed in a family of the nuclear pattern.

305

My father often used to give the example of a Hindu joint family, the Dewanji family of Dattapara, Noakhali, in East Pakistan. In that family as many as forty members used to take their food at the same table. Even in these days, this family had more than a dozen university graduates among its members. It conducted a school of its own where the girls and boys of the family excelled their counterparts in other schools in curricular and extra-curricular activities. My father used to say that the progress of that family had been secured by co-operation and joint action, and its motto had been: 'Each for all, and all for each.' He would add that if the members of his family worked on the same principle, his family also would be as renowned as the Dattapara family. He sometimes quoted the example of the unquestioning obedience of Lakhshmana (Rama's brother) to Rama, and used to express the hope that every member of his family should cultivate those same virtues too.

Thus in our childhood we were taught the habit of obedience not only to our parents, but also to our older brothers and sisters, including our cousins. This obedience and the mutual attachment gradually began to recede into the background with the entry of new female members and the break-up of the family group into separate nuclear units. At the moment my brothers and sister are all living separately. We have no common home, nor have we any common source of income. The majority of my brothers and my sister live in the city of Dacca. They usually, although not invariably, meet each other on social calls. Since the death of my father the common bond has been lost and the families of my brothers are, for all practical purposes, separate and independent units.

In the case of our children, the example of a joint family is no longer cited even as an ideal. On the contrary, whenever anybody speaks about it, he frowns upon it and points out how inconsistent the idea is with the ideals of our modern age. In spite of this, the parents still advise their children to obey their superiors, and to love and stand by each other in prosperity and adversity, even though they may be living in separate families. But this type of advice does not have the same appeal to them as it used to have for us.

Nevertheless, although it has been taken for granted ever since my father's death and the disintegration of his large family group that individualism is the order of the day and there can be no better ideal, yet we are beginning to realize that too much individualism is also of no value. We are beginning to feel that although living separately in separate households is good, yet there should also be an over-all solidarity, and that kinsmen should still help each other both in prosperity and in adversity. It is now clear to us that without some such over-all solidarity an individual may well find himself in a desperate situation, especially in a great city. In view of this, conscious efforts have been made in recent times to rebuild some kind of solidarity through the deliberate organization of shared social functions.

But it seems obvious that in the coming generations even this semblance of wider 'family' solidarity will disappear.

LOCATION

As we have said earlier, until recently the ancestral home of the family was in the village of Falgunkara, in the district of Tippera, in East Pakistan. At present only the vacant residential plot is lying there, without anybody to live on it. In 1901, my father, Moulvi Abu Rashid, was employed as a teacher in a government school, and later on he was appointed as sub-inspector of schools. This involved him in a considerable amount of travelling. He did not at first take my mother with him. On weekends and during holidays he would come home and look after his household affairs. My eldest brother was born in 1902. As he grew up, my mother felt that for the sake of better education and good company for the child she could leave the village. Thus it was that the family for the first time left its ancestral home. But the family members still visited the place from time to time, especially on occasions of marriage and other festivities.

In the later part of his career my father was posted to Feni, a subdivisional town, fifteen miles away from my ancestral home, and continued to stay there for about thirteen years till his retirement. His sons and other well-wishers insisted that, as Feni had a degree-granting college and other facilities for the education of children, he should settle there permanently, but my father preferred to come back to his ancestral home in Falgunkara, for which he had a great sentimental attachment. However, at the insistence of his sons and well-wishers, he purchased a plot of land at Feni and erected a house there before he left for the village home. Since then, for various reasons, my family members have often thought of settling permanently at Feni. In fact, one of the brothers, who is a physician, has been living there ever since my father left the place. Other brothers who are employed in various government posts or were studying at the college or university also thought of settling down at Feni after their retirement. But as our parents lived in the village home, we used to have to go there to visit them, and although we also visited Feni our ties there were not fully developed. Some of my brothers also considered settling near Calcutta to profit from the advantages of that city. However, we were not in a position to make up our minds on this point. About this time, in 1947, the partition of the subcontinent took place, and Dacca was made the capital of East Pakistan. As Dacca already had a university, it was undoubtedly the best place for the education of children, and it was felt strongly that now we should finally settle down in Dacca. At present out of seven brothers, five are serving in different jobs in Dacca, and have purchased land there. My sister has also settled in Dacca city.

After the death of my father, the buildings of my ancestral home were dismantled and brought to Feni. Since then we have lost all our connexions with the original village. There is practically no tendency on the part of anybody to return there, and although we still regard it as our ancestral home, we do not have any special attachment to it. For all intents and purposes the family has become urbanized. It is not likely that future generations will even regard Falgunkara as their ancestral home, far less that they will have any attachment to it.

What are the main reasons for the reluctance of the family members to go back to the village? In the first place, we should note here that as all the present generation grew to manhood outside the village home, they did not (as my father did) develop any special personal love for it. In the second place, although we used to visit our village after the retirement of my father, and thus developed some kind of attachment for it, we found that it was impossible to live in a village without joining one or other of the local power groups. The person who lives in the country but does not become involved with rural politics is likely to be harassed in so many ways. It was therefore thought that in an urban set-up, where relationships are more impersonal, we would be able to lead a more peaceful life. In the third place, female newcomers were particularly reluctant to go back to a village life, as there is less freedom for them there.

It is to be noted here that the change of location has done much to secure greater freedom for women. It is certain that it is this which has given them better opportunities for higher education and greater freedom of movement. They have also been entering various occupations. Thirty years ago, my sister was sent by my father to Dacca for elementary school education. At that time it was questioned in many quarters whether he was doing a good thing. It is surprising to note that in the course of a mere thirty years such a change has occurred that this same sister's daughters have not only received a university education, but one has even been to the United Kingdom, for still higher education. Yet even now in my village female education is looked down upon, and the freedom of women in many spheres is curtailed. Formerly, the ethos prevailing in the country was that as soon as the new bride came, she had to become part and parcel of the husband's family under the control of her in-laws. In the urban set-up the joint family no longer exists, and the newly-married woman becomes at once the mistress of the house. And the new family begins to revolve around her. Urbanization and the disintegration of the joint family have led to a great emancipation of women both in and outside the home.

RELIGION, RITUALS AND BELIEFS: MARRIAGE

Orthodoxy is on the wane and religion has been gradually losing its former hold on the family. As a result, the family has become more a secular association and less a sacred institution. This has brought about disturbances in family stability and peace. In the family we are discussing, we find in the earlier phases a combination of the ideals of Islamic and Indian womanhood. Both in this world and in the after-world a wife was thought of as existing solely for the husband, and for her there could be nothing beyond, above or against him. Today this unquestioned authority of the husband never goes unchallenged by the wife. A modern wife is no longer a *sita*. She is conscious of her rights and her separate entity. Obedience and faithfulness are now required not only from the wife but from the husband too. Movies, Western and modern Bengali novels, theatres, direct or indirect contact with Western culture—all these have helped to dethrone the ideal of *sita* in favour of that of Western womanhood, which insists on equal rights for both the sexes. It thus appears that women are becoming emancipated from their former subjection, although this may be at the cost of family happiness and stability.

Islam sanctions polygyny on special conditions. But it was not prevalent in the family under discussion, probably because even from early times it was essentially a middle-class family. It was in families of 'peasant proprietors' and those with a feudal background that polygynous tendencies were sometimes at a premium.

But there are other ways in which change in religious attitudes has vitally affected the institution of marriage. In the older days there were many formalities and ceremonies to be observed. In rich feudal families it was quite common for wedding festivities to continue for a month or even more. In middle-class and poorer families it was not unusual for the bridegroom's party to be detained even for a week or more for the sake of fun and formalities. In the rural areas even today no marriage can take place without the formal consent of the village elders. On every occasion of a wedding all the villagers, or at the very least the heads of all the families, must be invited, though poorer families may be absolved from these obligations. In addition to the villagers, kinsmen of the family come from great distances to attend the wedding ceremony. With the general decline in economic conditions, extravagance in marriage ceremonies has been curtailed.

Today, in the urban areas there are no such obligations to meet, and weddings are becoming as simple as possible. Recently there have been some weddings in Dacca where the whole ceremony concluded within an hour or two, followed by a dinner party. The observances involved in the formal meeting of the bride and bridegroom after the marriage contract has been completed have also been cut to a minimum. There has thus been a tendency to regard the marriage ceremonies more as a social and secular affair and less as a religious one. The result is obvious. In the former system religion used to provide a firm basis for the family; but today this is increasingly shaken. It is well known to students of sociology that ceremonies play a great part in giving stability to institutions. If marriages are performed with fewer rituals and ceremonies, it would not be unduly hazardous to predict that there may be an increased impetus to divorce, desertion, etc.

CONTRACTING A MARRIAGE

Until recently marriages were arranged by the parents, and neither

310

the bride nor the groom had a voice in the decision. In my generation the choice was made by the bridegroom, but the parents would have their say. So far as the bride was concerned, usually her formal consent was asked for, but she could not give a refusal. It seems that today when the choice is made by the groom he need not consult his parents. When everything is settled he will take the formal consent of the parents, and it is they who cannot say no. So far as daughters are concerned, marriages are still settled by the parents on their behalf. However, the tendency has developed among college and university-educated girls in the city of Dacca to arrange their marriages for themselves, even against the will of their parents. The boys of my family have already secured their freedom of choice. Will the girls remain for long insulated from the forces which are being generated among university and college-educated girls?

The prevalent idea in Moslem society is that there should not be a moment's delay in the marriage of a girl as soon as she comes of marriageable age. In the area which is now East Pakistan marriages used sometimes to take place even before puberty, though consummation would be delayed until later. My father was against the prevailing idea of child marriage, and maintained that no girl should be married before the age of 16. Today the girls of the family are receiving college and university education and later marriage is in vogue; but as a rule they marry between the ages of 17 and 20 and then continue their studies. This tendency towards later marriage has become possible because of the urban situation of the family. In rural East Pakistan the parents of a girl who remains unmarried after puberty suffer severe censure even now.

The change in the age of marriage has done much to affect the relations between husband and wife, and their relations to the traditional 'extended family'. Formerly, the young bride used to come to the family with a flexible mind. She used to accept without question the authority of her husband and her in-laws. Now this is no longer the case. She comes with a mind already formed, and she begins to draw the husband towards her side.

In the eastern part of East Pakistan where Moslem society has been less influenced by Hindu manners and customs, it was the husband's family, and not the bride's, which used to pay for marriage expenses and offer jewellery and other presents. This custom still continues in the rural areas. However, in recent times a tendency has been

311

developing in the rising merchant class and educated middle class for presents both in cash and kind to be demanded from the bride's family, after the Hindu pattern of giving a dowry. But whether the bride's or the groom's family will actually demand such presents, and how much, depends on the relative social status of the bride and the groom. In my father's day the groom's family had to offer presents of jewellery, etc., and would sometimes pay for the other expenses of the wedding. To-day in our family the major expenses of marriage are borne by the bride's family and the groom's is expected to offer a little nominal jewellery, the wedding dress, and some other presents, while the groom also expects some presents for himself from the bride's family. That the groom should demand presents in cash or kind has generally been disliked in my family.

Presents in the olden days consisted mainly of jewellery in gold and silver. The value was often quite considerable, depending upon the social status of the bride, and it worked as a security for her in times of adversity. But today gold and silver jewellery has lost its former importance as security for the educated girls, because they can depend upon themselves to earn a living if they have to. We may give a small, rather amusing, illustration here regarding the value attached to such ornaments in earlier days. In the twenties the provincial governor of Bengal, British by birth, once visited the sub-divisional town of Feni, where we lived. A ladies' party was arranged in honour of the governor's wife. The ladies of the town attended the party, attired in their best saris and adorned with all their heavy gold jewellery. Some of the ladies, who could find no more room for their jewels on their person, made a point of carrying them along in caskets in order to show them to the wife of the governor, if they could find any opportunity to do so. Display of this kind would not occur today.

An important part of the Moslem marriage contract is the groom's offer, known as *mehr*. This is a mention of a sum of money offered by the groom on the occasion of the wedding. The amount is determined by the social status of the bride, and sometimes it is a large sum. According to Islamic law, the amount has actually to be paid over by the husband to the wife. However, according to the custom of the country, it is generally never demanded by the wife. In effect it works as a check against ill treatment or desertion or threat of divorce by the husband, for the wife in such circumstances may demand her *mehr*. It also acts as security for her in the case of the death of the

312

husband, when she can realize her share of the *mehr* from the husband's property.

Besides this, the husband has to accept certain self-imposed conditions in the marriage deed or contract. He remains honour bound to respect those conditions (although they may not be always legally valid). These conditions also reflect the social status which a woman enjoys. I cite below the conditions which I found in the marriage deed of my parents:

DEED OF MAINTENANCE

pursuant to the deed of dower *(Kabinnama)* in favour of
Shamsun Neda Khatun, daughter of the late Munshi Sheikh Altak Ali,
Village: Joynaryanpur (known as Rajapur),
Pargana: Bhulua, Police Station: Feni, District: Noakhali,
Mussalman by religion, Talukdar by profession,
executed by Moulvi Abu Rashid (Nejamuddin Mahmud),
son of Munshi Kamruddin Ahmed,
Talukdar by profession,
Village: Falgunkara, Pargana: Tisna, Police Station: Chauddagram,
District: Tippera.

Whereas I have married you today by executing a separate *Kabinnama* in this assembly voluntarily of my own free will being in sound health and possession of my senses and fixed the dower at rupees 4,500/- (rupees four thousand five hundred only).

Now therefore to enforce the terms of the said *Kabinnama* I execute this Deed of Maintenance, and

I hereby promise that you will be entitled now and in future to the benefits accruing from the dower and the terms mentioned in the aforesaid *Kabinnama*. I shall not be entitled to lodge any objection against it in any criminal, civil or revenue court; if I do so, my objection will be held invalid by the courts.

To this end I execute this Deed of Maintenance to enforce the terms of the *Kabinnama,* with the conditions as mentioned hereunder, this the 14th Day of Kartik, 1306 (Bengali Era).

Condition 1. During the continuance of our marriage I shall teach you the rites and rituals of Islam. If the gold and silver ornaments of the value of rupees 500/- presented to you today be stolen or be broken as a result of wear and tear, I shall replace them at my own expense. I shall offer *Zakat* on these ornaments; failing which I shall be considered a sinner in the eye of God.

Condition 2. The amount of the dower will be payable by me on demand at your paternal house in the presence of your mother, brother and their heirs or descendants. Satisfaction shall be endorsed on the *Kabinnama,* failing which no credit will accrue for the payment.

Condition 3. I shall always pass my days in your company keeping you in enjoyment of food and raiment and the service of servants and maid-servants.

If in the pursuit of my avocation I have to go abroad to distant places, I shall take your leave. Before starting I shall provide you with maintenance suitable for a lady of status. My stay outside will not exceed six months. If on return I find that the maintenance provided by me having proved short, you had to incur debt, I shall clear off the debt; failing which I shall not be entitled to demand of you any duty as a wife. You will be competent to realize the unpaid amount by suing me in court.

Condition 4. I shall not give you any pain either by hand or by word of mouth. I shall not myself act, nor make you act in any manner which would be considered insulting to the sentiments of a lady of status.

If there persists misunderstanding between you and my relations, or if the climate of my place proves unsuitable to you, I shall construct a house or rooms according to your liking and pass my days there in your company.

Condition 5. As long as our marriage continues, I shall pay you rupees 15/- per month for your pleasure as pocket expenses. If I do not pay the amount voluntarily, you will be able to realize the same by suing me.

Condition 6. I shall not prevent you from paying visits to the houses of your father, mother, brother or near relatives. On the other hand, I shall myself accompany you on such occasions. If you incur debt for such visits, I shall repay the same.

Condition 7. I shall not marry a second time without your permission, nor keep any concubine. If I do so, they will be considered as divorced, once, twice thrice, i.e., finally. Children born of them will not be entitled to inherit my property.

Condition 8. God forbid, if I become mad, untraced, imprisoned or impotent or fail to perform my matrimonial obligations for a period of one year, or if there persist ill-feeling between you and me, or if I am otherwise considered unsuitable by you, you will be able to divorce me once, twice, thrice, i.e. finally (by virtue of the delegated power with which I hereby empower you) whenever you wish or wherever you may be.

The bond of matrimony between you and me will thereupon stand dissolved and you will be free to choose another husband. I shall no longer be entitled to demand any matrimonial duty from you.

To this end I execute this Deed of Maintenance pursuant to the *Kabinnama*
Given under my hand this the 14th Day of Kartik, 1306 (Bengali Era).[1]

OTHER RITUAL PRACTICES

A number of rituals and beliefs have long been current in East Pakistani society that are not strictly sanctioned by Islam. We cannot go into a detailed description of them in this article, but that they have

---

1. The Deed, of which the above is the original version in English, was registered at the office of the Sub-Registrar, Feni, on 31 October 1899.

served to strengthen familial relations cannot be denied. It is the woman who has domesticated the man. It is therefore natural that whenever the woman finds that her husband is indifferent in family matters or towards her, she should resort to certain rituals and practices designed to bring the husband under her control. In addition, there exist various rituals for the cure of diseases and for securing other kinds of welfare of the family or for thanksgiving, and on various occasions of festivities. These rituals have lain especially in the domain of women. Although my father would generally observe the religious injunctions of Islam, which were few and simple, he was against all the manifestations of these other rituals which constituted the popular religion. My mother used to observe some of them secretly; for instance, she would send subscriptions to the *pir*'s *mazar* (the shrine of the saint) without the knowledge of my father, or she would offer *shirni* (ritual offering) in the mosque or *mazar*, as a mark of gratitude for some good which had accrued to the family, or with the hope of preventing ill fortune from befalling any of its members. My father had to acquiesce in the observance of such rituals though he thought them useless and, in his opinion, the money would have been better spent on the health and education of children.

We thus find that in my father's time, although society as a whole was steeped in a multitude of traditional rituals and beliefs, there was a relative absence of them in my family. It seems that since Independence popular rituals and beliefs have been on the increase. I know a number of occasions when members of highly educated families have visited the *pir* for the healing of incurable diseases or for securing other kinds of worldly benefits. As we have earlier observed, these popular rituals are mainly the concern of women. It is thus natural to expect that with the greater freedom and emancipation of women popular rituals may come to occupy some place in the family in spite of modernism and rationalism.

With the rise of secularism, orthodox religious practices have been gradually losing their importance. However, religious festivals such as the two *Eids* and *Sab-i-barat* are observed, sometimes with even greater zeal than before. Moreover, these festivals are still taken as occasions for meeting relations, and thus strengthening the family ties. Sweets are exchanged on such occasions and juniors go to the houses of senior members of the family to pay their respects and to exchange greetings. In recent times, there has been a tendency to develop a few

315

more family functions such as the celebration of birthdays of children or marriage anniversaries or the death anniversary of my father. These social functions are beginning to assume a much greater importance than the above traditional religious festivities.

During my father's time men and women lived in two altogether different worlds. Women used to live at home and men would work outside. And the division of labour between the two sexes was as complete as possible. That women would remain inside the home and would not be required outside for work used to be thought of as a social distinction for women or relatively well-to-do families. For obvious practical reasons there could not be any absolute seclusion for working woman. Seclusion was expected of women of good social status, and they accepted the seclusion for the sake of their own prestige and for the maintenance of social distance. If they ever visited the houses of their neighbours or went to bathe in the outer pool, it would generally be done during the night. If the female members of such families were required to move from one house to another or visit distant places during the daytime, they would move by palanquin (frequently covered by the veil), or if it was not available they might walk carefully covered by some kind of veil as, for example, a *chaddar* (i.e., a long scarf). It should be specifically mentioned here that there was no use of *burkha*[1] in our family.

Women always used to cover their heads with the sari, especially in the presence of male in-laws. They were not generally expected to appear before the father-in-law and other uncles-in-law in the same relationship group at all, and also not before the elder brothers of the husband and other cousins-in-law of the same age group. If the bride should happen suddenly to find herself in the presence of such relations she would draw the head cover (i.e., the tail-end of the sari) over her face, and stretch it as long as possible. It goes without saying that she would not appear before any male outsider except the servants and others of the same category. Such were the prevailing customs among the Bengali Moslems during the days of my father and grandfather, and they used to be also generally observed by the female members

---

1. *Burkha,* the completely enveloping black 'sack', was especially in use among the women of feudal towns, such as Dacca, Murshidabad, etc.

of my family. However, so far as my family is concerned at least, they have lost their rigidity today. In the rural areas these customs are still in vogue. But in the urban areas they have almost disappeared.

None the less, although the free movement of women has increased, especially in urban areas, and women have been taking more and more to education, and increasingly entering various occupations and professions, they still live in a social world separate from that of men. They have their own associations, clubs and other sorts of social contacts. For instance, if any woman visits my house in Dacca on a social call, even though she is highly educated, it is expected that my wife, rather than I, will receive her in a separate parlour. Similarly, if a male visitor comes to my house, it is my duty, and not that of my wife, to look after him.

As regards the change in the mode of wearing dress, it is significant that the present style of wearing the sari was introduced by the female members of the family of the poet Rabindranath Tagore, in the latter part of the nineteenth century, and was later accepted by the Bengali Hindu middle class. In the present generation this is the prevailing style of wearing the sari in the Bengali Moslem middle class in East Pakistan as well. This way of wearing the sari is smart, dignified and elegant in style, and we should stay that it has given a greater expression to the freer movement of woman's body and her beauty. The use of cosmetics and the adoption of the Western art of make-up have also added to female beauty and elegance.

It is not only women's dress that has changed; male attire has undergone a considerable and even greater alteration. In the case of my family we find that women have discarded the veil and the old mode of wearing the sari, and have thus been coming closer to indigenous Bengali culture. In their make-up sometimes they use *tip* (a red mark on their forehead, which is another special trait of Bengali girls). But these are still Oriental fashions. By contrast, in looking at the males of my family, we find that we have been gradually discarding the Bengali mode of dress in favour of Western styles. My father used to wear the *lungi* at home, and when going out would wear *askan-payajama*, with a fez cap for head-dress. During our student days we were influenced by the Hindu mode of dress, and instead of our *payajamas* we would sometimes also use the dhoti. However, with the movement for Pakistan and the development of Moslem self-consciousness, we discarded the dhoti and took to *payajama*, shirt

317

and coat—this time dropping the head-dress, i.e., the cap. Recently, we have been taking more and more to trousers and shirt for ordinary occasions, adding a tie for special occasions.

Change in the mode of dress has something to do with the relations between men and women. The woman of former days in her veil was, so to speak, an object without free will, to be carried about by the husband. Today, along with the change in dress, she has a new personality and has been exerting herself more and more in every field. She wants to have a say in all family matters, including the question of how her husband will dress himself. The husband, therefore, must give up his former mode of dressing and take more and more to the Western type of dress which gives him a smart appearance.

But because of the Western style of dress, have we become more Westernized in our thoughts and ideas than our forefathers? When the youth of the nineteenth century for the first time came in touch with Western ideas, their minds became highly rationalistic and critical. Because of the freshness and newness of these Western ideas, the youths of that generation were naturally attracted towards them. Those who imbibed these ideas would accept nothing without question. In their thoughts, therefore, they were much Westernized, although in their dress they remained 100 per cent Bengali Moslem. But we find that the present generation sometimes accepts things without question, and thinks that it is better to spend time in material pursuits than to try to get answers for the basic problems of life.

DAILY LIFE

We have already observed in discussing various aspects of life in East Pakistan that the two worlds in which men and women lived and worked were different in so many ways. We hope to illustrate this aspect by describing a 'normal' daily routine. I will describe here the daily routine life of our family thirty years ago as I observed it in my childhood, and later on will contrast it with the daily routine as it is today in my own family.

My father used to rise from bed at about 4 to 4.30 in the morning, and would spend about two hours reading novels, etc. (Maria Edgeworth was one of his favourite authors). At about 5.30 or 6 a.m. he would call all of us to get up. The younger children would be asked to commit to memory arithmetic tables and also recite poems from

318

memory while still in bed. Afterwards, we would get up and go for our morning walk at about 6 to 6.30. My father would leave his study and perform his ablutions and morning prayer (he was not very regular about it). Meanwhile, we would return from the morning walk and have our breakfast, which consisted mainly of different kinds of indigenous preparations such as *chira, khai, muri, pitha,* milk (no tea), milk products and seasonal fruits. In my early childhood tinned food such as biscuits, pastry, etc., were very little used. All these items of breakfast were prepared by the women at home, which used to take up a good portion of their time.

After breakfast my father would sit down with us and give us lessons. Between 9 and 10.30 we would have our bath and morning meal, and after that would leave for school. Meanwhile, father would go to market and mother would prepare our food as quickly as possible, cooking only a few items because we had to hurry off to school. Mother would continue her work in the kitchen and prepare a full meal for those who were not going to school or office. This was a mid-day meal which would be served between 12 noon and 1 to 1.30 p.m. When all the male members had taken their meal my mother would eat afterwards along with the servants. Because of the pressure of work, she sometimes used to take her meal as late as 3 or 4 in the afternoon. According to the prevailing custom of the country, the mistress of the household was not expected to take her meal before the male members had taken theirs.

My father sometimes would leave for the inspection of schools quite early in the morning, and sometimes had to stay away for one or two days. If it was a holiday, or if he had not left for inspection work, he would spend his time in gardening and other household work in the morning and in the evening. At sunset he would perform his evening prayer. We would be at school from 11 a.m. to 4 or 5 p.m. On our return we would have a light meal and then go out to play. At sunset we would return home and study for about two hours. If father happened to be at home, he would give us a few lessons. Between 8 and 9 p.m. we would have our evening meal. The meal would be followed by conversation, gossip and story-telling, after which we used to go to bed. In the meanwhile my mother would take a nap (if the pressure of work allowed it) after her noon-day meal, and then begin again her work in the kitchen. She would look after all types of household work and in the evening, when all the male members had taken their meal,

319

she too would eat, once more along with servants and sometimes very late at night, say 11 p.m. or midnight. She might even miss out her meal altogether, if it was still later. Although she had the help of servants and maid-servants, there is no doubt that she was the hardest worker in the whole household.

In this daily routine there was hardly any scope for recreation, except that the children used to go out to play in the evening. Sometimes there would be functions in connexion with marriage ceremonies which, although enjoyed by the children and other members of the family, were rather colourless, because music, fireworks and other sorts of extravagant expenditure of this nature were all prohibited by religion. Sometimes a circus or a carnival or a *jatra* (open-air theatre) party would visit the town. Somehow or other we would manage to witness them, but generally these were disapproved of by religious people, and my father also did not like his children to take too much interest in matters which would distract their attention from studies. He used often to quote a Sanskrit verse which virtually meant *mens sana in corpore sano*.

Now, let us take the example of the daily routine of my household as it exists today. I generally get up between 6 and 7 a.m. Sometimes I go out for a morning walk, sometimes not. On my return from this morning walk I generally wait for about an hour for breakfast, which is served at about 8 a.m. when the daily newspaper also arrives. Items served at breakfast are simple; such things as *parata* or buttered toast, eggs and one of the following cereals: oats, cornflakes or *shuji*, sometimes *shewai*. In addition, there may be pastries, cakes or sweets bought from the market. The adults are served with tea while the children drink milk. At a quarter to nine I take my 9-year-old child in a rickshaw and leave her at school on my way to the university. I continue at my work there up to 1.30 or 2 p.m., and have my lunch, which is prepared at home and carried to the university. After taking a little rest, I continue my work normally up to 5 or 6 in the evening, at times even later. If I happen to come back by 5 or 6 p.m., I have my evening tea (a light one of tea and biscuits) at home. I then take an evening walk, in the course of which I do a little shopping in a modern market nearby. On my return home I receive visitors. With friends, the conversation is likely to continue up to 9 or 10 at night. In the meanwhile, tea and sweets may be served to them. After my friends have left I take my evening meal and go to bed.

320

The routine of work followed by my wife is almost similar to my own, except that she has to pay more attention to the children. My wife is professor of economics in a local girls' college. Thus she cannot, like my mother, pay full attention to the household work, which is performed by the domestic servants. Like me, she has to leave for her college quite early in the morning and leave the children in the care of servants. On her return from the college in the evening she looks after her children. Her friends call to visit her and she entertains them in the separate parlour reserved for female guests.

In comparison with my childhood, the scope for recreation has increased tremendously. We sometimes visit the various cultural functions organized by the student unions in the university or by other recreational organizations. But I have to admit that, although no doubt there has been a great increase in the scope for recreation, because of our busy life and great pressure of work, we ourselves can hardly find time to enjoy it. Nevertheless, my wife and I do try to go at least once a month to the cinema. Another kind of recreation is provided by the radio and gramophone. My eldest child (the 9-year-old girl) takes part in sports and games in the company of other children of the neighbourhood. On such occasions as birthdays and other festivities, my children organize tea parties, dances, etc., in my house. Whenever children's films, carnivals, circuses, music or dance parties, etc., come to the city, or some fair is on, I make it a point to take my children to them. It is interesting to contrast the opportunities for recreation for my mother and my wife. When there was less pressure of work, i.e., when there were fewer guests in the house, my mother would take some time off from her daily routine work at night and visit the neighbours' houses. That was the only kind of recreation or relaxation she had. Although my wife also has a heavy schedule of work, she has contact with the outside world and also utilizes her time for recreational activities. This was almost unthinkable in my mother's day.

We have seen earlier that my mother used to take her meal only after all the male members of the family had finished theirs. It was unthinkable, even thought to be a sin, in those days for a wife to eat before her husband. From the above routine it will be evident to the reader that it is no longer possible for us to follow that 'time-honoured' custom. Some years ago my wife and I were in New York, and every time I came home from work I would find that she would be waiting for me at table, because she could not take her meal before me. Thus we find that although the environment might have altogether changed, the older customs tend to persist. However, we are gradually realizing that, as the context has changed, we have to surrender our former values and attitudes towards life and replace them with new ones.

Combining marriage and career
in Karachi

by AMNA GANI

First you should know who I am. I am a Moslem by religion and a Memon by caste.[1] My family came from Bombay to Karachi in 1947 after the partition of India, to join our Moslem people in Pakistan, so I am an expatriate. I am 37 years old and am married, with one son aged 12 years and two sons (twins) aged 21 by my husband's first marriage. By profession I am a social worker. Although I am a Moslem, my mother was a Parsi, and she too was my father's second wife. Parsis are a small religious sect who worship the sun and fire, but they are one of the most highly developed communities of India, who have adopted Western culture and are leading industrialists and businessmen. My parents' marriage was a love marriage, a most unusual occurrence both from the point of view of the orthodox family from which father came and of my mother's family, whose religion forbids intermarriage and does not even accept converts. My mother became a Moslem before her marriage. Incidentally, I may mention that my father's first wife was still alive at the time he married my mother. Both the wives used to live together without any serious friction. My father died when I was 14. I received my primary and secondary education in a convent in Bombay, but graduated from the Moslem University in Aligarh. Aligarh is a small town near Delhi and is known only for the university, which is considered to be the seat of Moslem culture. I was sent there for graduation because my father thought I was becoming too Westernized due to my long stay in the convent. For a short period I was also a teacher in an Anglo-Vernacular school in Bombay, the Anjumane-Islam Girls High School. Three years after my graduation I was married, and a year later we moved to Karachi.

---

1. See Appendix on page 337.

My story is not, therefore, a very conventional one by Moslem standards. From the point of view of a conservative Memon, my Parsi mother, my education, my expatriation and now my work are all unusual. However, many drastic changes have occurred in most families in this great period of change that we are living through.

To understand these changes, I should first describe my father's family and also my husband's family, for it is family groups that shaped our lives.

My father was the younger of two sons of an orthodox family. He had two sisters. His father died when he was only 3 years of age, and he was brought up by my grandmother and his elder brother. He had a pampered boyhood and was educated mostly in religious teachings, as it was not considered essential that he should learn anything else. Education was not considered important in a man's life. Girls were kept as far away from school as possible. My uncle, after marrying, continued to live with his wife in the same house and he was in control of the family properties consisting of a salt mine and real estate. He had a domineering personality and was occasionally unmindful of grandmother's wishes, which was a source of irritation to my father. Therefore, on reaching maturity my father took grandmother and his two sisters (one a widow) and went to stay in a separate house.

In those days life was lived in a very conservative and orthodox manner. Strict *purdah* was observed by the women and mixed gatherings were unheard of. Separate arrangements existed for men and women on occasions of marriages, engagements, funerals, etc. Shopping by women was considered bad form, and only very old women or very young girls could be seen occasionally in the markets. Even the purchase of female clothing and jewellery was the concern of the men. Skill in cooking and looking after the children were considered the prime duties of a good wife. Incidentally, no doctors were permitted to deliver babies. Only semi-qualified indigenous nurses, called *dais*, attended at birth. All ordinary illnesses were attended to by old and tried home remedies, and it was only a chronic or serious illness that called for the services of a doctor. Living was a joint-family affair, and all near relatives stayed together and were jointly responsible for running the household.

Such were the circumstances in which my father was brought up. He was married at the age of 14 to a girl of my grandmother's choice, and for the first few years after marriage he was quite content to lead

324

the life of his forefathers. However, times were changing. The influence of Western culture and ways of life was being felt more and more. People were attending schools and colleges in increasing numbers and were joining the medical, legal and other professions which required high educational qualifications. In the course of business, my father came in contact with many such people and, being of a gregarious nature, he quickly made friends in such circles. The result was that he began to feel the inadequacies of his own life, the lack of any intellectual contact with his wife and, most keenly, the lack of his own education. He resolved that his own children, irrespective of sex, should receive the best education. During this time my father met my mother, and they quickly became firm friends. He found an intellectual companionship with her that he had not dreamed of, and the result was that father proposed and was accepted by my mother with full knowledge of his existing marriage. Mother was 18 at the time of the marriage, while father was 23 years old. It was a really happy marriage, and remained so throughout my father's life. Mother used to move about freely with father, and was an asset in his business also. My stepmother took the situation with very good grace indeed, and was quite content to look after the house and attend to household chores.

My father had two sons and one daughter by his first marriage, and my mother bore four sons and two daughters. I therefore had six brothers and two sisters. As stated earlier, father was determined to give us the best education and, therefore, as we reached school age, we were sent to English schools. At home we were given religious instruction and all of us had to pray five times a day as enjoined by the Koran. We had thus to lead two lives. At school we had to put on the prescribed dress, which for girls consisted of short frocks, but at home we had to wear the traditional long dress with a stole to cover our heads. In those days, girls over 8 years of age were not supposed to move about without *purdah* or to play with boys, but in our case this rule was not enforced, and I used to play freely with my brothers and their friends and other cousins and relatives. My aunts did not like the idea of my completing my secondary education, but father was adamant on my going as high as I could or would. Thus I was the first girl in our community to matriculate. Throughout those years I was given equal chances with my brothers who were older—in fact, being a girl gained me preferential treatment. I was allowed to move about

325

freely, attend cinema shows and picnics, activities which formerly were reserved for boys only.

However, my father drew the line at any of us becoming Western-ized. He cherished Moslem culture and the Moslem way of life. There-fore, from the age of 9 I had to grow my hair and put on long dresses and a stole to cover the head. English cosmetics were also dis-couraged. The reason my father always gave me was that I was the first girl of the community to reach the higher educational level, and I should not do things that would shock the community without any benefit to me. He wished me to become a pattern for the community's other girls to follow, and to illustrate that acquisition of English education, which was the need of the day, was possible even in a traditional set-up. In the course of years, this did have an effect. At the time other girls of my age did not attend schools, but the girls who grew up after that did go to schools, and this was continued. I do not claim that it was I who started the trend, but my father's insistence played a part in it. My two younger sisters automatically followed the same course and were brought up on similar lines. Now my brothers in turn are sending their daughters to school, although they have to face some slight opposition from their wives who were brought up in the old school of thought, though not to the same extent as my aunts.

I was encouraged to choose a career for myself and devote my studies to that end. In the beginning I was attracted towards the medi-cal profession. However, my mother vetoed the idea as, broad-minded though she was, she considered the primary role of the woman to be the home. Therefore, during the school vacations I was taught elemen-tary cooking, sewing, etc., and by looking after my two younger brothers I was able to gain experience in child care also.

My father died when I was 14. I was in the first year of college at that time. His death brought about vital changes in our family. The first one was the separation of my mother and my stepmother, since their ways of life were different, although it was decided that they should remain in proximity in the interests of the children. At that time, and even now, the source of the family income was a share in a picture house held by my father, and this has remained intact and joint ever since. Other assets, consisting of cash, jewellery, household effects, etc., were divided with complete goodwill according to the Islamic laws, which provide one-eighth for each wife and the remainder to be divided two to one amongst the sons and daughters. The older

326

children, including myself, took the separation philosophically, but the younger ones were not reconciled to it for a long time. The best of relationships has always existed amongst the brothers and sisters as well as between my two mothers.

The second change was that with the removal of father's influence and drive, no control was maintained over my brothers and sisters, with the result that their interest in education lagged, and my three elder brothers quit college after the first year. I myself failed by a narrow margin the inter-science examination, and I was further discouraged by the unfriendly attitude of the community towards education. My mother's health was also failing, and she was in no position to shoulder the responsibility of answering all the critics and continuing to encourage us. For nearly six months I did not attend college and became a helper to my mother, and it seemed that I too was destined to follow in the footsteps of other girls of our community. However, fate intervened in the shape of the principal of my college, a great friend of my father, who was good enough to visit us several times and persuaded me to take up a teaching job in a girls' school, which I did, as mentioned in the beginning. At that time there was a dearth of qualified Moslem teachers, and I was greatly encouraged by the then secretary of the school board. This job greatly helped to restore my interest in study, and by taking advantage of my free periods and by working at home I was able to sit for and succeed in the inter-arts examination. During these days I had also to shoulder the responsibility of running the home. As my elder brothers were away at Aligarh studying in college, I had to supervise the studies of the younger ones and also run errands and do shopping for the home, which was quite an unusual thing for a girl of my community to do. On the return of my elder brothers from college, I proceeded to Aligarh and graduated from there in 1943.

In 1945, my family had to decide about the marriage of myself and my younger sister who had also graduated by then. In our community, if a girl were not married by the time she was 20, she was looked upon with suspicion as having some physical or mental ailment. Also, her chances of getting a suitable match declined progressively as she grew older, and she had practically no chance at all after reaching the age of 30. In our case, many points had to be considered in finding suitable matches, as our upbringing was entirely different from the general pattern of the Memon community. One thing was agreed upon from

327

the first; we were to be married within the community. My father had also expressed this desire as he did not wish us to be lost to the community, but to be forerunners to lead the other girls. Also, mother desired to find conservative homes for us, regardless of any setback that we might have to suffer; we would have to adjust ourselves.

Generally, marriages in our community are arranged by the parents or, in their absence, by the elders. The parties to the marriage have no say in the matter. They never even meet till after the wedding, and contact with in-laws is also very formal. In our case, however, there was a slight deviation from this pattern. All the proposals that came were discussed with us, and our opinions were respected.

The proposal sent by my husband was accepted, although he had been married before and was divorced from his wife. He was also the father of twin boys. He was four years older than I. Another deviation from the rules was that my husband and I were given frequent chances to meet during the engagement. He was a regular visitor to the house and we even used to go out, although never without a chaperone.

My husband's family was quite interesting in its way. Very conservative and religious, they were quite well-off and lived in the heart of the Memon community district, steeped in tradition. The ladies of the house observed strict *purdah* and led a life of ease, mostly passing the time in gossip and occasionally doing embroidery work for their own clothing. There was no dearth of servants to attend to the household chores. Education was limited to religious teachings, and a slight knowledge of Gujarati, one of the local languages. The only exceptions were my husband and also my mother-in-law, about whom I will write later. Incidentally, you will be interested to know that the language spoken by the Memons, called Memoni, is oral only and possesses no alphabet. All written material is in Gujarati, which differs considerably from Memoni.

My husband's family consisted of his two sons by his first marriage, grandmother, mother, uncle and his wife and three daughters, one of them married with her husband, the other a widow with one child, and the third still unmarried.

My mother-in-law was quite a personality in herself. Though a widow at an early age, she was very courageous, energetic and possessed a lot of initiative. She was also well educated in Gujarati and Urdu. Having only two children and enough servants in the house, she devoted most of her time to reading books on Islamic literature and current novels. She had collected quite a good library and had even prepared an indexed list of the books. She also used to do a lot of social work. The council of elders of our community usually referred cases of matrimonial differences in the community to her, and even my husband's uncle took her advice and respected it. *Purdah* was no obstacle to her, and she would discuss family affairs with men even behind the curtain. She was known for her justice, and practically the whole community respected her for it. She would visit homes and patch up domestic quarrels. She had a natural instinct for such things and was always ready to help. She was instrumental in marrying off many orphans who would otherwise have found mates with great difficulty.

I was married in 1946 in the traditional way. We Memons were originally descendants of Hindus and, therefore, until recent times, quite a few Hindu customs were reflected in the ceremonies connected with births, engagements, marriages, etc. The actual wedding ceremony was performed by a *qazi*, an official designated by the community for the purpose, in the public hall used for such functions, in the Islamic manner. I was not present at the actual ceremony, but was confined with other ladies in a secluded part of the hall. However, the bride's consent is necessary, and this was conveyed to the *qazi* by an elder of my family and a witness. The questions asked by the *qazi* and the replies of the bridegroom are somewhat similar to those usual in Christian marriages, and so is the giving away of the bride, and the necessity for the presence of at least two witnesses.

After the ceremony the bride returns to her house, and late at night a procession of female in-laws comes to fetch her. They are feasted by the bride's mother and given a tearful send-off. On reaching her husband's house some coconuts are broken at the bride's feet and flowers strewn over her—typical Hindu customs. All this time the bride remains coyly shy and requires the support of her in-laws to walk to the bridal chambers where she is left. All this time, too, the bridegroom stays away from the house and comes home only after the bride is left alone.

Into such a home I was married. Although conservative, I realized that my in-laws were not fanatics. My mother-in-law especially, in her wisdom, was keenly perceptive of the changing times, and if properly persuaded she would change her attitude. My first step was to identify myself completely with them and their daily chores. Though cooking

329

was not an art which interested me greatly, I tried to learn their ways of preparing various dishes. This was greatly liked by the family. In the ways of dressing also, I temporarily discarded the sari which was not liked by the community, although very popular with the non-Memons. Instead, I used to put on the ankle-length frocks and pyjamas with a stole on my head. I was never forced by my in-laws to change my dress or put on the veil, but I thought it fitting to do so in view of the status enjoyed by my in-laws in the community, and so as not to hurt their pride.

At the time of my marriage, my stepchildren were 6 years old. One of them had been adopted by his uncle-in-law, who had no male child of his own. The other was looked after by my mother-in-law. During these days their real mother died at her parents' home, but it was not much of an upset for them. They had been brought up by the grandmother as was the custom in those days. Children of those times hardly ever stayed with their own mothers, if the grandmother were alive. They hardly recognized their real mother and did not even address her as such. There was not even much affection between the father and the sons, nor did he feel any responsibility towards them, as they would always approach the grandmother or the grand-uncle for their needs. The same pattern existed among my husband's married cousins and their children. To me, this state of affairs was very unsettling and a hindrance to my acceptance by my stepsons. However, I started to activate their interest in me by playing games with them and helping them at meal-times, and paying attention to their clothing, etc. I had to do all this very cautiously, lest my mother-in-law feel that I wanted to snatch the children from her.

Gradually, I brought up the subject of their education and the choice of a suitable school. The boys were constitutionally not very robust, and consequently my mother-in-law felt all the more protective towards them and did not wish to put them in any distant educational institution. Finally, however, the question of their education was left to me, and although our views differed as to their upbringing, both of us gave way. She had realized that those children could not be brought up in the same way as their father, in luxury and pampering, and therefore she always kept an open mind and made efforts towards the right direction.

Slowly the traditional pattern of home life changed. My mother-in-law, with her foresight and in view of my family upbringing, lowered

330

the conventional barriers between us and handed over more and more of her responsibilities to me. All my clothing and jewellery were under my own control. I had full access to the family allowance and was responsible for all home accounts. As regards my own studies, I very much wanted to complete my master's degree course, but this was just not possible on account of the lack of education of my cousins-in-law who, I realized, would be very difficult to convince of the need of higher education. Therefore, in spite of the means and the leisure that I had, I dropped the idea.

However, I used to take my unmarried cousin out with us to the cinema, shopping, and while visiting friends. Gradually I involved her in different programmes to keep her active, and she began to take more interest in learning Urdu, a national language, and also learned sewing and cutting, knitting and embroidery. Thus she became a definite contributor to the home. The other cousins-in-law had become too fixed in their ideas to change the least bit.

In 1947 my husband decided to move to Pakistan, and the whole family came over to Karachi. I was the first girl in my own family to move so far from them, but mother took it calmly. Generally, Memon girls are not wed to persons living in different towns. They have to be within a few miles of their parental homes. After our transfer to Karachi, my own sister's husband also decided to make the move and migrated to Pakistan in 1948.

Coming to Karachi brought other changes in our mode of life. This time, my husband decided to stay in a locality not made up entirely of Memons, but a more cosmopolitan one. Also, in contrast to Bombay, where we lived in a commercial area in flats, we were now residing in a completely residential locality with an independent compound. Previously we could not go out of the house without veils; now we used to move about with uncovered faces in the garden compound and also go outside without observing *purdah*.

My uncle-in-law, his wife and three daughters, together with the husband of one of them and one of my stepsons lived in a large flat with a common kitchen. My husband and myself and the other stepson lived in an adjacent flat. My mother-in-law used to stay with my uncle-in-law but used to have meals with us.

My uncle-in-law retired from business, and all the responsibilities of providing for his family as well as ours fell on my husband. There was more freedom for me, and my mother-in-law let me decide many

331

things for myself. Also, more of the responsibilities of the house and the upbringing of the children fell on me. However, she still continued to preside over the kitchen and the home budget.

In October 1948, I was blessed with a son. This was a rather critical period for me, as I did not wish to conform to the conventions and hand him over to his grandmother. I felt that my husband and I should have the burden and the joy of bringing him up. I began taking the initiative even before his birth when I started stitching a few clothes for the baby, and with my mother-in-law's permission, registered myself with a lady doctor for pre-natal guidance. I even had my delivery in a hospital, a most unusual thing for our family.

On my return from the hospital, I let my mother-in-law handle everything for the baby. She used to attend to his bathing, put him to sleep in the conventional swing cot, and, as I was ill and not able to nurse him properly, she put him on cow's milk in a feeding bottle and also accustomed him to the baby soother. She really loved him and did all she could according to her own beliefs. I tolerated all that she did so as not to hurt her in any way. However, during all this time she noticed that my husband and I were inclined to attend to the child in person and, therefore, she involved us also in his care. When the baby was about 6 months old, I was able to handle him better and gradually took over. I demonstrated to her that I could easily look after the baby under her guidance. She suggested my keeping a nanny for him (a practice followed in the family where the nanny did all the work and the mother and grandmother only supervised), but I declined the offer. Instead, I kept a young girl just to help me prepare his feeds and other things, and attended to him myself. Gradually I brought my mother-in-law round to the realization of the better nourishment in powdered milk for babies, and thus changed his diet. The soother and the swing cot were things very unpleasant to me, and I also did not approve of his regular use of the feeding bottle, but I continued with them as they were not harmful to the child and caused some satisfaction to my mother-in-law. However, when my son was over a year old, I took him on a visit to my own mother in Bombay, and there I made him discontinue these habits.

My son used to sleep with me and my husband and not with the old lady, as was the case with other children. Thus, gradually, I took him over entirely without antagonizing my mother-in-law, and she also had developed full confidence in me. Besides, she often had to go to Bombay to her married daughter, whose husband was not in good health.

We omitted many other customs also in the upbringing of my child. For instance, at the time of *aqiqa*, the first cutting of the child's hair, two goats have to be sacrificed according to the religious teachings. This we followed faithfully. However, there is usually a feast thereafter which is not enjoined by our religion, and this we omitted, distributing the greater portion of the meat of the sacrificed goats amongst the poor. Another custom was the circumcision, followed by a grand feast, which was held in the presence of a large gathering usually when the child was 3 years old. In this case the boy was quietly circumcised when he was fifteen days old, by the family doctor.

When my son was 3, I proposed to my mother-in-law that he be sent to a nursery school. She was at first horrified at the idea of sending such a small child away from home. However, I explained to her his need of company of similar age—he was very shy and disinclined to mix—and she reluctantly agreed. However, she could not bear his tears while being sent to school, and therefore she used to stay away at the time.

My son started being more attached to us, and he also became quite friendly with his step-brothers. I thereupon suggested to my mother-in-law that my stepson, who was more in her company, should also be allowed to live and sleep in our flat, to which she agreed. Thus we now have two children whose upbringing is our responsibility. The other twin, of course, stays with his adoptive mother and looks to her for all his needs.

As my son grew up, my mother-in-law and the other members of the family also changed their ways in keeping with the trend of life prevalent in the new State of Pakistan, and especially its capital. I was finding it monotonous to pass the days doing nothing, as my son was away at school and the servants and my mother-in-law attended to the house. In 1952 I had read of the first training course in social welfare started by the government, but was unable to join it because of the young age of my child. However, in 1954 when the United Nations and the Government of Pakistan sponsored another six-month 'on the job' training course, I prevailed on my family members to let me join, as it would keep me occupied and also give me knowledge of a subject of deep interest. With their approval I joined the course which was very interesting, and which gave me an opportunity to visit the poorer and

333

the slum areas and personally see the plight of my less fortunate sisters.

The course infused me with a zeal to work with and guide them in a more scientific way. In Lyari, a century-old slum area of Karachi, a pilot project was started and experiments were made to improve the lot of the residents through the technique of community development. At the conclusion of the six-month course, I again availed myself of a three-month 'follow-up' course sponsored by the same authorities. In this course, I gained a wider experience of case-work technique in a maternity and child health centre.

These courses helped me in many ways. Besides reviving in me the zeal for further studies, they gave me many new friends in the educated strata and in government circles. I also felt more patriotic and gained the feeling that we all should help in improving the country. Furthermore, it gave me an idea of the immensity of the social problems confronting Karachi, and I came to know of many social work agencies, both private and government-sponsored. I had lost contact with the outside world during my stay-at-home period. This work put me once more abreast of developments in the country and helped me come out of my pigeon-hole.

At the end of the course the government continued the pilot project at Lyari and started two more, employing the original trainees on a full-time professional basis. When the question of my becoming a professional worker arose, my in-laws demurred at the idea and my husband also was against it. At the time, it was unheard of for a girl of a respected family to go out to work, and even now my husband has occasionally to face sarcastic remarks from some of his acquaintances. Then it seemed quite certain that my husband's status in his particular community would be lowered, and his vanity hurt. I therefore sat at home with a heavy heart; I felt the disappointment very strongly. My former associates were all urging me to join the profession; there was a dearth of trained social workers and I could be of real benefit to the programme.

After some time, Fate intervened in that my husband's business declined owing to the depression then prevalent in the market. His responsibilities were also very great as he had to look after his uncle's family as well as his own. Under the circumstances, I thought I could help tide him over the difficult period by joining the profession in which I was trained, and thus contribute towards the family upkeep. It took me nearly six months to convince my in-laws and my husband that I could join the social work profession without disrupting family life, and at the same time contribute to the family income and be of service to the country.

My family at last agreed to my entering the service, and so after nine years of married life and stay-at-home atmosphere, I again ventured out as Social Welfare Organizer in the Ministry of Health and Social Welfare.

Our country being mainly agricultural, the government has launched a national uplift programme known as V-AID (Village Agricultural and Industrial Development) which covers the rural population, and full support and encouragement is being given to this nation-building activity. But the Ministry of Health and Social Welfare, through its Social Welfare Directorate, deals also with urban community development and social services, and my work lies here. The social services cover, with the medical social work, grants-in-aid programmes, training, research and the demonstration of new projects and services.

The urban community development programme was initiated in Pakistan under the joint auspices of the UNTAA and our government in the year 1953. The first experiment was carried out in Lyari Quarters, Karachi. At present there are twenty-five such community development projects working throughout the country, of which seven are in Karachi. The second Five-Year Plan envisages the establishment of ninety-eight projects in the country. Owing to the general segregation of the sexes, each project has two social welfare organizers, one male and one female, who work with their respective sexes to improve their lot. For the co-ordination and progress of all the projects in each city, a supervisor has been appointed. The over-all supervision on a national basis is the responsibility of the Deputy Director, Urban Community Development, while the co-ordination of all social welfare programmes on a country-wide basis is looked after by the Director. My own work is with the Khadda Nawabad Community Development Project, which covers an area containing mainly Sindhis and Memons, with a scattering of a few refugee families.

The Sindhis are mainly fishermen and hold a monopoly in this work. The Memons of the area originally came from Cutch and have been settled here for some four decades. They are mostly businessmen and shopkeepers. Owing to their close proximity, both the communities speak somewhat the same dialect, although they retain their own identities. There are no intermarriages between the Sindhis and the

335

Memons, and because of rivalry in politics and business between the leaders of the two communities, there is some aloofness, yet the ordinary people mix quite well. Since the establishment of Pakistan, Memons from Kathiawar, especially from Bantwa and Jetpur, have also arrived and settled down in this area.

A majority of the women in my area do not observe strict *purdah*, but there is segregation and they cannot move about freely, being confined to their homes or immediate neighbourhood. The elderly women do the shopping and the younger ones attend to all the domestic work. They assemble together mainly for marriages, deaths or religious gatherings. They are not very politically conscious and no organization or association for women exists. Through the community development programme, we are striving to fill vital gaps in their ways of life in order to assist in the social development of the area.

As I have said, the male organizer works with the men, while the female organizer works with the women in co-ordination with the men's programme, and in programmes meant for them and their children. In each project, programme contents have been designed to meet the socio-economic, cultural and spiritual needs of the residents of the area, and the main emphasis in my work is to bring about social changes in conformity with the traditional pattern.

In the initial stages I paid home visits intensively in order to get myself acquainted with the people and their customs. Gradually I was able to pick out a few potential leaders to help me in my work, as my main emphasis is to work through them, and thus create interest in them for organizing different programmes. In the beginning we worked on the felt needs of the women and started with adult literacy and needlecraft classes. Gradually the programme was expanded to cover group discussions on family life and problems of the neighbourhood. Health talks and demonstrations, documentary films, cooking classes and recreation were added later. Girls previously confined to their homes and passing their time in gossip have now started taking a greater interest in life, are regular visitors to the Social Education Centres (Mothers' Club) and participate in programmes which they themselves plan with the help of their teachers and myself.

To help them develop a democratic way of living, committees of the area and the central women's committee have been formed. Training in parliamentary procedure is given to members of the committee who were in the first instance chosen by myself. Thereafter they elected their

336

own members and are now handling their own immediate problems. They are taking over more of their own responsibilities and are able to gauge their own needs. For example, a Maternity and Child Health Clinic has been opened at their request by the members of a private social agency. I only had to guide them during the various stages of its establishment, but the pride of achievement is all their own. The mothers voluntarily take turns in looking after the children at the centres. As I am a member of their committee I am able to have an insight into their customs and traditions, and can appreciate the barriers which they have to face in making any progress. The biggest obstacle is their men, who fear that urbanization may lead to the uncontrolled freedom of the women and thus disturb family life. To banish that fear I have to move very cautiously and consult and convince the male members of the community on any programme that is to be started for women. As human changes are intangible and very slow, it will take a long time before any substantial difference can be perceived. But one thing is sure: the women do now have a broader outlook on life and now think in terms not only of their own families but of their neighbourhood also.

Coming back to my own family, I feel that my sons will not have to face many of the conventional barriers that my husband and I had to face. They will have more freedom in choice of profession and family life. The trend now is towards single-unit families, and they too will set up independent homes of their own.

When I look back, I see many of my college friends who have come over from India to Pakistan, and many of my colleagues on the social training course outstripping me in their careers. With their high education, better and earlier services and consequent earlier promotions, they have progressed ahead of me. But I have the satisfaction of having achieved my desire with the goodwill and through the understanding of the elder members of my family, and this in itself is a reward.

Appendix

A SHORT HISTORY OF THE MEMONS

The Memons originally were descendants of a sect of Hindus called Lohanas. They were concentrated in an area of continental India called Nagar Thatta, which now forms a part of Pakistan and is only sixty miles from Karachi.

Later on, they moved over to Kathiawar, a former independent state of India and occupied such towns as Porbunder, Kutiyana, Jetpur, Jamnagar, while a certain portion came down to Bombay. Throughout their history, it has been observed that the Memons were a close-knit group and settled in large groups only.

They were the backbone of trade at the time of the inception of Pakistan, pation has always been trade. They looked with contempt on service, and even when the poorer ones did enter service, it was with business firms and was meant only as a means to having an independent business later on. In search of business, quite a few of the more adventurous Memons migrated to foreign countries and established businesses there, but their families always stayed behind and their roots were in their native towns which they visited at least once a year. Vast fortunes were made by them, yet till recent times, their mode of living was simple and unostentatious.

They were the backbone of trade at the time of the inception of Pakistan, and it is no exaggeration to say that without their support, commerce would not have flourished so quickly in this new-born State. Their main business has always been in the basic necessities of life, such as grains and textiles, and in these they dominate the market. After coming to Pakistan, they entered the industrial field also, and now have become leading industrialists of the country.

The Memons have always maintained a joint family system. Marriages with members of the community living in different towns were not encouraged, as this would have meant the daughter going far away. Their women have always observed *purdah,* and with the exception of religious teachings they are devoid of any education. The job of the women has always been to look after the house, cook meals and bring up children, of which there is always a large number in every family. Marriages were made early in life, the girls about 14 to 15, the boys about 16 to 17, and the girls were taught to obey every wish of their husbands. The women do not go out shopping or on any independent excursion of their own. On occasions of marriages, deaths, births, etc., in connexion with their relatives, the women would go in family groups. They have become so much accustomed to this way that they feel lost and very uneasy if perchance they have to move about alone. In their leisure time, they do embroidery or sewing or simply gossip.

The children are brought up without much attention to discipline or education but most of them become excellent businessmen in later life. Boys are introduced to their father's business at an early age, and follow in their father's footsteps.

Being keen businessmen, the Memons do not take part in politics, but are friendly with all the parties. However, they were of considerable help to the Moslem League in pre-partition India, which was headed by Mr. Jinnah and which strove to establish Pakistan.

This devotion to business has deprived the Memons of any cultural heritage of their own. Owing to the segregation of the sexes, there is not even traditional folk-dancing, although the women do indulge in typical Hindu dances at times of marriage feasts. These dances are known as *rasras* and *garba,* and their musical accompaniment is provided by drums and the striking of sticks in time with the steps.

The men, when they are not absorbed in business, which is seldom, prefer attending singing parties, called *qawwalies,* in which professional male singers recite the praises of God and His Prophet.

There is one thing in which they take part wholeheartedly, and that is the affairs of their councils, which are called *jamats* (voluntary organizations). Migrants from each individual town of Kathiawar (their former birthplace) have their own *jamats.* This is a sort of council with certain office bearers, and all the other Memons of that town as ordinary members. In these *jamats* all domestic troubles of their members, such as divorces, separation, etc., are settled, and the policies of the community are decided upon. Also such social work as providing financial and material assistance to widows, putting the unemployed into business, providing scholarships to needy students is attended to. Funds for all this work are collected by donations and by membership subscriptions.

The Memons generally are very devout Moslems and follow the teachings of Islam and the Prophet faithfully. They abstain from prohibited foods and drinks, and regularly offer their prayers and fast in the month of Ramzan. They are also scrupulous in taking out *zakat* (a form of religious tax of 2.5 per cent of the total wealth to be distributed annually amongst the poor). Besides *zakat,* they donate large sums in *niaz* (offering for the Prophet) which is not compulsory, but which is used in preparing feasts for the poor. They take delight and pride in contributing to the construction of mosques, orphanages, public halls, etc. In their zeal they are many times duped by *pirs,* so-called holy men, who take advantage of their devotion to fleece them of large sums of money, but they take all this in good part and it has not lessened their zeal towards religion or charitable works.

In Pakistan, Memons from different towns of Kathiawar have come together, but they also have the opportunity of mixing with other communities such as Punjabis, Sindhis, Bengalis, etc. This has helped to broaden their outlook, and it has affected the outlook of the women also. Many of the girls are attending schools, though the majority still do not go beyond the seventh or eighth grade. A few have joined colleges, and the influence of the other girls there has affected their modes of dressing as well as their general outlook. Where once they were shy in mixing with others, they now take part in sports and social activities. The elders of the family, too, do not now attach any strings to the movement of the girls, and it is apparent that soon they will be competing with their sisters in other communities in every walk of life.

This is a very short history of the Memons. They have lived a contented and steady life, which, by modern standards, may be called antiquated. However, modern influence is at work. Their pattern of life is slowly changing; whether it is for the better or worse, is a moot question.

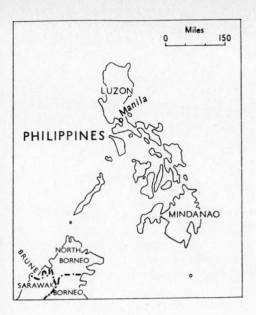

Philippines

Area: 297,487 square kilometres.

Population: 24,012,000 (census February 1960).

Recent history: 1898—Spanish Government cedes to United States of America; 1942-45—Japanese occupation; 1946—United States Government transfers sovereignty to the Republic of the Philippines.

Citizenship: Men and women have equal rights.

Religion: Roman Catholicism; there is a small number of Protestant Christians, and a Moslem minority inhabits some of the southernmost islands. Pagan tribesmen are to be found in the hills.

Inheritance and family patterns: Traditional inheritance rules do not differentiate between the sexes; nuclear families predominate, close ties being maintained with kinsmen of both spouses.

341

Men and women in the Philippines

by ROBERT FOX

FILIPINO CULTURE AND SOCIETY

The Philippines and its people are seemingly a paradox. Asian by birth and geographical setting, the people have matured within a Western matrix. And today they continue to value Western culture and its political and economic structure. Though Asian at heart they differ from other Orientals in many respects, and though they have absorbed a considerable amount of Occidental influences they are by no means truly Westernized. Rather, a generalized culture and society has emerged which is uniquely Filipino; a culture which, for thousands of years, including the recent Spanish and American periods, has abstracted, modified and elaborated diverse external influences to fit local needs and local developments. This process continues.

The twentieth-century Filipino men and women—their respective roles, relative status and patterns of behaviour and interaction—are understandable only when viewed as part of this complex heritage; and as part of a provident, tropical environment to which this heritage has adapted.

Though often thought of as a highly fragmented people with many languages and distinct cultures, a comparative study of the cultures of the eighty-odd cultural-linguistic groups which comprise the present Filipino population reveals far more similarities than differences, whether the groups are Christian, Moslem or indigenous religious groups, the latter peoples being those who have retained many pre-Spanish religious beliefs and practices. In 1960, at least 92 per cent of the 27.5 million Filipinos belonged to only eight groups (see

342

Table 1), and these groups show striking social and cultural uniformity.

TABLE 1. Major Christian groups ranked by size (1948)

Group[1]	Population
Cebuano (Sugbuanon)	4 759 772
Tagalog	3 730 028
Hiligaynon	2 373 566
Ilokano	2 340 221
Bikol	1 467 874
Samar-Leyte (Waray-Waray)	1 203 963
Kapampangan	641 795
Pangasinan	515 158

[1]. Mother-tongue speakers. Taken from *Statistical Handbook of the Philippines, 1903-1953*. Manila-Bureau of Printing, p. vii, 286. No figures are available for the 1960 populations of these eight cultural-linguistic groups.

These eight large groups (plus twelve minor groups) are Christian, predominantly Roman Catholic; live in lowland or coastal-riverine areas; and are engaged for the most part in subsistence agriculture supplemented by extensive, part-time, inshore and riverine fishing. The people of some communities are full-time fishermen. Many villages are found in regions where single crops predominate, such as the areas of coconut and sugar cane (these two crops form the principal export commodities of the Philippines), tobacco and rice. Generally, however, economic activities and the sources of family income to which both men and women contribute are highly diversified even in single crop areas.

A few urban centres have arisen—Manila, Cebu, Iloilo, and more recently, Davao. These cities are the focal points of social and cultural change, and when urban and rural culture and society are compared the activities and roles of men and women and the relationships between them show many differences. Manila has the classic characteristics of a metropolitan community—mobile social classes, economic diversity and cultural heterogeneity. It dominates the country from the standpoint of trade, educational facilities, and social, political and religious organizations. Greater Manila, which includes a number of smaller, contiguous cities as well as the metropolitan area, now embraces more

343

than 2.5 million people, approximately 10 per cent of the total population. Manila continues to grow with a continual influx of young
rural migrants, both men and women, who are eager for higher education and urban employment. This is a relatively dynamic group
receptive to change, new values and new ideas.

The great bulk of the Filipinos, however, still live in small rural
villages (*barrios*). These communities are characteristically small; in
1939, 76.5 per cent of the people lived in *barrios* of less than 1,000
and 46.7 per cent in *barrios* of less than 500. The rural Filipinos retain many of the characteristic features and qualities of a folk society
—highly personal face-to-face relationships; traditional theories of
disease and cause-and-effect explanation which antedate Spanish
times; as well as economic, social and religious activities centring on
the home and family, the family being the basic social unit of the
society. In the *barrios,* wisdom is equated with age, status is ascribed
not achieved, and an elaborate network of kinship forms, by and large
the organizational principle and model for all social relationship
within the community. Here in the countryside traditional life-ways
continue to inhibit programmes of social and economic development designed to meet the problems of an ever-expanding popula-
ting and increasing economic pressure. (The Philippines has one of
the highest rates of population growth in the world, over 3 per cent
annually.)

Social and cultural distinctions within the Christian areas of the
Philippines—distinctions which affect the roles, activities and behaviour of men and women—are largely the result of differences in
economic pursuits, such as in the contrast between the daily activitie
of fishermen, farmers and factory workers; between places of residence, whether rural or urban; and the degree of wealth which i
correlated with mobility and educational attainment. Though no
truly effective barriers exist to separate the people into 'classes' in the
greater part of the country where there really are no rich gentry to form
an exclusive group, certain provinces are still characterized by two
social classes: a small, highly mobile and wealthy land-owning and
entrepreneurial class; and a great number of landless farmers (tenanc
reaches 98 per cent in some areas of central Luzon) who are linked
closely to the soil. A middle class appears to be emerging in the few
cities.

It is important to point out that the many languages within the

344

Philippines act as the principal cause of social distance between ethnic groups and lead to the regional chauvinism and ethnocentrism which make casual observers picture the Philippines as socially and culturally diverse. Actually, the basic institutional differences between the many Christian groups are not striking. In other words, there are differences in cultural detail, but the fundamental features of the family and kinship structure, inheritance, religious beliefs and practices (both traditional and Christian), economic and political organization display strong affinities through the islands. Thus, it is possible to speak of, as well as to abstract for analytical purposes, 'a generalized Christian Filipino culture and society'. This model will form the basis for the subsequent treatment of men and women in contemporary Filipino society.

Many minority groups are found within the archipelago, totalling in all about 10 per cent of the present population. In the southern Philippines, specifically on the islands of Mindanao, Palawan, and in the Sulu archipelago, nine Moslem groups are encountered. The Moslem Filipinos comprise approximately 5 per cent of the total Philippine population, or some 1.2 million people (some estimates are much larger). A comparison between the roles of men and women in Moslem and Christian societies show fundamental differences and these will be considered briefly.

A number of Filipino cultural-linguistic groups retaining traditional life-ways and indigenous religions (they are usually spoken of as 'pagans'), are found largely on the islands of Luzon, Negros, Panay, Mindanao and Palawan, usually in the upland or mountainous regions. Apart from the many small enclaves of Aeta or 'Oceanic Negritos', more than forty such indigenous religious groups can be distinguished, including the Ifugao of northern Luzon who are famed for their towering rice terraces, the 'Sea Gypsies' or Bajaw of the southern Sulu archipelago, and the Manobo of eastern Mindanao whose ornate costume has attracted world-wide attention. Because of social and geographical isolation, many unique cultural traits have developed among the mountain peoples, but their institutions are basically equivalent to those found among the Christian lowlanders, particularly those of the folk societies in the rural areas. Brief mention, therefore, will be made of the indigenous religious groups.

The basic social, economic and ritual unit of Filipino society is the simple or elementary family composed of the father, mother and un-married children. The household (that is, the residential unit) is also usually equivalent to the family, but it is not uncommon to have one or more close relatives, usually unmarried siblings of the couple or a widowed mother or father, living in the household. A recent survey of Filipino households shows that the average family has six members (urban, 5.9; rural, 5.6).

Among a few Filipino peoples, such as the Maranaw who are a Moslem group living on the shores of Lake Lanao, Mindanao, com-pounded households are encountered in which more than one simple family share a common residence. Among the Maranaw, it is usu-ally the mother and father and their daughters' families who form the compounded household. In the cities, too, owing to economic pressure and crowded living conditions, the household tends to be larger, and even unrelated families may be found living under a single roof. But the prevailing practice and the ideal through the islands—even among the 'Sea Gypsies' or Bajaw of the Sulu archipelago who live on house-boats—is for the newly married couple and the simple family to have an independent residence.

Elsewhere the writer has described the Filipino family as 'highly centripetal' and Filipino society generally as an 'anarchy of families'. Thus, in Filipino society the personal obligations and responsibilities of men and women throughout their lives centre and focus on the family, and institutions which form the larger society, such as the government and church, receive little or only token support.

Community life and social activities within the *barrio* are also organized principally in families and kinship groups around common economic and ritual interests. On the village level, generally speaking, there have been no developed political structures or community-wide social organizations as such. Being fragmented, family and kinship oriented, the rural societies and communities present many serious problems for the administrator who is concerned with programmes of economic and community development.

Within the village a network of consanguineal and affinal kinship ties, and bonds of common residence and shared economic and ritual activities, do link a number of families together for co-action, for instance during the annual fiestas. Nevertheless, each family remains a highly independent entity and the focal unit of decision-making. The Filipino family displays an unusually great strength and solidarity, and the relationship between men and women and the roles which they play through life centre on the family and the kin world.

The family is the basic economic unit—mother, father and older children sharing specific responsibilities in extracting a living from the soil, sea and forest. When the father is a fisherman, for example, his older sons may be members of the boat crew, and the mother will engage in net-making or market the daily catch in nearby towns. With the exception of younger boys, each member of the family is a productive unit. Corporate businesses have emerged in urban areas, but many large companies—a surprising number—are actually family enterprises, staffed and managed by the family members, including the mother and children and close relatives as well as the father.

Religion, as a number of authors have noted, is family-centred rather than church-centred. Each family maintains a household shrine, and the beautifully carved wooden statues of saints which are carried in the processions of the villages are family owned and kept in the household. The small expenses paid to a parish priest for a wedding are commonly viewed as onerous, but extravagant feasts will be given in the household after the wedding with as many guests as possible even at the cost of debt—for such household functions enhance the prestige of the family. Church attendance, religious obligations and responsibilities, are commonly seen as familial rather than personal, the mother assuming these duties for the entire family.

Collective responsibility is extended to all members of a family, and respect and honour, or disgrace and shame, are equally shared. An offence against one member of a family is an offence against all members of that family; the shame of one is the shame of all. This collective responsibility is extended to all personal relationships, acting as a powerful mechanism of social control in a society which is highly individualistic. In many instances among adult men and women it is this consciousness of family ties and collective responsibility, rather than a moral conscience, which governs and controls interpersonal relations.

Each person in Filipino society is linked to many other persons by an elaborate and embracing network of kinship. The significance of kinship to the person cannot be minimized, for patterns of behaviour

347

which the child learns within the family and kin group provide the model for all subsequent interpersonal relationships. Like the family the kin group demands and provides emotional, psychological and economic support for its members. Within the secure kinship world formal behavioural relationships govern the interaction of the sexes and all age groups.

In all Filipino societies, kinship relations are reckoned radially or bilaterally; there are no clans or unilineal descent groups. A child (Ego) is considered related equally to the kinsmen of the mother and the father. The birth of a child may be viewed as formally structuring the family, for the child, unlike the parents, shares equal relationships with the maternal kin group and the paternal kin group. It is noteworthy that the term for 'family' in most Filipino groups is derived from the term for child: thus, *maganak* in Tagalog from *anak* (child)

All Filipino groups, like most Western ones, recognize consanguineal kinship relationships with and have separate kinship terms for parents, parents' brothers and sisters, cousins, cousins' children, grandparents, grandparents' brothers and sisters, and children and children's children. Among a few groups, such as the Ifugao of Mt. Province, uncles are addressed by the same term as father, aunts as mother, and cousins like siblings, thus emphasizing the generational characteristic of Filipino societies.

Formal kinship ties are usually extended to embrace third cousins and marriages prohibited within this degree. But the boundaries of 'being a kinsman' are not always clearly defined. As Father Lynch has pointed out: '. . . relatives are relative'. Thus, though the New Civil Code prohibits marriage between cousins, it certainly occurs and not infrequently among members of the upper class in order to prevent the dispersal of wealth and property. Likewise, a very close kinship tie may be felt with a fifth cousin or even with a person who carries the same family name but with whom an actual kinship relationship cannot be traced if there are common interests, occupation or residence. In short, distant relationships are often reaffirmed for self-interest, as for example when a man running for office seeks the support of his kinsmen regardless of the distance of their relationship.

MARRIAGE, INHERITANCE AND DIVORCE

Throughout the Christian region until scarcely a generation ago—and

348

among the Moslem and indigenous religious groups today—marriages were always arranged by parents, with primary consideration being given to the welfare and interests of the two families involved, not those of the bride and the groom. The custom of parentally arranged marriages is still encountered among some Christian families in the deep rural areas and always, even in the urban areas, the parents exert great influence on the final selection of their children's spouses. Common residence, and common economic and social status are the principal factors governing selection, the parents being aware of the need for providing a stable social environment for the new alliance.

Marriages are invariably performed by a priest in the town church or in the *barrio* chapel during fiesta times, for the great majority of the people are Roman Catholic. Civil marriages are not common, except in the urban areas. The traditional marriage ceremonies of Moslems and indigenous religious groups are also recognized by the new Civil Code. Marriages are prefaced by elaborate discussions between the parents, usually the fathers, in which go-betweens may be employed, and are accompanied by extensive (and expensive) gift-making. The actual costs of the wedding and the subsequent feast are borne by the groom, his parents and relatives. In some areas of the Philippines, the groom is expected to have an independent residence built for his bride before the wedding takes place. At present, even in the rural areas, there seems to be a growing number of elopements between young men and women, a reflection of their desire to select their own marriage partners and a rejection of the complications and expense of traditional marriage arrangements. After elopement and a civil marriage, the couples will still participate in a simple church ceremony.

Traditionally, the residence of the couple following marriage was either in the community of the bride's parents or that of the groom's parents. In some areas, particularly among the indigenous religious groups, it is obligatory for the couple to reside in the community of the bride's (sometimes the groom's) parents until a child is born, a traditional recognition of the instability of a marriage during the period when only affinal bonds are involved, and that it is only the birth of a child which formally structures the relationships between the two families. Throughout the Christian area, residence tends to be in the community of the groom's parents, but many factors in modern life tend to qualify this arrangement. Among these are: the place of employment of the groom, availability of land for farming, movements to frontier communities when neither the groom's nor the bride's parents have land, and the relative size of each sibling group. It may occur that the bride has no brothers and that land is available to the couple in the bride's community, and then even though custom dictates that the couple live in the groom's community, they will move to the place of the parents of the bride.

Children are expected as soon as possible after marriage and a large family is desired. Parents argue that many children provide economic security. Girls early learn household responsibilities—helping to cook the daily meals, cleaning the house and baby-sitting for younger siblings. The remarkable discipline and responsibility which Filipino women display in adult life is certainly conditioned by their childhood training. Younger boys are singularly free from obligations until they have completed schooling or become involved in economic activities. The eldest child, whether male or female, has a quasi-parental status which includes the privilege of disciplining younger siblings. As children grow older there develops a sharp separation between the sexes in recreation, interests and interaction. Teenagers take as confidants and friends members of their own sex only. Courting is highly formal and interaction between the sexes carefully controlled. This early distinction between the 'man's world' and the 'woman's world' continues into adult life, explaining many later patterns of behaviour and interaction between men and women.

Though marriage brings new responsibilities and obligations for the bride and groom, it does not dissolve or even minimize their ties with their respective families and kin groups. One's debts, as the Tagalog say *utang na loob,* to parents, siblings and kinsmen are life-long. Thus, the couple may expect to help their parents in their old age. No old-age homes are found in the Philippines. A person without a job can find a place with a relative to live and eat. A request for financial aid from a kinsman is granted if humanly possible.

In turn, the young man and woman continue to obtain support and protection from their respective families and kin groups. Thus, an argument between a couple will quickly involve their parents. In-law problems are not uncommon in the Philippines. If a young man were to abuse or strike his wife, he would be faced immediately by her father or brothers. This continuing support of the wife by her family and kin group accounts, in part, for the high social position which women enjoy in Filipino society.

350

Both by traditional custom and as now laid down in the new Civil Code, all children, whether male or female, receive an equal inheritance and provision is made also for illegitimate offspring. Generally, the family's dwelling will go to the youngest child and/or an unmarried daughter, for it is felt that the youngest child has not had the fullest advantage of the parents' past earnings. Though less so today than in the past, owing to the presence, even in rural areas, of an unusually large number of professional lawyers, custom law is still extremely important and is followed by a great number of rural folk. But the custom of equal inheritance among children is leading to many problems, such as the extreme fragmentation of a family's land, and there is a growing tendency for parents to will the land to those children who have remained at home and farmed it. If a will is made, it is not unusual for parents to favour the child with whom they have lived in their old age. Decisions as to the distribution of property are usually not made until the parents are very old, for it is argued that this is a means by which parents can control their children.

In sharp contrast to the law of the Spanish period—though in accordance with the traditional Filipino custom law—the new Civil Code lays it down that the property which a woman brings to marriage is her own, and she may exert full control over its disposition. When a woman dies childless, her property will usually revert to her sibling group or her parents. The control which women have over the property which they bring to marriage is another important factor accounting for the high position of women in Filipino society.

The laws of the Philippines do not recognize divorce but only legal separation. This is granted when adultery on the part of the wife, or concubinage on the part of the husband, has been established in court, or when one spouse attempts to take the life of the other. Largely because of the legal complications of a formal court separation, and the shame which might be brought upon the families and children in proving adultery or concubinage on the part of a parent, legal separation is not common. The interdiction against divorce must not lead to the inference that marriages in Filipino society are necessarily stable, for separation without benefit of the courts (called *hiwalay* in Tagalog) sometimes occurs in the cities or even in the rural areas, and one spouse, usually the man, may form a new 'companionship marriage' (the Tagalog use the term *kinakasama* from *kasama* (companion) for this type of alliance).

351

Divorce among the Moslem and indigenous religious groups is permissible and frequently common when a couple is childless (the writer has made one case study of a Tagbanuwa woman in Palawan Island who married and divorced seventeen times, and she had no children). These customary rural practices are generally tolerated by the government. Strong social sanctions against divorce are invariably applied in all Filipino societies when a couple has children. Many 'pagan' societies have developed sophisticated marriage counselling in order to prevent divorces in such cases.

THE RESPECTIVE ROLES OF MEN AND WOMEN
IN TRADITIONAL AND MODERN SOCIETIES

A comparison of the respective roles of men and women in traditional and contemporary society shows striking continuities, which go far to explain present-day attitudes and expectations, as for example in the acceptance of women in the economic sector of the modern community.

Although the woman's primary obligation is expected to be the maintenance of the household, raising children and caring for the needs of her husband, she has been and remains highly active in the economic sphere, sharing with her husband and older children the task of supporting the family. Men, women and older children work together in the fields; women doing the lighter work of planting, weeding, guarding the crop and harvesting, and men the heavier work of felling trees for clearings or building dykes and drainage ditches. When confined to the household because of pregnancy or the presence of small children, a woman will be busy with household crafts, such as basketry or mat-weaving, or involved in cottage industries, embroidering, making nets and so forth. Traditionally, women as well as men were economically active. The popular 'Maria Clara' characterization of the withdrawn, timid young woman, confined to the home, was a myth of nineteenth-century romanticism.

During the Spanish period, it is true, employment outside the household was almost impossible for women in the larger communities, prevailing attitudes at that time being that 'woman's place was in the home', though the women in the rural areas were certainly not restricted in this manner. There were also only very limited educational opportunities for women. With the advent of widespread education during the American period, available to girls as well as boys, a wide range of employment opportunities was opened to both sexes. From the early days of the American period until today there has been a greater and greater participation by women in the economic life of the community. This is intensified at the present time owing to contemporary economic pressure which literally demands that both the mother and the father be involved in full- or least part-time employment. In summary, there are no legal and few social restrictions, past or present, on the economic activities of women. The modern Filipina (like her forbears) is a highly competitive and aggressive member of the business and professional world. Nevertheless, the world has changed: in the past many of the religious functionaries and folk practitioners were women, today they are doctors.

In the mid-twentieth-century Philippines, there are few occupations, no professions, in which women do not participate, and they dominate many, such as pharmacy, teaching, nursing, chemistry, certain phases of commerce, merchandizing, and others. In the Christian areas women have been elected to every office of the land but that of President and Vice-President. They are respected as behind-the-scene leaders of industry. Women's organizations form powerful and feared pressure groups.

Yet, the Filipino family and society may still be described as patricentric. The father is the head of the household, and nearly all positions of authority within business, the professions and government are held by men. A large primary school may be staffed entirely by women teachers, but the principal will in many cases be a man. Leadership has been a traditional male function and it remans so. Family decisions may be arrived at by consensus, the opinions of the mother and adult children being carefully considered, but the decision will be formulated and voiced by the father. Discipline also remains largely the prerogative of the male. Here are the keys to the frequent failures of women in positions of authority.

It is the father who is primarily responsible for the economic well-being of his family; the income of the mother and older children are treated as supplementary. However, all income, regardless of source, is turned over to the mother, even among sophisticated urban dwellers, for it is she who controls the family budget. Woe betide the husband who is only a few pesos short in his pay cheque! Family counsellors in Manila have noted a growing friction among families where the

353

wife's income is greater than the husband's. And in traditional society it is still felt shameful if a man comes to marriage with less property or wealth than the woman. Generally speaking, however, the income obtained by the wife is not resented by her husband, for it represents greater security for the family and more opportunities for the children.

Striking differences in the roles of men and women are apparent when Christian and Moslem Filipino societies are compared. Islam entered the Philippines about the mid-fifteenth century, and by the time of the Spanish conquest of the islands (A.D. 1565) had swept over the Sulu archipelago, parts of Mindanao, and reached the major port communities such as Cebu and Manila. The Moslem Filipinos have remained a highly independent and conservative group. The basic social characteristics of Moslem and Christian societies in the Philippines are similar—the family, kinship, indigenous religious beliefs, and so forth—but Islam also established many differences, especially in the roles and relationships of men and women.

Among the Maranaw, whom we have already mentioned, the activities and roles of women are highly restricted. From early childhood girls are prepared for marriage and the responsibilities of the household—cooking, weaving, playing musical instruments, dancing and entertaining. As young ladies, and throughout adult life, they are confined to the household. They do no agricultural work, nor do they participate in trade and business. Even household shopping is done by the husband. Thus, among the Maranaw it is men alone who achieve professional status and participate in the economic life of the community. Girls are now entering public schools and the Madrasa or Arabic schools, and a relatively few are even obtaining a higher education (in 1957-58, twenty-four females, government scholars from Lanao, were attending schools in Manila: a sharp contrast with the 163 males from the same area), but their social world is still the home.

POTENTIAL CONFLICTS IN THE ROLES AND RELATIONSHIPS
OF MEN AND WOMEN IN CONTEMPORARY CHRISTIAN SOCIETY

Despite the social, economic and technological changes which are taking place in the Philippines, notably in the urban areas and the economic sector, there is little indication to date of any fundamental changes in the basic roles and relationships of men and women. This,

354

as we have noted, is due to a great extent to the continuity between the traditional roles of men and women and those of modern life.

There are, however, potential areas of conflict which will probably influence not only the future roles and relationships between men and women, but the basic institutions of the society, such as the family, too. Among these are: the likelihood of an even greater participation by women in economic activities outside the home; still greater educational achievements by women, as well as by men; further rejection of parental controls over marriage; the development of an independent type of simple family relatively free of obligations and responsibilities to the boy's or girl's family and kin group; greater freedom of interaction between men and women, both married and unmarried; and increasing mobility, both social and geographical, associated with urbanization and the emergence of a middle class.

The modern Filipina has displayed an amazing ability to manage a household, raise a large family, and carry on either a full-time profession or occupation at the same time. And we have seen that both traditional values and modern civil law support her involvement in the social and economic life of the community. In addition, urban Filipino society today shows high social mobility, and the woman's or mother's achievements, whether social or economic, bring added status to the family. Many a woman without economic need and with a large family continues to be involved in social and business activities for the prestige which they bring, but in countless instances it is poverty and economic pressure that force women, including mothers, to work, at least part-time. It is possible to measure the areas of low income and low productivity throughout the entire Philippines by utilizing one criterion, that is, the degree of emigration of young women (and men) to fill jobs in Manila as servants, waitresses and hostesses. Many of these young people—most are not married—contribute to the support of their parents in the provinces, or to siblings who are studying; others are simply finding income to support themselves.

But the active role which women play today outside the home is not without repercussions. In contrast to the harmonious sharing of the responsibilities of farming by husband and wife, it would appear that where money incomes are concerned the average husband feels that he should be the sole wage-earner; that his authority is challenged when his wife receives an independent income. As we have said, friction between husband and wife has been noted by counsellors when the wife's income exceeds that of her husband. Many a man feels embarrassed when it is necessary for his wife to work, particularly if it is soon after marriage.

It is only the availability of low salaried servants from the provincial areas (see above) and unmarried female relatives living with a family, or older female children who act as parental surrogates, which allows mothers with children to work full- or part-time. Not infrequently the eldest daughter is discouraged from going to school, even marrying, because of the help she can provide in the household. Although statistics are not available, it would appear that many old maids are the eldest daughters. The necessity for young girls, 11 or 12 years of age, to act as parental surrogates, performing fully adult tasks while the mother is working, is seen as a serious problem by some Filipino sociologists and psychologists.

The Filipina is continuing to invade more and more professional fields and will probably continue to dominate a number of these, such as pharmacy and primary and elementary teaching (see Table 2).

TABLE 2. Relative number of men and women passing professional government examinations in 1960-61

Examination	Number of passing candidates	Men	Women[1]
Certified public accountant	685	428	257
Physician	561	347	214
Pharmacist	288	3	*285*
Optometrist	209	62	*147*
Dentist	191	83	*108*
Nurse	172	2	*170*
Civil engineer	144	143	1
Chemical engineer	92	65	27
Chemist	82	10	*72*
Architect	54	48	6

1. The italic figures indicate more women participating in and passing the examination. No figures for the total number of candidates were available.

Again, for statistics are not available, there would appear to be a growing number of professional women who do not marry. Filipino men hesitate to marry women with an education higher than their own (or women with greater income and higher social status), for there is always the fear of domination by women who have social and economic advantages. When the wife is in a superordinate position, the husband is said to be 'under the *saya*' (the latter being the traditionally worn 'wrap-around skirt').

There are certainly emerging particular 'types' of marriages within the professional group; female pharmacists, for example, marrying male doctors with the wife then managing the family-owned chemist's shop. In the rural areas, marriages between teachers are common.

MARRIAGE AND THE YOUNG FILIPINO

Conflicts may be anticipated among the younger Filipinos as a result of changing attitudes towards parental influence over marriage. Marriages in traditional society involved persons from the same social and economic group and frequently young men and women from the same community. Parentally-arranged matches provided a potentially stable environment for marriage by bringing together two families and two individuals with common backgrounds and interests, and by stressing the responsibilities and obligations of the young couple to their families and kinsmen. Marriage was viewed as an alliance between two families and kin groups, not simply between two individuals. Thus, in traditional society, marriage ties were supported and strengthened by many factors other than the personal relationships between the young men and women—family and kinship pressures, the church, shared economic activities, common residence, similar values, attitudes and interests.

Filipino society was also characterized, and it continues to be, by a marked development of generational respect which requires deference and respect for the opinions, attitudes, values and decisions of all persons older than oneself, particularly one's parents. Voiced by the father, supported by the mother, decisions made as to the marriage, residence and occupation of the children were formerly irrevocable. Thus, great parental control was exerted by the parents over their children and this continued throughout their lifetime. Though consonant with conditions in a folk society, the equation of age and kinship with wisdom and leadership is not always effective in the mobile, modern society.

The young people of today, by seeking to minimize but certainly not to ignore parental controls over marriage, and in forming relatively independent families which are potentially mobile, allowing for the couple to seek the best economic opportunity, are placing the stability of their marriage squarely upon their own shoulders. If the thousands of young people who come to the cities from conservative rural environments to study, seek employment, and often to marry, are representative of traditional society, then it would appear that this background has not prepared them for the responsibility of marriage in modern life. It is no accident that marriage counselling has recently appeared in urban communities throughout the Philippines, or that colleges and universities are introducing courses on marriage and the family.

The relative freedom of action (and interaction) which is now developing among men and women—the chaperon system is being replaced by dating—focuses the responsibility of moral, social, economic and political decision-making upon the individual. This suggests that many areas of potential conflict between young men and women, and not only in marriage, which did not exist in the homogeneous traditional society, may appear in the future as a result of the potential choices between alternative beliefs and values which young men and women are beginning to express.

TYPES OF HOUSEHOLD IN RURAL AND URBAN SOCIETY

Among the Christian peoples of the Philippines differences in social organization and in the roles, activities and relationships of men and women may best be demonstrated by comparing rural with urban households, the differences between which are equivalent, by and large, to those between traditional and modern households. Among the lowland Filipinos, as we have said, sociological distinctions are not based upon affiliation with a particular cultural-linguistic group (such as whether a person is Tagalog, Ilocano or Cebuano), but on the economic base of the area in which the household is found, the size of the community and whether it is rural or urban, and the family income. Furthermore, distinctions between the rural and urban setting and households are not of 'kind' so much as of 'degree', for many rural enclaves are found in metropolitan areas. Urban migrants, moreover, maintain close ties with their home communities and with their parents and relatives in the rural areas which involve them in frequent visiting back and forth. Urban husbands and housewives are often heard to complain of the presence of relatives from rural areas who came to stay with them for a few days, even weeks, to shop or simply to vacation in the city. Many rural families of a higher income level maintain a second home in a city, particularly when they have a number of children attending colleges and universities. The attraction of city-living continues to lead to a growing absentee landlordism and an influx of rural people generally.

THE RURAL FARMING FAMILY AND HOUSEHOLD

Economic and household activities in the rural areas begin very early in the morning. When fields are being prepared for planting, the husband is off before dawn after perhaps a cup of coffee. The wife invariably begins the day by preparing the breakfast for the family with the help of her older daughters, and it is then carried to the husband in the field (or he may return to eat it). After breakfast, the wife continues with cleaning the house, feeding the animals in the yard, and plans for going to market. Marketing is a daily activity, as there are no facilities other than drying to preserve fresh fish and meat. Commonly this problem is solved by women vendors who go from house to house with vegetables, fish and meat, but the price will be higher.

The woman by this time has begun the noon meal, placing the rice on the stove to boil. Wood provides fuel throughout the rural areas; if only small kindling it will be chopped by the women, if large pieces are required, by the men and teen-age boys. The family usually has a supply of rice in the household, representing a share from their harvest or an agreed expenditure of family income after the harvest when the price of rice is low. Daily, however, the wife must worry about and plan for the daily *ulam* (food), such as fish or, more rarely, meat, which necessitates in many instances a cash expenditure by her. In provincial areas, owing to the small amount of cash on hand, when one family has *ulam* and a neighbouring or related family does not, it may be shared. This sharing of food tends to disappear in the city, for it is said to reflect upon the wage-earning ability of the husband. Frequently the wife (especially if she is an older woman) will fish with rod and line in the fields or nearby rivers, or when living along the

359

coast gather edible shellfish for the day's food. Men and boys also spend time trapping fish in the canals of the fields and in streams. Canned goods, such as squid, sardines and corned beef, are available at the local *sari-sari* stores, and if necessary may be obtained for *utang* (credit). (The common failure of many small, provincial stores is due to an excessive extension of credit, for storekeepers find it difficult to refuse to extend credit to relatives and co-villagers.)

During planting, harvest or when it is necessary to weed the rice or other crops, the wife works with the husband in the fields, leaving the care of the children to older siblings or to relatives and neighbours.

After the noon meal (the husband either returns to the household or the meal is carried to him), the wives commonly devote their time to cottage industries which bring extra income to their families: net-making, weaving mats and hats, weaving nipa shingles (for roofing) from the leaves of a palm, dressmaking, embroidering gloves, pillow-cases and children's clothing. Activities such as these are normally done in an informal group, the women chatting and gossiping while they work. During the day, the village becomes the women's world, for except during periods of bad weather or when there are no economic obligations the men are away from the household. And even when there is no work to do, men—far more so than women—spend considerable time visiting outside the community.

The evenings, a period of relaxation, also find women together with women, men with men; and younger, unmarried people forming their own group. The distinction between the 'man's world' and the 'woman's world' is learned early in life, as we have noted, and extends into adult patterns of recreation and social interaction. Husbands and wives rarely interact together during leisure time outside the home. In rural areas male visitors are entertained with native drinks *(basi* in northern and *tuba* in central Philippines); the same entertainment takes place during baptismal, birthday, marriage or other parties; in the cities men in small groups attend bars, night-clubs or a neighbourhood store which acts as an informal bar, to drink, talk and be entertained by waitresses and hostesses. In the central Philippines, serenading by young men is common, the group visiting the house of a girl to sing folk and modern songs.

Though the sexual division of labour is not sharply drawn in the Philippines—men may cook, tend to children, even go to market, and so forth—there are certain activities almost always performed by women. Among these are washing, sewing and cleaning the dwelling, which includes inside, under and around the house. The characteristic rural Filipino dwelling is built on stilts, the space under the house being a storage area, workshop and gathering place for women or men during the heat of the day. The family's dwelling and yard is kept immaculately clean, the women sweeping the earth in the yard each day with a stiff broom made from the mid-ribs of coconut fronds. Flowers in profusion, grown by the wife, are found around each dwelling, no matter how poor the family. An ill-kept yard or a poorly repaired roof reflects upon the prestige of the family. (We may add that the manner in which life in the Philippines centres on the family and household is vividly illustrated by the concept of sanitation traditionally held. Thus, the dwelling and yard are always clean while the community as a whole—roads, areas between households and so forth—does not appear so. Persons feel obligated to clean only the area of their own households, and the absence of effective community-wide organizations inhibit programmes of community sanitation.)

The rural mother and wife is busy; always busy. Her obligations, particularly if she has a large family, are never ending. The work behaviour of the men, generally speaking, is far more erratic, for during the period of the growth of the crops there may be relatively few economic responsibilities. Fishermen are confined to their community for days during bad weather, or during moonlit nights which make it impossible to use fishing techniques that employ illumination with powerful lanterns. Rural men are plainly underemployed except for limited periods of the agricultural cycle. During slack periods, many seek employment outside the community, men's much greater mobility than women's being reflected in their common ability to speak languages other than their mother tongue. Today in the rural areas wage-earning by men is becoming more and more popular, even though the wages are very low, for rural wage-earning can usually be co-ordinated with traditional agricultural responsibilities, and it brings a steady source of income to the family.

THE URBAN FAMILY AND HOUSEHOLD

Urban society presents today great variety in households and in the

361

roles and activities of men and women. Within cities are found the extremes of wealth and poverty, different levels of living and a variety of sub-cultures such as those of the Euro-American class, the Mestizos, and Chinese; all of these providing exceptions to almost any general characterization that can be made of the urban family and household. Moreover, many neighbourhoods in Manila have rural features, the people maintaining close ties with the surrounding rural regions. There are, nevertheless, certain growing differences between the rural and urban family which can be considered typical, and these we will illustrate by a discussion of a middle-income household, representative of the emerging urban middle class.

The urban family and household is first of all relatively independent of the embracing kinship groups and the respective families-of-orientation of the husband and wife, at least as regards daily obligations and responsibilities. This is due, in part to autonomous residence, to the existence of other, non-kinship, obligations created as a result of the occupation of the husband and/or wife, and to interaction with neighbours and co-workers who are non-relatives. Interaction within the urban setting involves many impersonal relationships (rather than the highly personal face-to-face relationships of the rural society), as well as daily tensions and stresses due to living in a highly competitive and mobile society with persons of different attitudes, values and beliefs. These influence the relationships between men and women, as well as husband and wife. In traditional areas of central Luzon, members of two different cultural-linguistic groups would be separated by a river, for example that between the Kapamgangan and the Tagalog, and there would be almost no intermarriage across the river. In the city, on the contrary, they live cheek by jowl, and marriages between persons from different cultural-linguistic groups and different faiths, even races, are not uncommon.

Secondly, in the urban setting both husband and wife spend a great deal more time away from the home, largely because of employment which demands fixed office or factory hours. The availability of maids even to middle-class groups allows the wife to work, to visit or join in recreational activities during the afternoons, which may include reading vernacular literature, listening to radio programmes, going to the movies, and indulging in games of chance such as *panginggi, sakla, mahjong* and bingo.

Statistics do not clearly reflect the great number of married women with children who work full-time in the urban areas (there is almost no opportunity for part-time employment). Market vendors, *sari-sari* store and retail clerks, are predominately women and usually married women. Many urban factories employ largely women—cigarette and cigar establishments, textile manufacturers and embroidery factories. The successful participation by women (and Chinese) in the retail trades which involve aggressive bargaining for the 'right price' is, in part, related to the sensitiveness of impersonal interaction between Filipino men. The Filipino male has a high concept of self-esteem (*hiya* in Tagalog), being sensitive to hard words and aggressive behaviour, a character trait which is not ideal for the cut and thrust necessary in bargaining with a stranger. Many married women set up stores on the ground floors of their homes—*sari-sari* stores, dress shops, beauty parlours—running both the household and a trade. Present economic pressures make it probable that a newly married wife will continue to work if she has a position in an office or factory, or if she is a professional, but husbands frown on their brides continuing with a job which involves interaction with other men, such as that of a waitress.

Urban husbands and wives are also involved in many associational groupings, sometimes together but more often singly, most of which are not directly related to family life. Among these are church groups, membership clubs, union activities, school programmes, professional organizations and women's and men's associations. These frequently obligate the husband or wife during evenings. Recreation, as in the rural areas, usually finds men with men and women with women.

Many of the activities and problems of the rural housewife are also encountered in the city. Though more and more families have electric refrigeration, allowing the wife to shop only once or twice weekly, the great majority of wives must plan the daily menu and daily marketing. When both the husband and wife work, the marketing will be done by a servant or another woman living in the household. Husbands still feel that if the wife does not prepare the meal—even though she is working full-time—it must be supervised by her. City families are also up early, for breakfast must be prepared, the children sent off to school, the house cleaned, clothes washed, the activities of the day planned and directed. When working, the noon meal will be taken away from home, but the husband and wife or mother and father are expected home promptly after work to dine

363

in the evening with the family. Despite the large number of working wives, however, townswomen in general do appear to have more leisure time than their sisters in the country, the greater responsibility of providing income for the family being assumed by the husband.

CONCLUSION

The relationships between men and women in Filipino society and the roles which they assume are remarkable equalitarian. The stereotype is that men dominate the society—sociologists have even called Filipino society 'patriarchal'—but in reality women as well as men enjoy and assume social, economic and legal freedom. The Filipino in both the traditional and modern setting is a dynamic and aggressive member of society. The basic social unit of the society is the simple family supported by the radially reckoned kindred groups of both husband and wife. The influences of the family extend to every facet of Filipino culture and society. Men and women, fathers and mothers, see as their primary obligation and responsibility their families. Changes are taking place in urban society, but modern Filipino men and women still view as the 'ideal', an economically sound, stable and large family with the father at work, the mother at home and the children in school.

A career-housewife
in the Philippines

by ANGELINA ARCEO-ORTEGA

The oldest of our four sons was 12 when I enrolled in college in the summer of 1949. The youngest was eighteen months old.

Because I attended only the morning and afternoon sessions in the university, more often than not I was the only married student in the class. (Married students were and still are more likely to be found in the evening classes.) My classmates were in their late teens or very early twenties. I wasn't a *rara avis* to them though. I created no stir as a college freshman at 31 . . . mother of four boys.

But I did stir up a little storm back home when I announced my plan to go to college. My husband (a college graduate himself) liked the idea of leasing the farm to his sister and migrating to the big city, Manila. He applauded my resolve to obtain a college degree and eventually become a career woman. My brothers were not so keen.

But after all, two post-war years had not brightened the future for us on the sugar-cane farm which before Pearl Harbour had seen us through handsomely for five years. We lost everything in the war— a guerilla force burned our bungalow (to prevent enemy occupation, they said); they (and later the enemy forces) expropriated all the product of the land; looters took whatever was left; and when the actual fighting got dangerously near to us, we fled to the mountains. There our second son, Jimmy, then two years old, became seriously ill and almost died from lack of proper nourishment and an almost complete lack of medicine. Yes, the war had been a stern, uncompromising teacher. It had seared me terribly and left me with a burning determination to fight back, to toughen myself against the hard blows of life. The first step for me was to learn to stand firmly on my own feet.

But go back to school? At my age? A woman's place was in the home! Wasn't I forgetting that I had a baby to take care of? (David, our fourth and youngest son was born in 1947.) Wasn't I being too ambitious?

My brothers' arguments did not stop me. My decision must have smacked a little of the rebellious, considering that we have always been a closely-knit family, more so after our parents died. But they were not narrow-minded; they were just surprised—not really hostile—to my idea.

My husband, our children and I came to Manila. I finished my A.B. in three years, during which time our three older boys went to school too. My husband had a good job in the city. Everything was fine and when, in 1952, I won a scholarship to the United States, everybody, including my once sceptical family, was happy.

Now I have been a college instructor for the last six years. This year I took the additional job of assistant-principal in the elementary department of a boys' school. My morning hours from 7.30 to 11.30 are in the principal's office. The boys' school is only a five-minute drive from our home, thus I can leave the house after having attended to several important things: see my husband leave for work, see the children off to school, and set things in motion for the household help. After lunch with the children (my husband takes his downtown) and a short nap, I drive to the university where my teaching hours are from 2.30 to 5.30. My husband, after a bus ride from his office in the afternoon, passes by the university and together we go home.

I am just one of the many career-housewives today. Our number is increasing, for even outside the big city women are discovering the glamour and advantage of being working girls.

Did I say 'advantage'? Well, it undoubtedly has its advantages, but sometimes as I go about my work, living my day according to schedule, I dream secretly of going back to my quiet life on the farm where I could gaze at the sky and daydream without worrying very much about the time. I envy my sisters who are full-time housewives—their time is their own. But now I am indulging in wishful thinking! I know I can't have my cake and eat it too. Maybe I'm just not a city girl at heart . . . perhaps I just need a good long vacation!

The career-housewife has contributed largely to the new portrait of the Filipina today. Fifty years ago, Grandmother with a large number of helpers put her house in order and watched the world go by, through her crochet spectacles, from her rocking chair, by the window. It was a rare occasion not to find Grandmother at home.

Mother had a more stepped-up schedule. For one thing she had ten children to raise and to send to school. Grandmother didn't have to worry much about her children's schooling.

Today's housewife? That's me . . . a human dynamo geared to to-day's hectic pace—wife, mother, wage-earner—'a new woman with the old heart'!

Our modern family is obsessed by the idea of a college education for the children. In a recent report on schools, Mrs. Geronima Pecson, Chairman of the Unesco National Commission for the Philippines, made reference to the great respect Filipinos have for education, stating that 'many families have mortgaged or sold properties to see their children through schools'.[1]

Three private universities in Manila each boast of an enrolment over 30,000, and the number shows no sign of decreasing.

This certainly is an attitude towards education very different from that in Mother's time. My mother did not go beyond the elementary grades. Nor did the mothers of seven out of ten of my colleagues. Our male parents did better, although there were still many who did not go further than the intermediate grades, much less the secondary or high school course. Parents then did not mind about their children's schooling very much, and whatever chance for education there was, was preferred for the boys.

In my country, as early as the seventeenth century there already was a 'new middle class' to which belonged 'well-to-do landlords, farmers, lawyers, physicians, teachers and government employees . . . (who) read books and periodicals, discussed public problems, and sent their children to colleges and universities in Manila or abroad'.[2] This is not surprising when one learns that 'university education in Manila antedated that in America and other civilized countries. The first university in the Philippines was the University of San Ignacio (1589-1768). . . . The second to be established was the University of Santo Tomas, which began as a college in 1611'.[3] It is one of the country's leading universities today.

1. *Manila Times,* 28 January 1960.
2. Gregorio F. Zaide, *Philippine History,* Manila, The Modern Book Company, 1947, p. 174.
3. ibid., p. 154.

367

The education of women was also taken care of very early. A college for girls was established in Manila in 1594, and in subsequent years many other girls' colleges were founded.[1]

Nor was education limited to the rich. 'The Educational Decree of 1863 established the first system of public schools in the Philippines. All children of school age were to attend. The schools were to be supported by the State'.[2]

What is surprising is that with all these opportunities, many women failed to obtain even seven years of schooling. The private schools did all right, turning out more serious students who obtained college degrees, teacher's or nurse's certificates. But in general 'the schools during the Spanish time were deficient ... (although) they were as good as the schools in Spain at that time, and were better than those in Latin America'.[3]

I suppose that my mother, like many other women, found it more convenient to stay at home and get her education from tutors or simply from books and association with the 'right people'. Anyway, it didn't really bother her parents whether or not she got serious about formal schooling. After all, she was a most accomplished lady who could play the piano, sew and embroider, cook like Grandmother, dance elegantly, converse intelligently, and blush prettily!

The family's pooled income today has brought about quite a change in money spending. The wife no longer simply waits for a dole from her husband. She has a big say in what, where and how to buy.

My husband and I contribute fixed amounts to the family budget. The rest is my responsibility—how much for this, for that, etc. So unless I want a big headache I stick as strictly as possible to carefully planned spending. My little whims and fancies are taken care of by my pocket-money. The same goes for my husband and his personal fund.

Since the modern family has two breadwinners, it has become a much-sought-after customer. Competing stores offer hire purchase schemes (not available ten years ago except on a few items) on almost anything to accommodate people who draw monthly salaries.

The career-housewife has more daring as a buyer than the man of the house who is the family's sole earner, certainly much more than

1. ibid., p. 154.
2. ibid., p. 155.
3. ibid., p. 157.

368

the housewife thirty or twenty years ago. (Of course, there were always the 'rich-in-their-own-right' wives who held separate purses and could spend their money as they fancied.)

I think it's a wonderful feeling to swoon over a lovely, stunning thing in a display window, and actually get it without feeling guilty about the budget.

How my mother would envy me this economic independence. And how she would love to buy the household appliances one can easily obtain today. In Mother's time a refrigerator was a luxury. So was an electric range, even a radio. Today all these, and many other things she never had in her time, are necessities in city living.

How does today's little woman feel about world affairs? Does she take an active part in affairs of the government? In politics?

I am wide awake to what's happening in my country and to the world outside. I am vitally interested in issues that affect my rights as a citizen. Generally, however, this awareness is accompanied by an opinion that even while I can be an intelligent participant in conversation about these matters, the cudgels are really for the men to take up. In fact, I feel out of place when the menfolk really get going in their discussions about taxes, political candidates, probes, etc. Then I welcome, even seek, the opportunity to leave the room and attend to something else.

I guess my attitude is that of the average Filipina. But one cannot discount the many women who do take an active and direct part in political affairs, and actually hold important positions in the government. Many wives are their husbands' best political campaigners.

Still, in comparison with Mother and Grandmother, I would be somebody for them to marvel at. For where they simply used to listen —in fact stay away from the men's sessions—I can today say my little bit freely, and in elections can back my opinion with a solid vote! This my elders could not do. Woman suffrage was granted only in 1937.

The Philippines is a predominantly Catholic country. Birth control is not a Catholic practice, but the demands of modern living have affected the size of the family.

My mother had five girls and six boys, plus one miscarriage. This was not a rare achievement in her time.

Looking at the situation through our family, one can say the modern family is smaller in number than yesterday's. All of us five girls have married. With the exception of one who has nine, each of us has only four children. Some of these numbers may yet increase, but it is safe to say that our trend today is toward smaller families.

This change has produced favourable results in healthier children and healthier parents. Of course, there is also the fact that the modern housewife has learned a lot about wise eating habits. Gradually the rich and many dishes are giving way to more simplified but carefully planned meals, with a generous emphasis on milk for the children— not only for babies.

The children themselves realize the importance of eating well; their heroes in basketball, football, baseball and other games take care of that. Hence, this generation's offspring are bigger and taller. Our son at 17 is a good three inches taller than his father, who is only 5' 5''. A Filipino six-footer in his teens is not news any longer.

And Mommie herself? Many of the chic fashionable women one sees downtown are housewives who are out shopping or doing part-time business. No longer is the housewife distinguishable from the rest because she is much bigger (oh yes, there were scrawny ones too, just as there are today), and wears clothes different from those worn by the younger women. She may not be a prettier picture, but she certainly is a smarter version of yesterday's housewife.

How does this smart housewife look at home? And how does she run her home?

Working clothes must be comfortable but stylish. The career-housewife does get more people calling on her than Mother did. Husband's business friends often drop in too.

Household chores are not very difficult to do when one has time-saving, labour-saving equipment and, moreover, a number of helpers to do one's bidding.

In the Philippines it has always been an ordinary thing to have two or three helpers. Many well-to-do families have many more. But in these last years securing domestic help in Manila has become increasingly difficult for many housewives. So far I have been lucky in having the services of a cook, a laundrywoman and a houseboy, maybe because our helpers have always been sons and daughters of tenants working on the farm back home. But I won't be surprised if five years from now I'll have to learn how to get along with just one or none at all.

This particular problem did not bother Mother or Grandmother, I am sure. Then there were many who would even beg to be taken in as household help for a very low salary, or even for only food, shelter and clothing. Today, in spite of the much bigger salary (about three times as much) and a weekly half-day off (a practice unheard-of before), the many factories, shops and stores offer much more attractive positions to people looking for work.

In some families relatives from the provinces who come to Manila eager to study, help out in solving this problem, but this practice is no longer very prevalent. Many are beginning to discover that this is not a very comfortable arrangement. In my family this practice has not been encouraged.

How does the Filipina react to something that threatens her home, her marriage? I suppose a loving wife is a jealous wife anywhere; jealous not only of other women but of many other things that militate against a happy, peaceful union. It is a healthy, normal jealousy that makes a women fight hard for the persons she loves, for the things she believes in. How she fights her battles is an individual and personal matter.

On the whole, the Filipina is a tolerant wife. She does not condone her husband's wrong-doings, but what can she really do? Even though a legal separation may work all right for the spouses, but what about the children?

Divorce is not allowed in my country. I'm glad. Maybe I'd feel strange and uneasy if it were. As it is, I feel secure and grateful in the knowledge that my marriage is to last for better or for worse. I must try all means to keep it for better. I must be worthy of a union smiled upon by heaven, of a union blessed by children. My happiness should be unselfish—the kind that thinks not of self, but of others. Thus it must embrace hardship, tears, deep joy, heartache, smiles, unkindness —everything! In this, Grandmother, Mother and I would have much in common.

Do I make the picture too ideal? What about the cases of legal separation? What about spouses who feel there is no other remedy but to part ways and 'get married' to others?

There are cases of legally separated couples, but not very many. To the other question the answer is simply that they are the very rare exceptions, and society condemns them.

Marriage customs are practically the same—today and yesterday. Courtship: theirs may have been a more strictly supervised affair, but we still believe in chaperons, too. Not the *duenna* who remained forever like a hawk in the background, but at least just another companion—a brother, a sister, a friend. Yes, safety in numbers.

Engagement: sometimes long (two years or more); sometimes short (about six months). The engaged people belong exclusively to each other, but the chaperon does not completely disappear. (Chaperons can be good sports anyway.)

Wedding: as in the good old days, it is the big day. Since the bride wears her very best on this day, the Filipina chooses—nine times out of ten—the elegant Filipino *terno*. All of us five sisters did so.

The honeymoon could be a two-week stay in Baguio (the summer capital of the Philippines) or, for rich newly-weds, a round-the-world trip.

The honeymoon over, the couple settle down in a home of their own (my husband and I did) or stay with the parents (either side) for a while until they get a place of their own. With the years, the tendency has been towards an independent start.

A marriage arranged exclusively by parents has never been the Filipino way. Parents advise, but do not force their choice on their child. They sometimes strongly object to their child's choice, but marrying off a daughter or a son to someone he doesn't care for is not likely. If any difference exists between yesterday and today in this regard it must be in the degree of outspokenness of the children in explaining their side of the matter. Certainly today's youngster is more candid and frank—sometimes to the point of being aggressive and (sad but true) disrespectful. In the past, the marriage of close relatives was encouraged, especially in wealthy families that were determined to keep their wealth strictly among themselves. This practice has been discouraged by a new law (effective in 1950) which prohibits first cousins from marrying.

A provision of the new Civil Code now entitles all offspring (legitimate or not) to inheritance from the father. May this help the men to think twice and hard before philandering!

For much as we women hate to admit it to ourselves, we do have different standards of sexual morality for men and women. It has always been so in my country. That is probably the reason why many of us have grown passive, even apathetic about it. Our mothers didn't make any fuss—why bother now? This is not a burning issue at present, to be sure, but a concern for this and other problems that face us today is growing upon the intelligent Filipina, who feels that she can be a mighty influence on matters of grave importance. I'd like to think that I belong to this group that believes sincerely in the decency of the individual, man and woman, and in the sanctity of the home as the answer to many ills.

Which brings the focus back on the little woman, the career-housewife, who figures prominently in this paper.

As a working girl I am aware that I can easily forget my primary duty as wife and mother in the glamour of working outside the home, in the economic independence that comes with being a wage-earner. How many cases of youngsters going astray can be traced to mothers too busy to care for their children! We reason that the hard-working mother pitches in because she desires only the best for her children, but alas, money is no substitute for motherly love! In fact, I think we are making it easy for our young ones to go wrong by giving them too much of the wrong things.

But the problem that confronts the modern woman is not simple. The standard of living has gone up; prices continue to rise; education means more expense. How can both ends meet unless both husband and wife are wage-earners?

I am in no position to offer an answer that will solve the problem for everybody. But this I know: next year I will give up my work as assistant-principal, not because I do not like working in this boys' school, but because I feel I must spend more time at home. And someday perhaps, I will realize my dream of going back to a quiet life on the farm where the grass is really green, and the sky is really blue, and the stars are clearly seen at night. Who knows? Perhaps in this atmosphere I may yet get to that book I have always wanted to write.

Wishful thinking again? Maybe I'm just getting old!

Singapore

(and the main
settlement areas
of the OVERSEAS
CHINESE)

Area: 741 square kilometres.

Population: 1,612,000 (estimated 1959).[1]

Recent history: 1942-45—Japanese occupation; 1959—British Government transfers full internal self-government.

Citizenship: Men and women have equal rights.

Religion: Among the Chinese of Singapore (as elsewhere) Confucian ethics hold an important place; many Chinese also adhere to beliefs drawn from Taoism, Mahayana Buddhism, and a variety of small cults. Malays, immigrants from Indonesia, Arabs and some Indians are Moslems; most Indians are Hindus. There are also Christian minority groups drawn from all communities, including Europeans and Eurasians.

Inheritance and family patterns: Chinese (who form 75 per cent of the population) have a strong tradition of strictly patrilineal inheritance, which has been modified to some extent by local legislation giving certain rights to widows and daughters. The traditional ideal of a patrilocal three-generation extended family was by no means common in fact among the less well-to-do in China, and is seldom found overseas where (especially in big towns, including Singapore) nuclear families are usual.

---

1. Latest official estimate of population as published in *The U.N. Population and Vital Statistics Report, October 1960.*

Chinese women of Singapore: their present status in the family and in marriage

by ANN E. WEE

There is evidence of centuries-old contact between China and Malaya, but it was only at the end of the eighteenth century that large-scale immigration began. From then onwards the numbers of new arrivals increased yearly until 1931, when economic depression and consequent unemployment forced a policy of restriction. The Japanese occupation put an end to all immigration during that period; succeeding governments have carefully controlled it. At first the overseas movement of Chinese was exclusively male with the result that even when women began to join in (in the latter half of the nineteenth century) the sex ratio was far from normal. Today it still shows some unbalance in Malaya, but approaches parity in Singapore.

The most recent figures for Overseas Chinese in selected South-East Asian countries are shown in Table 1.

TABLE 1. Distribution of Overseas Chinese in South-East Asia

Country	Date	Total of Chinese	Percentage of total population
Singapore	1960	1 230 000	75
Malaya	1958	2 415 000	37
Thailand	1947	835 000	5
Philippines	1956	145 000	1

The present-day position of immigrant Chinese women, though everywhere developed from a somewhat similar Chinese background (in which, however, there were quite marked local variations), depends

376

a good deal upon the general economic, political and educational conditions in the particular host countries, and also upon local legal provisions. In Singapore and Malaya the effect of British Colonial Law upon Chinese family and marital relations has been considerable, and unique. The following remarks do not, therefore, apply to all Overseas Chinese communities alike. Nevertheless there are many similarities.

THE WOMAN IN THE FAMILY

Patterns of residence and kin behaviour

While the Chinese have brought with them a rich heritage of traditional patterns, Chinese family life in Malaya is no mere replica of the homeland. It was only in the latter half of the nineteenth century that the immigrant wife began to take her place beside her husband. The move to Malaya meant great changes in her life. In the early days migration often was a release for her from the home of her husband's parents in China, where her status was the lowly one of daughter-in-law, the more lowly as her husband was away overseas and returned but rarely to give her support in the family circle. To escape from the domination of her in-laws in China and assume instead the role of mistress of her husband's home in Malaya must have been an intoxicating experience for many a young wife. Furthermore, it often meant sharing with him the building up of a young business, an experience from which she might emerge with additional status as trusted partner in the world of affairs.

All must not be thought of as gain, however. As time passed probably even more common was the experience of the woman who joined her husband and his parents in Malaya, leaving not her in-laws but her own kin in China. An overseas mother commonly travelled to China to seek a wife for her son—young wives from China were said to be more docile and domesticated. Without father or brothers in Malaya to come forward and fight her cause if she was ill treated, such a young wife had no alternative but to be docile, and adapt herself to the ways of her in-laws in the age-old style. 'I well remember mother's words when she persuaded me to accept her choice for me,' said Mr. G. 'She pointed out that my wife had no kin in Singapore and would be forced to look on her family of marriage as her only place of living, for better or for worse; besides, she would have no maternal uncle or close kin to bother us should any family quarrels arise.[1]

Tradition has placed the duty of the married woman to serve her parents-in-law even above her duty to her husband. In line with this tradition, many a migrant to Malaya left his wife behind in the family home in China, returning to her perhaps only once in years. This was for some a lifetime arrangement, with no permanent reunion until the man finally retired (if he ever managed this) to the homeland village. If his financial position was sound the man was not expected to wait long and celibate years for his wife's arrival. He broke no customary standard by taking another wife to be by his side in Malaya, while his principal wife served his parents in China. If, at a later stage of her married life, the principal wife was able to sail south to join her husband, she might well expect to find another established as lady of the household in Singapore.

In a traditional polygynous marriage the hierarchy of wives was unequivocal, and the inferiority of the secondary wife beyond dispute. But the circumstances of the immigrant society saw changes in this. The woman who married an immigrant on the understanding that, while he already had a wife in China, he was a 'bachelor' in Singapore, did not feel herself on a par with the ordinary run of secondary wives. Nor indeed did her neighbours so regard her. She would be referred to as 'the Singapore wife', a phrase which implies to the hearer that a principal wife existed in China, but that she was the head of the husband's home in Singapore. If the man married several women in Singapore, as custom indeed permitted, only one would have the rank of 'Singapore wife'. In the eyes of the community she held almost co-status with the principal wife in China though if the latter chose to move to the household in Malaya, then the status of 'Singapore wife' became open to dispute, and the final pecking order might be clear only after a battle of personalities, and depending on the husband's alignment. The tycoon whose business expanded to the stage of having branches in a number of centres scattered all over the South-East Asian region might find it suited him very well to have a wife established at each of these branches. On his visits she ministered to his needs, in his absence she tended his business interests, an arrangement which probably appealed to the lady as much as to her lord.

---

1. The quotation is from R. Goh's study, *Teochew Kinship in Singapore.*

The Straits Chinese have developed one pattern of residence which is singular in its breach with tradition. While far from universal among them, matrilocal marriage is none the less far from uncommon. This may arise when a Straits-born girl is matched with an up-and-coming young immigrant, whose diligence makes him an eligible suitor despite his lack of family connexions. Lacking a family of his own locally, it may be arranged that for some time at least the couple should make their home with his bride's people. But this is by no means the only circumstances in which matrilocal residence is found. When a Straits Chinese family has no son, or when relations with an already married son (or more often his wife) are so strained that the young couple live elsewhere, or merely when mother and daughter do not want to be parted, an effort is often made to persuade a new son-in-law to agree to live with his wife's people. It is often claimed that among the Straits-born this pattern does not imply the inferiority of status in the son-in-law which it most certainly would in China. The writer feels, however, that this claim does not quite correspond with the true state of affairs, and that usually the young man's family is of slightly inferior social and economic class; or else he himself is a distinctly undistinguished member of a family equal in rank to his bride's, with the result that his own family are glad to agree to a matrilocal marriage for him, so delighted are they that one so personally inferior has been able to marry within their own class at all.

Much of the foregoing argument implies the existence of extended family residence of some type or another. It is very difficult to assess the extent to which this is still typical for the Chinese in Singapore. If a narrow definition of the household as a group sharing common catering is taken, then most certainly the simple family household predominates. The 1953-54 Urban Incomes and Housing Survey, which covered a wide and carefully chosen sample of lower income families (no family including a member earning over 400 Malayan dollars per month was included) in the more crowded city wards, showed less than 6 per cent of Chinese households comprising 'couple with/without children, plus parents': almost 41 per cent of households were made up either of 'couple only' or 'couple and children', or 'widow or widower with children'—all variants of the simple family theme (just over 33 per cent of households were of single persons, either solitary immigrants or employees living in at their place of work).

But the writer feels that by limiting 'household' to a common budgeting group the picture of family life in Singapore is distorted. It is admittedly difficult to arrive at an alternative definition which could safely be handled by the large semi-trained team inevitably used in survey or census work. One can find almost any number of groups comprising, say, an old couple and one or two still unmarried children, together with perhaps as many as two sons each with a wife and children, which in present-day Singapore would be divided into three separate catering groups but all living in one house. There are many reasons for the separate catering, perhaps none more important than the unwillingness of the modern daughter-in-law to yield to her mother-in-law the role of treasurer and domestic manager; but there are also strong reasons both of filial duty and also of self-interest binding the whole group together. Yet by survey definition they are listed as three separate households, and so only their separateness is recorded, whereas the mutual help and co-operation which on many levels are likely to characterize such a group are ignored. This is an area of the web of kinship in which studies so far made shed little if any light and figures are not available.

In the absence of figures, it is possible that a consideration of some of the factors which enter into decisions about home-making may give us some information on this matter of family structure.

In the crowded city areas housing space is commonly rented by the cubicle. When the whole family lives in a partitioned (often window-less) space measuring about 6 x 10 ft., there is hardly room for the grown-up son to bring home his bride to live with his parents. Depending on the husband's place of work, however, the young couple would quite probably seek a cubicle for themselves in their neighbour-hood, and a great deal of coming and going between the two house-holds could be expected. Indeed, the writer has known of several young couples who returned to their own cubicle only at night, the daughter-in-law spending her day with the husband's mother, all meals being taken as if the two cubicle-units formed an extended family household. These may be extreme examples: but the writer feels that although crowded city tenements make large residential groupings well-nigh impossible for the Singapore poor, much of the spirit of family closeness has not in fact been lost.

Among the somewhat better-off sections of the Chinese community there is certainly still a strong sense of the rightness of having married children remain with the parents. However, many factors enter into the decision of whether the young couple will establish a home of their own or will accede to the wish of the parents to have them stay in the family house. Wealth is, as in most societies, a strong ally of authority, and moneyed parents will usually have at least one, perhaps even several, married sons and their families under their roof. But traditional duty may prevail even where pecuniary interest does not beckon. 'Yes, I am going to stay with my mother-in-law after my marriage: my fiancé says we will have to, until his younger brother marries. Then it will be up to him and his wife to look after the old people, and we will be able to start a home of our own.' Or 'We'll be staying with my parents-in-law for a year or so anyway: after all it is the custom and they will be very hurt if we don't stay there awhile, though they know we plan to have a home of our own eventually.' Such remarks can be heard often in the circle of young secretaries, teachers and nurses, girls with an education which has given them a sense of independence but who still recognize and will often be ready to comply with the duties tradition lays down for them.

The writer feels there is a marked correlation between family economic enterprise and extended family households. Where sons work together in a family concern, be it a small grocery shop or a large city firm, it is likely that the mother will head a household team just as the father heads the business. The girl who marries into such a group will know from the start where her husband's (and her children's) interests must lie, and that her parents-in-law, with the power to advance or reduce the young man's influence in the concern, must be deferred to as long as they live. If the young woman has ambitions for a home of her own, she knows she must put these aside for the lifetime of the old couple.

When patterns of residence are the subject of conversation among Chinese ladies, the tone always implies that it is the daughter-in-law who is making concessions by agreeing to live with her husband's parents; the emphasis is always on the loss of independence that this arrangement implies. The cost in terms of privacy and independence may be considerable, the task of fitting in with all the varied personalities of the family a great strain on her: but the returns may be great also. The young wife who passes these tests and makes these adjustments will never lack help when she or her baby is sick, and if anything calls her away from the home she will not need to rely upon servants and strangers to care for her husband and the children. The bride with a professional education does not damage her husband's prestige or comfort by continuing to work after marriage: indeed, in the extended family her being out at work may reduce the possible areas of friction, and the presence of a grandmother in the home frees the young wife from many of the worries about catering and child care which might otherwise burden her.

Although the mother-in-law is viewed traditionally as the bogey, likely to make life difficult for the young married woman, relationships with her are not necessarily the most difficult. 'I could manage with the old lady all right, after all she's getting on in years and we owe her respect. But when I think of my sisters-in-law, I get wild; we are the same generation, why should they be always interfering and making trouble?' Complaints like this are often heard, and the sisters-in-law referred to may either be the unmarried daughters of the house or the women married to the brothers of the speaker's husband. Quarrels between their little children, jealousies over favouritism by the mother-in-law, disputes over sharing household tasks—the sources of conflict among the younger women are legion. Here perhaps lie the greatest obstacles to extended family living, the paramount reasons why one son and his wife fairly commonly stay with the parents, but very rarely two or three.

The problems of the greater family household are widely recognized and much touched on in the conversation of women. But that kinsfolk should be perpetually visiting and helping one another in small ways is taken for granted. Within the circle of their kin the individual family members feel some freedom to choose those with whom they will mix more frequently, according to preference and common interests rather than according to traditional patrilineal principle. In traditional China a married woman was subject to all manner of pressures to keep contact with her own family of orientation and kinsmen to a minimum; to a very large extent this has ceased to be the case in Singapore. But her sense of belonging to her husband's group and her interest in that group may remain strong even under modern conditions. 'My mother has a sister in China,' said Mrs. P. 'She sends her food parcels in the name of my brothers who share the cost equally. My brother in Johore wrote to say he would contribute no longer as he had never known the China aunt. My mother asked a relative of hers to call on my brother and say she would cease to count on him for a share when he ceased to be her son. My brother's wife heard about this and quickly arranged to pay my brother's share to mother, on the quiet.' Here was a young woman hastening to heal a breach between her husband and his mother, and without any material gain in mind, for the older woman had no property to bequeath. Indeed, this anecdote throws light on a number of facets of Chinese family life in Malaya.

The attitude to daughters

The Chinese baby boy has always been assured of a welcome into the world. To a Chinese it would be almost unthinkable that any family should fail to rejoice at the birth of a son. But the baby girl cannot be so sure of a glad reception, and even today there is quite a risk that her arrival will be a source of great disappointment. If a number of older brothers have preceded her and she is the first girl to be born to her parents then they will almost certainly be delighted with her. Also her personality, if winning, her appearance, if charming, may secure her a favoured role in the family even though there are many daughters and few sons. The most unprepossessing little girl can become a cherished favourite if the family should prosper soon after her birth; for she then is seen as the precious harbinger of fortune.

In the old days only these were the fortunate, the daughters who, not by right, but through a combination of good luck and ability won status in the household. Much more commonly the birth of a girl was looked upon as either an unfortunate fact to be accepted with good grace or an outright tragedy. For the daughter-in-law in her first years of marriage to produce a succession of girl babies and never a boy, was in a real sense a tragedy. For the young wife's status in her husband's family was indeed marginal until she became the mother of a son: only sons ensured worship of the ancestors, only as the mother of a son did a woman become a potential ancestress, with prestige in her husband's family in life and the assurance of comforting rites for her soul after death.

> Sons shall be born to him,
> They will be put to sleep on couches;
> They will be clothed in robes;
> They will have sceptres to play with;
> Their cry will be loud.

383

They will be resplendent hereafter with red knee-covers,
The future kings, the princes of the land.

Daughters shall be born to him,
They will be put to sleep on the ground;
They will be clothed with wrappers;
They will have tiles to play with;
It will be theirs neither to do wrong nor to do good.
Only about the spirits and the food will they have to think,
And to cause no sorrow to their parents.[1]

There is a chilling note in those last lines, and neglect and rejection must have been the destiny of many a little daughter. Much of the literature, however, suggests that this was by no means universal: laments at her birth would not necessarily be reflected in the treatment a girl received.

These were the traditional patterns, and while some of the sharpness of distinction has become blurred among the modern Chinese of South-East Asia, yet much of the old feeling remains.

When we begin to understand the role that for hundreds of years the family played in China, and the family organization which made that role possible, then we begin to see how it is that sons stood for all that was desirable and auspicious, while daughters were at best a mixed blessing.

In a very real sense the dead did not cease to be members of their families, but only moved on to a more exalted phase of family life where they became the objects of worship and ritual attention from the living. But only male descendants together with their wives could perform these services for the parents: a daughter married out into another family in her teens and joined the ritual unit of her husband's family, ministering to his ancestors, not her own. The very salvation of a man's soul, and of that of his parents and ancestors, depended on his leaving male descendants to continue the ancestral cult. There are three unfilial acts, but the gravest is failure to beget sons, according to the sage. No wonder that even a weakly and unattractive son was to be preferred to the most promising daughter.

The basic fact of Chinese life is the struggle for existence, so wrote A. H. Smith in 1900. There is every evidence that the great majority of peasant families only managed to feed and care for their members

---

1. *Book of Odes,* Part II, Book 4, Ode 5, translated by Legge.

by dint of the greatest prudence and by a willingness to face any amount of hard work to produce even small additions to income or food supplies. Very commonly any sudden disaster, flood, drought or civil strife, could deprive the peasant of his tiny land holding and force the members of the family to wander off in search of work, to join the vast horde of 'floating people' who eked out a miserable existence as wandering labourers, in an overcrowded land with few opportunities.

Such 'floating people' were a major element in imperial society, and their plight well known to the great mass of peasantry who only barely managed to cling on to their tenure of land and to keep their families together. And each was constantly aware that some minor crisis or bit of ill-luck could mean the end of his status as a family man, a householder with roots in the village circle, able to tend in the approved way the souls of the ancestors, and with hopes of bearing male descendants to carry on the family line.

This precariousness of status, in this world and the next, left little room for sentiment in the organization of Chinese family life. Sons by their hard work, skill and thrift could help maintain and might well raise the standing of the family: by filial behaviour they could care for their parents in life and after death. The son was the investment on which the family's future depended. But what of the daughter? As soon as she reached her teens and the age when her labour could be most useful to them it was time for the family to arrange a marriage for her, with all its attendant expenses; and once married into another family her opportunities for visiting her own family were few, and the material help she could render limited to small formal gifts brought on the occasion of visits. And, worse still, the self-respect or 'face' of the woman and her family required that gifts of at least equal value be sent back with her to her husband's family. All in all, the Chinese saw girls as 'goods on which you lose'.

A girl would leave home in a few years in any case; it is not surprising that in times of crisis when poverty threatened the break-up of the family she could be spared a little earlier, an encumbrance of which the family could free itself. Disposal of immature daughters has always been a feature of the family life of the very poor in China, and it took a variety of forms. Female infanticide was much referred to in the old mission literature, and was undoubtedly one anguished response to the extremity of poverty in many areas, though by no means in all. The Chinese themselves have always condemned the practice, and the unbalanced sex ratio and consequent shortage of brides resulting from it in some neighbourhoods[1] was a social evil they recognized. The attitude of society to other methods of disposal was more neutral, and perhaps one can infer that these methods were, therefore, more likely to be resorted to.

Firstly there was outright sale, in which the family relinquished all rights over the girl in return for a cash payment. This might be pathetically little if economic depression was widespread, but in any case would tend to vary upwards in ratio to the girl's age. Sale might be direct to another family, but it was more likely to be to a broker when the girl's ultimate destiny would be unknown to her parents. Her purchasers might use her as a domestic slave, then in her late teens she might be given in marriage, or alternatively kept as a low status concubine of some member of the family or, at any stage after leaving her parents, she might be sold to a brothel keeper, who could profit from prostituting her even before puberty. The services of an immature, preferably virgin, girl were much sought by the rich and elderly because of the wide belief that intercourse with her had rejuvenating effects. Whatever the fate of the daughter sold out of the family, she was in effect entirely rightless and no ethical code effectively controlled the treatment meted out to her or served as adequate protection of her interest.[2]

Several writers have suggested that outright sale was particularly rife in times of widespread flood or famine, and was perhaps especially a feature of the life of those on the brink of joining or actually within the ranks of the 'floating people'.

Another device for disposing of daughters was common among the desperately poor, especially in certain dialect groups. This was the complete handing over of her in child betrothal to another family, to spend her childhood under their roof, and be married in her middle teens, by a quiet ceremony to one of their sons. Here the disposing family lightened themselves of the burden of a daughter and received a sum of money. The receiving family, almost certainly themselves not rich, ensured a bride for their son without having to meet the

1. As described for instance, in Isabel Crook's book, *Ten Mile Inn,* Kegan Paul, 1960.
2. A personal account of what it was like to be sold like this has been written in English by Miss J. Lim under the title *Sold for Silver,* Collins, 1958.

much greater expense of arranging a marriage for him later with an adult bride. They also, as she grew, benefited from the 'little daughter-in-law's' increasing ability to take a share of the work in the family. It seems that the parents of a 'little daughter-in-law' commonly failed to keep in touch with her.

The writer has expressed elsewhere her belief that there is much evidence today, particularly among the professional and clerical classes, of an attitude towards girls deviating widely from the traditional one. She recalls many cases where the birth of a second or third male child has called forth strong expressions of disappointment that the boy was not a girl: in one instance the young mother wept and refused to look at her baby, a third son, so greatly had she desired a daughter. Similarly it would be possible to quote from innumerable conversations expressing praise of daughters and their usefulness to the family: 'A young man has more to spend his money on, it's my daughters who give their mother the greater part of their wages.' 'If I was in trouble, it's to my girls that I'd look for help; my sons are so absorbed with their wives and children.' Congratulation of a mother on her four young sons brought the retort: 'To rear boys these days is to rear dogs to watch other people's doors.' (This reply presumably referred to the practice of young couples moving in with the bride's family, or, at least, setting up house by themselves.)

This does not mean that the traditional preference for sons is a thing of the past. It is still very strong indeed among most sections of the community, particularly, the writer believes, among the commercial and business classes. But there are other attitudes in existence as well. It is perhaps not fortuitous that conservatism in this matter appears to be found more among those classes who tend to organize their economic life in family units, sons following fathers into the business, whereas it is among those whose children, both boys and girls, enter salaried employment that the newer views are expressed. But we require more evidence.

MARRIAGE IN THE PRESENT DAY

Arrangements and rituals

Arranged marriages are by no means a thing of the past among the Singapore Chinese, although the traditional patterns have been modified. The bringing of pressure to bear on a girl to accept a marriage planned by her elders would be universally condemned and is indeed very rarely heard of. At an early stage it is customary for the horoscope, showing the details of the hour, day, month and year of her birth, to be asked for by the other family, so that together with the young man's it can be inspected by a 'fortune-teller' to ensure compatability on this mystic plane. (In fact, some small talk between client and fortune-teller usually precedes a consultation, and in this way it is relatively simple for the specialist to detect what type of verdict will be most welcome.) This is still very general in matches where parents are taking the responsibility of choice. Even where it is a love match, at the time he seeks his parents' approval the young man's mother may still insist on seeing the horoscope of the girl of his choice, though in these circumstances the custom is often dispensed with. The mother of at least one such young man most firmly refused to see the horoscope of his fiancée when a sister-in-law suggested she should do so: 'You know what young people are like now, they will go ahead whatever the horoscope says, so it is better not to see it and so save ourselves from worrying about the future.'

The girl is usually brought into the picture early in the arrangements and given the opportunity to meet the young man (albeit very superficially) at some social occasion before approaches have gone far enough to make retreat embarrassing. And certainly the young man in question expects at least similar latitude! These 'social occasions' are inclined to be agonizing. Everyone concentrates fixedly on the pretence that nothing at all is in mind, and the general tension withers every sprout of conversation. But one or two gallantly convivial souls will struggle on, with the matchmaker (almost always an aunt or close family friend these days when the professional is well-nigh extinct) feverishly encouraging each family to jump through those social hoops which will show the members off to the best advantage. Hardly the ideal climate in which to make the choice of a life partner. But the freedom of the young to say no is very real: indeed a young woman may reject a number of choices favoured by her parents. Once she has done so, however, her parents are likely to discontinue efforts to find a match for her, pointing out that they have fulfilled their duty and it is now her own responsibility. And in this last phrase perhaps lies the key to the parental attitude to arrangement of marriages: the anxiety is not so much to see her married as to feel that the obligations due from parent to daughter have not been neglected.

If the young couple favour each other at the first meeting arrangements will be proceeded with. Gifts will be exchanged, perhaps there will be some mutual family visiting, and the engagement will be formalized. Nowadays the young man will probably give his fiancée a Western-style engagement ring; and indeed she may in return also give him a diamond ring, which on dress occasions it would be quite in order for a man to wear. Only the most sophisticated would announce an engagement in the newspapers: publicity is more commonly assured by the distribution of cakes or sweetmeats traditionally suitable to the occasion among the circle of relatives and friends. After this the couple will be allowed considerable freedom to go out together socially without chaperonage.

An engagement of this kind is felt to be binding, and any breach after this point has been reached is attended with trauma on all sides. Even where both parties wish to back out they may consult a lawyer or the Counselling and Advice Bureau of the Social Welfare Department, for reassurance that the breach of engagement will be 'legal', and that each will be truly 'free' to enter a subsequent marriage with another partner. For a large part of 1957 the writer was acting in charge of the Counselling and Advice Bureau, and received frequent inquiries along these lines. The way in which, in such circumstances, the return of even valueless items like snapshots is mutually insisted upon, seems to illustrate the weight placed on an engagement and the need to obliterate every trace of the relationship if real freedom is to be regained.

Between engagement and marriage no fixed length of time must elapse, but in the vast majority of cases the wedding will take place within the year. Certain months of the lunar calendar are markedly more auspicious, especially those at the latter end of the year. At a specified time, a week or two before the marriage ceremonial, gifts are sent from the groom's family to the bride's. Prominent among these again are traditional cakes or sweetmeats, in quantities specified by the bride's family (through the matchmaker) as their requirements for distribution among friends and relations.

The gifts also include a sum of cash, the 'betrothal gold'. The amount, which the matchmaker negotiates in advance, is usually not less than $200 to $400, and may even be very much more. This is spoken of as a contribution to the bride's outfit, usually to augment the jewellery she will come adorned with to her marriage. A poor family, their resources taxed to provide their daughter with an adequate trousseau, will accept the entire sum proffered, and may even have bargained about the amount in prior negotiations. Where both families are well-to-do, the groom's may display their wealth by the offer of a large sum, while the bride's will respond by accepting only a token of perhaps $10, and politely returning the remainder. Some families make it clear, through the matchmaker, that they can dispense with the betrothal gold altogether. In such cases the groom's family may respond by pressing that a token sum should be accepted 'because it is the custom'; if they are modern and English educated they may acquiesce in the refusal, but offer instead to bear the expense of a certain number of 'tables' at the wedding dinner, to be reserved for guests invited by the bride's family. And this offer will almost certainly be accepted, nay, may even be bargained upwards without loss of dignity: 'With a social circle as wide as ours, what use would five tables be? We shall need at least ten.'

The Straits Chinese have the singular custom of handing over another item of cash besides the betrothal gold, a sum which is not negotiated and which is seen as an outright gift to the bride's mother. Although it has no equivalent in Singapore Malay marriages this gift is known by a Malay term which translates as 'breast money', a token of thanks to the bride's mother for the tenderness and care she has lavished on rearing the young woman whose skills and good breeding will now bring honour to her bridegroom's family.[1] Among the Malay-speaking Straits Chinese, the Chinese term for 'betrothal gold' is often not used. A sum of about $200 will be sent, along with the other ceremonial gifts, but this sum is called *wang belanja,* a Malay phrase meaning 'money for expenses' and referring to the gift given in Malay (Moslem) weddings to help the bride's family with the wedding expenses;[2] whereas the small sum, the 'breast money' will be accepted—it usually amounts only to $12—a better-to-do family should return the *wang belanja.*

Whatever the amount of the 'betrothal gold' itself, it is undoubtedly

---

1. J. E. de Young mentions an equivalent custom among the Thais, in his book, *Village Life in Modern Thailand,* University of California, 1958.
2. See the article by Michael Swift, 'Men and Women in Malay Society', above.

seen as a sum which the bride's family will at least double in their own expenditure on their daughter's trousseau—jewellery, clothes and furnishings for the bridal room. Any suggestion that the family has made a profit will imply to the hearer that the marriage is not quite above board, that the family is being bribed to accept a match for their daughter which honourable parents would have rejected: it may be rumoured that they are 'selling' her to an elderly man already much married.

What of the wedding itself? For the Singapore Chinese couple there are three alternatives. Firstly for the Christian Chinese, a minority, there is marriage in a church of one of the many denominations that flourish in the island. Secondly there is civil marriage before the Registrar of Marriages, available for couples of all races and religions, prepared to accept monogamy, and increasingly popular, though the registrar only performs a fraction of all the marriages which take place in the Chinese community each year. For the vast majority still favour the third alternative of 'marriage according to custom'. Essentially this consists of a ceremony in which the newly-married pair pay reverence to the elders of the groom's family and make obeisance before the family altar representing his ancestors; then finally the bride serves tea to the groom's parents and other relatives senior to her husband, as a symbol of her acceptance of her humble role in the family. And each in turn, as they receive her respectful offer of tea, express their welcome by handing her a gift which may vary from a few dollars to a valuable diamond ornament. The value of the gifts varies with the wealth of the family, but money or jewellery will always be wrapped in vivid red paper, symbol of happiness and prosperity. These are the commonest essentials, and no Chinese woman who could prove that her in-laws had accepted tea ceremonially from her need fear for the legality of her marriage. But various other features, some of long traditional significance, some belonging to the modern world, also usually feature on these occasions. A ceremonial combing of the hair of bride and groom, each severally at their own home in the early hours of the wedding day, is still performed except in rather modern families. And then for all with any pretensions to style there must be a car, hired or borrowed if need be, and festooned with pink ribbons, in which the groom together with a friend or relative (or sometimes just a male relative) should go to seek the bride at her home.

Even the girl who would never dream of wearing Western dress in everyday life will want a white wedding dress and flowing veil for the great day; and these items, too, can easily be hired. The bride will not go alone to her husband's home. Nowadays cars full of her girl friends, dressed in their best, but not formally arrayed as bridesmaids, often follow the bridal car. If the trousseau has not been conveyed to the groom's home on a previous day, there will be a whole procession of cars, some bulging with the friends, others bulging with dress boxes, embroidered pillows and blankets. With the whole neighbourhood assembled to look on, and amid cannonades of crackers fired outside her home, the bride's send-off is a notable occasion indeed. In the car with the bride and the groom will be the groom's 'supporter', perhaps the bride's schoolboy brother, and that most important lady, the 'bride's adviser'.

The 'bride's adviser' has always been a figure among the wedding personnel, right from traditional times. She is a professional, usually middle-aged, and hired for the day as an expert in the details of the ceremonies, and the procedures of dress. Her functions begin at the bride's own home when she helps the young woman to robe, and coaches her in the correct forms of leave-taking. She stays close by the bride throughout the day, keeping up a running commentary of whispered instructions through each stage of the ceremonies before the elders and the family altar.

Nowadays, although there is still a market for the services of such middle-aged traditional advisers, there are also serious rivals in the field in the shape of the make-up experts, the 'beauticians'. A small number of young women with training in hair-dressing or professional make-up (or in both) have built up for themselves both a high reputation and a lucrative business as bride-dressers. It is for their expertise in enhancing the bride's appearance, not for any knowledge of ceremonial procedure, that their services are sought: shrewdly, however, they have tended to equip themselves with a body of traditional knowledge, somehow incongruous with their modern and glossy appearance, in case their clients should require this of them also. Whereas the traditional adviser stays on right through the day's performances until evening, the modern beautician commonly disappears quite early—indeed on a particularly auspicious day of the calendar, when many marriages are being celebrated, she has probably accepted bookings from three or four brides one after the other.

Of great importance is the taking of a group photograph. It would be almost true to say that in no customary marriage where even the minimum of ceremonial is observed is this detail omitted. The photo of the bride and groom, the former resplendent in gown and veil, will almost certainly be framed and displayed in the home afterwards; it seems, especially among the less sophisticated, to have almost the status of being part of the legal formalities of the marriage. The writer recalls from experience in the Counselling and Advice Bureau, a number of occasions when, for a woman seeking help over quarrels with her husband, the focus of distress was his having torn up wedding pictures: he had destroyed something which in illiterate circles constituted the readiest proof that a marriage has been legally solemnized.

At no point is the economic status of the families concerned more apparent than in the feasting which attends the marriage. A dinner for kinsmen and friends, on as grand a scale as can be afforded, should ideally be given by the groom's family on the night of the wedding. Among the conservative this may still be divided into an early meal for the womenfolk, and a later evening sitting for the men: but if the women of the family are educated, one mixed gathering is much more likely. Various versions are given of what is the 'proper' role of the bride's family in this feasting. One stream of tradition would say they have no place in feasting of any kind at this time, for after all, what have they to celebrate? They have just lost a daughter. Another tradition would have the bride's parents invited to the groom's dinner and attending in the early evening, to withdraw before the feast is served. In middle-class and English-educated circles the dinner is now attended by relatives and friends of both families, although the organization and expense is primarily a matter for the parents of the groom, and they are essentially the hosts on this occasion. A restaurant is always asked to do the catering, though if the groom's family have a spacious home the feast is held in their hall or garden. At anything up to 80 dollars per table (of ten guests), together with generous servings of spirits and beer, a dinner can be ruinously expensive:[1] food for as many as fifteen or twenty tables may be needed. This is especially so where the modern, educated young people have each their own circle of school, college and office friends to think of beside their kinsfolk and family friends.

A compromise is sought in the Western custom of a tea-time

---

1. The Malayan dollar is worth about 35 U.S. cents.

gathering with suitable refreshments and the 'cutting' of a multi-tiered 'cake'—which is in fact usually a carboard edifice from the bowels of which are later lifted a myriad tinfoil-wrapped slices of cake for distribution to those assembled. Sometimes the cost of this kind of gathering may be borne by the bride's parents: but if the groom's father pays, he has still to give a dinner to his closer kin and acquaintances or risk being branded as tight-fisted.

So far only the arranged marriage has been mentioned. At one extreme is the marriage where all initiative lies with the two families and the boy and girl passively accept the choice made by their elders: at the other extreme is the couple whose meeting and courtship is on their own initiative, and parents are brought in only at a fairly late stage when their approval for an engagement is requested. Plenty of examples of both patterns could be found, the one common among the uneducated, the other more characteristic of those with secondary schooling, whether in English or Chinese; but this correlation is by no means complete and exceptions abound.

Between the two poles some interesting compromises flourish. In wealthy business and professional circles there is a great deal of social juggling to ensure that youngsters 'meet the right people'. And some parents make it quite clear to the young son or daughter whom they regard the 'right person' to be, and in which directions choice would be most auspicious. This situation has its Western counterpart and, as in the West, any suggestion that such steering does take place is met with shocked denials on all sides.

A compromise not found in the West occurs when a young couple meet fortuitously and, while each senses the other's attraction, neither has the confidence or social poise to initiate a courtship. This is where the young man can seek the sympathetic ear of a relative, probably an aunt or uncle to act, as it were, as go-between with his own parents, in the hope that they will be willing to find a way of approaching the girl's family. In a society where those with less than high school education have few accepted channels for social mixing with boys and girls of their own age, this modification of an old pattern serves an excellent purpose.

Even the most progressive couple who have conducted their own courtship always hope for parental approval of their choice, and usually seek every possible way of overcoming opposition and winning consent rather than risk plunging into marriage in the face of family displeasure. It is interesting to note that even in marriages of the most modern type (assuming that parents' consent is forthcoming) a relative often steps in to take over the final phases of the traditional matchmaker's role of conducting the negotiations regarding the style of the marriage and the gifts to be made by each side.

Polygynous marriage and modern trends

Polygyny in the traditional family pattern of China would appear to have followed a fairly standard pattern. The social background of secondary wives was always inferior to the standing of the husband and the principal wife, and the rights and authority of the latter were unquestionable in the hierarchy of women within the household. But perhaps even in olden times there were exceptions to this rigid structure. Certainly in Singapore, where plural marriages are still plentiful, a host of different patterns can be observed.

It would not be impossible to find a comparatively small number of polygynous households apparently adhering to all the 'rules': the secondary wives acknowledging the superior status of the 'great wife', training their children to address the older woman by the most honoured term for mother, permitting themselves to be addressed, even by their own offspring, by an inferior appellation. This is not the usual pattern, and it is rare enough to call for comment in Chinese circles; comment usually of amazement that any man can cope with the administrative problems of such a *ménage,* in an age when some measure of self-assertion can be expected of women. It does exist, however, at one end of the scale of plural matings.

At the other is the girl living in a room rented for her by a man who has a wife and home elsewhere and who visits her from time to time. He may have no intention of introducing her to his family, of acknowledging her as a wife, nor indeed of maintaining a relationship with her longer than passing fancy may dictate. But she may regard herself as a secondary wife. And if the man should die while the relationship is current, she may be able, especially if she bears a child, to establish before the courts a wife's claim in his estate. The writer can recall one such court decision which called forth ribald comments from among the friends of the departed on how incensed he would have been at the suggestion that the girl was anything more than a 'keep', a mistress of the moment.

Between these two extremes is the secondary wife in a relationship of some permanence, usually, in present-day Singapore, established in a home of her own where the husband, prepared to acknowledge her, spends a proportion of his time. Such marriages are rarely based on any ceremonial, being founded merely on the decision of the pair to co-habit. Where the first wife has been married according to custom, it is difficult to predict what her reaction will be to her husband's setting up with a 'number two' in a second establishment. Especially if she is generously provided for materially she may make no demur: but whether the reason for this acceptance is diplomacy, or merely lethargy, will be hard for outsiders to know. Perhaps it is significant of the times that it will be generally assumed that she objects, and her complaisance will be cause for comment. Perhaps the greatest bitterness is felt where the original marriage was entirely the choice of the couple themselves, and the wife suffers particular disillusion to find that what seemed to be a 'modern' marriage relationship is in fact drifting into the traditional mould.

When the two women have separate homes, they may or may not have any contact. The first wife may refuse to recognize the very existence of the second, and the latter, especially if she is quite sure of her hold on the common husband, may take a stand equally aloof. It is more often the second wife who presses for admission into the family circle, for the added security, the surer stamp of wifehood, that this gives to her otherwise rather vaguely defined status. Not that the junior wife will wish to give up her separate home; this independence and individual maintenance is one of the greatest benefits she enjoys *vis-à-vis* her counterpart in a previous generation. What she hopes to achieve is the status of family membership, manifested by her right to be present at great occasions, especially weddings, funerals and the like, when some public attention is focused on the household and her presence will be conspicuous. If her husband's parents are living she will be even more intent upon fostering their interest in any children she may have, assuming that the old people have some wealth at their disposal.

To bear children, especially sons, is important to any Chinese woman, who establishes her position in her husband's family far more securely by this than by the rite of marriage. This is all the more important for the secondary wife, whose marriage is very often not marked by rites of any kind. Additional descendants prove irresistible to grandparents and, whatever the background of the mother, she usually establishes herself in the family because of the children, who are thus an invaluable adjunct to her rather doubtful status as a wife.

Motives for secondary marriage: male

There is a fairly large body of reported court cases of women claiming secondary wife status in the matter of intestacy of their 'husbands'. It is interesting to note the number of these women with adopted children, rather than natural-born children. The total number of cases is too small, and the chances of further inquiring too remote, for any serious deductions to be made, but is there a possibility that secondary wives as a class have a high rate of infertility? It is difficult to see why this should be, for their background in Singapore does not have the uniformity which C. K. Yang noted in his study of a village where, with one exception, all secondary wives had been city prostitutes prior to marriage. Could it be that for the wives in some polygynous unions, while to bear children is important, to avoid being sexually *hors de combat*—through pregnancy, for example—is paramount?

Certainly it is true that although considerations of status and increased posterity may enter into secondary marriages, especially in conservative business circles, it is generally assumed that a man's motives for polygyny are at least in part amatory. The secondary lady is popularly seen as a temptress, as one who brings not the gentle, submissive ideal of a first wife but rather the spice of the courtesan's arts to her relationship with her husband. In the generalizations of gossip she is always a cabaret girl (professional dancing partner) or a glittering denizen of some other part of the lower end of the entertainment world. And in fact also, of course, she is often just that. But many secondary wives have more menial backgrounds with no claims to glamour.

In the older generation a man was free to take a *mui tsai* (girl domestic slave) as concubine, and after a girlhood of abject drudgery she was not usually a vivacious or very alluring personality: nor did marriage usually mean a release from domestic burdens. To a foreigner her lot would be seen as intolerable, the very lowest of all in the range of secondary wifehood, her children probably addressing her as roughly as the rest of the household, and under social pressure to detach themselves from identification with her. An immigrant Chinese would agree that this was certainly not pleasant for her; but, his social values conditioned by generations of peasant awareness of the ever menacing threat of destitution, he would also point out the good fortune that she, a mere slave, should achieve the security of acknowledged motherhood of a rich man's children, and enjoy the contentment of seeing their future assured.

Menial wifehood along these lines has more or less died out as, of course, has the institution of girl domestic slaves. But the writer can recall a number of instances where businessmen have taken as secondary wives factory hands or manual labourers. With the experience of earning a living in a competitive field these girls are not usually meek nor likely to accept a destiny of domestic drudgery; but like the *mui tsai* of old, they usually lack the finesse and charm of the typical *demimondaine*. Mr. Tan started life as a labourer, but in the hurly-burly of the Japanese occupation he moved up, and by the time of the postwar boom he was, at the age of 35, a well-to-do citizen with a substantial suburban residence. His first wife was already dead when the writer knew the family, but from her photo on the wall it was clear that she had been a plain and homespun creature. The household was presided over by the second Mrs. Tan, English educated and an excellent housewife—only her piquant beauty and sophistication gave a hint of her cabaret past. Although she described herself thus: 'I am the second wife'—implying secondary status and not chronology—she had to all appearances been promoted to first wife role on the death of that senior lady. Also in the household, though she later bestowed upon herself a separate establishment was Mrs. Tan number three, who had been a manual worker in a factory controlled by her husband. Adenoidal and with protruding teeth, she exhibited no grace, poise or any apparent charm, while her raucous speaking voice operated in perpetual fortissimo. And yet, when she got a little home of her own it was there that Mr. Tan spent most of his time. Ladies in-the-know were not at all puzzled by this: 'Ah,' they commented, 'when he was coming up "number two" suited him very nicely; she could entertain and her English was quite an advantage, while he knows not a word. But he probably never felt quite easy with her; "number three" is much more his type, just like his mother and sisters, the sort of woman he's used to.'

The conversation of ladies here in Singapore usually seems to accept that man is by nature inclined to polygyny and that it is the man not so inclined who is worthy of comment. 'I must say, I have never had any of that sort of trouble with X,' said the wife of a distinguished academic referring to her husband. Would we assume that she had had 'trouble', unless assured to the contrary? The lady's words seem to imply this. And indeed for the middle-class man, from at least the clerk upwards, the social pressures of his peer group and the blandishments of the entertainment world make philandering, the threshold of polygyny, a very real temptation. 'So your husband is going on his business trip alone? Wah! He's lucky!' said the businessman to his friend's wife: not on the face of it a very flattering remark, but it was intended as a compliment to the lady for her tolerance in not insisting on keeping her husband under surveillance.

If the senior wife in traditional society gained prestige from her role in the polygynous household, the vestiges of this have worn rather thin in Singapore society of today; and it is generally assumed that any woman would prefer to be a sole wife, other things being equal. On the other hand, other things are not always equal, and many women would undoubtedly choose to live in opulence with a shared husband than suffer extreme privations as a first and only wife.

Tradition did not ascribe a conspicuously erotic role to the first and principal wife. It was not exceptional beauty or charm that the elders sought in choosing a bride for a young man; evidence of health and a physique promising prolific conception and easy parturition were the qualities primarily demanded. The young wife's role was to bear children, especially sons to ensure the numerical strength of the family and the continuation of the ancestor cult. Indeed the development of a sentimental tie between the young married couple was actively discouraged as potentially dangerous to the unity of the extended family. A young principal wife with too strong a romantic hold over her husband might use her power to encourage him to defy his parents or even to break away from them and set up a small family household with his wife and children.

By the time he was older a man had an established vested interest in the extended family. Secondary unions promised an increase in descendants for it, and at the same time carried much less threat to its existence: thus it was possible to tolerate amatory motives in these relationships. Maurice Freedman in his book, *Chinese Family and Marriage in Singapore*, quoted from the Chinese: 'The domestic flower cannot attain the fragrance of the wild bloom', a saying which epitomizes the contrast between what was expected of the first wife and what was looked for in lesser ladies.

Perhaps the major changes taking place in the social life and manners of women of respectable background reflect to some extent a rebellion against this contrast and its implied acceptance of double standards. With, of course, some marked exceptions, the domestic flowers of the present over-45 generation have expected to do little about acquiring fragrance. The writer has often heard wives of this age group exchange grievances about the fickleness of husbands. And yet the speakers have patently made no effort to equip themselves as charming or attentive companions for their menfolk. In the traditional society a wife had much incentive to emphasize rather than play down her advancing years. Young wifehood meant subordination to the elders, but an increase in age entitled her to respect in the family hierarchy. Her interests in the family system were better served as an elder than as a symbol of erotic love. Cleanliness and a measure of neatness are universal to Chinese women. But the married woman of the older group apparently seldom gave much thought to the becomingness of what she wore, and assumed young the mien of staid and comfortable middle age. Again, the same woman who would be first to resent infidelity might ungraciously refuse to make an effort to accompany her husband on the social occasions required of him by his business connexions. These are, of course, generalizations to which many exceptions could be found, but the pattern is common enough to be worthy of note.

Since the middle 1950s an interesting phenomenon, in Singapore especially, has been the meteoric rise of the charm school, the modelling class and the beauty parlour. In 1950 the organizers of a beauty contest had a struggle, not to find pretty faces, which abounded, but to find middle-class girls with the poise and sophistication to take part in a parade. A glance at press photographs of such occasions at that time reveals a surprising lack of finesse for a city as modern in many respects as Singapore. But the 1960 platforms overflow with entrants, no prettier, for prettiness was never in short supply, but adept at emphasizing every quality they possess, poised, graceful and apparently prepared to take infinite pains to enhance their charms. The frizzy and shapeless perm has given place to a variety of styles not a whit behind the latest issue of *Vogue* or *Glamour*: one hairdresser described what she called the '7.30 trade', of business girls calling daily to have their 'sets' recombed and lacquered in bouffant glory, at 50 cents a time. (This probably implies a monthly expenditure, including setting, of about 20 Malayan dollars out of a monthly salary in the 150 to 400 dollar range.) Nor is hairdressing any longer the only service sought, and professional manicure (probably costing 2 dollars) and facial massage treatment (cost approximately 10 dollars) now commonly feature in the middle-class girl's budget.

Charm school courses and classes in modelling prosper. Large numbers of young middle-class women are prepared to expend sums in the region of 150 dollars for tuition in the social graces and the arts of self-adornment. A standard of gloss and sophistication is now common among young women in circles where first-and-only wife status alone would be acceptable. In so far as appearances are concerned, the *vrai monde* and the *demi-monde* are no longer distinguishable at a glance. Flowers of the domestic crop are rapidly acquiring a fragrance of which the wild bloom had once a monopoly. The modern young wife undoubtedly hopes her husband will conform to a Western pattern of marriage: she spares no effort to provide at home the perfumed and lacquered companionship of which the cabaret coquette was formerly the only purveyor.

Motives for secondary marriage: female

For a girl of working-class or entertainment-class origins, the motives for accepting marriage as a secondary wife are usually assumed to be economic. Certainly neither would be likely to achieve first/only wife status with a reasonably prosperous husband.

A desire for material security is not, however, a plausible explanation in all secondary marriages. The range of background of secondary wives is very wide and includes women of business acumen, skill and education—even professional training. Proprietresses of hairdressing establishments, clerks, secretaries, qualified nurses and teachers: it would not be difficult to find a small number of women in each of these occupations married to men with prior matrimonial commitments. And no-one would be surprised if these career wives supported themselves and any children of the union partly or largely from their own earnings. If the principal wife of her husband lives in some distant part of Malaya, or better still overseas, the secondary wife suffers little from her status—she assumes the role of 'Singapore wife' of earlier days. But the first wife is often embarrassingly imminent, in which case all her business and professional standing will not protect the secondary wife from some disparaging comment, albeit not to her face.

There is no body of material available to explain satisfactorily the readiness of a considerable number of economically secure women to accept this inferior status. Education in a woman is certainly no barrier to an eligible and advantageous match in Chinese society: probably the majority of senior professional women are married, often to men of high business and professional standing. (Incidentally, this is in marked contrast with Malay society where the average age of marriage is lower than among Chinese. The comparatively few Malay girls who go on to higher education often emerge qualified only to find the ranks of eligible suitors disquietingly thin.) The only explanation which the writer can offer as a possible solution of this anomoly lies in the attitude of society to secondary marriage.

In all three major communities of Singapore—Chinese, Indian and Malay—polygyny has been possible up till now, except for the small Christian groups and for the individual man of whatever community or religion who chose to marry in the Registry under the Civil Marriage Ordinance. Even for the Moslem Malays, whose law enjoins equality among wives, and certainly for the Chinese and Hindu Indian groups, the secondary wife is definitely inferior to the first wife in tradition. But she has a place, for secondary wifehood is a widely accepted and tolerated institution; and in the great flexibility of modern society a second wife may hope to raise her position in practice above that of the first wife, if she is skilful enough in her hold over the husband. So wide is this acceptance of the institution that the writer has even heard a Catholic Eurasian woman, complaining of her husband's perfidy, describe him as having taken a second wife. Questioned on this she was, of course, aware that as a Roman Catholic, married in his church, her husband could have only one wife; but her first thought was to describe her rival as a second wife.

A single girl finds herself romantically attached to an already-married man. In a monogamous society the alternatives for her are the heartbreak of parting or the tarnished status of mistress and potential mother of illegitimate children. For the Chinese girl a compromise has been possible which avoided both these unpleasant extremes. In a secondary marriage she could enjoy the undoubted legal status of wifehood, albeit not the most prestige-carrying variety; and children born of the union were free of the stigma of bastardy.

The availability of this compromise has, the writer believes, widely influenced the social behaviour of young women, even those with a measure of education and economic security—though it must be emphasized that only a small proportion of the total of middle-class and educated girls are ever in the position of secondary wife. Few middle-class secondary wives may have sought deliberately the emotional involvement which led to their marriage, but as long as secondary marriage is a possibility, the attentions of a married man are less than disastrous to the young woman who attracts him. It is the writer's contention that in Chinese society the single girl may allow herself to drift towards an attachment too strong to break; if monogamy were the rule she would have much less to hope for and much more incentive to flee from the relationship at an early stage. 'Dear...,' writes 'Perplexed' in the love-lorn columns of the local English press, 'I am deeply in love with a married man working in the same office. He wants me to be his second wife, but my girl friend says I should give him up. What should I do, I cannot bear to part from him?' This is an actual quotation, and a dozen similar could be extracted over any month of newspaper browsing. (A woman journalist assures the writer that she has no need to invent letters for her column, a steady stream comes pouring in from readers.) Perhaps in the act of writing the letter-writer betrays her doubts, but she by no means discards the possibility that there is a future in the relationship. It will be interesting to observe, in Singapore at least, the outcome of the Women's Charter (which is described below), and to see whether it results in a more circumspect attitude among young girls, or in the growth of tolerated concubinage in place of legal polygyny.

Legal status and secondary wives

As stated elsewhere, even for a first wife, only very scant ceremonies may mark the marriage in some circumstances. If it can be proved that the couple intended to enter into a marriage relationship this is, in the last resort, sufficient, although the majority of first marriages would not rest on such slight evidence. A secondary marriage may be marked by some ceremonial, but the writer believes that in the majority of such unions the couple merely commence cohabitation, and, then, as in the case of a first wife, if it can be proved that both intended the union to be a marriage, the legal status as such is established. With the law, as

403

it has been administered heretofore in Singapore and Malaya, recognizing the polygynous customs of the Chinese, a secondary wife can sue for maintenance for herself and for her children in the same way as a first wife. She can also apply for letters of administration on a basis of equality with the first wife, and can claim half of the widow's share on the intestacy of the husband; indeed, if six women can all prove status as wives this share will be divided into six equal parts. Thus, as Freedman has pointed out, British colonial law, with the expressed object of respecting custom in recognizing polygamy, gave to the secondary wife rights to ownership in property where, in the traditional society of the homeland, she, and indeed the first wife also, could have claimed adequate maintenance only.

The main legal disability suffered by the secondary wife in Singapore is her vulnerability to divorce. In reported case law where the question of divorce was relevant (usually in disputes over rights in intestate estates) expert witnesses have been unanimous that the secondary wife could be repudiated at the will of the husband. The same authorities repeatedly expressed doubts as to whether a principal wife could be divorced at all, except for grave misdemeanours. But they usually conceded that, in practice, agreements to separate with freedom to remarry have, if drawn up by mutual consent, been accepted in Chinese society as amounting to divorce, and in fact in Singapore anyone who has been married by Chinese custom but can produce such a document of separation is accepted by the Registrar of Marriages as capable of contracting a civil marriage.

In practice the fear of mere desertion may worry the secondary wife most; but it is the ease with which she can be divorced which can nullify the protection which the law seeks to extend to her in recognizing polygyny for the Chinese community. Mr. Tay, a wealthy but almost illiterate merchant, sold the house in which his secondary wife, a well-educated teacher in a Chinese school, and four children were living: the purchasers sought to evict the lady. As she insisted on her right to remain, the purchaser sought a court order to force her to leave. Through her lawyer she pressed her claim to a matrimonial home. Mr. Tay was called as witness, and although he had registered the children at birth as his and letters were produced in which he spoke of the lady as 'my wife', he claimed that he had never intended a marriage. On the basis of this last claim the judge found in favour of the purchasers and ordered that the lady quit the premises—as a mistress she had no right to a matrimonial home. The lawyer representing 'Mrs. Tay' was sure that on appeal he could establish her claim to wifehood—the husband's vested interest in the case could be used to discredit his oral evidence *vis-à-vis* the other evidence available that the Tays were in fact man and wife. However, the lawyer advised against appeal: of what avail to prove she was a wife if Mr. Tay retained entire freedom to repudiate her at will and deprive her of the right to a roof by that means?

Recent reforms

The peoples of Malaya have been aware of changes in the marriage laws of other Asian countries. In theory at least, polygyny ceased to be legal in China in 1929 with the promulgation of the Nationalist code of law. In practice this code is said to have left the problem to all intents and purposes untouched save in some ultra-modern circles. The People's Republic has, however, tackled the question more vigorously. The code of 1950 enjoins strict monogamy, among other reforms in the field of domestic relations. The Hindu Marriage Law 1955, of India, established monogamous marriage for all Hindus in that country.

There followed then some expressions of public opinion that Singapore law in permitting polygyny to the two major immigrant communities had, in a sense, fossilized their customs at a point now obsolete in the respective homelands. The People's Action Party's 1959 election platform included promises of marriage reform: these have now been incorporated (along with a large number of other measures in the interests of women's status) in the Women's Charter, an ordinance which passed the Legislative Assembly and came into force on 15 September 1961.

The charter provides that from 2 March 1961 the only form of marriage permitted in the State will be monogamy, whether the rites be civil, Christian or customary. A man who already has one wife will be unable to marry another unless his previous marriage is brought to an end by the death of his wife or by divorce. Polygynous marriages already in existence remain valid and the children of these unions legitimate. But no new secondary marriage can be embarked upon and children born of a man other than by his legally married wife or by secondary wives married prior to 2 March 1961 will not be his legitimate issue. Moslems, whose law permits polygyny, are excluded from these provisions of the charter. In practice this means Malays are excluded. The number of Chinese Moslems is negligible.

Prior to the charter, only civil and Christian marriages were registered. It will now be required that customary marriages be reported to the Registrar and a record of them kept. The penalties for failure to register a marriage are by no means negligible, the maximum being a fine of 1,000 Malayan dollars combined with one year's imprisonment. The government of Singapore appears to intend citizens to take the new marriage laws seriously.

Divorce

Up till now, the High Court has only had jurisdiction over civil or Christian marriages, the parties to which could seek remedy by means of divorce under provisions very similar to English law. For those married by customary rites no Singapore court had any jurisdiction in divorce matters. Mutual consent separations, generally accepted as amounting to divorce, have been referred to elsewhere in this paper. The status of these has never been pronounced upon definitively; the writer knows of no reported court case in which the status of such a divorce has been an issue in the proceedings.

Although these mutual consent divorces have had no confirmed legal standing, in a certain sense the colonial government gave them the stamp of its approval. The Department of Chinese Affairs came to have the role of arbitration court in all manner of disputes involving the Chinese community. In no formal sense had it the standing of a court, but Chinese brought their disputes to the department voluntarily and tended to accept advice from the head as if this carried the force of law. In the course of handling matrimonial disputes, the practice arose of drawing up, within the department, mutual consent separation documents, copies of which were kept on record.

The period following the Japanese occupation of Malaya and Singapore saw the setting up of Departments of Social Welfare which took over many of the functions previously fulfilled by the Departments of Chinese Affairs—among others the role of arbiter in family disputes. And so the mutual consent separations continued to be drawn up and recorded within a government department. About 1954, however, the Directors of Social Welfare, in Kuala Lumpur and Singapore, after consultation, ruled that this practice should be discontinued. It was felt that while a welfare department's role in settling disputes was unequivocal, to preside at the dissolution of marriages was too onerous a responsibility to be discharged without any statutory basis.

This change in departmental policy by no means terminated the practice of mutual consent separation among the Chinese. Many such agreements had, even before that date, been drawn up in a variety of settings. Clan or family elders of the spouses might be asked to preside at the drawing up and signing of the documents, or a lawyer's services might be sought for this purpose. (Many lawyers would charge approximately £3 for a straightforward agreement completed at one interview: all but the poorest would regard this as within their means for so important an issue as divorce.) At one time it was not uncommon for a couple merely to publish in a newspaper notice of their intention to dissolve their marriage, though these 'divorces' had in fact no legal standing, and were never held in respect among Chinese, and the press has now become wary of accepting these notices for fear of possible legal repercussions. Only in the comparatively rare instance of a lawyer suggesting the publication of a notice announcing the signing of mutual consent separation documents does the press now play any part in customary divorce. Here it is the name of a legal firm at the foot of the advertisement which emboldens the newspaper approached to insert the notice.

The Women's Charter will bring as decisive changes to divorce as to the whole framework of customary Chinese marriage and its legal standing. As we have seen, it states: 'Every marriage solemnized in Singapore after the coming into operation of this ordinance shall be registered . . .' by a public officer appointed to act as Registrar. Likewise from now onwards the High Court of Singapore will be authorized to make on appropriate grounds a decree of divorce 'where the marriage has been registered or deemed to be registered under the provisions of this ordinance'.

While it remains to be proven that the charter is without loopholes, it would appear that the element of doubt concerning the validity of marriages and divorces among Chinese in Singapore will in time be entirely removed. In so far as divorce is concerned the new procedure will involve very radical reform. The charter enjoins specifically that in granting divorce the court shall conform 'as nearly as may be' to the principles applied in the High Court of Justice in England. Mutual consent until now has been the prerequisite of the only form of divorce available to the customarily married Chinese. In future mutual consent will not only have lost its potency as a step in effecting divorce, it will also bear the ugly stamp of collusion. Where the court is cognizant of such an agreement it will close the door to divorce in the face of the couple wishing to dissolve their marriage.

It should be stressed that the Women's Charter is an ordinance applying to Singapore only. In the Federation of Malaya the position of customary marriage and divorce remains as it has always been. Nor does there seem any likelihood that the government of the Federation will take any immediate steps to follow Singapore's lead. The question of reform in family law is potentially highly controversial, and there are strongly entrenched pockets of Chinese conservatism in the Federation. Moreover, the official religion of the Federation is Islam and more than half the population Malay and Moslem. Little wonder if monogamy for the Chinese is a question unlikely to rouse much interest in government circles. The People's Action Party government of Singapore, which swept into power with such a vast majority of seats in 1959, owed much of its strength to the drive and enthusiasm of the young Chinese-educated of both sexes. Markedly socialist in ideals these young people were strongly influenced by the puritanism and the family law reforms of the Chinese communist government. Their influence in the ruling party and the latter's firm control in the Legislative Assembly, where it held forty-three of the fifty-one seats, made possible the bold legal measures embodied in the Women's Charter.

To have two entirely different systems of family law in territories as closely linked as Singapore and the Federation of Malaya seems likely to give rise to some complicated legal problems. Although the two States have entirely different governments, movement to and fro across the mile-long Causeway linking them is almost unimpeded. A customs check at the Federation end of the Causeway is in effect the only impediment which the law-abiding citizen has to take note of and no papers or identity cards are normally asked for on either side. Furthermore, a strong movement towards political integration is already in existence.

In 1950 the Singapore government introduced a system of stricter control in the application of Moslem family law than exists in the Federation. For example, a *kathi* may no longer officiate at the marriage to a second wife of a man already married, unless evidence of

408

the consent of the first wife is produced. But a mile away across the Causeway in Johore no such formality is required, and a Moslem man has complete freedom to take wives up to the permitted four. There is some concern in responsible Moslem circles that illicit nuptial flights across the Causeway (the bus fare costs 80 Malayan cents) could bring to nought Singapore's attempt to raise the status of the Moslem wife. Whether such flights take place is merely a matter of rumour, but the determined Moslem polygynist would be breaking no law if he sought this means of carrying out his purpose in the face of his first wife's protests.

Whether the Women's Charter will provide more effective protection for Chinese women remains to be seen. Not until its provisions have been in force for some time will it be possible to measure the effects of Singapore's proximity to an entirely different system of family law. Nor, at this stage, can we do more than record the passing of the new legislation. Its effects in practice still lie in the future.

A Chinese family
in Singapore

by FOONG WONG

In the early 1900s a Chinese male emigrant from Kwantung with a
teenage son stepped on to the shores of Singapore Island. The older
man was my husband's great-grandfather, the young boy his grandfather. The two immigrants were equipped with only a small bag containing a few tools, because Great-grandfather was by profession a
dentist—not college-trained, but with skills acquired through appren-
ticeship to a 'craftsman dentist'. What he lacked materially, he compensated with a will to make good in this *entrepôt* port. His ambition
was to start a business, make a competence as soon as possible, and
return with it to China to live at a standard rarely attained by his stay-
at-home compatriots in the village, leaving his son here to carry on
the business. This they both accomplished, owing largely to their industrious, intelligent and thrifty natures, and to the fact that they arrived at a time when opportunities for men of their calibre were many.
But little did Grandfather know he was to establish a flourishing large
household, extending to four generations, and to die here.

   Grandfather's business prospered and soon he returned to China to
get married. Like an obedient son, he left the choice of a wife to his
mother. After marriage he hurried back to Singapore to tend his
business, bringing out his wife. She was rather slow in bearing him
children, and Grandfather considered this a calamity. He quickly
remedied the matter by going back home again at the earliest opportunity to acquire, in one visit, not one but two secondary wives to bear
sons. He wanted to be sure he would have sons by them, and to save the
possible expense of having to make another trip should his second
wife have no son or few sons. (This proved to be a wise foresight on
his part because Second Grandmother bore him a number of children,

but only one son!) On their voyage to Singapore with Grandfather, the two women were entirely ignorant of each other's presence in the same boat. Following their arrival in Singapore, the traditional 'tea ceremony' was held, in which a newly-married secondary wife acknowledges the authority of the principal wife by serving her tea. Then, and only then, did Second and Third Grandmothers learn of each other's existence.

At about the same time as the third wife, who was my husband's grandmother, gave birth to her first son, the primary wife at long last also bore a son. Grandfather was very pleased with Third Grandmother, attributing to her the change of good luck in having two sons at the same time, and when she had borne four boys she became his favourite. Grandfather was the patriarchal head of the family, full of authority and financial power, and he strictly limited the amount of household expenses. At first all the wives and children lived together under one roof, and Chinese customs and traditions were observed, for example, the husband as the breadwinner, and especially a well-to-do one, was waited on 'hand and foot' by his wives, and was greatly respected by his children, who stood in awe of him. He dominated his wives and was strict and stern towards his children. Grandfather's wives were all illiterate women, and he seemed to regard them simply as physical vehicles for the continuation of the family line. They, on the other hand, did not have romantic feelings about Grandfather, or at least they did not show them to us in their memories of him. Third Grandmother always described him as very severe of countenance and manner, and she said he would not have allowed me and my husband to go out as freely as we do if he had been alive. She illustrated this by telling me how she had had to beg him for hours to allow her to go down the street to see the *wayang* (Chinese opera) which was being publicly performed during a festival. Finally he agreed to let her go alone, on condition that she must not take any of his sons with her in case a fire should break out during the show and they might be burnt to death in the ensuing stampede. He implied that she could take the risk if she wanted to, but not his sons. Grandfather seldom allowed his wives to go out by themselves, and even more seldom went out with them. Their activities were mainly confined to bearing and caring for their children, household work, ancestor worship and religious rituals.

Grandfather's primary wife was a forceful figure in the home. She was vested by him with a certain amount of domestic power over the

411

secondary wives, who held rather inferior positions in the household. It was she who was in charge of the household expenses, and it was from her hands that Second and Third Grandmothers received their personal allowance of 25 cents each per month. A Chinese man had to give 'face' (i.e., respect due to one) to his principal wife, otherwise he would excite the private censure of his kinsmen and friends. Thus the principal wife was able to command the services of the secondary wives, who had to do much of her bidding. I shall mention a few of their tasks; a secondary wife should offer to dress the hair of the principal wife; she should wait on her during meals; should fan her when she was hot and massage her limbs when she felt tired. Second and Third Grandmothers recalled doing all that, but they did not object at the time.

Grandfather's attitude towards his children showed his distinct concern for sons. He made sure the boys were educated by sending them to an English school in the mornings and in the afternoon to a Chinese school to learn their native language. He did not care for girls. Second Grandmother said that when she informed him she had given birth to a daughter, he just grunted and did not even enter her room to look at the new-born baby. But if it was a son, he would certainly go and look at him. The daughters were never sent to school, but they surprisingly managed to learn enough Chinese from their brothers to be able to read and write. Following the Chinese customs of that time, on reaching marriageable age they were taken back to China, where they were married off and settled down as housewives.

To a large extent Grandfather reproduced the ideal family pattern of his homeland. But as the years passed, the first rift came when he found himself faced with the problem of maintaining order and harmony among his three wives. There were differences, grumblings and rumblings, although there was no open conflict, owing in all probability to his wisdom in listening to them but not repeating anyone's complaints to the others. Eventually, however, he had to agree reluctantly to allow his wives to live separately in order to have domestic peace. Hence, on the flimsy excuse that one of her sons did not 'agree' with the house (because a god said so), Third Grandmother moved out, followed later by Second Grandmother. There were perhaps other underlying reasons too. With a growing family, the first floor of the shop-house they were occupying was becoming overcrowded, and there was not enough room. We have to remember that at that period

412

in Singapore it was by no means easy to find a spacious house to live in in the centre of the town. It was different from the village in China where many people had big ancestral houses. Had such a rift happened in China, it would have put an affront upon Grandfather. But since this was a 'coolie town' and traditions were not so rigid, conditions brought changes which were overlooked because people here directed their energy and time to the field of economic activity, and were too busy to mind the affairs of others. Grandfather's business enterprises were also expanding, and in this prosperous atmosphere he could afford to maintain three separate households instead of one.

A very serious impact of the English legal system on the family occurred on Grandfather's death. He died intestate. Now the traditional Chinese rule of inheritance is that sons only inherit and share equally in a father's estate. Wives, even the principal wives, are traditionally entitled to maintenance only, and daughters to their upkeep while single and to the expenses of a wedding in keeping with their social standing. But the legal rules enforced in Singapore, although they treat sons as equal inheritors in cases of intestacy, also ascribe the same rights to daughters and, furthermore, give a widow a third share in an intestate's estate. Where a man leaves several widows they share the one-third share equally amongst them. Without recourse to the courts, this non-Chinese principle was applied to Grandfather's estate, but with a variation. There was some private agreement among the three households so that the estate was finally divided among the sons and three widows. The daughters signed away their full rights of inheritance in return for a certain sum in cash.

After Grandfather's death each widow looked after her own family's affairs—financial and otherwise. Third Grandmother's eldest son, who is my father-in-law, had already married during Grandfather's lifetime. 'At his father's command' he and his half-brother by First Grandmother were packed off to China in the early 1920s with their respective mothers to marry China-born wives chosen by their mothers. This was the common practice and was considered definitely preferable to marrying local girls for two reasons. Firstly, China-born wives cut off from their kinsmen proved to be more obedient and submissive to their mothers-in-law than local girls; and secondly, there was the fear among immigrant parents that if the sons married local girls they would remain and settle down here permanently instead of returning to China at a later date. It remained for Third Grandmother

413

to make three more trips to China to choose a wife for each of her three other sons. All her sons having married, the family under Grandmother swelled quickly with grandchildren, forming an extended household of three generations. It comprised Grandmother, senior generation; four sons and four daughters-in-law, middle generation; ten grandchildren, younger generation; there were also four *mui tsais* (adopted unpaid servant girls) and a cook; a total of twenty-four in all. Grandmother was, of course, the matriarchal head of the family. And in this as in the other two households of the single lineage, the rights and obligations between the members were determined by the ties of kinship. The relationship between brothers was governed by their relative ages, the younger showing deference to the older. As for their wives, they were dominated by Grandmother. They meekly obeyed her, partly because of their social upbringing, and also partly because there was much competition among them for Grandmother's favour. In such an atmosphere, it was inevitable that some jealousies should exist among the members of the household. On the surface, however, the family was united and harmonious, though not very solid.

Then came the war clouds of 1942. The fear of the extinction of the entire household by bombing was so great that Grandmother reluctantly consented to spread her family out into four separate households, all occupying strong brick houses, she herself following her eldest son and his family. This splitting-up of the extended family was primarily attributable to the political events of the second world war. After the Japanese occupation Grandmother made a few attempts to regroup her family together, but met with no success. She found that her sons and their wives, having tasted and enjoyed freedom and privacy, did not share her enthusiasm for living collectively under one roof again. The other factor was economic. Grandmother no longer wielded the economic whip over her married children as each of them not only had a share in his father's estate but was also managing it himself. The sons therefore could and did assert their independence. So until her death she remained with only her eldest son and his family under her roof.

The process of the breaking up of the large extended family led to a severe attenuation of social relations. The sons and their wives came occasionally to see Grandmother, and she at times went down town to visit them in their homes. Meetings of the entire family were confined to formal visiting and special occasions such as marriages, funerals, Chinese New Year, ancestor memorials and so on. On Grandmother's death the dissolution of the extended family was complete, in that the final parental link was broken.

Grandfather's two eldest sons were, in their turn, polygamous. My father-in-law has a principal wife, who is my mother-in-law, and three secondary wives. Like his father, my father-in-law also failed to attain to harmonious co-residential polygamy. Legal enactment in Singapore had by now raised secondary wives to the same status as the principal wife, with the result that they no longer felt themselves to be in an inferior position, no longer had to be accepted by principal wives or to live collectively under them, subjecting themselves to humiliations. Thus secondary wives in Singapore have often assumed a significance unknown in China. At the same time, the principal wives have often lost much of their domestic power. Nevertheless, a woman does usually lose some social prestige by becoming a secondary wife. From the beginning my father-in-law has kept his secondary wives in separate establishments, and for a considerable length of time—about eight years—my mother-in-law also succeeded in her resistance to recognizing them, in the hope that they would be discarded. Indeed, it was not until a doctor pronounced the imminence of the death of old First Grandmother that my mother-in-law formally recognized them. We have a custom that if an aged parent of a man is likely to pass away, his secondary wives seek recognition by his family.

I married my husband during the Japanese occupation, during Third Grandmother's lifetime. It was a love match, and instead of obeying our parents' command, we told them of our intention to be engaged. (Years later Grandmother told me that had it not been for the war she would have tried to persuade my husband to go to China to marry a China-born wife, as his father and grandfather had done before him.) At once Grandmother become active again; she consulted her gods as to our compatibility for each other. They must have given a favourable reply because she set about making the necessary arrangements, such as the gifts to be presented on our engagement day to my family, whose comment on these traditional procedures was: 'What a big fuss!' The form of marriage we went through was a combination of traditional and reformed style (*Kuomintang*) ceremony. We were married in a restaurant by a prominent Chinese scholar and leader in our community. The wedding was publicly witnessed by both my husband's and my families and friends. We signed two marriage

415

certificates, which also contained the signatures of our respective fathers, the two 'introducers' (representing the traditional 'go-between' or 'match-maker') and the Chinese scholar who officiated at the wedding. After this ceremony light refreshments of cakes and tea were served in Western style. On the same day in the evening and in the same restaurant, my father-in-law held a dinner party for 500 people to celebrate the occasion.

Immediately after this ceremony, my husband brought me to his parents' home where we had to go through the traditional marriage ceremony amidst his family, relatives and close friends. We paid respect to the household gods and then to the ancestors, followed by the 'kow-tow and serve tea' to First, Second and Third Grandmothers, my parents-in-law and the numerous uncles and aunts in order of precedence. We then settled down to live with my husband's family, which then consisted of Third Grandmother and my parents-in-law, my husband being an only child.

When our first child, a son, was born, we formed a household of four generations. Although nothing approaching very warm affection grew up among the three generations of women, Third Grandmother and my mother-in-law made some allowances for my sake, while I adjusted to some extent to their personalities and traditions, thereby enabling us to live together satisfactorily. Filial piety is still practised but not exaggerated as it was in the time of my husband's grandfather who, on returning home from Singapore, went straight into the presence of his parents, fell on his knees and knocked his head twice on the floor before them (the 'kow-tow') and thrice before the family tablet, the memorial inscription to deceased ancestors, carefully kept and revered in all traditional Chinese households.

My English education stood me in good stead; I had learnt to think for myself, and what little knowledge I had obtained I put to good use in domestic affairs. I neither agreed to all their opinions about things nor disagreed with them on every occasion. Often I had to bargain for a compromise. I meet them half-way in many matters, but have not obeyed unquestioningly their superstitions and other unreasonable demands. For example, although I am not a Christian I feel no reverence for the traditional gods and I have resisted the pressure put on me to worship the numerous idols (fourteen in all), which they have installed in the house. However, I agree to uphold the practice of ancestor worship which I interpret as ancestor commemoration. This

416

has some meaning to me because we of the younger generation have often been attached to our ancestors during their lifetime.

Another example of a difference of opinion was in the matter of style of clothes. My mother-in-law told me to wear loose and long dresses as she believed that close-fitting dresses were indecent. I compromised by wearing looser and longer dresses at home and in her presence, but more fitting ones for going out. A very important area of possible dispute concerned my children's milk diet. We were all happy when I was breast-feeding my first baby. He was weaned at three months and was fed on Lactogen powdered milk, as advised by our doctor. My mother-in-law distrusted the powdered milk, saying it was 'heating', and doubted that it could be made into a feed straight from the tin. 'Don't you have to cook it?' she asked. And when she saw the many bubbles on top of the milk she groaned that her grandson was taking in extra 'wind' together with that awful powdered milk. She had never seen a three-month-old baby taking fruit juice every day either. And when I was training him to move his bowels daily, Grandmother chimed in to say merrily: 'I only do it once in four days and look, I'm healthy and strong.' At times my baby's stools were hard, and this gave my mother-in-law another opportunity to blame the milk for it. I ignored their comments, knowing they had good intentions, and since I was in sole charge of caring for him, I could put my own beliefs into practice. Gradually it became obvious that my baby was thriving and all was well again in the family.

On many other minor matters I bow to my mother-in-law's wishes. For example, I follow her taste in cooking—lots of pork oil is used for steaming fish and fried vegetables (two tablespoons of oil for a six-inch fish, three tablespoons for a ten-inch or bigger fish), and we make no hot and spicy curry dishes to tempt the appetite. I also found out about her amusing peculiarity of wanting to sit next to my husband when he is driving the car. As a local-born girl I was as a matter of fact in a stronger position than my counterpart from China would have been, in spite of the largeness of the family group I had married into, for I could have counted on my parents' support and, if the domestic relationship had proved too intolerable, I think I could have persuaded my husband to move out and set up our own home, or to permit me to find employment in the day to escape from them. Realizing that these channels were open, Third Grandmother and my mother-in-law did not press their authority beyond what was their rightful due, for which I have always been grateful to them. I once overheard one remarking to the other: 'I have not seen a young person so argumentative!'

My husband and I are more free and at ease with one another in our marriage relationship than were our grandparents-in-law. We address each other by name and treat each other as equals. This was definitely not so with them. Overt affection between them was not displayed, even in the family circle. Their behaviour towards each other was stiff. My parents-in-law were less stiff but still formal; my mother-in-law in her early married days could not call my father-in-law by his name, but had to address him by the same term as a servant would use. Now in her late fifties, she still does not call him by name, but follows his children in calling him Ah Bah (i.e., Father). Like other English-educated Singapore-born Chinese, my husband takes me to parties organized in the European style with dancing and sitting-out in mixed company. Even now some of the men and women of a generation above us prefer to sit separately at dinner parties and public or social gatherings.

There is much evidence all round us that the traditional pattern of behaviour between husband and wife has undergone some modification in response to the changed social conditions of overseas society in the mid-twentieth century. We are also more outspoken to each other, and mature enough to discuss birth control and practise it accordingly. In Singapore, family planning is officially recognized and recommended by the government. I am a strong advocate of family planning, and am never too busy to explain to anyone who wishes to know about it. This was unheard of in my grandmother's days, but it was not unknown to my own parents, who are more advanced than many of their generation. My mother has had six children and I have two. My husband and I believe in quality rather than quantity of children. We have limited the size of our family in order to have a higher standard of living, and to enable us to give our children a good education to equip them in life. We hope they will make the grade and become useful and economically independent citizens. Unfortunately for my husband, my father-in-law did not believe in professional training and so was not prepared to spend money on his education. He only thought of putting his son into the family business. The university education my husband went through was due to a scholarship.

My having only two sons and no daughter caused a certain amount

418

of uninvited comment and advice from the relatives of both sides. They said that there should be 'ins' and 'outs' (daughter-in-law marrying in and daughter marrying out respectively), and that daughters are more attached to their mother than sons. My own opinion is I have no preference for either sex and am thankful to God for His blessings.

I wish to digress a little and contrast my own parents' family with my husband's family. Unlike my father-in-law, my father encouraged his children—sons and daughters alike—to study hard. He is not a rich man. But as he did not indulge in the distasteful practice of acquiring secondary wives, he could afford to give four of his children a college education. Except for my youngest sister who is staying with my parents and my grandmother, all of us are married. My mother is modern in outlook, as evidenced by her attitude towards her two daughters-in-law. She did not mind very much when they hinted that they would like to live separately from her. This was a departure from the traditional pattern of family organization. (In my own case, if I had not consented to live with my in-laws it would have caused some ill-feeling.) My own grandmother was not happy about such arrangements at first, but my mother cheered her up by saying 'they will surely come and see us'. My first brother and his wife are both doctors, and he is provided with quarters about a mile away from my parents' home. My sister, a university graduate teacher, and her husband, also live by themselves. Both my sister and first sister-in-law are working—thus showing that the more education and economic opportunities they have, the more duties and responsibilities they shoulder. Each of them employs two servants, one for housework and the other to look after the two children. With no mother-in-law problem, they have instead a servant problem, particularly with that all-important figure, the baby amah. The baby amah is an indispensable and bossy person in such a simple modern household and she knows it. 'She is like my mother-in-law' is the usual cry of many a young wife. Nevertheless, baby amahs must be tolerated for the sake of the very young children left at home while their mothers have gone out to work. Fortunately domestic servants are readily available in Singapore, but they are by no means cheap and a good one is difficult to get. If the cook or the baby amah were to leave, my brother (or brother-in-law as the case may be) would help his wife to look after the children or help with the washing up. Though they are men, they no longer hold themselves aloof from female chores.

My second brother and his wife live by themselves about two miles away from my parents, but they go to my mother's every evening for dinner and sometimes for lunch at weekends. This domestic arrangement was first started immediately after their marriage, because this sister-in-law could not cook and it was not worthwhile to employ a servant as they did not go home for lunch. It is an arrangement which has proved very satisfactory to both young and old. It is more economical for the young couple, although they pay something to mother every month. The old grandmother sees her favourite grandson every day, almost as if he is still living with her. My mother encourages her married children and their wives, husbands and grandchildren to visit her, sometimes just for a chat, sometimes for a mahjong game, or at times to eat some delicacy she has specially prepared at the weekends. In this informal way, family relations are maintained in a happy and healthy atmosphere. My brother- and sisters-in-law and my own husband follow their spouses in calling my parents 'Father', 'Mother' and my maternal grandmother 'Granny'. In contrast, I myself am not allowed to use such familiar forms of address to my in-laws.

In the old days almost all Chinese married women would say to their husbands: 'I am married to you but I will not follow (or use) your surname.' This custom has taken a reverse turn, and now very many Chinese married women, both among the English and Chinese educated, are addressed by their husbands' surnames in the Western style, for example, Mrs. Tan, Mrs. Wong. (Our ancestresses would turn in their graves if they could hear such forms of address.) This change may be attributed to couples marrying in Christian churches and mixing in Western society.

It will surprise Western readers to learn that I know more of the English language than my own written language. This paradoxical situation arises from the fact that an English school education opened —and still opens—the door to professional training and a wider economic world for both men and women, whereas Chinese education in Singapore, even at the secondary level, is no secure route to employment. The use of the Chinese written language is mainly confined to Chinese businesses which employ a small number of secretaries imported from China easily and cheaply. I began my education in a language which is not my mother tongue, and though I speak my own dialect to my mother, grandmother and servants, I use English to my father and among my brothers, sisters and friends. By the English-educated Chinese of my generation, written Chinese has been sadly neglected, with the result that there is a whole host of Chinese men and women in Singapore and elsewhere overseas who cannot read their own language. My father is well versed in both English and Chinese and it was our own fault that we did not bother to learn from him, for he was willing to teach us. My husband, coming from a more conservative and stricter family, studied Chinese from his childhood days.

In Singapore there is no doubt that English education, with its concomitant economic independence, has done much to uplift and strengthen the position of women *vis-à-vis* men. It has also played its part in reducing the complexity of the Singapore Chinese household. Another effect of education on family structure here is on the age of marriage for both men and women. General age levels for marriage are higher than in our grandmothers' days. My own grandmother and mother were both married at the age of 16; I was married at 22; my first sister-in-law at 30 because her medical studies were interrupted by the last war.

In contrast with the business pioneers like our grandfathers, whose ambitions were to make money and return home to China with it, we have since taken roots in Singapore. The second-generation Chinese, such as my parents-in-law, still have ties with people in China, but when they were contemplating whether to retire in their old age to China, Fate in the shape of war and revolution decided for them, and they could not go. We of the third generation are here to stay.

The Singapore Government is shortly to pass a new law requiring all marriages to be registered; this will affect my husband and me too, since our marriage was a customary one. That being the case, it is our wish to marry again under the Civil Marriage Ordinance. A week ago we went to the Registry of Marriages to give notification of our marriage. And so after sixteen years and two sons, my husband and I will be married again. All this goes to show the changing social conditions that can affect Chinese family structure in Singapore.

Thailand

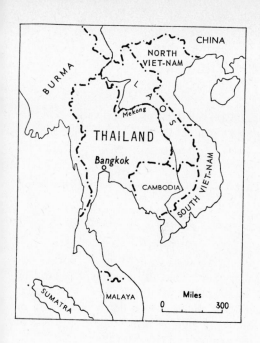

Area: 514,000 square kilometres.

Population: 22,718,000 (estimated 1960).[1]

Recent history: 1941-45—Japanese occupation.

Citizenship: Men and women have equal rights.

Religion: Theravada (Hinayana) Buddhism; there are minority groups of most of the other world religions, and also some pagan hill tribes.

Inheritance and family patterns: Customary rules of inheritance do not discriminate between the sexes. Nuclear families predominate, the new home being set up near the parents of one or both spouses if possible.

---

1. Latest official estimate of population as published in *The U.N. Population and Vital Statistics Report, October 1960.*

Thailand:
equality between the sexes

by Lucien M. Hanks, Jr. and Jane Richardson Hanks

THE FAMILY BACKGROUND

A rural home

On the central plains, for almost everyone, the growing of rice for the market shapes the way of life. For eight months of the year the waters of the Chao Phraya River cover the land to a depth of a metre or more. The comfortable houses are high on piles, in shaded groves of bamboo and fruit trees. The poorer cottages with thatched roof and walls stand directly on dirt mounds which in some years may be flooded. In the wet season all transport moves by canal; boats carry vendors with their wares or children to school. A single high road bridges the larger canals, permitting bus connexion with Bangkok in all seasons. During the remaining four months, February to May, the water ebbs so that only the larger canals remain navigable. In the country, seasons are clearly defined. The monsoon periods—hot-wet, cool-wet, and hot-dry—are less important than the divisions based on agricultural work. There are two heavy work seasons: first, ploughing and planting; later, harvesting. These are separated by two 'rest' periods, the first during the growing season with its high water, and the second during the dry season when nothing grows. Actually, the farmers do not rest but turn to other tasks: house building, repair of equipment, ceremonies, visits, pilgrimages, and today, especially, work for wages. A typical day in a Thai farmer's life is shown in Table 1.

With greater detail let us describe such a day in the life of a husband and wife with five children ranging in ages from a baby to a girl of 10

TABLE 1. Typical day of a farming family

Time	Occupations
4 to 4.10 a.m.	Wife nurses baby; may chew betel.
4.10 to 5.30 a.m.	Wife (or a grown daughter) cooks while others sleep. Husband arises at 5 to care for water buffalo.
5.30 to 9 a.m.	Husband, wife and older children work in fields. Between 6 and 8.30 children eat, help in household, feed buffalo and prepare for school. Priests collect alms.
9 a.m. to 3 p.m.	School for children 7 to 14 years old; younger children cared for by wife, older kinsman or hired girl.
9.15 a.m.	Field group returns for breakfast.
9.30 a.m. to 2 p.m.	Field group again does farm work.
2.30 p.m.	Field group may eat a light lunch.
2.45 to 4 p.m.	Wife prepares evening meal.
3.30 to 6 p.m.	Children return from school; bathe, fish, care for buffalo. Husband does chores near house, organizes co-operative work ahead.
6 p.m.	Evening meal.
7.30 p.m.	To bed; occasionally chat, plan work. Winnow or pound rice.

and a boy of 12; the wife's mother also lives with them.

Two hours before dawn, by the dim light of a kerosene-soaked wick, a woman named Chua boils the rice over an open wood fire. Her curry-pounding echoes over the silent canal. It is harvest time. On the preceding night Chua and her husband Waj planned their work as usual. 'Will the neighbours be ready to harvest our last field on Friday?' Chua asked. 'Yes,' said Waj, 'I have already spoken with five. We'll see the others tomorrow when we work on Cham's field. You'll have ten to feed. Then our crop will be harvested. School vacation begins tomorrow so our son can help thresh.'

Now, by the grey light of dawn, the family is stirring. The oldest son takes the baby, while the 10-year-old daughter rolls up sleeping mats, sweeps and helps her grandmother feed the younger children. Chua

425

and Waj are off to work without eating. Though the food is ready, they do not eat it, and, anyway, grandmother must first offer some to the priests when they come gathering alms after 6 a.m.

Paddling off in the boat, Chua feels glad to be out of the house. Though she has often said to friends, 'I am not bright, I can only farm', she still accepts farming as her way of living. Housework also is her responsibility, but she finds it rather boring. She is fortunate to have her mother living with them, for an extra pair of hands in the house makes it easier. Without grandmother there she would have to wait until her husband returned before leaving the house to fish, or even fetch firewood, and her older children would have to take turns staying home from school to care for the little ones. As to cooking, four hours a day is long, but in five years her daughter will be old enough to do it all. At 10 she can already cook some dishes. 'Caring for babies is really hard,' Chua exclaims to herself, 'they are tender little things, but my hip hurts from carrying them around so much. It's too bad they have so little sense that they may fall into the water or burn themselves in the fire, but they have their good sides too. We shall have the reward for our trouble when our children are big enough to work in the fields, get jobs and bring home money to us; when we can rebuild the house, marry them off well, and often invite in the priests.' Her thoughts are interrupted by shouts from approaching boats. Down the canal race two long boats, paddled furiously by crews of laughing young men and women. They met by chance and are now having a gay race on their way to harvesting.

At Cham's field Waj and Chua set to work with the rest, cutting and tying the sheaves of rice. Each has his own section of the field to cut. Planting time was more sociable, for one could talk with a fellow-worker, moving together down the long rows, but harvest is happier, for the crop has come through all the dangers. Cash and rest are in sight. At 10 a.m. the gang goes to Cham's house, for he as host must feed them. After breakfast Chua leaves the group and goes home to look after the children.

Back at the house, the children have already set off for school. Grandmother has fed all except the infant, and is busy making decorative flags for the sheaves as they come to the threshing floor. After nursing the infant, Chua puts the baby in the swinging cradle while grandmother goes over to a neighbour to return some sugar she had borrowed. Chua tells the 6-year-old boy to look after the two younger ones while she stretches out on the floor for a brief nap. Soon she is up again paddling back to the field. The gang works today right through the noon-day heat to finish the work before evening. Cham's children, kept home from school, load the sheaves into the boat to take them to the house. By 4 p.m. the field is finished.

When Waj and Chua arrive home, the children are back from school, and the baby is crying. Chua takes him from grandmother, and a second later he is quiet. The two girls take the family boat to cut grass for the buffaloes. Waj and the oldest boy turn to plastering the threshing floor with mud to renew the surface. Later they bring out the winnowing machine. As the sun dips low, the water buffaloes have been fed. Waj bathes his toddler in the canal in front of the house.

After the evening meal, Chua and Waj turn to planning.

'I am thinking of raising eggs to sell,' observes Chua. 'My older brother said he would show me the new way to take care of hens in cages. Will you build me some?'

Waj replies: 'Yes, but don't forget that I am going to try for a job on the highway during the slack season. It will take money to buy wood for the cages, yet we must have something left to help my younger brother when he becomes a monk this year at the temple.'

Chua answers: 'I understand, but if we put our money into raising eggs, we are not spending it. We shall be using, instead of losing, it.'

'I know you,' Waj teases, 'you want to find a reason for going off to market. You just want to chatter with the women there.'

'You men are much worse,' retorts Chua. 'You don't even earn any money. You just spend it at the coffee house. Well, I am tired, and going to bed.'

A city home

A few miles from the golden spires of the old royal palace lie Bangkok's modern suburbs. The main roads until recently cut past ricefields, but today blocks of stores with their coffee houses, restaurants, and shops of artisans and garages rise on both sides of the well-paved street. On the side-streets behind their garden gates stand the houses of government officials, prospering businessmen and occasional foreigners. Farther along, these side-streets peter out into unpaved lanes lined with wooden houses where poorer people live crowded into one or two rooms.

427

Inside one of the garden compounds are four dwelling houses, each in the slightly different style of the decade of their construction. Concrete walks between flower-beds connect the houses, and a two-car garage is near the entrance. The house in the centre is occupied by an old lady who, except for two servants, lives alone. Two of the other houses serve as dwellings for two married daughters. In the fourth lives a foreign family.

By 5 in the afternoon all the residents of this compound have returned from their work in the city. Nang Suphab, the youngest daughter of the old lady, is drinking tea on the upstairs verandah together with Nai Sawad, her husband, their 16-year-old son and 12-year-old daughter.

Nai Sawad is speaking to his wife: 'Khun Chub and I had lunch with two foreigners from the International Bank. That was the only interesting part of the whole day. One of them told us about hunting ducks in Scotland.'

'Was the Minister there?' asks Nang Suphab.

'No, he went out with their chief of mission. These two men were his assistants. Besides, the Minister doesn't eat with us, just as the Minister of Education doesn't eat with you.'

'Oh, you don't know the Minister of Education!' she replies. 'He is very democratic. One day he had coffee with us when we were all lunching with my boss. By the way, you know that your younger brother and his wife dine with us tonight. He likes to drink whisky and we have none left in the house. Won't you get some from the store on the main road?'

'Yes, but I'll have to hurry because I want to plant those gladioli that your older sister brought us.' Addressing his son, Nai Sawad asks: 'Have you studied enough for your examination so that you could help me for an hour in the garden? I know you haven't; I won't ask. And Nu, I suppose you want to see the movie actress on television; so I won't ask you to help either. Khun Suphab, could you spare me the cook's boy from setting the table, and get along with her girl this evening?'

'Anything to keep you happy. But don't become so interested in your garden that you forget to buy the whisky and run in covered with dirt like a farmer to greet your sister-in-law. I must go and tell the cook a few things about dinner.'

About 6.30 the guests arrive and for fun they set up a card game.

428

Though dinner was to be served at 7.30, it is well after 8 before their spirited game is finished. Then the television programme is turned off so that Nai Sawad's children may join the guests at table and the cook's children may serve the dinner.

Nearly an hour later, as coffee is passed round, Nai Sawad's younger brother observes: 'I don't drink coffee after dinner. Did you come to like it when in Rome on Ministry business? That was when you brought my wife that gold necklace that she likes so much.'

'No. I learned to like coffee after dinner during my six months in The Hague. But you wanted to ask me about your new business,' Nai Sawad replies.

'My wife is running that. You had better let her tell you. I am not very familiar with the details,' says the younger brother.

His wife then says: 'Khun Sawad, I did want to talk with you. Five of the motel units are nearly finished, but you remember the plan calls for ten units. Building costs are higher than I expected, and I don't see how we can finish. You are the family's financial expert. What should I do?'

'You are not the only one short of money,' Nai Sawad says with a smile, 'I am short too. That is why I am lecturing after hours at the University. That is why Khun Suphab is working every day at the Ministry of Education. And why did her older sister rent her house to foreigners? All of us are hard-pressed.'

'It is nice to have a financial expert in the family,' the sister-in-law teases. 'He tells his family members to move out of their houses and work harder. I hope you don't recommend this to the Minister of Finance when he needs money.'

'You know very well that I cannot refuse my younger sister. But I hope you don't need much. Seriously, don't you know that everyone in the whole country from the Minister down to the farmer is deep in debt. You must try to cut costs. Can't you build those four remaining units a little more cheaply or just build two more this year? I think I can give you ten thousand, but you'll have to wait a week or so until Khun Suphab and I can call in a few loans.'

Nai Suphab's sister-in-law is pleased: 'That is going to be fine. I know you are generous to everyone. Now I can build two or maybe three more units this year, I can finish the rest next year.' Soon thereafter the guests leave, and the parents join their children who have become too sleepy to wait for their elders.

In the morning they begin again the daily round dictated by their government positions and the children's schooling. Over the weekends they enjoy visiting relatives outside Bangkok. The annual two-week vacation is spent together at the seaside.

A typical working day is summarized in Table 2. Some schools begin at 8 in the morning, and some offices continue later than 4 in the afternoon. The times of arising and retiring vary an hour or more on weekends and holidays. Marketing and house-cleaning are done by the servants, and if the children of servants are of school age, they too may attend school but help before and after school with the housework. Alms to monks are not regularly given. Rather, monks are invited to the homes for special occasions to preach sermons and to be fed.

TABLE 2. Typical day of a city family

Time	Occupations
6 to 6.30 a.m.	Family arises, prepares for day.
7 a.m.	Breakfast, previously prepared by cook.
7.30 a.m.	Wife plans meals and house work for servants.
8 a.m.	Family departs by motor-car, driven by husband, for schools and government offices.
8.30 a.m.	Schools begin work.
9 a.m.	Government offices open.
12 to 1.30 p.m.	Luncheon, often eaten at school or in government-run restaurants.
3 p.m.	Schools out; children await parents.
4 p.m.	Government offices close. Husband fetches wife and children, drives home.
5 p.m.	Tea. Husband follows hobby, visits or works to produce extra income. Wife oversees work of the servants and then turns to diversions. Children study or play.
7 p.m.	Dinner followed by diversions.
8 to 8.30 p.m.	Children retire.
10 p.m.	Adults retire.

These two families differ considerably. Nai Waj's family is poorer and probably has a less constant food supply than Nai Sawad's. In the country, such needs as firewood for cooking or grass for the buffalo require the labour of some family member, whereas in the city many common needs, such as water or light, are supplied mechanically. There is more leisure in the city and it occurs more rhythmically because of the regular hours of the work day and work week. Nai Waj's and Nang Chua's leisure is less predictable. Also the presence of servants relieves the city family of many tasks which the country family must itself perform. The city home has such luxuries as television and coffee, and had we seen the kitchen we would probably have found an electric refrigerator and a gas cooking stove. These commodities are rare or missing entirely in the countryside. Certainly no-one in Nai Waj's house has travelled much farther than Bangkok, which perhaps the ageing grandmother has never even visited. Nai Sawad's family, on the contrary, lives in a broad world, not only through more extensive travel but through contact with foreigners.

Though differing in many ways, the two families still have much in common. Both occupy stations on the same social ladder which organizes Thai society. They stand on this ladder somewhere between the king at the top and a lone hunter of the hills at the bottom. Nai Waj could point to the richer farmers of his own community a step or two above him. He would also know of city artisans and merchants with statuses above those of any farmers. He is well aware that government officials stand above merchants, though he could not distinguish clearly the official ranks that lead up to Nai Sawad and beyond him to the higher officials and the king. Both know that the ease of living is greater for those higher on the social ladder than for the lower. Those of higher station are wealthier, more influential and urban. Both families recognize that their positions are not fixed. With good fortune Nai Waj might become a rich farmer, and Nai Sawad might some day become a Minister. Of course, Nai Waj is already too old for a great leap up the social ladder, but one of his sons might equal or surpass Nai Sawad. Every year a few farmers' children at the invitation of some kinsman already in government circles do move to Bangkok. There some enter middle school and, passing their examinations, move to the university. A successful graduate may enter a middle position in government. The rest depends on his skill in the job and his wit in making himself known to officials who can help his advance. Likewise, by loss of their government positions, financial reverses, drinking or excessive gambling, people like Nai Sawad have been known to lose their stations on the social ladder, just as farmers for the same reasons sometimes lose their houses, fields and farming equipment.

Both families also share a similar understanding of the meaning and justification of this social ladder. As Buddhists they believe that in living they must suffer through thirst, hunger, fatigue and death. But this suffering continues for aeons, since after death one is reborn into one painful existence after another. With such a view of life the Lord Buddha asked why creatures must suffer such endless pain. Eventually he discovered the answer: creatures suffer because of their sins; those who live virtuously are reborn to a life of less suffering; those who sin are reborn to greater suffering. The completely virtuous no longer suffer because they are no longer reborn but enter Nirvana.

People summarize these sins and virtues simply by saying that Nai Sawad in his more comfortable station has greater 'merit' from past lives than Nai Waj. Those who rise from lower to higher positions in a single life, they add, do so because they have greater merit than those who rise a little or not at all. Thus, Buddhism makes the inequality of Thai society understandable and bearable.

The two families are alike also because of their ladder-like internal organization. The Thai vocabulary of kinship specifies the age of every family member as younger or older than the speaker, and in all Thai families every elder is in a position of authority over every younger member. Parents command children, and elder brothers or sisters command their juniors. A parent may enfore his will by threats or actual punishment, but more effective and more stressed in Thai families is love. A parent shows his love by giving food, clothing, shelter, protection and comfort to his children. An older brother or sister similarly shows his love by gifts and companionship. We have seen a small girl feeding her younger brother a longed-for ice cream cone, waiting until he was completely satisfied before she gulped eagerly the soupy remainder.

Love or threats alone do not enforce obedience. Command and obedience require two persons, a commander and a follower of commands. Thai say: 'If the elder who commands is not obeyed, he may withdraw his kindness; if the younger is dissatisfied with the tokens of love given him, he may disregard the command.' Thus we have seen a mother restore order to a chaotic scene of disobedient children simply by walking away from all of them. She acts effectively because the children recognize their dependence. In sum, the loving care of an elder in return for the loving obedience of a younger family member, reinforced by the threat of withdrawing either love or obedience, forms the principle on which family living rests.

With a slight change of emphasis this principle organizes all groups in Thai society. Let us substitute the words 'patron' and 'client' for 'parent' and 'child'. Command and obedience are still present between patron and client, but there is less love and more tangible economic advantage in the relationship. In this sense a landlord is a patron to his tenants because he supplies them with the land they need. He expects them to pay the rent and such other services as he may wish; as long as they are willing to obey, they may continue to use the land. Similarly, the employees of a factory consider their employer as a patron and obey his orders as long as they receive benefits.

It is this patron and client principle which makes the social ladder work. The king is patron to his subjects because he offers them protection against enemies and the use of his land. A teacher is patron to his pupils because he offers them knowledge. Wherever two people meet, an inequality in wealth, power or knowledge must be found, so that one can be patron and the other client. This relationship differs from the European moral type, where a man of inferior station helps a superior in distress because of a sense of duty and expects nothing in return. It also differs from another European concept of 'equals in a bargain', where employers receive the benefits of a worker's skill in return for the wages they agree to pay.

Just as a parent may withdraw his love, or a child his obedience, so a patron is free to withhold his benefits and a client to cease to obey. Then the relationship ends. Here again Thai society differs from those societies in which accepting the benefits of another presumes a moral obligation to continue rendering obedience. Though Nai Sawad may have been raised by his superior to his present position in government service, he might leave this service any day without question of loyalty or the feelings of remorse that moral obligations presuppose.

We can now see how a kinsman differs from other people. The trust between kinsmen establishes a more enduring relationship than between non-kin. Parents and children do not lightly terminate their bonds. Because of this trust, kinsmen can participate with kinsmen in affairs of greater risk and importance. In contrast, the foreman of a labour gang who briefly hires unknown workers specifies exactly the price for each cubic metre of earth removed or for other services rendered with as much care as if he were framing a written contract. Much greater latitude, and flexibility as well as continuity, exist in the relations between kinsmen, as our illustrations have shown.

Who are the kinsmen that make up a family? The Thai think of the family as the group that eats food from a single hearth; the husband, wife and children; possibly an aged parent and/or a younger brother or sister of either spouse. Though the ageing parent is actually the oldest and will be consulted on many affairs, the working authority rests with the active generation according to seniority. Old people are said to have earned freedom from responsibility through the life-long giving of benefits to their children, so they may come and go at will, helping mainly during emergencies. Hired workers fall under the direct authority of the head of the hearth group. They may share their meals and sleep with the family, or, like servants of Nai Sawad's household they may have separate living quarters but eat from the same kitchen.

Thai family arrangements hinge a good deal upon warmth between brothers and between sisters. Their long association tends to breed particular trust. We have seen that Nang Suphab lives next to her two sisters and that Nai Sawad's younger brother came to him for financial assistance. In the country, where daily subsistence requires more labour, the households of brothers or sisters may help each other even more with baby-watching and sharing of food and equipment.

Since cousins are not separated by the use of different kinship terms from children of the same parent, the Thai system offers a whole generation of brothers and sisters. In addition, persons entering a new family after marriage group their own brothers and sisters with those of their spouses. This adds another indefinite number of elders to be obeyed and younger ones to command. But which of these many potential brothers or sisters become trusted intimates is not laid down. In practice all depends upon the personal taste and experiences which can build trust between two of these individuals. Then, once established, this trust must be sustained with frequent loving gifts from the elder, returned by frequent appreciative signs of respectful obedience.

The founding of a new hearth usually occurs at marriage. Parents with wealth in which their child may eventually share prefer to arrange the match for their child. They seek to assure themselves of the economic and social suitability of the prospective spouse of their child before entering into a formal contract between families. On the wedding day, money and property are settled on the new couple in the presence of witnesses. Title to land is never conferred until the stability of the marriage is assured. Poor young men and women frequently elope without parental knowledge. They seek in advance some kinsman who can provide at least temporary shelter. The groom then begs forgiveness of his bride's parents who ordinarily accept his petition after a few days. Poor families often encourage their children to elope as the cheaper way of marrying.

Either mode of marrying is considered a private contract. One must marry outside one's own hearth group, but marriage between first cousins is permitted and even encouraged in order to keep property in the family. The new couple may live with the parents of the bride or the groom or separately. Usually they seek to reside where the opportunities for a secure living are greatest. Every couple hopes eventually to have its own house. If and when this finally occurs, a few husbands take additional wives. Though laws have been passed by the Thai Government withholding recognition of more than one marriage, the law seems to have little influence. In keeping with the private nature of the wedding contract, either party may decide on his or her own volition to end a marriage. He or she simply takes his own property and departs. Older children join their preferred parent, though younger ones ordinarily stay with their mother. Jointly owned property is divided and, to settle difficulties, an intermediary may be called in.

Thus we have seen that both the country and city families live within a social system of inequality, viewed by the Thai as necessary for forming harmonious relationships. The system is justified by Buddhist views on life and gains flexibility by the right to withdraw at will from an unsatisfactory relationship whether with a superior or an inferior. The fairly stable bonds within families are cemented by the trust which long association may offer.

THE SIMILARITIES BETWEEN MALE AND FEMALE

Though Indian Buddhist tradition holds that rebirth as a male indicates greater virtue than rebirth as a female, the Thai minimize this

435

evaluation. Since they expect many hundreds of rebirths before release from suffering, all are believed to take turns as male and female. Life, they say, is no more difficult for a man than a woman. A wealthy woman is better situated than a poor man, and so being born to a less painful position on the social ladder is more important than one's sex.

In turn, parents express no consistent preference for a son or a daughter. A daughter is considered a little easier to raise when young, helps with the cooking, is more obedient, more apt to stay at home and care for her parents in old age. A son, on the other hand, is needed for farm work and can increase his parents' store of 'merit' by becoming a Buddhist monk. Neither sex is considered stronger or weaker, so parents hope to have children of both. Childless couples who wish to adopt a single child tend to adopt girls, because they are more immediately useful about the house.

As children, boys and girls play the same games, and both look after their younger sisters or brothers. Boys know how to cook a meal. Girls can cut grass, tend animals and work in the fields, for all children perform the same tasks restricted only by their physical strength.

Nor is esteem or privilege accorded to one rather than the other. Regardless of sex the same ceremonial procedures occur at birth. Male as well as female midwives assist the delivery. Childhood names differ little. Both sons and daughters grow sickness-preventing top-knots of hair which are cut ceremonially before puberty. Nor are there special privileges within the family. Girls and boys sleep together as children; priority of eating or receiving gifts is determined by age rather than sex. Achievements in school are applauded equally, and permission to continue education to a higher level is granted to daughters as well as to sons.

In adulthood, the division of labour between the sexes is flexible. In city or country, when necessary, men care for children and cook. Farm women plough and harvest in the fields beside the men. Nai Sawad gardens, and purchases food in the market.

In terms of rights there are no marked sex distinctions. The bride's consent is as necessary for marriage as the groom's. Indeed, a woman may prefer to remain single, just as a man may think of advantages in remaining a bachelor, though bachelors are rare in Thailand. In marriage the wife retains as her own the property she brings to the marriage. As a divorced woman, or as a widow, her freedom is in no way limited.

Almost all social relationships in Thai society define a superior and an inferior. In marriage, on the contrary, the relationship between husband and wife is a partnership between equals. Their authority over household, children, or other matters of common concern outside the household is equal. Though the work divides into areas of special interest, consultation is necessary, particularly in the poorer families, in order to allocate funds, arrange working schedules, share workers and render needed assistance.

Because the two are equal partners in marriage, we can understand the special efforts that Thai parents make to ensure a balance of tempers in the marriages of their children. Traditionally, horoscopes are compared so that a boy born in the year of the cat, for instance, will not marry a girl born in the year of the mouse or the dog for obvious reasons. A considerable number of books and many practitioners add further qualifications in helping select a mate who will complete a union 'of the ten transcendant virtues'. At the wedding day the ceremonial leader calls for blessings, saying: 'Let the wife know how to please her husband, saying sweet words to him and admonishing him only in private, not before others. Let the husband perform his duty of loving and protecting his wife and never use harsh words to her.' Such a ceremonially expressed hope differs considerably from the woman's vow of dutiful obedience, found in many European countries. At marriage the young couple kneel side by side while kinsmen pour holy water over them. Their heads are encircled with a sacred cotton cord. At the end of the ceremony the bride and groom race to remove the cord from their heads, and the winner is expected to be 'boss' of the household. Noteworthy here is that the two not only compete with each other, but they compete on identical terms.

Some of the strengths and weaknesses of Thai marriage may be due to the fact that it is the only equal relationship which exists in Thai society. Elopement is more widely approved as a manner of marrying than one might expect if one considered only its disruptive aspects. People say that since the motivation of elopement is mutual love, elopement provides a good basis for a partnership; after an arranged marriage, however, the growth of love is considered problematical. If a marriage survives the first few years and becomes a compatible union, people praise it highly, saying: 'They were a couple in a former life.' Happily-married men delight in times when they talk freely with their wives about mutual accomplishments and plan joint activities for the future. Thus, a successful partnership becomes a valued achievement because of its contrast with the usual inequalities.

On the other hand, this optimal relationship is difficult to achieve with partners accustomed to inequality. Marriages break apart not so much because a spouse fails to do his full share nor even because of infidelity, though both of these acts certainly damage a partnership. Rather, separation occurs when one spouse uses the property of the other or turns common property to his own private ends. Between unequals, inferiors expect to make their private property available to a superior, and a superior may legitimately demand it. In marriage the standard is different. This is illustrated by the following husband's tale: 'During the war I sold pork, but the business failed because my wife was untrustworthy. She was unfaithful and took all my property. Then she chased after her former husband and went back to him.' One wife accused her husband of pawning her gold necklace in order to pay for presents to another woman. As a final result this husband committed suicide.

These two examples also indicate that susceptibility to error is not considered the weakness of one sex only. Women enjoy gambling and drinking as much as men, and people do not condemn female vices more severely. Boisterous gaiety is as much a female as a male characteristic, and at festivals more than one mixed boatload of tipsy men and women may be seen clowning in a manner that brings roars of laughter from the bystanders.

The path of virtue is also open to both sexes. To be sure, a daughter does not become a monk at the temple when she comes of age nor receive the praise of the community for increasing the 'merit' of her parents. But even here Thailand introduces a considerable measure of equality. Where boys traditionally learned about sin and merit at the temple, girls learned a version of these same rules from their mothers. At the festivals where all come to the temple for blessings, no distinction is made between men and women either in seating or participation. Moreover, though comparatively few enter them, special temples are available for women who wish to take the vows of poverty and follow the discipline of Buddhist monks.

With old age, women as well as men are relieved of responsibility for house, fields or earning an income. Many turn to religion, inviting Buddhist monks for a meal or feeding them every morning on their rounds of alms collecting. People of either sex may spend several days at the temple each month. At death the sexes are again equal, for, from the first washing of the body to the great cremation ceremonies, men and women receive identical attention. Afterwards, their children inherit equal shares of their property.

TRADITIONAL DIFFERENCES

Though girls and boys differ little in childhood, Thai society does recognize certain differences later on. Menstruation, occurring about 14 or 15 years of age, receives minimal attention. A girl merely remains at home and abstains from heavy work. Women hope for regular occurrence and duration because then they feel better. A girl is advised to avoid certain foods so as not to prolong the flow, and if it continues beyond a few days, a physician will be consulted. The few prohibitions, such as those upon cooking, are phrased aesthetically rather than in terms of dirt or ritual contamination. A menstruating woman should stay away from the temple because soiling the floor where she sat would be impolite. In itself menstrual blood has little power. To be sure, women should not touch certain amulets, for fear their touch will negate the power, yet other amulets exist which must be wrapped in cloth from a woman's skirt in order to preserve their power. Still other amulets may be worn by either sex, or are only for women, such as those aiding child-birth.

Behind the flexible and lightly-marked division of labour between the sexes, one may detect a certain formulation of male and female natures. In a sermon at a country temple two priests spoke of the rice goddess, Mae Prasob (*mae* is the Thai word for mother). Because her presence makes the rice grow, she is thanked in ceremony after a good harvest. From their elevated chairs two monks addressed in dialogue the country folk who bowed their heads and listened from their positions on the floor:

First monk: 'What does Mae Prasob mean?'

Second monk: 'It means rice. There are many kinds of rice in the world, such as milled rice, popped rice, etc., but these are not called Mae Prasob. Mae Prasob must be the spikes of rice or the stalks of rice in the field which can grow and spread out. Popped rice and milled rice cannot grow up; so they are not considered to be Mae. Mother means one who can provide for children while Prasob means rice. Mother is the person to whom we should be grateful.'

First monk: 'Why do we not call her father?'

Second monk: 'Mother means one who is our benefactor, but father means a person who has power. Things having power, influence and hardness are supposed to be masculine. Rice has no power or influence. On the contrary, it feeds all creatures in the world and lengthens their lives; so it is placed on the side of the female. Human beings who are born to be mothers are very sweet and polite to their children. In comparison, fathers have hardness and scold.'

Here softness and hardness, pity and indifference, nourishment and power offer clues to the Thai conceptions about masculine and feminine nature.

Two kinds of task are necessary for preserving the group around the hearth. One, the man's, deals with the world beyond the hearth. Men must bring into the home what is needed from outside. As hunters once brought home their game, so Thai farmers bring crops from the field; so the government official returns with his salary and the news of his promotion to a better position. The job of climbing the social ladder or securing connexions with a new patron is his, and so is the responsibility for losing a patron through inept services. These tasks require hardness, self-centredness and power.

The second task is to hold the group around the hearth together. The farmer's wife cooks rice for her children, while the city wife manages her servants. Traditionally, through her softness, pity and nourishing, a woman distributes to the group the benefits which her husband has brought her. Her femininity increases the group, not only by her bearing children, but by the amplitude of benefits she gives.

At the time of a girl's first menstruation the saying is: 'Now you are a complete woman.' Her feminine nature is felt to be clearly manifest. To be sure there are earlier signs, for girls are said to be more obedient as children than boys. When possible, parents assign cooking and baby tending to growing girls because 'they have pity'. Only at the first menstruation are girls moved from the mat where they slept with their brothers to separate mats. From then on they should not roam about like boys. When they leave home, they go in company, for 'females lack power'. Temptation to wander is usually slight for their duties leave them little leisure. The degree of supervision varies with the economic level.

For boys also puberty passes with little notice. In the countryside the lad of 16 is needed in the poorer homes as much as his sister. He must help during work seasons, but these periods occur only twice a

440

year. Other work such as fishing, dyke mending or boat repair can be flexibly scheduled. Thus for many hours or even days he is free. His taste for wandering can often be indulged by visiting distant relatives, even if his parents do worry when he is away too much. Then groups of young men move about in the country as well as the city, testing their strength and talking of their conquests.

Male aggressiveness and self-indulgence are recognized as problems for which a period of special training at the Buddhist temple offers a solution. All males are supposed to take the vows of a monk or novice for at least a few months in order to learn the evil consequences of their natural inclinations. By receiving food from alms-givers, eating only before noon, sleeping only until just before dawn, saying prayers, and by other methods of discipline, male nature may be fitted for living in society. Before he takes monastic vows, a man is called 'raw', but after his year at the temple he is 'cooked'—and ready for marriage.

Learning at the temple is a heritage from India. Through it men traditionally learn the ceremonies necessary for blessing a new house, calling spirit protectors, curing illness and various types of magic. These skills presuppose knowledge, which is masculine because knowledge gives power. Following Indian precedent, women are excluded from participation. Indeed, until 1932 women could not receive formal education of any sort, for Buddhist monks, prohibited by vow from contact with women, were almost the only teachers. Hence learning was a masculine undertaking, and the vast majority of Thai women were illiterate.

The Thai tendency to minimize sex differences has, however, dulled the sharpness of this distinction. Many bits of ceremonial knowledge, magical formulas, prayers and remedies for sickness are passed within the family from mother to daughter. In several instances, perhaps even before King Rama IV engaged Anna Leonowens to teach the royal children, fathers have taught their daughters to read. We know of one woman who has become a physician indirectly; when patients come for a cure, this woman becomes possessed by the spirit of a dead physician and thus conducts a thriving practice.

Though parents supervise their unmarried daughters with care, supervision is not sufficiently rigorous to prevent them from meeting young men. At harvests or co-operative work parties a young man may whisper times for meeting the girl he seeks to court, just as in the city, where rendezvous are more difficult to arrange, boys pass notes through the hands of a younger sister. The slightest glance may affirm a plan to meet. At such times, both sexes distinguish between a meeting for satisfying sexual appetites and a meeting that may lead to marriage. Equipped with love magic, some young men try to ensure favourable replies from their sweethearts of the minute.

These escapades sometimes result in a girl becoming pregnant. Parents, particularly those who hope to advance their position on the social ladder through a marriage, do not look favourably upon this conduct. Eligible young men and women should not acquire a reputation for promiscuity, for habits of this sort are associated with unstable marriages. In this way parents lose their bargaining power in contracting a marriage. If a daughter does become pregnant, abortion is possible, but Buddhists consider this a sinful taking of life. More frequently the child is born, and its arrival tends to cool familial anger. Then the child is accepted into the family of its mother on a status equal to children born in wedlock. Of course, efforts are made before the birth to identify the father of the child and, if he is acceptable, arrange a marriage. Differences in wealth between the family of the bride and groom then offer an opportunity for the poorer to form an advantageous alliance. Thus, the problem of children conceived out of wedlock is viewed more as an economic than a moral question.

Whether marriage is arranged or by elopement, the groom, once recognized by the bride's parents, makes an offering to the dead ancestors of his bride and petitions to be accepted by them. Such a ceremony suggests that newly-married couples traditionally live with the bride's parents and that the husband becomes a member of the bride's family. The traditional marriage contract reaffirms this practice, for the newly-married couple receive land from the bride's parents where a house is erected at the groom's expense. People also say that it is easier for a man than a woman to live in peace with his mother-in-law. Despite many exceptions, we detect here an underlying tendency for continuity of the generations to take place through mother and daughter.

Such an inference is consistent with the tendency to assign work within the household to females and the preference for adopting girls rather than boys. Girls contribute more to this continuity between generations than boys. This agrees with the conception of the nourishing function of females. The separation of the sexes at puberty and the

442

gradual weaning of a boy from dependence on his parental hearth are also congruent with such a view of the social scene. Thus brothers do not normally interfere with a married sister's management of her household, yet a sister may still stand close enough for them to give her needed security in case her husband fails her. In this manner a woman in marriage can move towards a key position of leadership as well as responsibility at the hearth. If the husband separates himself from his wife, he may take the moveable portion of the joint property plus whatever cash may be needed to make up the value of his share and leave his wife with the house and land, where a woman and her sisters can live very comfortably without a husband.

Of course, life is fuller for a woman in the partnership of marriage than single. Children contribute to the security of a household through their labour, for traditionally they as well as her husband bring their earnings or produce to her. Her sons contribute to her store of 'merit' when they become monks. A husband adds not only the immediate product of his own labour, but, by affiliating himself with a patron, he can advance the level of his family's living much more than a woman can if left to herself. She is said to lack the strength and hardness required for securing these advantages.

Several subtle weightings help protect women against male domination in the marriage partnership. Freedom to break the partnership is always a safeguard, yet beyond this important sanction lie others less tangible. For example, Thai farmers believe that sexual relations are difficult, tend to exhaust a man, and are often insufficient to satisfy the greater sexual appetite of a woman. The tendency for men to avoid touching or passing beneath the garments of a woman reinforces the idea of potential loss of power. A woman who dies during pregnancy is especially feared as a ghost because, having died 'violently', her angry spirit has double strength to disturb the living. As soon after death as possible the foetus is separated surgically from its mother. Though few tasks are designated for a single sex, certain critical portions of the ceremonies for the rice goddess Mae Prasob can only be performed by a woman. The goddess is said to be so beautiful that a man cannot resist her seductive beaty. Either he will run off with her from home or she will be frightened away. Then the stalks may grow, but within the hollow flower will be no rice. In these supernatural ways femininity assumes certain positive and exclusive aspects which, despite its traditional lack of power, prevent domination by a male.

This position is not diminished in the least by a husband's right to take more than one wife. Ordinarily in such marriages the husband gives each wife her own living quarters to manage independently. Co-wives are sometimes able to co-operate sufficiently to lighten each other's work, so that the arrangement is advantageous. But if a wife finds herself at a disadvantage, she may always leave, and in some cases a wife may find herself in such a strong position that she can demand that her co-wife be sent away. A woman's loss of privileges occurs not because of her sex but because of her bargaining position. A secondary marriage is most frequently with a poor girl, whose family finds a tie to a rich man the best possible security for a daughter. Such a co-wife, who ordinarily brings little or no personal property to the marriage, may have to accept abuse from other wives and neglect from her husband. As soon, however, as she earns some property, perhaps by petty trade, she can bargain more effectively.

TRADITIONAL SEX ROLES AND ANXIETIES SUMMARIZED

Two main roles for women can be discerned from the foregoing account. On the one side a woman may emphasize her feminine aspect as nourisher. On the other side she may emphasize her equality and the slightness of the differences between herself and her husband. Traditional circumstances favoured the nourishing aspect. Like the compound where Nang Suphab lives, the rural hamlet was a nearly self-sufficient cluster of sisters, sometimes with the addition of brothers, cousins and their spouses. The duty of nourishing was of acknowledged importance, requiring much skill. Indeed, a recurring anxiety of many women centred on the adequacy of their performance as nourishers. This traditional fear was perhaps voiced in an indirect way in our hearing by a son speaking to his aged, senile mother. The old lady grumbled when visitors came to spend the night in her house. She was somewhat reconciled only when her son said: 'Never mind them, mother. They will not eat your food. They have brought some of their own.'

Traditionally, then, partnership between the sexes was defined in terms of performing complementary functions, the man in the field, the woman in the kitchen. Farmers, since they dealt with rice, enjoyed the most secure living, but even they might fall upon evil times and during years of poor crops women might have to brave the outside world in order to feed their children. A woman describes her experience during one year as follows:

After the flood all the crops in the fields were destroyed. I took some of the children in a boat and went to many places to earn a living. I went to places where the crop had not been destroyed, so that I could earn money by harvesting. Then I was hired to carry straw left in the fields after threshing. People wanted it to cover vegetables in the gardens. I worked about three months at this. From time to time I brought food and rice to the children at home with the money I earned. Every place I went I bought things and took them to sell in the market. I sold some of that straw to a Chinese at Wat Phajten. At the end of three months I bought some seed rice before going home. So I knew that I never need fear starving. I can always go and sell something, even if it is just straw.

This woman has proved her capacity in triumphing over the fear of leaving home and of starving, and this became a significant step for the new era. But here we must emphasize the fear that in traditional times kept her sisters at home except when they were forced to move away. Men under these circumstances were usually concerned to save the farm equipment and water buffalo, which always represented a considerable investment. The children remaining at home were cared for by a grandmother or aunt during the emergency.

Looking at male anxieties, we see in contrast concern with loss of power. Lack of power implies that a man cannot properly serve a patron, or if he is a patron, that he cannot provide adequately for his clients. Failure in either of these respects leads to his deep-lying fear of isolation, hunger and sexual impotence. The amulets that men carry testify to these concerns, for men's amulets have power to give invulnerability and success in one's undertakings. Though women do not wear amulets with these powers, they, like men, do wear others empowered to make people kind.

THE NEWER SEX ROLES

Many of the changes in Thailand during the past century are due to influence from the industrially-transformed West. Some, such as freeing the slaves, are nearly a century old. Others, like the commercial production of rice, have occurred within the present century. Universal education reached Thailand when the monarchy became part of the constitutional government in 1932. The appetite for consumer goods appears to have mounted particularly during the prosperity following the second world war. We shall not try to describe the historical sequence of these changes.

The impetus to produce in quantity for the domestic and world markets, together with the introduction of machinery and increased use of currency, have directly affected life around every hearth. The traditional female tasks of pounding the paddy in a mortar and winnowing the husks on a tray have largely been replaced by taking the family rice to the mill for processing. Similarly the home manufacture of mats, ropes, baskets, hats, fish soy (a kind of sauce) and other commodities has been supplanted by buying from the neighbouring market, thus freeing women from time-consuming work. In the cities, canned spices and store-purchased foods, though not yet widespread, help to reduce the time required to prepare a meal. A husband's work, too, has become more productive with the advent of more efficient tools, such as the winnowing machine and the gasolene motor, or the motorcar and the calculating machine. Along with these changes, living has become more comfortable with illumination at night, a greater abundance of cloth, insecticides and soap.

The time gained from these savings has contributed little leisure for either sex. Since the desire for cash has increased, people work as long as ever. Men now cultivate larger acreages, or work at new occupations after their shorter days in the city offices. Women, freed from home-centred work, engage in petty trade, home industry or salaried office positions. Both men and women are driven to acquire the new labour-saving and comfort-bringing commodities.

This reorganization of work has made more radical changes for women than for men, because it has moved them out of the kitchen. In the countryside women engage increasingly in vegetable and market gardening, poultry production and retail buying. The emergency measures of the past have become full-time occupations which bring countrywomen frequently to the city markets for purchasing supplies or delivering produce. Many city women engage in these same activities, but, in keeping with their greater wealth, some have also become heads of firms, founded and managed by themselves. All enjoy the greater freedom of their new occupations, but some must toil harder than others. The women who may once have said: 'I work hard to feed my family' now say: 'I must earn cash to feed my family'. In many cases these new occupations differ from those of their hus-

446

bands, who do not ordinarily interfere with the work of their wives.

Despite the traditional equality of the sexes, imported standards from the West have resulted in certain gains for women. Chief among them has been their admission to education at all levels. The legislative measures that established secular education were accepted enthusiastically. Thus, technical occupations requiring education, such as medicine, scientific research, finance and education itself, have been opened to women as well as men. Thai standards admit women to professional schools in equal proportions to men, and only recently have medical schools reduced to one-third the proportion of females to males, a measure introduced on grounds of national medical needs rather than sex discrimination. Crowded medical schools, insufficient physicians, and the proclivity of many women to give up medical practice during the years of child-bearing brought about this limitation.

Western doctrines of sex roles include a sharper distinction between the sexes than has traditionally been the case in Thailand. Little boys were once almost indistinguishable from little girls by dress or coiffure. Today sex distinctions are being cultivated. A little girl, otherwise naked, may wear a silver mesh apron over her genitals; 4-year-old girls may be seen stopping to bind their skirts tighter before chasing after their brothers clothed in shorts. The hair that once was cut short is allowed to grow long. The Ministry of Education has followed Western practice by encouraging the wearing of 'uniform' middy blouses and skirts for girls and shorts and shirts for boys. Formerly both wrapped a few yards of cloth about their loins, in a form resembling the Indian dhoti. The elementary curriculum makes further distinctions: while boys engage in Scouting, girls occupy themselves with needlework; boys play football while girls run races. Lipstick, jewellery and permanent waves help further to accentuate femininity, while trousers, fountain pens and cameras have become associated with masculinity. Special hospitals for women, the separation of men's and women's wards in unspecialized hospitals, public toilets distinguished for the two sexes, all help now to emphasize a person's sex.

Among the importations have come occupations clearly labelled for one sex or the other. Tailored clothing has brought tailors for men and seamstresses for women. Nursing the sick is a female occupation; dentistry, a male occupation. Garage work, radio or electrical repair are masculine domains; needlework, beauty parlour operation and pre-school education are women's.

One cannot yet say that these occupations have undermined the hearth group. The population of Thailand remains very predominantly rural. Though retailing, new crafts and services are increasing rapidly in the country as a whole, the majority of these occupations remain home-centred. They are represented by the country store where husband and wife share the work, or perhaps by the city establishment where half is a barber shop for men and the other half a beauty parlour for women. Here the partnership of husband and wife is continuing. But a good portion of the future may be represented by the home of Nai Sawad and Nang Suphab. Here new kinds of problems may arise.

One dilemma is posed when earning power becomes the measure of authority. Whether in the city or the country, women are not as free as men to sell their services beyond the hearth. Their special duties as nourishers of the hearth group still limit them. After work Nang Suphab must supervise the household, look after the needs of servants and children. In contrast Nai Sawad remains free to earn extra money after his government office has closed. Nang Suphab cannot compete with her husband as a money-earner. If money becomes the source of authority in a world increasingly inclined to judge in accountant's terms, Thai women are in danger of losing their position as equals in the marriage partnership.

Their dominant influence over the hearth group may also be dwindling. Even in the countryside today young men and women who live at home are less inclined to turn over their earnings to their mother. Some try to preserve the old form, saying: 'My children are good. They give me the money they earn, even if I have to give it right back to them.' Yet many young earners do not preserve even the form, but spend their earnings by themselves. They may recognize a duty to contribute to the household, for they give to the mother who feeds them the occasional blanket or pillow, radio or kitchen cabinet, perhaps bring regularly some items from the market to eat. But her authority over these hearth members has diminished, since she no longer makes the decisions as keeper of the purse and store-room.

On the new scene women appear to be emphasizing their role as partners at the expense of their role as nourishers. With the increasing concern of government in welfare, women are no longer worried about food sufficiency, but instead feel burdened by their household responsibilities. Being home-bound with children and cooking is regarded as hampering. Bottle feeding occasionally replaces the more limiting

448

breast-feeding; early weaning offers an escape. Exhilaration comes when a woman is engaged in some stimulating occupation beyond the hearth. Nang Chua is glad to have her mother take over the baby-tending and the cooking; she looks forward to the time when her daughter can replace her in the kitchen. As an egg dealer she will not only enjoy the relief of moving freely along the canals but also some day, if successful, be able to hire a girl to bear her domestic burden, like the servants in Nang Suphab's household. Thus, she maintains herself as an equal partner with her husband at the expense of her nourishing role.

In comparison, the form of man's life has changed less. His work has always drawn him away from the hearth. That his patron is the owner of a garage instead of a land owner has not altered his social position, nor the kinds of obligations owed a patron. He is perhaps freer to move on his own because of the greater variety of new occupations. He need not always remain a farmer or an artisan, but even though education does offer a means of rising in the social ladder it does not alter the basic plan. A man's fears of impotence and hence of isolation occur as readily in a Bangkok traffic jam as on a paddy field.

CONCLUSIONS

We may distinguish two aspects of social change: a disruptive and a constructive one. We have noticed particularly the disruptive aspects. We have seen families struggling to hold their members close to the hearth. Economically, costs have risen faster than income or ability to produce income. The hearth group must have benefits if it is going to remain a unit, and many of these are consumers' benefits such as more varied food, more comfortable housing, better illumination, etc. At the same time the productive capacities must be increased not only to support these new consumer goods but also to purchase such new productive equipment as the farmer's winnowing machine and the gasolene engine. The symptoms of strain are to be seen when Nai Waj must work for wages and Nang Chua sell her eggs, when Nang Suphab accepts a regular job outside the home, and Nai Sawad works at special jobs after office hours. The disruptive aspect has gone farther on the land, for the large group of co-operating relatives is disappearing when Nai Waj appeals to his neighbours and a few kinsmen among them to help him on his farm. In the city Nang Suphab's sister has had to rent her house and move away, though two other sisters live nearby.

Let us turn to the constructive aspect of the change. In the country-side, when land becomes divided to the point where it is no longer able to support a family, it is purchased by a wealthier farmer who adds it to his existing holdings. The richer farmer is adding to his wealth, so that he may be able to hold his daughters at home by giving them and their husbands land to work. Similarly, the operator of a home industry may be able to employ his sons or sons-in-law and increase his productive powers. Nai Sawad held his sister-in-law in the larger family circle by helping her finance the houses she was building. Conceivably the extra efforts of Nai Waj and Nang Chua will enable them to hold their children when they become less dependent.

Here are only the beginnings, for modern production occurs in factories, requires capital of considerable size, and demands a power of organization greater than Nang Chua with her twenty or thirty hens can command. To survive in a newer world she must at least join an organization of other wives who can win their way to the market.

We believe that the impersonal corporation that developed in the West is poorly suited to Thailand. Co-operation under abstract articles of incorporation demands pre-conditions that are not found there. Where freedom to enter and leave a relationship between superior and inferior is the recognized guarantee against excess, a corporation is too inflexible. When a slowly-established mutual confidence has to be built before co-operation between two persons is truly possible, a corporation is too impersonal. Labour unions, co-operatives, and political parties with a national programme have all failed to function in the Thai climate.

To cope with the complex problems of the present a new organization of family members is developing, and may be more successful. The new type no longer occupies a single compound; its hearths are dispersed. Each hearth group has in its charge one or more large enterprises, and the co-operation of various hearth groups at a distance is necessary for their survival. For example, a brother in the country manages the family lands and sends produce to his sister who operates a hotel in the city. A brother in the bank helps provide capital for his brothers and brothers-in-law in a variety of businesses. We have seen this co-operation occur informally when Nai Sawad's sister-in-law solicited money for building houses which she intended to let.

In these circumstances, the role of woman regains importance. She is again a nourisher of a group, but a larger one which extends beyond her children and servants. Also in it are the cousins and nephews who help her manage a portion of her larger enterprise. By holding them together she gains in responsibility with the result that she may become again an equal partner in a common enterprise. Once she has tasted the greater freedom of movement and sensed the excitement of management, only necessity can insist on her returning to cooking and child care. Though some women must accept these tasks, the lot will fall to those born, as they say, with a smaller store of 'merit' who occupy lower positions on the social ladder. The wealthier woman can enjoy greater freedom because she has a greater store of 'merit'.

Thai women are taking advantage of the new standards of equality of opportunity for both sexes and the new economic order. Education has given them access to positions of influence in a more specialized society, and although if their status in marriage is measured in terms of their earning power they may be thought to have lost some of their traditional equality, nevertheless this equality is bound to be regained as the group to be nourished grows in size. Moreover, the nourishing function is no longer restricted to feeding, clothing and sheltering, but extends also to such things as marketing produce, buying raw materials, meeting pay-rolls, etc.

At present Thai women appear to be willing to accept the Western conception of the proper roles of men and women, with its clearer distinction between the sexes. This is not likely to go unchallenged, however, if it leads to a true loss of freedom. A modern Thai woman can manage her growing hearth in the most 'feminine' of European costumes, for these outward trappings are not signs of a limited authority, nor does wearing feminine apparel signify an acceptance of seclusion or an indifference to new privileges. The Thai idea of femininity does not make it necessary for a woman to use seductiveness and ingratiation in order to make her way in a male-dominated world. Instead, the proper feminine task is conceived of as the nourishing of a group, and this is seen as complementary with, rather than subordinate to, the proper masculine task of advancing it. Moreover, the manner of the nourishing being left unprescribed, a woman is free to perform it through any of the very wide variety of occupations open to a group of growing size.

My life history in Thailand

by PRAMUAN DICKINSON

A couple of years ago when I asked my parents' approval of my decision to get married, my mother said: 'If your grandmother were still alive she would be shocked by this.' This was due to the fact that I decided to marry a young man from a place not only very far from our community, but also very far away from our hemisphere—in Canada. This was a very unusual thing for my people. So a strong protest was naturally expected, at least at first. 'But the world has been changed a great deal,' said my father, 'how can one resist such a great change?' And the discussion went on and on for some long time before I got complete agreement from both of them.

As a matter of fact, such an important matter must be taken up for consultation among all of our close elderly relatives. It was a pity that my grandmother had died only one year before. I missed her so much. I would have liked to hear whatever she might have said.

Coming back to my father's words. He was right. The world has been changing a great deal from my grandmother's days to our present time. My grandmother married a man from the same community, but a man who she had never met before. The marriage was arranged by parents of both sides. My parents were somewhat different. My mother became a little acquainted with my father before they were married, and my father came from a place very far away from her community. That was more or less a shock to the family, too, because my mother as a daughter of a community in the north-east was to marry a man from the central part of the country—a man who spoke a different dialect and who was from a place nobody had heard of before.

In the days when my parents married, communications were very difficult, and one part of the country seemed almost like a foreign country to another. A wild mountainous jungle between the north-east and the central districts made it very difficult for people to travel back and forth. It used to take my grandfather at least two months to cross this jungle by elephants. By my parents' time there was a railway running through. It took my father a whole day to cross the jungle by train, but he still had fifteen days more to go by ox carts to my mother's home town. Now, on a modern highway, one can cross the jungle within two hours by car.

In my grandmother's days it was unusual for women, especially unmarried girls, to travel very far from home. My grandmother, like all girls of her age, was educated at home only. She was taught by her mother to work in the household—cooking, spinning, weaving and sewing. Once in a while during Buddhist festivals she went to the temple accompanied by her parents or some other elderly people from the household. My grandmother did not learn to read and write because it was thought to be not proper for girls to do so, but she told me that one of her elder sisters could read because she was a very 'obstinate' girl who got her own way by finding somebody to teach her. Her youngest sister learned to read and write even in Bangkok style because she was the most favourite daughter and therefore could do everything she wished. My grandmother was the third child among five children. Her position as a middle child was likely to make her more obedient to her parents.

I used to ask my grandmother why she did not try to have her own way like her elder and youngest sister did. She remembered she had once tried in secret to learn how to read. Her younger brother, who was the only boy of the family, secretly provided her with literature in the local script. She hid it among the branches of the trees in the mulberry plantation. In those days raising silkworms was one of the important home industries, and mulberry leaves were used to feed the silkworms. Usually my grandmother was sent with some servants to pick the mulberry leaves in the evening. That was her opportunity to study by herself. Her brother, who was staying in the monastery to study with the monks, called from time to time to teach her. But my grandmother said that she could not pay close attention to her study, because the work in the plantation was her responsibility and she had to see to it that just the right type of leaves were picked. Running back and forth like that made it impossible for her to study. So she went on very slowly. Her brother became more and more impatient with her. Finally my grandmother gave up her studying for good.

This grandmother had nine children altogether. The first one was a boy. He was sent to study with the monks in the monastery when he was about 12 years old. My mother was the second child. My grandmother did not object to her daughters learning to read and write at all. Therefore my uncle, who had some spare time from the monastery, was encouraged to teach his younger sisters to read. The only thing that barred girls from having equal education with boys at that time was that the monasteries were the only institutions that provided academic knowledge, and the teachers were all monks. Girls, even very small ones, were not supposed to be close to the monks. Physical touch has always been a taboo for both parties. When a girl is giving something to a monk, he is not supposed to take it right from her hand. He must put down a piece of cloth on the floor. The girl is supposed to put the offering on the end of the cloth while the monk is holding the other end as a sign of accepting her offering. So one can see how impossible it is for the monks to teach girls.

Boys had no problems like that. It was right for them to stay at the monastery. They closely attended the monks who in turn taught them. They were allowed to go home once in a while. From the time of entering the monasteries, boys had a different type of education from girls. Their roles were now clearly set apart. Education for boys emphasized academic knowledge; girls were concerned with homemaking.

My grandmother had nine children. When her fifth child had reached school age there was a change in women's education. A school was set up for girls in the community and a male teacher who used to be a monk was hired. My grandmother sent my aunt, who was then about 10 years old, to this school. My mother was too old to go, so she continued with her self-study at home until she married my father, who helped her to learn both reading and writing in Bangkok style.

At that time there were two types of Thai script. The old script was influenced by Laos and Khmer (Cambodian) letters. Words were written on a type of palm-leaves, bound together with cotton string and protected by two pieces of wood on either end, thus forming a book. Only a skilful man could write and make such a book. In my grandmother's days, therefore, most people learned only to read, not to write. The new script was in Bangkok style, which is at present used all over the country. This was usually written on paper, and was more convenient for everybody to read and write. The new school for girls started to teach this type of script.

Even though there was a permanent school for girls, education was not compulsory. My grandmother's sixth daughter missed going to school in spite of great encouragement from her parents simply because she did not see more fun in going to school than in going to the rice-field. She used to tell me that when she was older she felt so sorry for not having gone to school because one of her relatives, about her age, who went to school and then on to further study in Bangkok later on came back to be the first woman teacher appointed by the government to teach in the girls' school of her home town. That was the first time that a woman in that place had a career outside the home. This woman teacher was looked up to by all the girls in the community.

In my generation education was compulsory up to the fourth grade. Most parents were not satisfied with only that. Those who could afford it liked their children, boys and girls alike, to go on up to the end of secondary school which was available in the home town, and if possible to have further study in Bangkok. Communications had improved and travelling to Bangkok was no more a problem. Since Bangkok was the only centre for higher education in the country, every year young people came into the capital from all the provinces. Boys still had a better chance, because they could stay at the monasteries in Bangkok while they were going to school or college. It was difficult for girls to come to study in Bangkok, unless they had reliable relatives there with whom they could stay. Otherwise they had to go to boarding schools, which were too expensive. Only rich people could afford to send their daughters there to receive higher education, but every year the government granted some scholarships to both boys and girls to study in the field of education. This was the only chance for girls of poor families to go to school in Bangkok, and only provided that they were very bright. At present it is quite different. The opportunity of receiving an education has become much wider for girls. A girl may now choose to make a career as a teacher, doctor, lawyer, or in many other professions.

When I was of school age, my father's profession as a merchant was disturbed by the depression after the first world war. A family friend suggested that the business in precious stones was not too bad.

455

There was a great demand for precious stones in Burma at that time. My father decided to take up this line of business by running a precious stones mine. That meant the family had to move into the wilderness of the jungle where those precious stones existed. Then the problem of my education arose. There was no school at the mine, which was at least one week's journey by elephants to the nearest town. Therefore, my parents had to leave me with my grandmother. I was very sad to see my parents depart, but my grandmother was very kind to me. She helped me to overcome my sadness within a short time.

As a matter of fact I did not feel too lonesome living with my grandmother, because I had stayed with her before. As my parents were very busy at that time, I was very happy to be once in a while with my grandmother, who was very gentle and understanding. I slept in the same room with her, and she was always telling me interesting tales and real stories of the old days. To me she was a rich book of different types of knowledge. We enjoyed each other's company very much.

The time came when I had to leave my grandmother for further study in Bangkok. I was very sad indeed. I was sent to a well-known boarding school for girls. That was my first experience of living with people of my own age. Until then, being an only child of the family, I had been used to living with only grown-up people. It was quite an interesting experience for me to be among young people from every part of the country. I was the first girl of the family to come out of the home to a school that far away. It was even farther later on when I was given a Unesco fellowship to study in the University of Toronto (Canada), where I met the man who became my husband.

Looking back at the family history, I can see a tremendous change in the expectations about women's roles in the family. My grandmother used to tell me how she was selected as a daughter-in-law for her husband's family when she was young. One day as she was weaving under the house, an elderly lady whom she knew very well dropped by to look at the material woven. That lady watched her working so closely that it made her feel embarrassed. She became more suspicious when it dawned upon her that the lady had a son who was just at the right age to get married. He had entered the monkhood for one period of the Buddhist Lent, and was now accepted as being a mature man who was ready to 'have family' (to get married). It was the mother's duty to look for a suitable wife for her son. First of all, girls of good behaviour all over the community were taken into consideration. If the mother had some girl in her mind, she would make a thorough check as to whether the girl was good at home-making, especially cooking, weaving and spinning—the handicrafts that were expected of her. My grandmother was right. A few days after that, her mother told her privately that the lady had asked for her to be married to her son.

I told my grandmother that if I had been in her position I would have been angry. 'But why?' asked she. I said because nobody seemed to care what the girl herself might feel, and the girl should have her right to select her husband also. My grandmother laughed and said: 'Grandchild, we girls at that time did not bother very much talking or even thinking about "rights" as much as you do now, but still we were very happy. There is an old saying, "A woman is the hind legs of an elephant." That means you are supposed to be the follower only, and I had done my duty as a good follower. That's all.'

I did not have an opportunity to meet my grandfather, who died very young. According to my mother, her father was highly respected by his children. It was he who disciplined them. My grandmother, to whom all the children turned when they had any troubles, was very warm and gentle. My grandfather alone worked outside the home. He then gave all the money he earned to my grandmother who kept the budget, ran the household, looked after the children and made cloth for the whole family. The home seemed to be everything in those days. Besides being the place to live in, it was a school and a small factory in itself. It was the only place for a wife to work in most of the time.

My grandmother was very good at weaving. She said that it was a shame for housewives to use imported clothes, since we could make them at home. While I was living with her, I was taught to weave and spin cotton. I enjoyed doing that very much. It was interesting to make cloth, starting from picking the raw cotton from the trees and working on it till it turned into a very beautiful material. It is a pity that since I came to school in Bangkok I have never had an opportunity to go back to the loom again. My grandmother used to tease me by saying that I was then studying to be a career girl, so there would be no more weaving and spinning jobs for me.

So far as father-child relationships are concerned, my mother said that I was closer to my father than she was to hers. My father, although he did not take part in running the household, always helped in taking care of me. My grandfather, so I was told, never played with his children. He was very firm and his word was law to them.

457

My father used to run a shop selling books, stationery and a few other things. That was the first book store in the town. Most of the books were textbooks to supply the newly-built 'modern' school of the town. My mother shared responsibility with my father in running their business. In addition to the shop my father started bus services to some towns nearby. Until then people used ox carts or horses to travel from town to town. Later on, rough highways were built and that caused some motor-cars to be introduced. People then travelled more often. My mother no longer did any home-making. She had some relatives doing that for her, and my grandmother always took care of me when my mother was away from home on business. My mother often accompanied my father to Bangkok, in contrast with my grandmother who, at least when she was young, never left her home town for any other place at all.

In my mother's days, the majority of women still stayed at home as their mothers had done before them. Very few women had independent careers. Even my mother, who was involved with my father's business, acted only as his little assistant. It was my father who took responsibility for the whole business. Wage-earners were almost all men. There was only one woman (whom I mentioned before) who had a job as a teacher in the town. There was another woman, a nurse who was working in Bangkok. She came to visit her parents who were running a restaurant in our town. The two women were highly looked upon. I remember my mother once said that I should study to be a nurse like them when I grew up.

At present, it is not unusual for women to earn their own living. Most young wives and mothers take jobs outside their homes. All my female cousins of my age are now wage-earners. Families have become smaller than those in my mother's days. The old saying: 'Plenty of men are handy to be used; plenty of wood is handy to be selected', which means the more persons there are the better for the household, is not heard now. Most families can no more take in all distant relatives as dependants in the households. In most cases of working mothers, servants must be hired instead. Unfortunately, those who are servants are not very well qualified for their jobs, and many complicated problems about domestic help arise.

In my grandmother's days, most households had their permanent servants or so-called 'slaves'. Later on, slavery was abolished all over the country by the order of King Chulalongkorn. By that time my

458

grandmother's children were old enough to help her with housework. With their help she could run her home very well. My mother had many people to help her to do housekeeping, but she did not hire any servants. She just brought in relatives both close and distant as they were available. It is not so now. My family is very lucky to have a relative to stay with us to look after the baby, but all of my cousins have to hire servants. My grandmother used to say at times that she herself would have no idea of how to run a household where the wife had to go out all day long as well as the husband, leaving their home to be run entirely by servants. On the other hand, one of my cousins once said: 'I'm glad that we girls are more free than those of grandmother's days. I don't think I could stand being kept permanently in the house, prevented from seeing the moon or the sun.'

My grandmother always quoted the old saying: 'Your husband is a shading umbrella to protect your head. He makes you look pleasant and respectable to all eyes. Therefore, obey him.' At present, some wives might say: 'But the world has changed a great deal, man and wife must be mutually dependent toward each other, and there is no such thing as absolute obedience on the wife's part now.' My grandmother would not be happy to see my husband washing dishes while I was doing something else. She used to say: 'It's mean to "use" your husband, and his place is not in the kitchen at all.'

Within our three generations—grandmother, mother and myself—roles expected of men and women, boys and girls have been tremendously modified by the great change of the world. The rate of change has increased rapidly. I believe there was little difference between the social life of my grandmother and her own mother. During the time of my grandmother and her children many new things were introduced from the other communities and the world at large. As for my mother and myself, one can see a big gap between the social life of the two generations, and the change is still going on very rapidly.

By the time my own children are grown up, what will they think of their great-grandmother's days? It should be very interesting to know.

Viet-Nam

Area: 326,034 square kilometres.

Population: 30,200,000 (1960 estimates).[1]

Recent history: 1954—Complete independence of French Union established. Partition between North and South Viet-Nam at seventeenth parallel.

Citizenship: Men and women have equal rights.

Religion: Confucianism; other religions are also present, including Mahayana Buddhism, Taoism, Christianity (mainly Roman Catholic) and a modern cult which draws its doctrine from both East and West: Cao-Daism. Pagan tribes exist, especially in the hills.

Inheritance and family patterns: Traditionally inheritance was strictly patrilineal, and a well-to-do man always strove to maintain a large patrilocal extended family. Nuclear families also existed in rather greater numbers, and are at present increasing.

---

1. Latest official estimate of population as published in *The U.N. Population and Vital Statistics Report, April 1962.*

A woman of Viet-Nam in a changing world

by LE KWANG KIM

'I am thoroughly bored with this essay on Voltaire! I have no desire this evening to emulate his caustic wit. Saigon, in this stormy May weather, is oppressive; in the hot and humid air the body is damp with sweat and the mind is incapable of effort. Nevertheless, I must finish my essay or else I know what I shall hear from the professor on the subject of the usefulness of higher education for girls, on their proper place in the home, on the quality of their intelligence. . . .' It should be remembered that at the time these words were written girls who wanted to continue their education beyond the primary stage had to study at the mens' college. Thus every year four or five courageous—or foolhardy—young women adventured on the road to a bachelor's degree. It was indeed an adventure. The powerful and inflexible Confucian tradition forbade any companionship, any familiar intercourse between the sexes. They never exchanged a word except on occasions of urgent necessity. Nowadays, after 20 years, if I meet one of my former classmates, bald, stout, married, the father of a family, we cannot help laughing when we recall the past. How things have changed since the morning when our group of girls, wrapped in a haughty and dignified silence, arrived for the first time at Petrus Ky College, and made our way along the corridors, following the red arrows which would direct us, as we supposed, to the lecture room, but which in fact, to our great confusion, led to the lavatories!

At 18, like most of my companions, I wore my long, straight, black hair in a heavy knot at the back of my neck. Out of doors I wore silk trousers—black or white according to whether or not it was raining—beneath a flowing high-necked tunic. A wide conical hat of plaited palm-leaves protected my complexion for, paradoxically enough, while

Europeans get themselves tanned and bronzed by the sun till their skins are amber-coloured, we who are naturally brown-skinned endeavour by every means, including face creams and large hats, to preserve a clear complexion. My lacquered wooden shoes clattered at every step. I rode to my classes every morning in a rickshaw which, by my mother's orders, conveyed me four times a day to and from my home. Mothers in those days exercised a strict supervision over their daughters.

This was in 1940, when Viet-Nam, together with Cambodia and Laos, was part of French Indo-China. It comprised Tonkin in the north and Annam in the centre, both French Protectorates, and Cochin China, a French colony, in the south. As citizens of Cochin China we learned French and were educated in the French manner like young girls in France, although at home we lived according to the Confucian traditions and oriental customs of Viet-Nam. This circumstance may make it easier for women of other countries to understand our reactions and behaviour, which sometimes might surprise them.

Now on that May evening, while I was struggling with my essay, I heard my father coming upstairs. Good heavens, what could I have done to displease him? Whenever he came up to my room it was to scold or lecture me—reminding me of a young girl's duties to her parents and her family. This might go on for hours for my father, like every self-respecting, well-educated man, was never in a hurry. In these circumstances there could be no thought of my essay; as usual I should have to listen, sitting motionless with downcast eyes, looking as docile as possible. In Viet-Nam, filial piety is the first and fundamental principle engraved on our hearts. My father came in and sat down on the large couch of polished wood, without mattress or pillows on which we used to sleep, our heads resting on those oblong, wickerwork blocks which, though very pretty with their brightly coloured covers, were very hard and most uncomfortable. He looked at me over his spectacles and quietly said: 'Tomorrow you will take your books back to the librarian at the college and give this letter to the vice-principal before giving up your studies. Your mother and I, with the approval of your grandparents, have arranged a marriage for you with the sixteenth son of Madame H. The young man is one of the most eligible *partis* in the country. They are Catholics and have asked that you should become one, and therefore you will do so. It is of no importance since, as a girl, you would not have to be responsible for the cult of the ancestors. Your brother will undertake this honourable duty. The day after tomorrow you will attend instruction at the Cathedral of Saigon.'

Thus speedily, clearly and without discussion, the two most important decisions of my life—my conversion and my marriage—were taken by my parents. Obviously, when my future mother-in-law asked me, at the joint family council, if I agreed to become a Catholic, my reply would be 'Yes' without hesitation, since my parents had already signified their agreement. After all, did I not admire the style and the distinction of those Catholic institutions for young girls maintained by the Augustinian Canonesses at Dalat?

Do not be surprised that a girl of 18, educated in Western culture for many years, should submit with such meekness to decisions of great moment affecting her personal life so closely. In Viet-Nam the family ruled everything, decided everything, but also took all responsibility for the consequences and supported all its members in any trouble. I still have a very vivid memory of my sixth aunt, who was unhappily married and who, unable to bear the misery caused by her mother-in-law, came back to the family home. All the marriage gifts were returned on that bitter occasion, and my aunt's twin sons were brought up in exactly the same way as we were ourselves in the Great Family. Having lived in these surroundings and having seen such obvious and reassuring instances of the authority of its head, I could not help trusting to the unshakeable system constituted by the family. At that time I was not an independent person responsible for my own future. I was only the grand-daughter of the Great Nobleman of Binh-y, daughter of his second son, existing not on my own account but in relation to my family. I could not, therefore, live my own life as an independent and responsible person.

In the turmoil of the months before my marriage I was scarcely able to apprehend the change which had taken place in my life, to question or to understand the real significance of events. One thing struck me, however, the presence beside me of the man with whom I was soon to share my life. As he had not been able to get the bishop's permission to take part, he merely stood respectfully by while, on the day of our bethrothal, I carried out alone the customary prostrations before the altar of my ancestors, presenting my future husband to them. After the ceremony he asked me affectionately if I was pleased with the jewels his mother had given me. These were a pair of ear-rings set with diamonds—the traditional betrothal gift, like the ring in the West—with a pendant and bracelet to match.

I had barely time to reply, for my mother called me and bade me prepare the quid of betel for my mother-in-law to chew; this finicking and delicate operation required skill and care. From a round silver box I took a freshly-gathered betel leaf; having cut off the small end with a brightly-polished knife, I took a spatula and carefully spread on part of the leaf lime which had been washed and rinsed several times to soften it; then I rolled up the leaf thus prepared, and with a bit of its rind I fastened to the little roll an areca nut and a ball of tobacco. As my mother-in-law was very old and nearly toothless, I also had to pound the preparation in a mortar before giving it to her in my two hands. My mother, being younger, preferred to have hers served on a saucer. First she chewed the areca nut, then the rolled-up betel leaf and, when the mixture was thoroughly masticated, she daintily spat out into a chased silver spittoon the salivated juice, bright red because of the oxidizing action of the air on the betel-lime mixture. Then she rolled the tobacco between her fingers with their long, well-kept nails, making it into a ball which she slipped over her teeth before tucking it away between the gum and the upper lip. How beautiful my mother looked then! Her lips grew redder, her eyes shone, and the colour in her cheeks grew brighter. Years afterwards I understood the cause of this physical transformation when I learned, from my study of pharmacology, about the stimulating properties of betel, its power of overcoming fatigue and producing an air of liveliness and awareness. It would seem that there has been little progress, if one considers that to produce the same results women today have recourse to a whole range of different operations even more complicated than the preparation of a quid of betel, using for example, rouge, cosmetics, coffee, cigarettes, among many other things.

Three days after our marriage we went to visit all our relations, in both our families, offering to each one the customary cakes, betel and areca fruit on the bough, symbols of the four classical good wishes: Happiness, Health, Wealth and Longevity. Thus we spent two days with my grandfather, a forceful little old man, who differed scarcely at all in appearance from his wife, with her small chignon of white hair, except for the black turban which he wore out of doors with a tunic of the same colour, shorter and stiffer, over full white trousers, the outfit completed by shining, flat black slippers. Grandfather was a man of few words, who thought a great deal, never took advice, and nevertheless lived in perfect understanding with his three wives and fourteen children. My grandmother was the chief wife, or 'wife of the highest rank', and thus took precedence over the other two who had to obey and submit to her. My grandfather's other two wives were evidence both of his social status and of his considerable wealth, which required a number of trustworthy persons to assist him faithfully and efficiently in the administration of his affairs. Grandfather took his meals alone or with his grown-up sons in the room at the front of our house where were placed the altars dedicated to the smiling and grimacing spirits of fortune, of the earth and of the village, and also, of course, the yellowing portraits of our ancestors with their grimly-set faces.

Grandfather spent most of his daylight hours lying with crossed legs on the teakwood bench which served as his bed, meditating or reading, with his spectacles comically perched on the end of his nose. My grandmothers—for so I called them, adding, in the case of grand-father's second and third wives, the number indicating their respective rank—took their meals with all my young uncles and aunts in the back part of the house where they could keep an eye on the running of the household. In Viet-Nam all food is chopped into small pieces and served on saucers. You take up these pieces with your chopsticks, place them skilfully on your ball of rice and quickly pop the whole into your mouth in one rapid movement of your chopsticks. At every meal there used to be one boiled dish, a stew, generally very salty, and some soup or broth, for we never drank at meals; some kind of pickle always accompanied the food. As Viet-Nam has 2,400 kilometres of coast and innumerable canals, fish was naturally our staple food, as well as large and succulent fresh-water prawns. Our dishes were highly seasoned, pimentos appeared at every meal as well as pepper which we used lavishly. Today, in spite of attempts to improve our diet, we still enjoy our fish sauce well spiced with pimento, *nuoc-mäm* and dishes seasoned with lots of salt and pepper.

Southern Viet-Nam, before the second world war, was a country of huge rice-fields, which at harvest time spread a golden carpet as far as the eye could see. Here and there small hamlets or trim peaceful villages lay in the shade of clumps of trees or green bamboos. A luxuriant, fertile and prosperous land! That was why its children, like many children of wealthy parents, were gentle, amiable, and smiling;

466

too gentle, indeed, to be energetic or pugnacious, too amiable to be firm and decisive, too cheerful to be sober and ambitious. The Chinese, who ruled us for a thousand years, were not far wrong when they called our country 'Annam'—the peaceful South. The easy life, the bland Confucian ethic, the tropical heat, inimical to effort—all these conspired to make us what we were in those tranquil and peaceful days. But one is never sufficiently distrustful of still waters. These same Annamites (as we were called), good, generous and peaceable, suddenly exploded into savagery, as witness the events of 1945, when the people of Viet-Nam, supported by Japanese troops, rose with incredible violence and put an end to eighty years of French rule.

This was the classic story of the insurrection of a dependent territory against foreign domination, with guerillas, massacres, bloodshed and martyrs. It was also the awakening of a people who had become enervated by prosperity. Finally, it was the prelude to a shock which affected every member of the community without exception and rocked the very foundations of society. But after years of disorder, insecurity and bereavement, of the disorganization of clans and the destruction of fertile land, this stricken people, intelligent and skilful but still adolescent, began to grow up. The disappearance of prosperity and of the artificial sense of stability and security led to a general awareness—more or less acute—of individual responsibility, entailing a fundamental change in our ideas about life, the family and the individual. The family shrank to its simplest expression—father, mother and children. Individuals generally, and women in particular, no longer protected within the framework of the Great Family, began to measure their capacity to cope with life. As a result, there was a frantic rush to secure diplomas and enter professions. The young girl's future had indeed changed; marriage still was to be hoped for, but was no longer the one and only end.

For me personally the 1945 revolution was a harsh ordeal. I was then a widow with a 2-year-old son and, after a life of leisure and luxury, without a profession, without an income, and with our land devastated during the disorders. I had to take refuge with my parents who, when our property had been destroyed by fire, had gone to live in a small house they owned in the capital. Alas, old age and the sorrow caused by the destruction of his possessions took toll of my father's delicate health and in due course he died, leaving my mother, seventeen years my senior, and my young brother of 13. He was at the awkward age and had never submitted to discipline, except from my father, who had devoted himself to training him to be the future guardian of the cult of the ancestors.

I spent three years of my life in this atmosphere of mourning, insecurity and increasing disintegration, while my mother continually bewailed the cruelty of fate, the heartlessness of friends, and the outlook of post-war society; to the end of her life she never succeeded in adapting herself to the changing world. All this was too much for me at the age of 22. Nevertheless our troubles quickly matured me. When I considered my brother, my child and my mother, I realized that if I did not quickly take action, if I did not decide to be 'the man of the household', we should soon find ourselves adrift. What does a person do who has to support a woman not equipped for the battle of life, to educate a boy, to bring up a baby? She works. So be it, I would work. But a rapid assessment of my capacities clearly showed that I could achieve very little by that means, and who would help me to carry out my heavy responsibilities?

To marry again was out of the question; it was not considered fitting for a woman to marry twice. Was my reluctance to marry due to a desire to show myself worthy of my mother-in-law, that indomitable woman who, though widowed, was bringing up her children alone? No, I think rather, though I was unaware of it at the time, that the fact of being able at last to take my life and my future into my own hands, having no longer either father or husband in authority over me, liberated me from my bonds, so that I intended to preserve my newfound freedom at all costs. I was, so to speak, intoxicated with the sense of being no longer a minor, no longer under tutelage, being able at last to make decisions for myself. I experienced to some extent the feelings of a person who, having just learnt to drive, takes the steering wheel of his new car. It was the exhilaration of emancipation. It was, however, a time of groping, of feeling one's way, the discovery of life, of reality, for until then I had lived only at second hand. It was not without pain and suffering, but for me it was a time of great enrichment. Soon I realized that in order to fight one must be armed, and well armed, and that in every field my weapons were inadequate. To educate two boys one must oneself be educated, and I had not learned nearly enough; therefore, it was here that I had to begin.

By selling all the trinkets that I still possessed I managed to collect enough money to enable me to go abroad and begin my studies again, at the same time supervising those of my brother and my son. Through this close contact with Europe I became, without noticing it and in spite of myself, progressively Westernized; this was inevitable. The culture I had partially acquired, now freed from the inhibiting influence of the family, gradually developed and took root in me, soon permeating me entirely. I became completely adult, in the Western meaning of the term; making decisions for myself, assuming responsibilities, engaging in undertakings, discussing, persuading, settling questions, becoming daily more sure of myself and of my capacities and my potentialities; already I was able to manage my two boys with some competence and authority. This went on for seven years, at the end of which I believed myself to be trained for life.

Having taken my degree, I returned to Viet-Nam with my son. Viet-Nam, in the meantime, had become the Republic of South Viet-Nam as a result of the disastrous Geneva convention. Thus, the disintegration of the family was followed by the dismemberment of the country. And I think this was what we, who had lived before and after the war, felt most deeply—this sense of a decisive break which affected people and things alike. Certainly similar changes had occurred in Western countries, but more slowly, more gradually, operating over a long period, giving people time to evolve. In Asia, although the rhythm varied in different countries yet, in general, changes took place with the suddenness of revolution. In Viet-Nam particularly the speed of change was stupefying. By reason of its geographical situation—the pivotal point of an Asia suddenly risen to importance—Viet-Nam is at the exact centre of the South-East Asian countries. Her capital, which had been French when I left, had when I returned become cosmopolitan. Nevertheless, cutting across all the penetration by different civilizations, and the wider opening towards the West, there was a persistent and definite return to the traditions of the past, as if the people, alarmed by so many new things and new influences, were conscious of a need to rediscover themselves.

Deeply influenced, in spite of ourselves, by Western culture, we now found ourselves in a completely different environment, divided between two opposing trends. Readjustment was not altogether comfortable. It is impossible to define the effect on one's mind of the passage from an organized society to a society in course of organizing itself—as ours is today—while in spite of everything it is still part of ourselves. One is conscious of being at once strong and weak, at home

469

and at the same time foreign, doubtful and also assured. It took months for us to adjust ourselves to the pace of the new Viet-Nam. After having learned to advance, we learned to retreat, which we thought useless but which, nevertheless, is necessary. It is only when one has learned to move in both directions, that one really knows how to drive.

It has taken me several years to achieve that delicate balance—'the golden mean' of Confucius—between the frenzied urge towards Westernization and the simultaneous need to cling passionately to the old traditions, both of which are characteristic of Viet-Nam today. This gives me a sense of fulfilment and satisfaction which one can only experience when one's personality has become finally integrated. It is a strength and a stimulus to feel that one has at least achieved stability in a changing world.

PART III

The history of female emancipation in southern Asia

by ROMILA THARPAR

'A woman should never be independent. Her father has authority over her in childhood, her husband has authority over her in youth, and in old age her son has authority over her.' This statement is to be found in the famous *Laws of Manu,* the basic source of law in Hindu society.[1] The book was composed in the early centuries A.D., and its application has continued up to recent times. It was written originally in order to preserve some of the finer values of Hindu society, but through the course of centuries the spirit of the book was lost. The rigid application of ill-digested ideas, taken from this book, led to the emergence of a society which, ostensibly chasing an ideal, ended up by becoming a minor hell for some of its members. This was possible because political and social authoritarianism clasped hands with religious authoritarianism, as so often happens in the history of any civilization. The laws having been imbued with religious sanctions, there was no escape for those condemned to suffer in these societies. In the case of India, this social code affected not only the lowest of the four castes, who have traditionally been regarded as the unfortunates of society, but it also led to attacks on the position of women in society, and to their being regarded as inferior in every possible way.

This was the picture in India, in certain areas and at certain periods.[2] It is certainly not possible to generalize from this and state that this was the picture for all time, or in all the countries under consideration in this book. The geographical area covered by these

1. *Laws of Manu,* Dharmasastra, IX, 3.
2. When mentioned with reference to events prior to 1947, 'India' refers to the entire sub-continent.

473

countries is far larger than that of the whole of Europe. Consequently there were many changes and modifications in each society, as new ideas arose. It is impossible to regard the region of South and South-East Asia as one unit. In tracing the emancipation movement of women in this region, I shall consider the area in three groups. The sub-continent of India, Pakistan and Ceylon comprises the first. This is the largest in the region and has been subject to two main waves of social thinking, one dominated by Hinduism, and the second and later wave dominated by Islam. The broader aspects of the Indian pattern are applicable to some of the other areas as well. Ceylon, with its Buddhist faith, provides a kind of bridge to the second group, which consists of Burma, Thailand, Laos, Cambodia and Viet-Nam. This region has been subject to only one religious code on the whole, that of Buddhism. The third group consists of the South-East Asian peninsula and islands: Malaya, Indonesia, Borneo and the Philippines.

The societies of all these countries have at some stage been moulded by one or two of the three main religious ideologies, Hinduism, Buddhism or Islam, though Confucianism in Viet-Nam and Roman Catholicism in the Philippines form exceptions. The development of social ideas has therefore been fairly similar in many countries, for example, there is a fairly close parallel between the position of women at various stages in Indian and Indonesian society. The urges for and against the emancipation of women, and the events connected with the spread of these ideas, have been remarkably similar. A brief chapter such as this cannot contain a detailed consideration of the status of women in every country. A representative example from each group may suffice. Indian society has been moulded by the impact of Hinduism and Islam. Indonesia presents in the main an Islamic society with elements of earlier Hindu and Buddhist culture.

The opening up of opportunities for women has been accelerated in the last decade in nearly all Asian countries. In ex-colonies which have now become independent, this is part of the process of national reconstruction, in which the role of women is being increasingly recognized. Nevertheless, traditional attitudes take a long time to pass away, and there are always traditionalists who insist on going back in time in order to provide the model, whether this model be relevant or not. Therefore, many Asian countries today show a strange mixture of enlightened ideas on the position of women co-existing with opinions that demand their rigid seclusion and subordination.

Contemporary India may be cited as an example. Theoretically the equality of women has been recognized, yet social opinion takes a long time to change and, in practice, the older attitudes are not dead. These attitudes still prevail in the middle classes of the urban centres, where modernization is either still a fringe development or else is an imitation of the West indulged in only by the men: in rural areas too, the better-off families cling to these traditions in their entirety.

More often than not, the birth of a boy is welcomed with greater delight than that of a girl—at least one son being necessary for the various rites performed after the death of the father, and for the continuation of the family. A further rationalization of this lack of enthusiasm for too many daughters is that parents have to provide dowries for the daughters, which is a heavy financial liability, whereas sons bring in both money and goods. Starting life with this somewhat negative reception the girl has, however, a carefree childhood. This is the only time of her life when she is permitted liberty of movement and expression. At puberty she is considered ready for marriage and has to be trained accordingly. Now she can be free only with other young girls of her age. The company of boys is strictly forbidden. If she has been sent to school (and this is by no means the general pattern), then in most cases she will discontinue her schooling at this age.

Childhood in a joint family system or where many sections of a wide family live together, is not unpleasant. There are always many cousins and young relatives to provide companionship. But later it begins to be irksome when individual whims and fancies have to be suppressed. In Hindu families marriages have to be arranged in order to preserve caste requirements. Marriage has not only to be within the caste, but very often preferably within certain sub-castes, since a person's caste is determined by his or her being born into it. If young men and women were permitted a free choice in marriage it would be impossible to maintain caste endogamy. Once a girl is married, either she is absorbed into the large family of her in-laws or she lives with her husband. Her relationship with her husband is one of extreme deference towards him, since she has been brought up to believe that her sole purpose is to minister to his needs. It is only when she becomes a mother-in-law in her own turn, or a grandmother, that she can assert her position and assume some authority.

Middle-class families in some cities are becoming a little less particular about following this pattern. A small percentage do send their daughters not only to schools, but even to universities, where the girls remain until they graduate. However, their activities at university remain circumscribed. Many admit quite frankly that they are there simply 'to mark time' until a 'good match' is found for them. Being at a university does not provide much opportunity for social activity unless it be at a college for girls alone. Mixing with male students is generally embarrassing to both sexes. In the few co-educational centres there are, on the whole, just a handful of students of both sexes participating in university activities.

This brief sketch of the average city-dwelling young woman applies only to present-day India. In the past a variety of social patterns existed. The process by which the present pattern was arrived at was a long and complicated one. In India the code of Manu did not prevail from the very beginnings of Indian culture; it was a later development. The earliest information available on Indian society is to be found in the famous Vedic hymns of the Indo-Aryan tribes; these go back to about 1000 B.C. From then until the early centuries A.D., it would appear that Indian society had a flexible social structure, which changed and took shape as the needs of the moment demanded. None of the rigid features known to later Indian society held sway at this time. There appears to have been no bar on young men and women mixing with each other before marriage. Marriages were determined by individual choice, and early marriages were not the norm. The remarriage of widows was permitted. Women were respected, and although it was a male-dominated society, women were given the privilege of being recognized as co-workers in the moulding of society.

The radical change which Indian society was to undergo was completed in the mediaeval period, that is, sometime after the seventh century A.D. After the invasion of India by the Arabs, Turks and other Islamic peoples to the West (post-A.D. 1000), the marriageable age for girls was made even earlier by Hindu theorists. Marriage was now to take place before puberty, and no woman was allowed to remain unmarried. By the seventeenth century A.D., early marriages had become the vogue. This was followed by the other practices which were to be condemned by later reformers. Women were reduced to a subordinate position both socially and legally, and the code of Manu was cited as the theoretical basis for this subordination.

Perhaps it was because of current attitudes to sexual life that Hindu social legislators were insistent in precipitating this situation. The

476

Hindu attitude to sex had been an enlightened one in the past. There was no guilt complex with regard to sex, such as there is in the Judeo-Christian tradition, since there was no belief in original sin. The purpose of early marriage was theoretically explained to be the preservation of caste. Another reason may be suggested, that of avoiding sexual frustration among young people, a problem which European society has up to now failed to solve. But the comprehension of this idea appears to have been lost at a certain stage in India, when perversions such as marriages before puberty (even if they were not consummated) were introduced. The sexual guilt complex first came to India via Islam, which had borrowed it from the Judeo-Christian background in which it originated. The impact of Christian Europe on India intensified this new development. Today the idea has permeated fairly deeply into Hindu society, particularly amongst the urban middle classes, who are now incapable of even appreciating the earlier Hindu attitude, let alone practising it.

The position of women further deteriorated in this period when the consolidation of family holdings became a regular feature of Hindu life. According to the various laws regarding property rights which governed the joint family system, daughters could not inherit the family property, since it was the maintenance of the family property as joint property that was the material basis of the family structure, and daughters always left their natal families at marriage. Women were compensated by being given a dowry at marriage. A portion of this was regarded as their personal property which no-one could take from them without their consent. In point of fact, a woman was hardly ever able to maintain her rights over this property once she had gone to the home of her in-laws. Being in a subordinate position, she could not fight to keep intact her own possessions.

The treatment of widows was another stigma on latter-day Hindu society. In certain circles the widow was held responsible for the death of her husband and was treated as an outcast. She was not permitted to marry again, and was denied normal social activities. Her head was shaved and she was expected to wear white all the time, so that her widowhood was immediately apparent. She was believed to be an inauspicious person and was therefore excluded from family ceremonies and festive rites. It is not surprising that some preferred to die by becoming *satis* (that is, attaining merit by 'voluntarily' being burnt alive on the funeral pyre of their husbands), rather than live in this fashion.

477

The coming of Islam to India did not in any way alleviate the position of women. It brought with it the *purdah* system, which merely continued the downward trend at a faster rate. *Purdah,* which means literally a curtain, required the complete curtaining off or seclusion of women. Even close male relatives in a large family are often not permitted to look upon all the women in the family. The women usually live in a separate part of the house, known as the *zenana* (women's quarter). When in public, the women have to veil their faces or else wear a large tent-like garment called a *burkah,* which covers them fully from head to toe. In the case of well-to-do families there is at least a garden attached to the house where the women can move freely, but in the poorer sections of the cities this fencing in of women was harmful to their health as well.

Yet the surprising thing is that legally Moslem women had a better status than Hindu women. They were permitted religious education (not that this stressed anything but their subservience), divorce and remarriage should the marriage not work, and rights of inheritance. The divorce or *talak* is thought to be unfair on the women, since it was the husband alone who had the right to divorce his wife. The divorce itself is a fairly straightforward matter, the husband merely repeats the word *talak* thrice in the presence of his wife and a few witnesses. It meant that a wife had no real security in the marriage. The inheritance laws were about the only real privilege that the Moslem woman had, though the application of these is also a debatable point. The laws were not always applied in her favour, nor could she always gain her rights. Polygamy was allowed in both the Hindu and the Islamic systems, the difference being that the Islamic code limited the number of wives to four, whereas the Hindu code did not specify any limit. Polygamy has generally been a luxury indulged in only by those who could afford to keep more than one wife. This naturally tended to reduce the status of the wife officially, if more than one wife was possible in an otherwise largely monogamous society.

Indonesia has followed a pattern similar in some ways to that of India. Indonesia is a predominantly Moslem country and Islamic ideas had a constraining influence on the women. Many of the modern emancipation movements among Indonesian women have been for the abolition of the *talak* or divorce as envisaged by Moslem law. In some places it has been modified. A wife can now make a petition before a judge, and the husband may be called upon to explain why he wishes to divorce his wife. The *purdah* system was also common to both India and Indonesia, but in the latter country the veiling of women was not insisted upon so strictly, and they were not kept in seclusion as soon as they were of a marriageable age.

Thailand presents a different picture from those of India or Indonesia. Theoretically women are subordinate to men, but owing to the absence of the joint family system, women have a considerable say in family affairs. The family units are small and the position of the wife and mother is one of privilege and independence. There are no caste restrictions either, so that young people are more in a position to choose their marriage partners, although the parents influence the choice. The ideal Thai woman may be described as hard-working in the rice-field, a capable woman in the house, respectful to her husband, efficient with children, devoted to religion and a shrewd businesswoman in the market. This stress on being a good worker is not without fortunate effects on the status of women. Much of the trade in the small country markets is handled entirely by women. This results in their providing a sizeable portion of the family's income. The knowledge of this financial independence creates in the women the necessary self-confidence, and in the men the necessary respect, for there to be a fairly equal relationship between the two sexes. Inheritance laws provide equal shares for sons and daughters, so that there is no need to give a large dowry to the daughter. A similar situation exists also in many sections of Burmese society, and in Laos and Cambodia.

Part of the reason why Thailand has managed to avoid a rigid social code is because it has not been subject to orthodox Hindu or Islamic codes. The main religion in Thailand today is Buddhism. The type of Hinduism which earlier received favour amongst the Thais was a much modified religion that found its way into folk sentiment. Ceremonies were adopted largely because they were believed to be auspicious. The more authoritarian aspects of Hinduism, particularly its social code, were dropped. Although Buddhism accepted the idea of women being an inferior species, it had a far more humane and liberal attitude towards the female sex than either Hinduism or Islam. Women were not thought of simply as child-bearers. It is the only one of these three religions that permitted women to become nuns. Although nuns have the lowest rank in the religious hierarchy, nevertheless the fact that a woman was permitted the alternative of becoming a nun is significant.

479

In Laos, Cambodia, Thailand and Burma, the attitude to marriage is based on a considerable amount of commonsense. Young people meet at local gatherings and on festive occasions. Courtship is permitted provided the parents of the girl are in the vicinity. Choice of a marriage partner is not restricted by any caste rules. The marriage itself is regarded as a secular and social affair, and there is no necessity for any religious sanction. In most cases an elder of the community presides and blesses the union. Divorce is regarded as a solution to a marriage that has failed. The termination of the marriage may be announced to the village headman or the heads of the two families concerned. A complete separation lasting for a period of about three years can also be regarded as sufficient ground for divorce. Inheritance laws are generally simple. In Burma, property is held jointly. The surviving partner inherits the property and, at the death of both parents, the property is equally divided between all the children.

Countries such as these have not seen any marked agitation in favour of female emancipation. Within the existing socio-economic framework, women have long had a position of prestige and respect. When the occupations begin to change in large numbers, for example, when women stop being merely petty traders and take to professions of various kinds, there may well be social upheaval, but it is likely to be of a less fundamental nature than in other countries, since the condemnation of working women as such is not found.

EARLY REFORMERS IN INDIA

The unequal position of women in India had its critics even in the early stages. Mediaeval India saw a number of movements, which, though often religious heresies in origin, advocated social reform. Religious reformers of the time attacked the rights which the priests had assumed as the guardians and interpreters of religion. In some ways similar to the leaders of the Reformation in Europe, they wished to bring true religion to the uneducated. They used the everyday speech of the people and not the court language, and were thus able to reach a large audience. It is significant that women were encouraged to participate in this new religious expression and to attend gatherings for prayers, and so on. Unfortunately, none of these movements conducted systematic campaigns against the various social injustices. Thus, their protest weakened through the years, and orthodoxy once more established itself. Organized movements for social reform did not start until the early nineteenth century. The impetus then came from a group of thinkers of remarkable perception, and also from the fact that the socio-economic structure of Indian society had begun to change, as indeed had that of practically all Asian societies. The intrusion of Europe into the history of Asia in the seventeenth century had hastened the downfall of the traditional social structures in Asia, and had introduced a new set of ideas, those that were current at the time in Europe. It was to take a couple of centuries for these ideas to grow in Asian soil, but by the nineteenth century Indian society had begun to respond to them.

In India, the history of the emancipation of women began with a number of people who questioned their existing status in Indian society. The questioning originated in two sources of thinking. One, known as Revivalism, objected that the existing status of women was not in keeping with the very ancient tradition, which was far more liberal. This group spoke of a Utopian past and desired a return to it. They stressed the gentle and submissive qualities of a woman, assuming that emancipation, or rather liberalization, was to come as a gift from the male section of the community. But the second group, known as the Reformers, objected to the subordinate position of women because they believed in the equality of the sexes and individual liberty. They took it for granted that a society was not healthy as long as women were kept in a state of subjugation. The Reformers were impressed by the humanism and application of rational thought in the European philosophy of the eighteenth and nineteenth centuries. The works of Mill and Bentham were favoured by this group. They were interested in the speculations of European intellectuals on society and social patterns. They were convinced of the necessity for social and political reform in India, and of this being the only means by which India could once more emerge with a civilization that she could be proud of.

By far the most outstanding person amongst the Reformers was Ram Mohan Roy. Roy was, in a way, the man who launched the ideological movement for the modernization of India. He published his own journal in which he discussed his ideas and explained the controversies that were current at the time. In 1828 he founded the Brahmo Samaj, an organization of people who had ideas similar to his own, and who were in favour of reform. Roy and his supporters

481

strongly attacked inhumane practices such as the burning of widows. They supported the social reforms planned by Lord Bentinck, the then Governor-General of India. It had been suggested that the government should forbid such customs as female infanticide, the burning of widows, and so on. Roy also demanded that the inheritance laws be changed so that women should have the right to inherit property.

Another vexed question on which the early Reformers spent much time and discussion was that of the age of consent. Some were of the opinion that the marriage of a woman could be arranged any time between the ages of 16 and 24, and that the marriage should conform to the old ideal of *svayamvara* (free choice), under which eligible bachelors were selected by the parents and the young woman was permitted to choose from among them. The possibility of divorce was not allowed at this stage even by the Reformers. According to Hindu custom marriages are sacred and only death can part a husband and wife. In 1860, after much agitation, the age of consent for girls was raised to 10 years. Previous to this it was permissible to marry a girl below the age of 10. In 1891 the age of consent was raised to 12 years.

During the latter half of the nineteenth century, the debate continued with men such as Ranade attempting to change public opinion. Ranade attacked not only child marriages but also the ban on the remarriage of widows. The orthodox were willing to grant that a child-widow (i.e., a girl who had been widowed before reaching puberty) could be permitted to marry again. But any other widow would be regarded as an adulteress if she remarried. Between the years 1860 and 1901, a total of 138 cases of widows remarrying was recorded, and this in itself was an achievement. Another supporter of widow remarriage was the novelist Premchand. Regarded as among the most outstanding writers in Hindi and Urdu during this period, this writer's novels and short stories, generally carrying a theme in support of social reform, were another factor in influencing public opinion.

Ranade was also keen that there should be an organization devoted to the cause of the emancipation of women, so that the movement should cease to be a local battle in certain areas, and should become a national cause. This was achieved to some extent when the National Social Conference was inaugurated in 1887. The founding of this organization was assisted by the emergence of another aspect of the main problem—the demand for education for women.

The lack of facilities for the education of women had already caused much controversy. It was recognized by some thinkers, such as Vivekanand, that women should be fully educated so that they could participate in social reforms and assist those who were propagating these reforms. His argument was that women alone know best what improvements are most urgent. In 1875 the Arya Samaj was founded by Davananda Sarasvati. Although this group had a traditionalist (Revivalist) character, it mobilized opinion in favour of reform. Education for women was one of the slogans of the Arya Samaj. Dayananda himself insisted that girls should be educated until the age of 16. The educational course was to emphasize languages, sciences, practical handicrafts and physical fitness. It is interesting to notice that he did not advocate domestic science alone for women, but demanded an all-round educational background, similar to that given to men.

Traditionally if women were given schooling at all, it ceased at the primary school stage. The nineteenth century saw the opening up of a few private institutions for girls. These were organized by various societies, such as the Brahmo Samaj, the Arya Samaj and also by some of the Christian missionary societies. The latter were made somewhat ineffectual by the fact that no girl from a 'respectable' family was permitted to attend them. It was also feared that the mission schools would try to convert the girls to Christianity. It was not until fifty years ago, when a 'European-type' education became a definite asset in upper-class society in India, that convents and mission schools began to enrol a large number of girls from 'respectable' families. The biggest obstacle in the way of large-scale schooling for girls was that of early marriages. Thus, the two problems went hand-in-hand. The raising of the age of consent also meant the possibility for more opportunities of higher education.

The British-India Government was on the whole slow in encouraging women's education. In the main, government-sponsored schools were for boys only. It was not until the last quarter of the nineteenth century that emphasis was placed on the possibilities of encouraging schools for girls. The real advance in this direction had to wait until the twentieth century. It has been suggested that the Indian uprising of 1857 was partially responsible for the timidity of the British-India Government in matters relating to social reform after

1857, for the government thought that earlier attempts at reform had been interpreted as unnecessary interference in Indian society, and that this had been one of the causes of the uprising. A more probable reason for the slowness of development is that the emancipation of women even in Europe was still a comparatively unheard-of idea. In 1865, when John Stuart Mill placed women's suffrage in his election address, it was thought to be quite revolutionary.

The situation was similar in both the Hindu and Moslem communities. The nineteenth century saw a number of Moslems, prominent among them Sir Sayyed Ahmed Khan, advocating more educational facilities for women. But this consciousness took a somewhat longer time to mature in Moslem society, and the concessions were, therefore, granted at a later period.

Another argument in favour of educating women was that if women were encouraged in this activity, it would provide a means of employment for them; and once women were given economic independence, then their social equality would follow as a natural course. Facilities for women's education were, until fairly recently, restricted to school education. In 1916, a Women's University was founded in Bombay by Karve, the idea coming originally from a similar experiment which had been tried out in Japan. In the first year only six candidates appeared for the examination. Gradually the numbers grew and it became a centre for women who wanted university education.

Women's organizations in India

By the end of the nineteenth century these various ideas had begun to link up. It was then that the most important development of all took place in the movement. Women themselves came into the forefront and took over the leadership and, further, the issue of the emancipation of women was brought into the wider movement of national independence. One of the first women to express this change clearly and sharply was Annie Besant. Her attitude to the emancipation of Indian women was quite unequivocal. She demanded this emancipation because, she maintained, the progress of India depended on it. It was essential because the time had come when the women had to understand in an intelligent manner what the men were fighting for in the movement for political independence. Not only were women required to understand, but they also had to participate. The wisdom of this attitude was brought home to the leaders of the political movement. From this point onwards the women's emancipation movement ceased to be the eccentric ideology of a few reformers and became a part of the bigger struggle for political freedom.

The plan of amalgamating the social and political movements was discussed at the first session of the Indian National Social Conference in 1887. This was a stormy and controversial session. Ranade and his group believed that these were merely two aspects of the same problem, and that social reform should go together with political reform. Another debate began over the methods to be followed. Here the age-old problem arose. Some held that the government should legislate reform. Others regarded this as interference and insisted that the reform should come from the people themselves, as a result of rousing public opinion. This debate was to continue for many years. The main outcome was the realization that a women's organization was necessary, to be responsible for propagating social reform. At the same time, this organization would work in conjunction with the various important political organizations. In 1917, the Women's Association was started. This was guided by Sarojini Naidu, who, apart from her political perceptiveness, was also known as a poet, writing in English.

An even larger organization was founded in 1926, when the All-India Women's Conference held its first session at Poona. Thereafter the Conference met annually, and became one of the foremost bodies working for social reform. Although it did not actually align itself with any particular party, it was sympathetic towards the independence movement, and a number of its members became active in the political struggle. The concern of the Women's Conference was not confined to the problems which have already been mentioned. Its activities included an attack on adult illiteracy amongst women through the use of the radio and films, and a campaign for better conditions of work wherever women had begun to take up professions, such as nursing and teaching. Efforts were also made to insist on legislation that would ensure a minimum of welfare facilities, such as adequate basic wages, the right to join trade unions, equal pay for equal work, maternity benefits, etc., for women working in the factories. A few years after it was founded it voiced the demand for female franchise. Other more revolutionary ideas were included in its programme, as, for example, family planning. It tried to fight increasing prostitution and, although this was not successful, demands were made for legal action to be taken against the ill-treatment of prostitutes by brothel-keepers, pimps and others.

Women and the independence movement in India

In order to prove their worth in the political struggle, women were willing to take on any responsibility that the political committees of the various parties required of them. Particularly after 1920, when the programme of the National Congress Party was clearly defined in terms of fighting for complete independence, they showed a tremendous and eager interest in the political movement. They organized themselves into groups, and were willing to join processions, face police firing and go to prison. They formed an important section of the passive resistance movement started by Gandhi and his colleagues. This entailed anything from squatting in rows across a street or a railway track in order to obstruct traffic, to picketing liquor shops and shops that sold foreign manufactured cloth. The last was part of the *swadeshi* movement, which advocated the use of only those goods which had been manufactured in India. Women were also known to have joined the terrorist groups throughout the country, which being illegal were forced to go 'underground', and some helped in the distribution of banned newspapers and similar literature.

The women were not slow to recognize the fact that they could use their participation in the national movement for advancing their own emancipation. Since political activities were not objected to, women took to them with a remarkable sense of responsibility. Sometimes this existence was very trying. Women with children went willingly to prison, yet conditions in the prisons were by no means comfortable. Picketing a liquor shop also meant being able to stand up to the jibes and scorn of male passers-by on occasion.

The result of all this activity was that many of the taboos and restrictions which had been placed on women were either lifted or were quietly overlooked. As the pace of the national movement quickened the single goal of national independence was the sole concern of both men and women. Gradually women came to be accepted as political comrades. All this gave them great self-confidence. Women had also begun to be elected to the Legislative Assemblies and other constitutional bodies, which gave them additional training for political leadership. It is not surprising therefore that a number of women did emerge as political leaders.

Until the early years of the twentieth century, the Indian national movement was largely a liberal middle-class movement. The widening of its scope, largely by leaders such as Gandhi, brought into its ranks the participation of industrial workers and certain sections of the Indian peasantry as well. It was during this period that Gandhi in particular encouraged the participation of women. He had firm ideas about social reform. Although he may have had reservations as regards the complete equality of men and women in society, nevertheless he demanded a far greater degree of emancipation for Indian women than existed at the time. Under his leadership women came out in large numbers and joined the Non-Co-operation Movement in 1921, and the Civil Disobedience Movement in 1930.

The second world war also played its part in the emancipation of women, although its effects were not by any means as wide or as deep as those of the national movement. The influence was almost entirely on women of the urban middle classes. The mobilization of men in the armed forces caused vacancies in the professions, and these were partially filled by women. This did not occur at the same rate as in Europe, but on a sufficiently perceptible scale. Such professions as nursing and medicine became quite popular, and women doctors were commissioned in the medical services of the armed forces. Secretarial work, both in civilian offices and military centres, attracted the type of young woman who preferred to work for a while before she got married. Male opinion was thus beginning to change by slow degrees. The idea of a 'working woman' was no longer something unheard of.

Legislation in favour of women's rights was also beginning to move in a less timid manner. Women working in factories had their working hours reduced to forty-eight per week, with nine hours per day as a maximum. Maternity benefits were introduced. The fight for improved wages still continues. Although the constitution of independent India declares that there shall be equal pay for equal work for both men and women, discrepancies are still fairly frequent, and women are paid less.

A number of acts had been passed (1874, 1929, 1939), relating to the right of inheritance for women. Each act was a step further. But it was not until 1955 and 1956 that the matter was finally settled on the basis of equal rights of inheritance (unless specified otherwise by a will) for sons and daughters. Three bills were passed in these two years, the Hindu Marriage and Divorce Bill, the Hindu Adoption Bill and the Hindu Succession Bill, which gave the Indian women a considerably emancipated status, at least legally. Marriage in Hindu society is now monogamous and divorce is to be permitted. Daughters are co-heirs with the sons. The practical consequences of these acts are familiar only to those who know about them; it will necessarily take time for the full realization to filter down to all levels of society.

INDONESIA

In Indonesia the need for an improvement in the status of women was first expressed by the agitation for social reform and against the lack of proper educational facilities for women. The parallel between the Indian and the Indonesian movements is very striking. The significant difference between the two is that in the early stages the Indonesian women were far more active than were the Indian women. The reason for this may be that the Indonesian movement began somewhat later in the nineteenth century. As in India, social reform and the establishment of educational institutions went hand-in-hand in Indonesia. Devi Sartica started the first private school for girls in Bandung in 1904.

The memoirs of a young Indonesian woman, Kartini, were published in the late nineteenth century. They described the seclusion and suppression of women in traditional Indonesian society. The book created an immediate stir in Indonesia and inspired many of the early feminists. Much of the support for the emancipation movement in the earlier period was enlisted with the aid of literature. Indonesian novelists of the twentieth century took the theme of the suppression of women and wrote a fair amount on the subject. The novels were largely attacks on what were thought to be social evils, the forced marriage, for example, and were eulogies of the newly-aspiring woman, the working woman who was economically independent, and women patriots.

The organized movement in Indonesia began in 1912 with the founding of the Putri Mardika (The Independent Woman) at Djakarta. This body worked in association with a professional men's liberal society, the Budi Utomo, which aimed at gradual independence through constitutional means. A number of other women's organizations were established. Some of these were concerned with the dispensing of charity and some with education. Journals were brought out regularly in which the social code was analysed and existing conditions were discussed.

Some of these organizations were of a secular nature, and worked with all communities. Others were purely religious and traditionalist in character. These were concerned only with Moslem society, Islam being the predominant religion in Indonesia. In the 1920s a number of girls' schools were opened at mosques and other Islamic centres. However, in 1928 these various religious and secular movements were amalgamated into one important organization, the Perikatan Perempuan Indonesia. For the first time an Indonesian women's congress had been held at a national level. The inaugural meeting pressed for more education for girls, greater security against wilful divorce by husbands in an Islamic marriage, and assistance to widows and orphans.

The most interesting development at this stage was the awareness that women's movements had started in other Asian countries. The reforms of Mustafa Kamal in Turkey and the meetings of the All-India Women's Conference in these years were watched with growing interest by the Indonesian organizations. A further source of support emerged when the women's organizations began to participate in the national movement, the political struggle of the Indonesians against the Dutch. Once again the pattern was similar to that of India. Men were willing to concede the demands of women when they recognized in them fellow workers in the political movement. It was no longer the fight of women against men, but of Indonesians against Dutch, at least for that period. Having once put a wedge in, as it were, it was easier for the women to push forward with their demands after that.

The repeated nomination of Dutch women to municipal office was resented by Indonesian women. It led to a determined demand for the franchise at a meeting in 1941. But the coming of the second world war and the Japanese occupation of Indonesia diverted some of the energy of the emancipation movement. A change was also taking place within the movement. Until this period it had been dominated by the women of the cities, largely from middle-class backgrounds, who were more concerned with the rights urgently needed in middle-class circles, such as marriage and divorce laws, etc. The participation of women working in the rural areas and on the plantations and in factories was not considered. The forties saw the coming together of the women from the rural areas with those in the cities. The common aims of both (the ending of the Japanese occupation and the attainment of political freedom) modified class barriers and demanded that women from all backgrounds share the work. This naturally resulted in a far stronger women's movement at the end of the war, when a new organization was formed on a wider basis which drew in most of the existing women's associations.

In 1948 was held the important session of the women's congress at which a definite programme for the achievement of concrete results in improving the status of women was adopted. The new women's organization was established as an official body representing women's rights and, as one observer has remarked, it took on the character of a political party. The climax came in the following year with a conference at Djogjakarta, which was attended by women from all over the country. This was a feat in itself, since some parts of Indonesia were still held by the Dutch at that time and others were under Indonesian authority; and, as the Dutch regarded the Indonesians as rebels, travel from one section to another was immensely difficult. The importance of this gathering lay in the fact that it no longer demanded individual social reforms or the removal of local grievances. Instead, there was an insistence that women should in principle have equal rights and equal privileges. This was again an expression of the new self-confidence that Indonesian women had acquired in the last ten years.

A comparison of the movements in India and Indonesia reveals three stages common to both. The first was confined to changing the religious basis of certain social conventions and applying humanistic criteria to them, as for instance, child marriage or the *purdah* system. The second stage saw the movement widening into one of liberal ideas. Education for women came to be seen as a necessity and the working woman was no longer regarded as an oddity. The entry of women into the political field acted as the pressure which led to the third stage. This was the demand for equality as a perfectly natural outcome of the new social structures which were to emerge with independence. By contrast, the British suffragettes had had to follow a somewhat different course. For them, agitation in Parliament was the first step. When this appeared not to be succeeding or moving at a fast enough pace, a certain section of the suffragettes took to breaking the law and courting arrest, thus drawing attention to their cause. This step has fortunately not been necessary so far in Asian countries.

With regard to the other group of countries, Burma, Thailand, Laos and Cambodia, none of these have had a women's emancipation movement similar to the ones discussed above. This was partly because, as we have seen, their social pattern was different, without too many restrictions. Thus, the first stage of fighting against the religious sanctions of a rigid social code was never necessary in these countries. There was no child marriage, no forced marriage, divorce was equally open to both men and women, inheritance laws were not unfair to the women since property was held jointly by husband and wife. Discrepancies between theory and practice were not so great as in, say, India or Indonesia. Some social injustice against women existed and still exists, but because women have apparently always had a certain position of independence it has never been permitted to reach the extremes which it did in India and elsewhere.

Whatever agitation there was in these countries has been centred much more on the second stage, that of demanding greater facilities for education and various political rights. The question of education was a difficult one since most of the schools were run by monasteries and consequently only the boys received regular teaching. Girls were expected to pick up learning at home as best they could. The Christian mission schools had some success in this sphere when they started schools for girls. Political rights consisted largely of demands to take part in political life, to stand for election, and to exercise the right to vote. In 1927, the women of Burma objected to the fact of their not being able to stand for election to the Legislative Council. Within two years this right was granted to them. Similarly in Thailand, the need for the general education of women, in addition to the learning of domestic science, has now been accepted. Only recently women have been admitted to professions which had been generally regarded as the monopoly of men, such as teaching in schools. Recent figures show that a quarter of all the village school teachers in Thailand today are young women.

Since there was no colonial power in Thailand, there was no national movement of the conventional type similar to that which existed in most other Asian countries. But the battle for modernization was certainly fought in Thailand as much as anywhere else. As a result a number of social reforms have been introduced over the last twenty

491

years which have considerably improved the status of women in legal terms. Polygamy was forbidden, a woman could continue her profession without getting the consent of her husband if need be, property was generally to be held jointly except where specified otherwise, divorce by either party was possible. Although women have equal rights, yet in urban society social equality is not practised. The upper class believe it to be traditional for the women to be subservient to the men. This is all part of what is regarded as gracious living. It is only the rural society that comes near to the idea of equality.

SOUTHERN ASIA TODAY

The position in contemporary Asia is, therefore, one in which most countries have granted equal status to women legally. In this they are in advance of some of the countries of Europe, such as Switzerland, where women still do not have the right to vote in national elections. Nevertheless, the gap between theoretical equality and the actual conditions is still very wide. Present-day China is about the only Asian country which has come close to equality at every level. Elsewhere this discrepancy is still apparent in the simplest of situations. The social mixing of men and women is still viewed with distrust. A woman is expected to remain in the background and certainly cannot assert the same degree of social independence as can a man. The term 'career woman' referring only to the fact of a woman having a profession, still carries a strong undertone of condemnation, almost as if this was an abnormal species of woman. The picture is not dissimilar to that of certain Catholic societies of southern Europe, where traditional ideas on this subject remain so firm as to prevent any but the more daring of women making use of the rights which they legally possess.

Fortunately, social attitudes and values are not everlasting. Although the change is slow, there is some change in Asian opinion from year to year. A number of professions are now being opened to women. Medicine, nursing and teaching have the longest history. The seclusion of women necessitated women doctors, since male doctors were not permitted to see women patients. Secretarial work in offices is another recognized profession for women. The reluctance to admit the intellectual and professional ability of women is gradually being modified. In India, the government services have allowed the recruitment of women, and indeed many have here attained the highest positions.

A woman earning her living by joining a profession related to the arts, acting, dancing or singing, is not automatically classed as a prostitute in disguise, as she was in the nineteenth century in India. This attitude was particularly current in Indian middle-class society which had eagerly imbibed many Victorian values, some of which are retained to the present day. The influence of films on the ambitions of adolescent girls in the cities has been quite remarkable. The presentation of a romantic ideal can be very vivid on the cinema screen and the appeal to the sentiments of the young cannot be ignored. Films advocating the relaxing of social rigidity and attacking the more useless social traditions have been frequent in recent years.

Being permitted a profession is not enough, for emancipation must also exist for the woman who chooses to make the rearing of a family her career. For her there is no emancipation until social equality is also established. This is not a one-way process. It is essential that women be educated to understand the meaning of their rights. This is particularly important in countries where the status of women has been low in the past. Women should be educated in the ideas of emancipation and should know why they are important and how they can be applied. Lack of even a formal education still remains a barrier to this understanding. The percentage of literacy amongst Asian women varies considerably, from 7.9 per cent in India (1951) to 40 per cent in Thailand (1947). One belief held widely in Asia is that if women are educated they will want employment and that this will merely raise the present high rate of unemployment. The long-term effect of raising the whole standard of a people by providing parents who are educated and conscious of their responsibility is often completely overlooked.

The commonplace that the bicycle assisted the emancipation of women in Europe is not without relevance to Asian countries. Not necessarily the bicycle, but improved means of communication in general bear many advantages. It is far easier for a woman to travel alone in a train than in a bullock cart or on a donkey. The possibility of travel brings with it the possibility of new ideas.

In many ways the actual fight for the real emancipation of Asian women has only just begun. The attaining of political rights and legal equality has been no small achievement. But the assertion of these rights in everyday life is a far more difficult and frustrating matter. The granting of legal rights tends to assuage public conscience. The frequently heard remark made to feminists, 'You've got your rights, now what more do you want?, sums up this feeling. The natural tendency amongst Asian women now is to put these rights into practice. And here they meet with opposition. The desire of a daughter or a wife to be economically self-supporting, or to insist on an equal social position, is regarded with great indignation by the men. 'Women', one hears, 'are getting too forward these days.'

Change in the social climate will have to come. Even if the legislation concerning women's rights were, by some misfortune, to be reversed, there are other factors which will compel this change. Since many Asian countries have now adopted democratic forms of government, socialist patterns and planned economies, the structure of society in each country cannot remain static. It must undergo change in relation to the political and economic changes. Older institutions such as the joint family system and the caste system in India will either have to be modified or they will fade out. Principles such as the freedom of the individual and the rights of man, if they are accepted, cannot remain pretty phrases in any country anywhere in the world, without attempts being made to apply them in practical terms. The emancipation of women is no longer the isolated ideal of a few eccentrics; it is closely bound up with the functioning of social systems all over the world.

There is much conflict in Asian society at the moment. Old forces are dying, but the new have not replaced them. Often the new are not understood, they are condemned as mere imitations of the West. It is a conflict not only between generations but also between the sexes. Fortunately there are no immutable standards in the organization of social patterns. Each society has to change its pattern in keeping with the new elements that constitute political, economic and cultural change. No single one of these factors can be isolated. If a people chooses to follow a certain pattern which requires the emancipation of women, then this emancipation must come about. Today, in the mid-twentieth century, Asian countries have chosen patterns which require the emancipation of women. Therefore, movements in this direction cannot be stopped.

Appendix I

FOUR INDIAN REFORMERS

Of the many who have been instrumental in furthering the cause of women's emancipation in India, the following four have been selected for illustration.

RAJA RAM MOHUN ROY, 1770-1833

Raja Ram Mohun Roy was amongst the earliest of Indians who may be described as 'modern Indians'. Born in 1770 into an orthodox Bengali family, he was responsible for setting in motion a new trend of thought, often in opposition to his own family traditions. Quite early in life he became conscious of some of the less attractive aspects of certain Indian institutions. He was shocked when a woman in his family became a suttee on the death of her husband. Expressing his disapprobation strongly, Ram Mohun Roy left home to travel for many years in northern India. In the usual manner of many thinkers of the time in India, he wandered from place to place seeking a solution. He also spent the time in learning various languages, eventually becoming fluent in Sanskrit, Arabic, Hebrew, Greek, Persian and English.

On completing his wanderings he returned to Calcutta, where he took employment with the British and thus came into direct contact also with European thought. He was soon singled out as having a particularly good mind. For the next sixteen years he devoted himself to a campaign in favour of social reform in India. He attacked what he regarded as backward social institutions, such as suttee, the caste system and the ban on the remarriage of widows amongst Hindus. He also made a strong plea for the freedom of the press in India. In this connexion he edited a paper, *Sambudha Kaumudi,* which became the main organ for his ideas. As his fight for social reform gathered momentum, he began to support the idea of inheritance rights for women. He felt that economic dependence made a woman weak.

In 1816 he founded the Hindu College, or Vidyalaya, which was to provide a new or modern type of education. His biggest success in terms of organizing public opinion in favour of reform was the founding of the Brahmo Samaj in 1828. This consisted of a group of people with similar ideas who believed that a more organized stand was necessary if there was to be any progress in achieving reform.

In 1830 Ram Mohun Roy left for England. In orthodox Calcutta circles this was regarded as a rebellious act, since a Hindu was believed to lose caste if he travelled overseas. His object in coming to England was to plead the cause of the Mughal emperor, who was by now a pensionary of the British-India Government. He also used this opportunity to appeal against the decision of the Privy Council to maintain existing laws relating to the burning of widows in India.

Ram Mohun Roy's chief aim in supporting the reform movement was to assist in the spreading of modern culture and thought, which he felt was greatly needed. His stand in favour of new ideas was backed by rational arguments and the use of appropriate quotations from traditional literature.

He died at Bristol in 1833.

ANNIE BESANT, 1847-1933

Annie Besant was one of those rare persons who, though British by nationality, spent much of her time in assisting the Indian national movement in its struggle against British rule. For Annie Besant the motivation came from her interest in religion and her activity in the Theosophical Society.

She was born Ann Wood, in 1847, and came from a middle-class family. Being interested in religion from her early youth, she married a clergyman, Frank Besant, in 1867. She believed that she had found her true vocation in life as she could now serve the Church. But this idyllic life was not to last. Two factors changed the pattern of her life. The first was her introduction to politics, when she began to take an interest in the Irish movement. The second was more personal: she began to doubt the authority of the Bible and questioned the existence of God. It soon became impossible for her to live with her husband, still an ardent Christian. She separated from him and went to London.

While in London she met Charles Bradlaugh, the atheist, and worked with him on his paper, *The National Reformer*. She also took to public speaking which was to stand her in good stead later in her public life. Her interests widened to include participation in the women's emancipation movement, support for the landless tenants in Ireland, pacifism and the movement for the abolition of capital punishment.

Her contact with India began in 1878 when she started reading extensively on the subject of India. During the 1880s her interest shifted to theosophy and, on reading Helena Petrovna Blavatsky's book, she felt that she had found the religion she had been seeking and threw herself into it wholeheartedly. So great was her enthusiasm and the amount of work she put into theosophy that in 1891 she was put in charge of the Eastern section of the Theosophical Society and sent to India. Her experience in India so overwhelmed her that she became a devotee of things Indian.

Although she did not approve entirely of all Hindu social institutions, nevertheless she was keen to revive traditional Hindu ideas and thought that they were needed in modern conditions. In 1898 she was instrumental in the founding of the Benares Hindu University, which was to dedicate itself to furthering Hindu culture. She was a supporter of the women's movement in India and assisted it by starting the Central Hindu Girls School in 1904, together with a number of schools for Harijans or out-castes. She made her ideas public through her journal *The New India*.

Her participation in the political movement resulted in her being elected president of the Indian National Congress, largely because of her efforts in creating the Home Rule League, a political group concerned with fighting for greater independence, in 1915. However, her association with the Congress became weaker with the years owing to a disparity in aim. Annie Besant was too imbued with Hindu ideas, and sometimes overlooked the fact that there

496

were other ideologies side by side in India: Moslem, Zoroastrian and Christian. Even more important was the purely political factor that, whereas Annie Besant was content to rest at having dominion status conferred on India, the Congress was aiming at complete independence.

Despite these differences of opinion, her death in 1933 was regarded as a loss to the Indian national movement in India as a whole, and certainly a considerable loss to the women's emancipation movement.

Iravati Karve, 1858-

Karve was a close contemporary of Mrs. Annie Besant. He belonged to the generation who worked in the period after the Indian Rebellion of 1857. He was born in 1858 in Maharashtra. From an early age he became keenly interested in education and the improvement of educational facilities for Indians, particularly for Indian women.

At the age of 14 he was married to a girl of 8. She died of tuberculosis before long, and the entire experience of a young marriage and the girl-wife's death made a lasting impression on him. Later, he donated a large sum towards the education of girls, and started the system of setting aside one pice in every rupee as a fund for this purpose. Some years after this he supported the movement for the remarriage of widows, and to prove the strength of his conviction he married a widow. His family, being orthodox, immediately excommunicated him but, undaunted, he merely redoubled his efforts in support of the movement.

He started his career in education as a school teacher. With this he combined social work, associating himself with various women's social welfare schemes. In 1891 he was offered a lectureship in mathematics which he eagerly accepted, and also became a life member of the Deccan Education Society; both these steps enabled him to concentrate even more upon improvements in education.

Karve revived the Widow Remarriage Association in 1893. This body consisted of men who had either married widows or who were willing to dine with others who had done so. (The question of dining was of significance, since eating with ostracized members of the community was a severe infringement of caste laws.)

The next twenty years of Karve's life were spent in active and accelerated work aimed at reforms of various kinds, particularly those connected with the education of women. Karve believed in organizing new institutions himself if none were available. Thus 1896 saw the opening of the Hindu Widows Home Association, which concentrated on giving education and practical training to widows, thus enabling them to secure at least a minimum of economic independence. In 1907 he opened the Mahila Vidyalaya, where unmarried girls could be given schooling.

Karve was elected president of the National Social Conference in 1915. It was at this time that he heard of the Women's University in Japan, and the idea occurred to him that a similar institution would be most useful in India. He planned a large-scale college teaching arts and sciences, and providing a university education for women. With the opening of the Women's University

497

in Bombay in 1916, his dream was fulfilled. The university is still in existence, and has been recognized as having university status.

SAROJINI NAIDU, 1879-1949

Sarojini Naidu began life with one advantage over most of her contemporaries. Although she too belonged to an orthodox family from Hyderabad, nevertheless her family were sufficiently liberal to permit her to participate fully in intellectual pursuits and indeed to educate her in London and Cambridge. To this extent it may be said that she came from a liberal background. In fact, when Sarojini Naidu was born in 1879, some of the early battles in favour of women's education had already been fought with success. Her father, a doctor with a flair for the humanities, understood his daughter's desire for education. During her stay in London and Cambridge, Sarojini Naidu spent much of her time writing poetry (in English). Edmund Gosse read her verse and thought highly of it, encouraging her to take her writing seriously.

On her return to Hyderabad in 1898 she married Dr. Naidu, a marriage which was not accepted by her family as Dr. Naidu was of an inferior caste and therefore the marriage upset caste laws. Hyderabad prided itself on being a cultural centre of some repute, and here Sarojini Naidu established herself as a leading poet. Much of her best poetry was written during this period. A collected edition was later published under the title of *The Sceptered Flute*.

But gradually through the years she saw the greater need for able women in the political movement, the movement for national independence for India. She began to spend increasingly more time in the political movement at the expense of her future as a poet.

Sarojini Naidu chose to participate in the national movement by working in the Indian National Congress. In 1919 she played an important part in the protest against excluding women from the franchise. But her activities were not limited to supporting women's movements alone. She participated in the national movement on every plane. Not surprisingly, she was elected president of the Indian National Congress in 1925. When Gandhi was imprisoned for his political activities by the British-India Government, Sarojini Naidu took up the responsibility of organizing the Civil Disobedience Movement. This led to her being imprisoned as well in 1930.

The following year she accompanied Gandhi to England in connexion with the round-table conference, which was held in order to discuss what form Indian independence should take. In 1932 she spent a further period in prison, after her re-election as president of the Indian National Congress which had then been declared an illegal body. As the momentum of the national movement increased, its leaders were inevitably thrown into a whirl of activity. It was the same for Sarojini Naidu during the years until 1947, when the national movement achieved its aim and India became an independent country. She was permitted a brief spell of comparative quiet when she was appointed Governor of an Indian province. She died in 1949.

Appendix 2

The honour of granting the first women's voting rights in the world belongs to Sweden (1863) and the United States of America (1869). These earliest voting rights were, however, restricted in various ways. The chronological order in which completely equal voting rights were granted was as follows:

1893	New Zealand	1946	Albania, Cameroon, Guinea, Japan, Mali, Panama, Rumania, Togolese Republic, Yugoslavia
1902	Australia		
1906	Finland		
1913	Norway		
1915	Denmark, Iceland	1947	Argentina, Bulgaria, China, Venezuela
1917	Byelorussia, Netherlands, Ukraine, Union of Soviet Socialist Republics	1948	Israel, Korea
		1949	Costa Rica, Chile, India, Indonesia
1918	Canada, Luxembourg		
1919	Austria, Czechoslovakia, Germany, Poland	1950	El Salvador
		1951	Nepal
1920	United States of America	1952	Bolivia, Greece, Lebanon
1922	Ireland	1953	Mexico
1928	United Kingdom	1954	Colombia
1929	Ecuador	1955	Ethiopia, Honduras, Nicaragua, Peru
1930	Union of South Africa		
1931	Spain, Ceylon	1956	Cambodia, Laos, Pakistan, Viet-Nam
1932	Brazil, Uruguay, Thailand		
1934	Cuba, Turkey	1957	Ghana, Haiti, Malaya, Singapore
1935	Burma, Philippines		
1942	Dominican Republic	1958	San Marino
1944	France	1959	Tunisia
1945	Italy, Liberia		

In the following countries the rights of women are subject to restrictions not imposed on men: Egypt, Guatemala, Monaco, Portugal, San Marino, Sudan, Switzerland, Syria.

In the following countries women have no voting rights and are not eligible for election: Afghanistan, Iran, Iraq, Jordan, Libya, Liechtenstein, Paraguay.

In the following countries neither men nor women have voting rights at all: Saudi Arabia, Yemen.

In certain of the above countries restrictions other than those based upon sexual discrimination exist.

---

1. Most of this information is taken from a United Nations memorandum entitled 'Constitutions, Electoral Laws and other Legal Instruments relating to Political Rights of Women', 27 July 1960 (Ref. A/4407).

Population characteristics
of South and South-East Asia

by T. E. SMITH

In its past history, Asia has seen the rise and fall of civilizations and of empires, the migration of peoples over vast distances, the growth of population during periods of peace and prosperity and the decline of population during periods of famine and strife. It is fascinating, but ultimately unprofitable, to speculate on the possible size of population of some of the Asian empires of the past and compare the figures with the present population of the areas which they covered. All we can say with certainty is that in past centuries, in the countries of Asia as in other continents, there have been alternating increases and declines in population totals and that the history of population growth has hitherto been determined by wide variations in the death rate rather than by any large fluctuations in the birth rate. Calamities such as war, famine and epidemics have caused temporary lulls in population growth in parts of Asia even in this century; during the influenza epidemic year of 1918, for instance, there were many more deaths than births in some of the countries of South and South-East Asia. In the past a high birth rate has been necessary to satisfy most parents' desire for a family, because a large proportion of the children died in infancy and early childhood.

Most of the people of South and South-East Asia are dependent on agriculture for a living. The standard of living of the people of the region is low, even if allowance is made for the fact that, in a warm climate, less food and less heating are required to keep body and soul together. In general the family is both the social and the productive unit. State systems of social security in the Western sense do not exist or are in their infancy in South and South-East Asia and the care of the sick and the welfare of the aged are family responsibilities. Usually the family undertakes collectively the various productive activities that support its members. Healthy children who can make a significant contribution to the family income at an early age are an economic asset. Only in the large towns and cities, and in some of the areas in which a wage economy has replaced the old-style subsistence agriculture, is this picture of the role of the family no longer applicable. Urban life in particular tends to give new importance to the individual and less importance to the family group and, in the town setting, the costs of family maintenance are usually increased and the economic advantages of large families greatly reduced.

Today the countries of South and South-East Asia together contain rather more than one-quarter of the world's population. In 1955, the region had an estimated 685 million people out of a world population of some 2,690 million.[1] Well over half of the people of the region live in India, whilst Pakistan and Indonesia together account for nearly one quarter of the total; the remaining countries, as Table 1 shows, contain under one-quarter of the population.

TABLE 1. Estimated total 1955 population of the large countries of South and South-East Asia (and of some Western countries for comparison)

Country	Estimated population (in millions)
India	386.0
Pakistan	83.2
Indonesia	81.9
Viet-Nam (South and North)	26.3
Philippines	22.1
Thailand	20.5
Burma	19.4
Other countries of the region	45.6
United States of America	165.3
France	43.3
United Kingdom	51.0

1. *The Future Growth of World Population,* United Nations, 1958.

There are over 40 births each year for every 1,000 persons who live in the region; this means that about 30 million babies were likely to have been born in South and South-East Asia in 1960 and, as the population grows, the annual number of births will increase if birth rates remain at the current high level. In the United States of America there are only 24 or 25 births each year for every 1,000 persons and in Western Europe the figures are even lower—18 or 19 in France and only 15 or 16 in the United Kingdom. Death rates, unlike birth rates, have been declining quite rapidly in recent years in most of the countries of the region, and as a result, the growth of population is alarmingly rapid. The rate of growth is now rising towards 2 per cent per annum and it has been estimated that, by 1975, the inhabitants of the region may number between 939 and 1,017 million in the absence of war and major natural disasters. This high rate of growth of population must be compared with a rate of about 0.5 per cent per annum in the United Kingdom and 0.6 or 0.7 per cent per annum in France; the rate of natural growth of population (i.e., without taking immigration into account) in the United States of America—about 1.5 per cent per annum—is much higher than in France and in the United Kingdom owing to the somewhat higher birth rate and the very low death rate in the United States.

It is in some of the smaller countries of the region that the most rapid rate of population growth can be observed. In the Federation of Malaya and in Singapore, the rate exceeds 3 per cent per annum and this growth, if continued, will involve the doubling of the population in under 25 years. In Ceylon and the Philippines, too, the rate of growth is now close to 3 per cent per annum. These countries have been able to afford intensive and successful work in the battle against disease and famine; the spectacular decline since the second world war in levels of mortality in Ceylon, largely as the result of a vigorous anti-malarial campaign, is an example of the effectiveness of properly planned and conducted public health programmes in bringing about drastic reductions in death rates and corresponding advances in the direction of the acceptable goal of good health. There is every reason to suppose that the larger countries of the region will continue to experience a general decline in mortality rates as sanitation and drinking water supplies are improved, anti-malarial campaigns are extended in scope, and other public health programmes get under way.

It may be easier to visualize the present demographic situation in South and South-East Asia if, instead of talking in terms of so many millions of people and about percentage rates of growth, we look at details such as the distribution of the population by age groups and by sex, the marriage rates and age at marriage, the size of families and the expectation of life of the 'average' man and woman. Let us first examine the age structure. Obviously the age composition of a given population at any moment is determined by past births, deaths and migrations, but, where gains or losses of population by migration are negligible, it is, in the long run, primarily the levels of fertility which shape the age distribution of the population, whilst levels of mortality play something of a secondary role. In the countries of South and South-East Asia, where birth rates are high, the ratio of children to total population is much higher than in the countries of Western Europe and North America, where birth rates are low; and, conversely, persons of working age form a rather small percentage of the population in the region under consideration as compared with the West. Table 2 outlines the position for four countries of the region and for three industrialized countries of the West and it is clear from the figures given, firstly that the great majority of the dependents in the four countries of South and South-East Asia are children in contrast with the Western countries, where there is a far larger percentage of aged people, and secondly that the total burden of dependency is greater in the Asian countries than in the West. The general poverty of the people of the region is accentuated by this heavy burden of dependency. As a decline in mortality coupled with the maintenance of high fertility has the effect of increasing the proportion of children slightly and to that extent increasing the dependency burden, the forecast is that the percentage of people in the most productive age groups will continue to decrease, so that each working person will have to support an increasing number of dependents. This high ratio of dependents to working population slows down the rate of economic development, because it means that a larger proportion of the national income must be spent on food and other necessities than would be the case if a larger proportion of the population were of working age.

In Asia, as in other parts of the world, the population of cities con-

TABLE 2. Number of persons in dependent age groups per 100 persons of working age

Country	Year	Persons in dependent age groups per 100 persons aged 15-59		
		Under 15	60 and over	Under 15 and over 60
Ceylon	1955	72.8	6.3	79.1
India	1951	65.8	9.9	75.7
Philippines	1956	85.9	9.0	94.9
Thailand	1947	79.1	7.8	86.9
France	1956	41.5	28.8	70.3
United Kingdom	1956	38.3	27.0	65.3
United States	1957	53.5	22.2	75.7

Source: Economic Bulletin for Asia and the Far East, Vol. X, No. 1.

tains a higher proportion of young adults and a lower proportion of children than the rural population. It would be false, however, to conclude from the statistics that the real burden of dependency of persons of working age living in the cities is necessarily less than that of their contemporaries in the rural areas. Most of the cities and large towns of South and South-East Asia are overcrowded and a feature of the composition of urban populations is the predominance of younger males, bachelors and married men often separated from their families. Many of the bread-winners in the urban areas support or help to support families or relatives in the rural areas, and because the family is a closely knit social and economic unit in many countries of the region, this flow of assistance in cash and kind may continue even when the working man and his wife and children are permanently settled in the town or city.

DISTRIBUTION OF POPULATION BY SEX

If census statistics are to be believed, the ratio of men to women is higher in some of the countries of South and South-East Asia than in other regions of the world. No census of population is absolutely accurate, however, and in countries in which the social position of men is superior to that of women, there may be a much larger omission of women than of men in the census count. Indeed, all census statistics —and particularly those relating to underdeveloped areas—must be used with the greatest caution. Where immigration has been a significant factor in recent population growth, as in Ceylon, the Federation of Malaya, Singapore and British Borneo, a preponderance of males is to be expected because of the high proportion of males in the immigrant stream in past years. Singapore, which is perhaps an extreme example, has grown from a mere 10,000 in the 1820s to about 1.5 million people and the sex ratio, although still about 11 men to 10 women today, is nevertheless far smaller and more normal than it has been at any time in the last 130 years, as the figures for selected censuses shown in Table 3 indicate.

TABLE 3. Singapore's total population at various censuses (in thousands)

Census year	Males	Females	Total
1823	7	4	11
1860	70	12	82
1901	172	58	230
1921	292	139	431
1947	552	425	977
1957	763	683	1 466

Sources: Report on the 1947 census of population of Malaya and preliminary releases on the 1957 census of population of Singapore.

In countries of high mortality there is often a greater death rate for adult women than for adult men, in part due to the large number of deaths of mothers in child-birth. In India, for example, the estimated 1951 death rates for males between 5 and 35 are lower than the corresponding rates for women, though infant mortality is believed to be higher for male than for female babies and death rates for the over-35s are higher for men than for women. Although death rates have been declining rapidly, it would not be surprising, therefore, to find a high ratio of adult men to women in the countries of South and South-East Asia in view of the mortality levels current in the past. As death rates get lower, the mortality of women usually declines more rapidly than the mortality of men and the ratio of males to females in the population thus tends to be reduced. Indeed, in most economically developed

505

countries, the number of adult women greatly exceeds the number of adult men and, in the United Kingdom for instance, there are more women than men at every age over about 17. Assuming, then, that international migration is not an important factor in future population growth in the countries of South and South-East Asia and that mortality continues to decline in the region, we would expect the present excess of males in the population of many of the countries of the area to be replaced in the not too distant future[1] by an excess of females. There is no demographic evidence which suggests that female infanticide is of sufficient importance anywhere in the region to make a noticeable difference to the sex ratio of infants and small children. It is possible that, in some countries, girl children are more neglected than boy children and that this may result in a higher proportion of girl deaths than would otherwise be the case; but any such discrimination, in so far as it still exists, is likely to be of diminishing importance.

If the ratio of men to women is high on a national basis, the disproportion in the two sexes tends to be even more marked in the large urban centres of the region. We have already noted in discussing the age distribution that the population of cities contains a higher proportion of young adults—and particularly young males—than the population of rural areas. 'The tendency for the population to become more masculine as localities become more urban reflects, primarily, the sex composition of migrants from rural areas and villages to towns and cities, although in some cases relatively high mortality of females in urban areas may also be a factor. Rural-urban migration in the Asian countries is primarily a movement of males. In many of the countries of South-East Asia, tradition does not sanction the employment of women outside the home.'[2] The ratio of men to women in urban areas tends to be greatest between the ages of 15 and 39.

AGE AT MARRIAGE

This general excess of males is undoubtedly one factor in making

---

1. But not in the next 30 years. United Nations population projections for various countries of South-East Asia as given in Annexes II and III of the United Nations report *The Population of South-East Asia 1950-80* indicate a continued but reduced excess of males by 1980.
2. *Proceedings* of the joint United Nations/Unesco seminar on urbanization in Asia and the Far East held in Bangkok in 1956.

marriage almost universal for women. A recent study prepared by the Secretariat of the Economic Commission for Asia and the Far East states that the available data indicate that 97 to 99 per cent of all women in the age group 45 to 49 years in the ECAFE countries are or have been married and that only in Singapore and the Philippines is the proportion as low as 93 per cent.[1] In economically developed countries, the proportion varies from 85 to 92 per cent. The higher mortality in Asian countries is, however, responsible for a greater degree of early widowhood than in the West, and, although remarriage of widows is permitted in some of the countries of the region, the Hindu custom is to forbid widows to remarry. Thus, although the proportion of ever-married women in South and South-East Asia is, for any age group, higher than in Western countries, the proportion of currently married women in South and South-East Asia may well be less for the older adult age groups than in the West; on this subject, the statistical data is, unfortunately, inadequate but, from the point of view of fertility and population growth, the marital status of the younger adult women is obviously of far more importance.

It is quite clear that the average age at marriage is lower in South and South-East Asia than in the West, for the proportion of women married in the 15 to 19 and 20 to 24 age groups is far higher in Asia than in Western Europe and North America. There is in fact a considerable variation in age at marriage within the region, for only some 15 to 25 per cent of girls aged 15 to 19 are married in countries such as Ceylon, the Philippines and Thailand compared with 40 per cent in the Federation of Malaya and some 70 per cent in India and Pakistan. Custom is naturally of the greatest importance in fixing age at marriage in these countries; among the Malays of Malaya and their ethnic cousins, the Indonesians, women commonly marry at the age of 17 or 18; among the Chinese in Malaya, and also the Chinese in Taiwan, the average age at marriage is rather higher; in India, the average age at marriage of women was only 14.6 years in rural areas and 16.4 years in urban areas during the period 1946-51. There are some indications that the average age at marriage of women in some parts of the region is increasing—for instance in Ceylon and in India— but it is rather unlikely that such an increase in age of marriage will have been sufficient to have any lowering effect on levels of fertility.

---

1. *Economic Bulletin for Asia and the Far East,* Vol. X, No. 1.

Only in the Philippines and Singapore among the countries of the region does the proportion of ever-married women in the 20 to 24 age group compare with the corresponding proportions in the countries of the West; in Singapore, the proportion of ever-married women in this age group is just under half and this figure is almost identical with that of the United Kingdom.

SIZE OF FAMILIES

Because birth rates are high and the proportion of children who die in infancy and early childhood is gradually decreasing, large families are typical of South and South-East Asia. In any society there are, of course, numbers of married couples who are unable to have any children or as many children as they would like to have, and there is no reason to suppose that sterility is any less common in Asia than in Europe or North America. But the average size of completed family in the countries of the region is of the order of five to eight children (not all of whom will survive infancy and childhood) in contrast with the two to four children who make up the average completed family in the countries of Western Europe and North America. One hundred and fifty years ago, large families were the rule rather than the exception in the West. Families in colonial America were comparable in size with those of present-day South and South-East Asia. The small family emerged gradually during the nineteenth century and the early years of this century along with the growth of urbanization and industrialization; the decline in birth rates in the West started in the cities and large towns and gradually spread to the rural areas as country people came to accept more and more the social values of the new wealthy industrial societies.

It must be emphasized that the drop in the birth rate in the West was due to social rather than to physiological factors. In urban surroundings, the costs of child maintenance were increased, the income contributed to the family in cash or in kind by children was more limited and education inspired hopes in the individual for his own and his children's advancement and opened up new material aspirations. Above all, urban life changed the role of women by enlarging the number of activities in which they could take part outside the home.

Only in Japan among the countries of Asia has there been a decline of fertility comparable with that of the West; crude birth rates in Japan have dropped from over 30 per 1,000 population in the years immediately after the second world war to well under 20 per 1,000 population now, and this decline has in fact been far more rapid than that which has taken place in the industrial countries of the West. In South and South-East Asia, birth rates have been fairly stable at a level rather over 40 per 1,000 population (with some variation from one country to another) and, in the general absence of the practice of family limitation and with the near universality of marriage at an early age, there is no reason to expect any early substantial decline in fertility. The available information relating to fertility is not sufficient to state any broad generalizations with regard to differences in birth rates between urban and rural areas in the region and between various socio-economic groups in the community. All that can be said is that, whilst birth rates of both urban and rural populations in the region are high, there is some evidence of lower fertility in just a few of the cities of the region—for instance, Bombay and Colombo—as compared with the rural areas surrounding each one of them. Possibly, then, some of the cities of the region are the centres from which a small family movement may ultimately spread.

EXPECTANCY OF LIFE

It is, as we have said, the spectacular decline in mortality rather than any pronounced trend in fertility which has led to the current rapid rate of growth of the population of the region. Some ten years ago, a team of American demographers were still able to write that 'there is no reason to believe that in the Far East as a whole more than two-thirds of those born reach their fifteenth year, or that more than one half reach their thirtieth year. By contrast, in the best Western experience, one half of those born reach their seventieth year'. It is doubtful whether this dark picture of the toll of mortality would still be quite accurate even in respect of India and Pakistan, which are among the countries with the highest death rates in the region.

The expectancy of life at birth at any given period measures the average number of years which a group of persons born at the same time will live if they are all subject to the rates of mortality at successive ages current at that period. In India, life expectancy at birth has increased from an estimated twenty years for the period 1911-20 to approximately thirty-five years in 1955, whilst in Ceylon the increase is from about thirty-six years in 1910-12 to approximately fifty-four years in 1955. In no country of South and South-East Asia is life expectancy yet quite as great as in the industrial countries of the West, where expectancy of life at birth now averages about seventy years, but the gap between the figures for the smaller and more highly developed countries of Asia and those for the Western countries is rapidly diminishing.

INFANT MORTALITY

The most important single component in the reduction of death rates has been the decline in infant mortality, which is measured by the number of deaths of infants under 1 year of age per 1,000 live births. The exact measurement of infant mortality is difficult in any circumstances and particularly so in the countries of Asia, where there is a considerable degree of under-registration of births and deaths. As a rough guide, however, it seems likely that one baby out of every four or five born alive died in infancy in the region in the years between the two world wars, but that a level of infant mortality as high as one-fifth of the live born children can be found now only in countries with the highest general death rates, such as Burma, India and Pakistan. For India, the census actuary has estimated the infant mortality rate for the period 1941-50 at between the upper and lower limits of 240 and 155 deaths per 1,000 live births, whilst an independent estimate has put the upper and lower limits at 250 and 200 deaths per 1,000 live births. In the Asian countries with the most rapid growth of population, however, an infant mortality rate of well under 100 deaths per 1,000 live births is now the regular experience. In Ceylon, for example, the rate has fallen from the 150 mark shortly after the first world war to under 70 in 1956 and 1957; and, in Singapore, the infant mortality rate has been under 50 per 1,000 live births since 1955. For purposes of comparison, the rate in the United Kingdom is now just under 25 deaths of infants under 1 year of age per 1,000 live births, whilst the French and German rates are in the thirties. Given a static birth rate, of, say, 40 births in a year for every 1,000 population, a reduction in the infant mortality rate from 200 to 50 deaths per 1,000 live births will in itself reduce the crude death rate by 6 per 1,000 population.

We must now examine the distribution of the population between town and country and between agriculture and industry. The overall population density of any but the smallest of the countries in the region is of limited interest because of the variations in density between different districts in the same country—for instance, between Java and Madura on the one hand and the outer island of Indonesia, between the well-watered riverine and coastal plains of India and the centre of that country, and between the paddy plains and rubber areas of north and west Malaya and the jungles of central and south-east Malaya. The population density per unit of arable land is somewhat more meaningful, and in almost every country of South and South-East Asia the density measured in these terms is much higher than the world average. Areas of very dense population are mostly those in which there is intensive cultivation of rice.

Let us look at the position of agriculture in India, the largest country in the region. In 1951, the proportion of the population engaged in or primarily dependent on agriculture was about 70 per cent. Prior to that year, the total acreage of land under cultivation had increased slowly, but not rapidly enough to keep pace with the growth of population. Farming techniques were primitive and crop yields were low. Food production was insufficient to meet minimum nutritional standards for the maintenance of health. India was, and indeed still is, a living example of the dangers of over-population in a densely settled country with an economy primarily dependent on agriculture. Those responsible for economic planning in the Indian Government hope to double the total 1950 agricultural output by 1971, partly by improvement in agricultural methods and partly through land reclamation. But, owing to the expected growth of population in this twenty-year period, even this very ambitious target will make rather little difference to the standard of living of the people of India unless there is an even bigger increase in non-agricultural production. A decrease in the proportion of the population dependent on agriculture side by side with a rapid rise in agricultural productivity are two of the necessary conditions for real economic growth in India, taking into account the expected growth of population. If things go in accordance with India's development plans, then although there may be an absolute increase in the numbers of people engaged in agricultural activities yet the

511

proportion of the total population engaged in agriculture will fall well below the present figure of about 70 per cent and there will be a very rapid rise in the number of people engaged in industrial activities and, with it, a higher proportion of the population living in cities and large towns. The Western countries have been going through this same process of industrialization and urbanization for the past century.

Most of the other countries of the region are, like India, in an early stage of the process of urbanization and industrialization. Apart from city-states like Singapore the percentage of the total population living in urban areas[1] nowhere in the region exceeds 22 per cent (the figure for the Federation of Malaya at the 1957 population census) and the average is not much above 10 per cent. In India, where, as we have seen, 70 per cent of the population was engaged in agriculture in 1951, the percentage of the population living in urban areas was 12 per cent. Countries like Burma (10 per cent living in urban areas of 20,000 or more), Indonesia (9 per cent) and Pakistan (8 per cent) are even more rural than India.

Although the urban population is still small in relation to the total population of South and South-East Asia, the proportion is increasing. In India, the percentage of the population living in towns and cities of 20,000 people or more grew from 4.4 per cent in 1900 to 12 per cent in 1951; in Malaya from 8.3 per cent in 1911 to 17 per cent in 1947 and 22 per cent in 1957; and in Ceylon from 7.9 per cent in 1900 to 11.4 per cent in 1947, but back to 9.8 per cent in 1953. In some of the countries of the region, urban growth has been concentrated mainly in a few large towns, whilst elsewhere the smaller towns have been absorbing their full share of the increase of urban population. Some of the towns of the region—particularly the smaller ones with a population of between 20,000 and 50,000—are merely overgrown villages and their only industries are small-scale handicrafts. Many of the larger towns are merely trading and distributing centres dependent for their prosperity on primary production in surrounding rural areas rather than on the growth of secondary industries. In some countries of the region urban growth has been accelerated by difficult living conditions in rural areas rather than by any positive economic pull towards the towns and cities; under-employment (as opposed to

---

1. Defined as places containing a population of 20,000 or more.

512

unemployment) is very common among the agricultural population, whilst political and civil disturbances have at times made life particularly unpleasant for the inhabitants of the countryside. In general, the region is already rather highly urbanized in relation to the degree of economic development and the small proportion of the labour force (30 per cent in India) engaged in non-agricultural activities. Certainly the rather rapid pace of urbanization in recent years can only partly be explained by industrialization.

ECONOMIC ACTIVITIES

We have said that in South and South-East Asia it is usually the family which undertakes collectively the various productive activities that support its members. This is true of both rural and urban areas—but particularly the rural sector—for the peasant and his family together cultivate their land holding and tend their animals, and in the urban sector, there are very many small family businesses in which the head of the household relies to an important extent on his family for assistance. It is not, therefore, surprising to find that the percentage of employers and self-employed persons in the labour force is far higher in the region than in the industrial countries of the West. Even in Malaya, with its important rubber plantation industry and tin mines, there are about as many people in the labour force working on their own account as there are salary- and wage-earners. In India, wage-earners form less than a third of the total employed population—about two out of every seven members of the labour force in the rural areas and about four out of every seven in the urban areas. Only in modern cities like Singapore do wage- and salary-earners attain something approaching the relative importance of this group in the countries of the West; in Singapore, nearly 75 per cent of the working population are earners of wages and salaries.

Young people start working and join the 'economically active' population at an earlier age in Asia than in economically developed countries. 'Among males of 10-14 years, only a small fraction takes part in economic activities in industrialized countries—in Australia and the United States about 3 per cent and in Japan 5 per cent. But in the less developed countries the rate is much higher. In Ceylon, China (Taiwan) and the Philippines 14-23 per cent of males 10-14 years old are in the labour force, and in India perhaps as many as 40 per

513

cent.'[1] The percentage of economically active males has, however, been on the decline, largely because of 'an extension of formal school education beyond the age of 10 years, and to some extent by the earlier retirement from economic activity of persons of advanced ages in urban or industrial surroundings'.[2] Obviously self-employed persons living in countries without any form of State old-age pension are likely to go on working until they are physically quite unable to continue to do so.

The extent of the economic activities of women in the region is very hard to assess, because of the difficulties which arise in interpreting the statistics and the lack of comparability of the data. The main problem centres around the inclusion or non-inclusion in labour force statistics of the large number of unpaid family workers in Asia. Women are engaged in housekeeping and bringing up children, but they often give part of their time to work in the fields or in cottage industries. All that can be said with certainty about the economic activity of women in South and South-East Asia is that only a fairly small proportion of them are earners of wages or salaries. In India, for instance, only some 10 per cent of the female population are classed as employees.

We have seen that agriculture is the principal economic activity of the people of the region. Manufacturing, building and other secondary activities employ but 10 per cent of the labour force, whilst transport and communications, commerce and other services engage from 15 to 30 per cent of those employed, the actual percentage in any one country of the region being largely dependent on the importance of production of cash crops for export. In Malaya and Ceylon the proportion of the labour force engaged in these 'tertiary' activities is relatively high, whilst in large countries with poor communications and much subsistence agriculture, such as Burma, India and Thailand, the proportion of those engaged in this group of activities is relatively low. Although the statistics on economic activity and type of occupation are, for a variety of reasons, most inadequate for almost all the countries of the region and are not strictly comparable as between one country and another owing to differences in classification, the general picture which emerges is fairly clear. Agriculture is even more important to the region than the division of the labour force between the main

---

1. *Economic Bulletin for Asia and the Far East*, Vol. X, No. 1.
2. *The Population of South-East Asia, 1950–80*, United Nations.

branches of economic activity would imply, for not only do the peasants and the agricultural wage labourers depend directly on agricultural production for their livelihood, but many of those engaged in manufacturing are processing agricultural produce and many of those engaged in commerce, transport and communications are marketing and carrying the fruits of the soil.

A number of the countries of the region have no census statistics on economic activities of their population and, where such data are available, they do not reveal the degree of under-employment in the rural areas and the extent to which those gainfully employed have secondary occupations in order to improve their standard of living. Many paddy planters, for instance, will become fishermen or offer their services as labourers during the four or five months in which there is little work to perform in the rice-fields (this applies only to areas which do not attempt to harvest two crops of paddy in a year). It is this seasonal characteristic of agricultural work which causes so much under-employment in the rural areas of Asia, and this, combined in some parts of the region with land-hunger, undoubtedly encourages the drift of population to the towns.

MIGRATION

The movement of peoples from the rural areas to the town is, of course, only one of the possible types of migration. At various times migration from continent to continent, or from country to country, or even from densely settled areas to places where the land is not being fully utilized, has been advocated as a means of relieving population pressure. It is undoubtedly true that international migration from the United Kingdom and from other countries of Western Europe to the United States of America, Australia and elsewhere was of considerable help to the countries from whom the migrants came in the nineteenth and early twentieth centuries, when the populations of these countries were expanding very rapidly; emigration helped to ease the strain on the economy. It is equally true that, without large-scale immigration, the United States of America, Canada and Australia could not have become the prosperous countries they are today. Within Asia, Malaya could not have become as rich as she is today by Asian standards without large-scale immigration in the past from China and India, and, forty or fifty years ago, when the populations of these latter countries were nearly stationary, such migration may well have had a temporary effect in relieving the burden of over-population in particular areas—for instance, in the Tamil-speaking areas of India and the southern coastal provinces of China. As a general statement, population growth provides an impetus to economic growth both in sparsely settled areas (where a denser population will reduce the costs of transportation and marketing and increase the division of labour) and also in more densely populated areas in which there is already a fair degree of development of manufacturing and secondary industries and the money is available for further investment in industry to satisfy the demands of a wider market. But, in most of the countries of South and South-East Asia, the problems involved in improving living standards to a satisfactory level in the face of population growth of unprecedented intensity are huge. It can, then, fairly be asked whether migratory movements across international boundaries would help to relieve the population problems of Asia today, but the answer must be that, even without considering the political and social implications, the scale of emigration from the overcrowded countries of the region could not be large enough to have any real effect on the net rate of population growth in these countries. Even if large-scale migratory movements from India and China to Ceylon, Malaya and Indonesia were permitted today (which they are not), they would not play more than an infinitesimal part in relieving population pressure in the countries of emigration. Moreover, those countries of the region which used to receive immigrants are now faced themselves with acute population problems, for Ceylon, Malaya and Singapore are among the countries with the most rapid rate of natural increase of population in the world.

The movements of population from more densely populated areas to districts still sparsely peopled inside the same country is officially encouraged in some countries of the region. In Indonesia, the movement of people from Java to under-populated areas in other islands of Indonesia is organized by the government. This movement is known locally as 'transmigration'. The net effect of 'transmigration' on the problems of over-population in Java has been negligible, simply because the movement each year of a few thousands of people represents the removal of but a tiny proportion of the annual increase of the Javanese population. There have also been movements of rural families under government sponsorship from densely populated areas in Luzon in the Philippines to the island of Mindanao. Officially sponsored resettlement schemes have had some effect on local population distribution in the Federation of Malaya, but there the reasons for official action have been in the desire to clear troubled areas or to find cultivators for newly irrigated or newly opened-up land, and not because of a wish to relieve population pressure on a particular district.

THE PROBLEM OF POPULATION PRESSURE

Because migration provides no satisfactory answer to the problems created by the greatly accelerated rate of population growth of recent years in South and South-East Asia, the solutions must be found in rapid economic development and in a lowering of the birth rate. It is clear that, though the process of urbanization is likely to continue, it can only be on a scale sufficient to relieve the pressure of population on the land in the overcrowded countries of South and South-East Asia if it is accompanied by a high rate of increase of productive employment in the towns and cities—and this can only take place if there is a major growth of industries in the non-agricultural sector of the economy side by side with improved productivity in agriculture itself. Economists can find no universally applicable formula for the balanced development of the economies of densely populated underdeveloped areas, but all are agreed that a major growth of indigenous industry is desirable. Not every country can have steel mills and heavy industries, but most countries can achieve some degree of industrialization, if necessary with the assistance of protective tariffs or quotas. It is, however, only the larger countries, such as India, which can hope to achieve any major degree of industrialization in the next few decades. The majority of the countries of South and South-East Asia are likely to remain primary producers, and the degree of expansion which can be obtained through a fuller exploitation of natural resources will define the limits of economic development.

If migration cannot be of much assistance to Asian countries in finding solutions for their population problems and if industrialization is not likely to be on a scale sufficient to achieve a full measure of prosperity, one is forced to ask whether there are any other measures which a community or a government can take in order to relieve population pressure and influence the future trend of population growth. India is the only country in South and South-East Asia which has so

517

far made family planning the subject of government policy, though other governments in the region—notably Ceylon and Singapore—give financial support to family planning activities. In India, the First Five Year Plan adopted in 1952 stated that: 'A programme for family limitation and population control should: (a) obtain an accurate picture of the factors contributing to the rapid population increase in India; (b) discover suitable techniques of family planning and devise methods by which knowledge of these techniques can be widely disseminated; and (c) make advice on family planning an integral part of the service of government hospitals and public health agencies.'

In the Second Five Year Plan, this programme is being intensified, but the allocations still seem small when considered in relation to the size of India and her population. It is too early to form any estimate of the likelihood of a substantial decline in the level of fertility in India as a result of the government's declared policy, but it is perhaps significant that some recent surveys in that country have indicated a marked interest by married couples in methods of family planning.

Judging by the experience of Japan during the last decade, it is conceivable that a positive governmental programme for population control combined with a desire for smaller families on the part of a large section of the people of the country could lead to a very spectacular decline in fertility. In Japan, the government embarked on its postwar policy of restraining the rate of population growth in 1948 with the enactment of the Eugenic Protection Law, which extended the grounds for legal sterilization and abortion considerably. The reported number of legally-induced abortions increased 2.5 times between 1949 and 1951 and, following further liberalization of the law relating to abortion in 1952, it is now estimated that abortions are approximately equal in number to live births. However, the frequency of abortions appears to be declining as a result of more widespread knowledge of contraceptive methods. The fertility of Japanese women is now much lower than that of women in the United States of America and rather lower than that of women in most of the countries of Western Europe.

Although the level of fertility is likely to decline eventually with improvements in standards of living, it is rather unlikely that the experience of Japan in the last decade will be repeated in the near future in any of the countries of South and South-East Asia, with the possible exception of Singapore. As a recent ECAFE report on population trends and related problems of economic development in the ECAFE region says:

'... a number of factors exist which may delay the decline in fertility or even increase fertility temporarily. Customs, social values, and attitudes towards marriage, family and children may change as slowly as in the West; the low level of living, widespread illiteracy and the existence of ignorance and superstition may be delaying factors. The decline in fertility is expected to take place first in a few socio-economic groups and gradually filter to others. In the developed countries of the West, the decline in fertility began among the well-to-do families and spread gradually to the lower income groups; also it began sooner in urban communities than in the country.... There is little sign as yet of any major rural-urban differences in fertility patterns in most ECAFE countries. Various studies have also shown little indication of fertility differentials among other socio-economic groups....

'The control of malaria and other diseases, the maternity welfare programme, and the improved health and sanitary conditions in general, may tend to increase fertility by reducing the still-birth rate, the risk of spontaneous abortion and sterility. Further, the decline in mortality among men will tend to reduce the high rate of widowhood prevailing in several countries in the region and so tend to increase fertility.

'It should also be noted that a rising age at marriage does not necessarily mean a decline in fertility....

'The drive for family planning which is being made in a number of countries in the region cannot therefore be counted on to lower fertility substantially in the near future. It is true that as these activities are mostly sponsored by governments, they are likely to give results sooner than they did in the West where the movement was often opposed by the official authorities. But the fact that the ECAFE populations are predominantly rural, illiterate and poorly housed and fed will delay the dissemination of information on family planning. Considerable research is still required to develop a contraceptive which is inexpensive, easy to apply and acceptable to the large majority of people in the ECAFE region.'

FUTURE POPULATION

As the Government of India (like the Governments of Japan and Mainland China) has realized, positive planning and vigorous effort

519

are required both in order to improve the standard of living of a growing population and to reduce human fertility to a level more nearly in equilibrium with the new level of mortality. We cannot be certain what the growth of population will be in the second half of the twentieth century, but the estimates in Table 4 indicate the potentialities. These figures, prepared by the United Nations, give four estimates for the population of certain countries of the region in 1980, based on varying assumptions regarding the future of mortality and fertility rates. The first estimate is based on the assumption that mortality will decline rapidly and fertility remain constant during the period 1955-80; the second assumes that mortality will decline normally and fertility remain constant; the third that mortality will decline normally and fertility will decline moderately; and the fourth assumes that mortality will decline normally and that fertility will decline rapidly. It will be seen that even the fourth assumption implies a population increase of about 50 per cent in countries with currently high mortality and an approximate doubling of the population in countries with a fairly low level of mortality already.

TABLE 4. Estimated total population and per cent increase of population in selected countries of South and South-East Asia, 1955-80[1]

Country	Estimated 1955 population	Estimated 1980 population (percentage increase in brackets)			
		1st assumption	2nd assumption	3rd assumption	4th assumption
Burma	19.8	45.3 (129)	32.3 (63)	30.5 (53)	28.7 (45)
Malaya	6.0	14.4 (141)	14.0 (134)	13.1 (118)	12.1 (103)
Indonesia	82.2	159.7 (94)	138.5 (68)	131.0 (59)	123.4 (50)
Philippines	23.0	57.0 (148)	50.8 (121)	47.6 (107)	44.3 (92)
Thailand	20.9	47.5 (127)	41.6 (99)	39.1 (87)	36.6 (75)

1. Population figures are in millions.
Source: Economic Bulletin for Asia and the Far East, Vol. X, No. 1.

Another and quite different assumption could well have been made regarding the future levels of fertility and mortality. It is possible that, if fertility remains high and economic stagnation results in lower standards of living, mortality may reverse its present decline and climb back to a high level. The present rapid growth of population in South and South-East Asia, though unprecedented in the region, could at least in theory be followed by a decline in population as the result of war, famine or disease. A nuclear war would probably have a disastrous effect of this kind. It is not beyond the bounds of possibility that, even without war, the problem of attaining the minimum standard of living necessary for the maintenance of health and strength will be insoluble in the face of rapid population increase and that the largely agricultural population of South and South-East Asia will wage a losing battle in the attempt to wrest a living from the soil. Certainly it is true that, in the long run, either the birth rate must decline or the death rate must rise; the present rate of population growth in the region is too high to last for more than a few decades.

Recent events in Asia have shown that death rates can be reduced very considerably without any very substantial economic development. Apart from Japan, there is little evidence as yet of the conditions under which birth rates are likely to decline, but the combined evidence from Europe, North America, Japan and elsewhere does indicate that a reduction of fertility can be quite rapid if there are greatly increased opportunities of education, improvements in the status of women, and real chances for the individual to assert his individuality and improve his social and economic position. As long as a community retains traditional social attitudes which tend to favour a high human reproductive performance, however, little decline in fertility can be expected. In rural Asia, children can contribute at an early age to family production and the cost of educating them is small because schooling ends at a low level; without children, the parents would lack security in old age; the status of women in much of Asia is that of subordination to the men, who have learnt from past experience that the community must have a high birth rate to balance the high death rate. For these reasons, it is unlikely that the old-style peasant societies of rural Asia will generate within themselves the social changes which may ultimately bring population expansion to an end, but it is much more possible that the new and forward-looking societies of the big towns will be the nuclei from which the evolution of the required

521

magnitude will emerge. Although the growing urbanization tends to be disruptive of the traditional form of family life and brings with it evils which were virtually unknown in the old rural communities, it seems reasonably certain that the changes of outlook involved in the widespread acceptance of family limitation must start in the towns and affect the reproductive habits of the majority of the urban population before the small family movement can spread to the rural areas.

The next fifty years are likely to show whether South and South-East Asia can move in the direction of the demographic equilibrium based on low birth rates and death rates with which the West is already familiar or whether the ultimate future is to bring economic catastrophe and demographic disaster.

Appendix

FAMILY PLANNING IN SOUTH AND SOUTH-EAST ASIA
by BARBARA CADBURY

During the winter of 1960-61 I accompanied my husband when he visited ten countries in Asia, on behalf of the International Planned Parenthood Federation, but the views expressed here are my own, not necessarily shared by him or the Federation. The mission was one of organization, and was intended to strengthen ties between the Head Office in London and national volunteer societies already in existence, and to bring workers for birth control into closer touch with each other for mutual help. We were not trying to convert people to family planning, nor studying their reasons for accepting or rejecting it. Nevertheless, I have returned with two inescapable conclusions on these two questions, and one of these is specially relevant to the subject of this book. My first conclusion is that in those countries where the employment of women for wages is the usual pattern of life the ordinary citizens are anxious for birth control and are persistent in its practice. Where it is not the custom for women to be gainfully employed outside the home, they and their husbands may be awakened to an initial interest in birth control by the pressure of their poverty, but the women lack persistence in limiting and spacing their families. My second conclusion is that the failure of the World Health Organization to include birth control in its medical help to underdeveloped countries has an enormous checking effect on the confidence that all classes of Asians feel in it. In emerging countries WHO stands for all that is sensible, scientific, modern in public health and practices not endorsed by it are looked upon with dubiety.

The mission took us to Japan, Korea, the Philippines, Taiwan, Hong Kong, Indonesia, Singapore, Malaya, Ceylon and Burma, and we also visited the Indian cities of Delhi, Madras and Hyderabad, where we attended the fourth All-India Family Planning Conference.

ATTITUDES

In India, Japan and Singapore the governments were greatly committed to the promotion of family planning, making help available to everyone through the health and adult education services, and giving large grants to the voluntary associations devoted to it. In Japan the people's own determination to limit their fertility had preceded their government's action, and more than kept

523

pace with the government's interest. Of all Asian countries Japan is the one where women are most completely integrated with the economic productive activity of the nation, with the possible exception of mainland China, which we did not visit. In India the people's interest does not match the concern of their government. The political and psychological position of women in India, certainly as far as the intellectual and governing classes are concerned, is one of complete equality with men, but Indian women in the main do not work for wages and so do not fear pregnancy as an interruption of earnings. In Singapore, although the government had taken the initiative with a crash programme of propaganda, the citizenry appeared to follow their lead. In Ceylon the government recognized the threat of their population explosion, and the Prime Minister's husband had been the first to move in the World Health Assembly for the inclusion of birth control aid. The government gave a large grant to the voluntary family planning association, and its blessing to all public health officials who wished to promote the service, but racial tension between Ceylonese and Tamil was beginning to bedevil family planning work, each ethnic group fearing the limitation of its own numbers. In Ceylon a scheme of unilateral aid in birth control, between the government and the Government of Sweden, was in progress.

In Indonesia, where there is a small voluntary organization, there is antagonism to family planning at government level, but the independence of the women and the pressure of poverty led to great interest wherever ordinary people become aware of the possibility of birth control. There is believed to be widespread abortion, and much smuggling of contraceptives from Singapore. While we were there the attitude of other Moslem countries, notably Pakistan, seemed to be softening the attitude of the Indonesian government, and should Egypt endorse birth control this would have much influence in Indonesia. The country supports a very large army and we did find interest in the Army medical authorities for the idea of teaching birth control to soldiers' wives, since the Moslem soldier sometimes has more than one wife and the Army paymaster makes allowances to all his resulting children. In Malaya the government was sympathetic to the voluntary organization, made it a money grant, and would have been prepared to do more if birth control were part of the programme of WHO. All racial groups seemed reasonably interested in the service; the Chinese the most so, the Malays the least. Burma has no population problem at present, other than the one of having a fertile and uncrowded land sandwiched between other huge land-hungry populations, and the government therefore is not interested in family planning except as a health measure for the reduction of high maternal mortality. The people, however, are extremely interested in limiting the numbers of their children. One of the main reasons for the formation of the Burmese Family Planning Association by a group of doctors in Rangoon was their distress at the great number of male sterilizations which were being sought and performed privately. They hoped to replace these, and abortions, with contraception.

In the Philippines, a Roman Catholic country, there is a small group of birth control workers, mostly Philippine Protestants, but including a few Catholic doctors, and their work was welcomed by the poor of the cities. Contraception is common among the well-to-do.

524

Japan has achieved her demographic miracle by abortion, to which the people resorted themselves after their defeat in war and the economic disruption of their country. For economic reasons the government has welcomed this, legalized and facilitated it, but for humanitarian and health reasons is anxious to replace it with contraception, and the Public Health Departments and the Japanese Family Planning Federation were actively promoting the use of the diaphragm, the condom and a successful and reliable foam tablet, which was made under licence from the government. Next to abortion the condom was apparently the most used method. The contraceptive propaganda and education was done through newspapers and women's magazines, and through people's places of work. Sterilizations for both sexes were available through the public health services.

India is the country which has discovered, to everyone's surprise, that there is no great reluctance among its peasant and worker menfolk to being sterilized, and the central government, and many of the provincial governments such as that of Madras, are promoting this on a great scale. It is not possible to be so active with female sterilizations on account of the lack of hospital beds. India could make use of a very simple contraceptive, such as a reliable suppository, or an injection, the inadequate housing and lack of privacy making other methods difficult. In Singapore the government offered, and the people accepted, all medically approved forms of family limitation. The government doctor in charge of the campaign was opposed to legalized abortion, but illegal abortion was common. Male sterilization was not popular and female was. In Malaya, where living conditions are very simple, there is need of a simple contraceptive. Difficulty in importing contraceptives, because of a general ban on foreign manufactured 'non-essentials', or a high tariff on them, was met in Ceylon, Indonesia and the Philippines, and great use could be made of a simple contraceptive that could be locally made if a reliable one could be devised.

In some countries a method of using a piece of sponge dipped in salt solution had been suggested by individual Western enthusiasts, and this had antagonized the local doctors, particularly in Burma and Taiwan, who felt that something inferior was being passed off on Asians. They felt that, used continuously, it could be harmful. On the other hand, a public health doctor in Thailand (which we did not visit) advocates this method and finds it acceptable. If family planning were a WHO service there could be a standard of advice on this and other home-made methods, some of them originating in the countries themselves.

The rhythm method was all that the voluntary organization was able to offer to most of their contacts in Indonesia. It was offered also in all the countries we visited. It is particularly unsuitable for countries where marriages are very early and pregnancy and lactation fairly continuous. WHO had once sponsored a pilot scheme in India with the rhythm method, and this was adjudged a failure.

525

In all these countries, even in the Roman Catholic Republic of the Philippines, there is little opposition to birth control from ordinary parents on religious or any other grounds, but where women have no occupation outside the home there is a lack of sustained interest, so that inertia might be called the chief opposition. A sociologist in Ceylon said that it should not be concluded that a rising standard of living in Ceylon would result in a reduced birth rate—as in some Western countries, for unless this were accompanied or achieved by women becoming wage-earners the effect might be the opposite. It is difficult to see what the wives of India, married in their teens, would do with their lives, if they had only the two or three children their government advises. Convictions of nationalism, racism and militarism also made for opposition in high circles in some countries, but did not influence individuals in their decisions. Some religious leaders in Moslem communities feared the spread of immorality, but did not condemn the idea of family limitation with appropriate safeguards. Moslems everywhere were much influenced by the lead of Pakistan. In some countries Roman Catholic missionaries have suggested or hinted that charity might be withdrawn if birth control became a government activity.

HELPING THE CHILDLESS

The infertility services, whereby childless couples can sometimes be helped to become parents, are part of the work of every voluntary association affiliated to the International Planned Parenthood Federation.

Suggestions for further reading

Additional titles and references to more detailed studies will be found in the
bibliographical sections of the books suggested.

GENERAL AND SOUTH AND SOUTH-EAST ASIA

APPADORAI, A. (ed.) *Status of women in South Asia.* Bombay, 1954.
COUSINS, Margaret. *The awakening of Asian womenhood.*
INTERNATIONAL INSTITUTE OF DIFFERING CIVILIZATIONS (INCIDI). *Women's role
in the development of tropical and sub-tropical countries.* Brussels, 1959.
LEMAY, R. S. *The culture of S.E. Asia; the heritage of India.* London, 1954.
MEAD, Margaret. *Male and female.* New York, 1950.
MYRDAL, Alva; KLEIN, Viola. *Women's two roles.* London, 1956.
Report of the Asian Women's Conference held in Bangkok, 1958.
UNESCO. *Urbanization in Asia and the Far East.* Calcutta, 1957.
WOODSMALL, Frances. *Women of the New East.* London, 1960.

BURMA

KHAING, Mi Mi. *Burmese family.* London.

CAMBODIA

STEINBERG, David J. (ed.) *Cambodia; its people, its society, its culture.* New
Haven, 1959.

CEYLON

RYAN, Bryce. *Sinhalese village.* Coral Gables, Florida, 1958.

INDIA

ARTEKAR, A. S. *The position of women in Hindu civilization.* 1938.
DESAI, Neers. *Woman in modern India.*
DUBE, S. C. *Indian village.* London, 1955.
— *India's changing villages.* London, 1958.

KAPADIA, K. M. *Marriage and family in India.* Oxford, 1955.
KARVE, Iraveti. *Kinship organization in India.* Poona, 1953.

INDONESIA

GEERTZ, Hildred. *The Javanese family.* New York, 1961.
SUBANDRIO, Hurustiati. *Javanese peasant life.*
VREEDE DE STUERS, C. *L'émancipation de la femme indonésienne.* Paris, 1959.
WERTHEIM, W. F. *Indonesian society in transition.* The Hague, 1956.

LAOS

Introduction au Laos.
RENAUD, Jean. *Le Laos.*

MALAYA

DJAMOUR, J. *Malay kinship and marriage in Singapore.* London, 1959.
FIRTH, Rosemary. *Housekeeping among Malay peasants.* London, 1943.
WINSTEDT, R. *The Malays; a cultural history.* London, 1947.

PAKISTAN

EGLAR, Zekiya. *A Punjabi village in Pakistan.* New York, 1960.
KARIM, A. K. Nazmul. *Changing society in India and Pakistan.* 1956.
LEVY, R. *An introduction to the sociology of Islam.* 1931.
ZAIDI, Syed M. H. *The position of women under Islam.* 1955.
The Koran.

PHILIPPINES

GUAZON-MENDOZA, Maria Paz. *The development and progress of the Filipino woman.* Manila, 1951.
HUNT, Chester (ed.) *Sociology in the Philippine setting.* Manila, 1954.
MACARAIG, Serafin E. (ed.) *Philippine social life.* Manila, 1954.

SINGAPORE

FREEDMAN, Maurice. *Chinese family and marriage in Singapore.* London, 1955.
KAYE, Barrington. *Upper Nankin Street, Singapore.* Singapore, 1960.

THAILAND

BLANCHARD, H. (ed.) *Thailand.* New Haven, 1958.
DE YOUNG, John E. *Village life in modern Thailand.* Berkeley, 1955.

528

TIRABUTANA, Prajuab. *A simple one: the story of a Siamese girlhood.* New York, 1958.
VORAVEN, Rudi. *The treasured one.* New York, 1959.

VIET-NAM

BRODERICK, A. H. *Little China.* Oxford, 1942.
HUY LAI, Nguyen. *Les régimes matrimoniaux en droit annamite.* Paris, 1934.
VAN HUYEN, Nguyen. *La civilisation annamite.* Paris, 1944.

DEMOGRAPHY AND SOCIOLOGY

BARNES, J. A. 'Kinship', *Encyclopedia Britannica.* London, 1955.
COALE, Ansley J.; HOOVER, Edgar M. *Population growth and economic development in low-income countries.* Princeton, 1958.
MITCHELL, Duncan. *Sociology.* London, 1958.
UNITED NATIONS. *The future growth of world population.* (ST/SOA/series, A/28.)
—. *The population of South-East Asia 1950-80.* (ST/SOA/series, A/30.)

DATE DUE
